VOCABULARY

OF THE

TONGA LANGUAGE

ARRANGED IN ALPHABETICAL ORDER:

TO WHICH IS ANNEXED

A LIST OF IDIOMATICAL PHRASES

BY

THE REV. S. RABONE
WESLEYAN MISSIONARY.

ISBN: 978-93-5128-595-3

First Published in 1845
Indian Reprint in 2017

Published by

Kalpaz Publications
C-30, Satyawati Nagar,
Delhi – 110052
E-mail: kalpaz@hotmail.com
Website: kalpazpublications.com
Ph.: +91-9212142040

Cataloging in Publication Data—DK
Courtesy: D.K. Agencies (P) Ltd. <docinfo@dkagencies.com>

Rabone, Stephen, 1811-1972, **author.**
Vocabulary of the Tonga language, arranged in alphabetical order: to which is annexed a list of idiomatical phrases / by the Rev. S. Rabone.
pages cm
English and Tongan.
"First published in 1845"—Title page verso.
ISBN 9789351285953 (HB)

1. Tongan language—Glossaries, vocabularies, etc. 2. Tongan language—Dictionaries—English. I. Title.

PL6531.Z5R33 2017 DDC 499.4820321 23

A

VOCABULARY,

TONGA AND ENGLISH.

A, THE first letter in the Tonguese Alphabet. Its sound is that of *a* in *Father*.

A, A prefix used before the names of persons in the nominative and oblique cases; as *Oku mohe a Jone; ave ki a Jone; omi mei a Jone.*

A, *prep.* Of or belonging to.

A, *s.* A fence, hedge.

A, *a.* Awake, not sleeping; open, not shut; liquid.

A, *v.* To heat as a stick, in order to straiten it; to supple by heat; to surround.

A, *v.* To be awake.

Aa, *v.* To ford; to pass without swimming.

Aaaga, *s.* A ford; any passage that can be forded.

Aau, *pron.* Yours, thine.

Aau, } *v.* To mesh, to net; to
Aaua, } cast or spread a net; to compass; to divulge, to reveal; to cast the young.

Aauliliki, *v.* To make a full and unreserved confession or statement.

Aaba, *part.* Afraid.

Aabi, *a.* Straight, small, confined, wanting room.

Aafa, *v.* To rise rapidly as full tides; to overspread, prevail.

Aafaki, *v.* To keep others awake, to keep awake.

Aafakihau, *s.* Various heathenish amusements performed in the night, to excite attention.

Aafu, *a.* Oppressively close; rash, headstrong.

Aafu, *v.* To work without judgment, to drive at any thing without thought.

Aaga, *s.* A watchpost or watch-tower.

Aagi, *a.* Changeable, not fixed.

Aahi, *v.* To visit; to look after, to inspect.

Aahi, *s.* A visitor.

Aahu, *a.* Smarting, pungent.

Aaku, *pron.* Mine.

Aala, *a.* Beautiful, shining.

Aali, *a.* Transparent; deep; just visible in water.

Aalo, *v.* To paddle, to row; to sit orderly and in state.

Aalu, *v.* To hunt with a dog or dogs.

Aana, *pron.* His, hers, or its.

Aana, *a.* Deep and large, as applied to ulcers or sores.

Aano, *v.* To think; to say, applied to what is the general opinion.

Aanu, *v.* To spit.

Aanu, *s.* Spittle, saliva.

Aanua, } *v.* To spit at or upon;
Aanuage, } to bedawb.

Aanuaga, *s.* A vessel for spittle.

Aata, *pron.* Mine, a familiar term.

Aata, *a.* Ripe, mellow; transparent.

Ae, *art.* The.

Aefe, *pron.* Which, whether?

Aeha, *pron.* Which, what?

Aena, *pron.* That, those?

Aeni, *pron.* This, these?

Aeva, *v.* To walk, two or more.

Ai, *v.* To put, to place; to burn circles on the body.

Ai, *ad.* There, in that place.

Ai, *pron.* Him, her, or it.

Ai, *s.* A tree, also its fruit; circles burnt on the body.

Ai, *v.* To surround, to enclose; to defend.

Aia, *pron.* He, she, or it; who, which, that.

Aiga, } *s.* The place of any thing,
Aiaga, } a term of general application.

Aiagakai, *s.* A table, crib, manger.

Aiagatohi, *s.* A bookshelf.

Aitoa, *int.* An expression of pleasure at the misfortune of others.

Ao, *s.* A cloud, presence; the front or most frequented part of any island; the inside of native cloth; a head dress.

Ao, *v.* To repeat a game, to play over again.

Ao, *v.* To seek suitable trees in a forest; to chase.

Aoao, *s.* Sovereign, sovereignty.

Aoao, *a.* Supreme.

Aoao, *s.* The eighth moon in the Tonga calender.

Aoao, *v.* To bind round and round; to hew timber in order to its being straight.

Aoaofia, *a.* Cloudy, overcast, as the moon.

Aoaokimajijiva, *a.* Kind, thoughtful to the poor.

Aofagatuku, *v.* To play another game and then give up.

Aofi, *s.* Lining, covering.

Aofi, *v.* To line, to cover.

Aofia, *v.* To screen, to shield; to intercept.

Aofia, *s.* A screen or shield.

Aofibaba, *s.* The front part of the wood on which the native cloth is printed; a covering for a shelf or table.

Aofinima, *s.* The palm of the hand.

Aofinima, *v.* To cast the net in a certain way.

Aofivae, *s.* The sole of the foot.

Aoga, *a.* Worthy, useful, profitable, needful, acceptable.

Aoga, *s.* Use.

Aokai, *v.* To beg food; to beg provisions.

Aoniu, *s.* The name of the wood band which surrounds a Tonga house, to which all the rafters of the roof are fastened below.

Aoniu, *a,* Omnipresent.

Aotuku, *s.* The last game of the *Ao.*

Au, *s.* Old people; weak and aged persons.

Au, *a.* Old, ripe.

Au, *pron.* I, me.

Au, *v.* To arrive at; to flow rapidly, as the current; to reach.

Au, *s.* A current; the sugar cane leaf.

Aua, *int.* To be sure; it is just so.

Auau, *v.* To shell; to pick out bones.

Auaukolo, *s.* An uneasy state of the bowels; gripes.

Auautonu, *s.* To declare without reserve.

Auaga, *s.* The cause, the origin of death or destruction.

Auia, } *v.* Take it, it is yours,
Ouia, } answering to *atamai* or *otamai:* which see.

Aubito, *ad.* Very; in an eminent degree.

4

Aubito, } Superlatively;
Aubito aubito, } the superlative degree.

Aufau, *a.* Distant, out of reach.

Aufoe, *v.* To peel off.

Auga, *v.* To appoint; to agree to meet at a specified time and place.

Augalua, *a.* Hungry.

Augamokaunaga, *v.* To fail in an agreement from unforeseen engagements.

Auha, *part.* Destroyed; extinct.

Auhani, *v.* To prune; to lop off.

Auhagataa, *a.* Difficult to make an end of.

Auhagofua, *a.* Easy to get through or make an end of.

Auhakaua, *ad.* Astray, as a fish that feeds near shore.

Auhatamaki, *a.* Difficult to accomplish.

Auhe, *s.* A wanderer, a vagabond; one deserted or forlorn.

Auhe, *v.* To wander or rove about.

Auhi, } *v.* To surpass, to outdo.
Auhia, }

Auhia, *v.* To be carried away by the sea.

Auhiaamotuafanifo, A phrase, one in trouble, but expert at extricating himself.

Auhulu, *v.* To strip off dry leaves from trees.

Aujia, *v.* To arrive at or come up to.

Aukai, *s.* A fast.

Aukai. *v.* To fast, to abstain from food.

Aulologo, *s.* Roar, echo, sound.

Auna, *v.* To conquer, to overcome; to be conquered.

Aunoa, See *auhe.*

Aunofo, *v.* To sojourn.

Aunofo, *s.* A sojourner.

Autau, *a.* Unsold; not bartered, implying it was offered.

Autaki, *v* To lead into; to conduct; to head a party; to arrive at.

Autalua, *s.* End, termination.

Auto, *v.* To fall away; to leave; to disappear.

Autua, *v.* To try to catch fish that have escaped from the net.

Aba, *v.* To venerate, to make sacred.

Abaaba, *s.* The master of the the ceremonies in a cava party; the Alofi of the Tuitoga's cava party.

Abaabai, *s.* A war weapon, made from the rib of the nut leaf.

Abaabai, *v.* To proceed; to move in a row. as soldiers.

Abai, *s.* The name of certain rafters in a Tonga house.

Abai, *v.* To uphold; to render prompt obedience.

Abagofua, *a.* Not sacred.

Abaabagofua, *s.* Liberty, unrestraint, applying to any thing that has ceased to be forbidden.

Abajia, *s.* Reverence, respect.

Abajia, *v.* To reverence, to respect; to hinder, to prevent.

Abe, *ad.* Perhaps.

Abe, *v.* To linger, delay, hesitate.

Abi, *s.* Habitation, home, lands.

Abiabi, *a.* Crowded, straight, narrow.

Abifaatoetuuaieteve, An *abi* that have plenty from their work with the addition of fruit trees.

Abiji, *v.* To tie together, to bundle up; to be wrapped or tied up.

Abijia, *v* .To remain at any place, detained by adverse circumstances.

Abita, Similar to *abiji.*

Abitaga, *s.* A temporary residence; resting place.

Abo, *ad.* To night.

Abo, *v.* To burn lights in the

night with one very ill or one dead; to feast upon the reception of something valuable.

Aboabo, *v.* To take aim; to poise as a spear.

Abogibogi, *ad.* To-morrow.

Abuanea, *a.* Mouldy; rotten from being wet.

Afa, *s.* A hurricane, a storm.

Afa, *s.* A wonder maker; one who appears to wonder at every thing.

Afa, *v.* To wonder, to appear astonished; to wish to astonish others with what is of daily occurence.

Afaafa, *a.* Strong, healthy, robust; full, as the tides.

Afaki, *v.* To cook food so as to be done by the time of waking.

Afe, *a.* A thousand.

Afe, *ad.* When, only used in the future tense.

Afe, *v.* To turn aside.

Afeafei, *v.* To warp or coil round the body.

Afeafefua. *a.* Semicircular, half round.

Afeafetata, *v.* To turn short; to go and turn again.

Afega, }
Afeafega, } *s.* The turning of a road.

Afekafu, }
Afeafekafu, } *v.* To wrap anything several times round the body, and lie in it.

Afeitui, *s.* A serpentine winding path.

Afeitaulalo, *v.* To espouse the cause of the weak.

Afeitaulalo, *s.* One that helps the downcast or the weak.

Afia, *v.* To watch.

Afi, *s.* Fire.

Afii, *v.* To open; to stretch.

Afio, *s.* Majesty.

Afio, *v.* To behold; to regard; to attend to.

Afioaga, *s.* The residence of majesty.

Afiona, *s.* Majesty.

Afo, *s.* A measuring line; a small rope; one course or range of the thatch on a Tonga house.

Afu, *v.* A word used when the fire is made for baking food.

Afu, *s.* The spray or mist of the sea, when breaking upon the rocks; the shoots or saplings of the *Hiabo*.

Afu, *a.* Overdressed; a term applied to food that has been too long in the oven.

Afu, *s.* Hot, redhot; thoroughly heated.

Afua, *a.* Fair, dry; not raining or wet.

Afua, *v.* To long or desire, as in pregnancy.

Afuafu, *s.* Small rain; mist.

Afuafu, *a.* Rainy.

Afueina, *a.* Dry and pleasant weather during the performance of any work.

Afugi, *v.* To tease, to annoy with importunity.

Afugia, *v.* To feel oppressed with heat; to wither from heat.

Afuha, *s.* The grain of wood; the temper or propensity; the direction or course of things.

Afuhataha, *v.* To go together in one direction.

Afuhi, *v.* To make damp or moist; to madefy, to sprinkle.

Afuhia, *a.* Wet from driving rain or mist.

Afuluga, *a.* Mouldy; foisty.

Afuluga, *s.* Mould.

Aga, *s.* Manner; disposition; behaviour; nature; habit; state.

Aga, *s.* The shark.

Aga, *a.* Clever, knowing, sagacious.

Aga, }
Agaaga, } *v.* To challenge.

Agaaga, *s.* A corpse, dead body.

6

Agaaga, *s.* The name of a shell fish.
Agaaga, *v.* to interfere; to intermeddle.
Agaagaki, *v.* To increase or grow in bad habits.
Agaagamoana, *s.* The name of a shell fish.
Agaagamofai, *s.* The name of a fish, a species of shark.
Agaaeiki, *a.* Chief-like in disposition.
Agaamua, *a.* Gentlemanly, becoming a *mua.*
Agaatu, *v.* To face, to look towards; to incline in an opposite direction.
Agaatua, *a.* Mean, low; like a *tua.*
Agai, *v.* To make, to correspond; to finish off; to reward.
Agai, *a.* Alike..
Agai, *s.* The principal in any department; the finishing stroke; the corresponding opposite.
Agaofa, *a.* Kind; loving.
Agaofeina, *s.* One generally beloved.
Agaua, *a.* Clever with both hands.
Agabauu, *s.* A rogue; a bad character.
Agabauu, *a.* Mischievous; roguish.
Agabago, *a.* Disgusting, hateful.
Agaboto *a.* Clever; righthanded.
Agafajia. *a.* Insinuating.
Agafakaotua, *s.* Godliness; the Divine nature.
Agafakaotua, *a.* Godly, godlike.
Agafakabotoboto, *a.* Prudent; careful.
Agafakabuaka, *s.* Swinishness; filthiness.
Agafakabuaka, *a.* Swinish.
Agafakafefine, *s.* Womanishness, effeminacy.
Agafakafefine, *a.* Womanlike, effeminate.
Agafakakakano, *s.* Fleshliness, carnality; sensuality.

Agafakakakano, *a.* Carnal, sensual.
Agafakalaumalie, *s.* Spirituality of mind.
Agafakalaumalie, *a.* Spiritually-minded.
Agafakalielia, *s.* A depraved, polluted, and filthy disposition.
Agafakalielia, *a.* Abominable; disgusting; depraved.
Agafakamakukaga, *a.* Prudent.
Agafakamanu, *s.* Beastliness.
Agafakamanu, *a.* Beastly.
Agafakamolakau, *s.* An angry, petulant, unforgiving disposition, literally the disposition of a centepede.
Agafakamolakau. *a.* Peevish; waspish; unforgiving; centipede-like in temper.
Agafakatagata, *s.* Manliness.
Agafakatagata, *a.* Manly.
Agafakatamajii, *s.* Childishness.
Agafakatamajii, *a.* Childish.
Agafakavalevale, *a.* Childish; foolish.
Agafatu, *s.* One kind of the *Ifi.*
Agafefeka, *s.* Stubbornness, obduracy.
Agafefeka, *a.* Stubborn, perverse.
Agafehianekina, *s.* One generally disliked.
Agahaohaoa. *a.* Perfect; free from charge or complaint in disposition.
Agahake, *v.* To go upwards; to be raised.
Agahala, *s.* Sin; sinner; transgressor.
Agahala, *a.* Sinful; estranged from God.
Agahala, *v.* To sin.
Agahia, *s.* Sin; sinful; wickedness.
Agahia, *a.* Wicked; sinful.
Agahifo, *v.* To go downwards.
Agahiki, *s.* Pride; highmindedness.

Agahiki, *a.* Proud; lifted up.

Agakehe, Agakehekehe, } *a.* Different; dissimilar in disposition; opposed.

Agaki, *v.* To air or dry anything by the fire; to fire off a large gun.

Agakoloa, *a.* Lucky, fortunate.

Agakovi, *s.* wickedness; a wicked person.

Agakovi, *a.* Wicked, bad; ill natured.

Agalahi, *s.* Selfwill, obstinacy.

Agalahi, *a.* Obstinate, determined.

Agalelei, *s.* Goodness, kindness.

Agalelei, *a.* Good, obliging, kind.

Agama, *s.* Modesty; bashfulness; shame.

Agama, *a.* Bashful; modest.

Agamaa, *s.* Purity, cleanness.

Agamaa, *a.* Pure, clean, spotless.

Agamai, *v.* To approach; to be drawing near; inclined this way.

Agamau, *a.* Fixed, settled; unchanging in disposition.

Agamaha, *a.* Empty; the cocoa nut when all the milk is absorbed.

Agamaka, *s.* Perverseness, obstinacy.

Agamaka, *a.* Hardened, perverse.

Agamalau, *a.* Noisy, talkative; open, free.

Agamalohi, *s.* An ungovernable disposition; fierceness.

Agamalohi, *a.* Ungovernable, violent.

Agamalu, *s.* Meekness, mildness; softness of disposition.

Agamalu, *a.* Meek, humble, mild.

Agamamao, *a.* Thoughtless; distant.

Agamamili, Agamioi, Agamimio, } *s.* A twisted contorted disposition.

Agamousaa, *a.* Bad, unkind in disposition; libidinous.

Agamolu, *s.* Softness, tenderness.

Agamolu, *a.* Soft; tender in disposition.

Agamua, *s.* The old or former disposition.

Aganoa, *a.* Foolish.

Aganofo, *s.* Submission, submissiveness.

Aganofo, *a.* Submissive, obedient.

Agataeofa, *a.* Unkind.

Agataha, *s.* A oneness of disposition.

Agataha, *a.* Unanimous; of one mind or disposition; singular; determined in disposition.

Agatala, *s.* Conformity; imitation.

Agatala, *a.* Imitative; desirous of imitating another.

Agatala, *v.* To copy after; to imitate.

Agateia, *a.* Unlucky; often beat or struck.

Agatouia, *a.* Easily wounded.

Agatonu, *s.* Uprightness, honesty, faithfulness.

Agatonu, Agatotonu, } *a.* Upright, faithful.

Agatua, *a.* Humble, applied to persons of rank who are unassuming.

Agatofoi, *a.* Exceeding in wickedness.

Agatuu, *s.* Rebellion, opposition to lawful authority.

Agatuu, *a.* Rebellious.

Agatuu, *v.* To rebel, to oppose.

Agavaivai, *s.* Humility, gentleness.

Agavaivai, *a* Humble, gentle.

Age, *v.* To give.

☞ *Age* is used only when the third person follows the verb, as, give him, give them. When the first person follows the verb, as, give me; *mai* is used instead of *age;* and when the second person follows, as, I give you, *atu* is used.

Age, *ad.* Towards.

☞ This, like the above, can only be used when it has relation to the third person, as, *alu age*, go towards him, her, or it.

Agi, *v.* To superintend, to oversee; to come from.

Agiagi, *v.* To begin; to spring up as a breeze.

Agiagina, *s.* The motion of any thing light moved by the wind.

Agiga, *s.* That point of the compass from which the wind blows.

Agimui, *v* To follow after, to imitate.

Agina, *v.* To be carried away with the wind; to be full as the sail with wind.

Agini, *a.* Wrinkled; shrivelled from cold.

Ago, *v.* To line or mark; to chalk.

Ago, *s.* A mark, a chalked line; a shrub.

Agoago, *a.* Quite empty; perfectly dry.

Agoi, *s.* A spot on which the foot is placed in certain games.

Agoi, *a.* Anxious to know and do many things.

Agoi, *v.* To use all sorts of means to accomplish an object.

Ahai, *pron.* Whose?

Ahaga, *s.* A ford, see *Aaaga.*

Ahi, *s.* The sandle wood.

Ahiahi, *s.* An attempt, endeavour, experiment; trial, temptation.

Ahiahi, } *v.* To tempt; to en-
Ahiahii, } deavour; to make an effort.

Ahiahikovi, *v.* To tempt to sin.

Ahiahikovi, *s.* A temptation to evil.

Ahiohio, *s.* A wirlwind; a waterspout.

Ahitua, *v.* To look up laggers and idle persons.

Ahitua, *s.* One who does as above.

Aho, *s.* A kind of shark.

Aho, *s.* Day.

Ahoia, *v.* To overtake by the day; to see another day.

Ahoaho, *a.* Bright, shining, as the moon in a clear night.

Ahofakaua, *s.* A term used when the moon is full; literally, one day made two, or a double day.

Ahohiva, *s.* A heathen festival.

Ahotetea, *s.* Morning light.

Ahu, *s.* The gall; soot; smoke.

Ahu, *v.* To smoke, as a fire.

Ahua, *s.* The moving of earth by fish under water.

Ahua, *v.* To rush at random.

Ahuina, *v.* To be smoked; to be smoke dried; to die from suffocation by smoke.

Aji, *v.* To penetrate, to pass through; to peep.

Ajiaji, *v.* To spy, to look out.

Ajiaji, *s.* A spy.

Ajiu, *s.* A kind of shrub.

Ajiga, *conj.* Notwithstanding.

Ajigai, } *v.* To change ones
Ajiajigai, } conduct; to simulate.

Ajigaki, *v.* To make earnest and repeated attempts to accomplish an object.

Ajili, *v.* To increase. to grow.

Ajilojilo, *a.* Transparent, clear.

Ajinijini, *a.* Clear, lucid; cloudless; guileless; unspotted.

Aka, *s.* The root of trees; the name of a shrub; a kick.

Aka, } *v.* To kick; to take
Akahi, } root in the earth.

Akaaka, *s.* The wide-spread and branched root of a tree; the rays of the sun.

Akaaka, *a.* Rooty, full of roots.

Akaaka, } *v.* To kick repeat-
Akaakahi, } edly.

Akau, *s.* A tree, a plant; a general word under which all kinds are comprehended; also, timber; a club; a common term applied to medicine, either alone or qualified by another word, as, *foi akau*, a pill.

Akauia. *a.* Abounding in trees.

Akauola, *s.* The *toutai* of the King of Tonga; *i. e.* the chief officer in his canoe.

Akafiji, *s.* Restlessness; continued motion with the legs.

Akafiji, *v.* To be restless.

Akatuu, *s.* The principal root of a tree.

Ake, *s.* The name of a tree.

Ake, Akeake, } *a.* Convalescent.

Ake, *v.* To be convalescent, to revive.

Akeaga, *s.* The origin or cause of a reviving; a reviver.

Akeakeloto, *a.* Rooted in the mind.

Akefuu, *part.* Swollen, arisen.

Akefua, Akefuu, } *v.* To rise or swell as the waves of the sea; to be inflated.

Akega, *s.* Variety; dispensation; epoch.

Akegafoou, *s.* A new plan; a new era.

Akegamotua, *s.* The old plan; the former dispensation,

Aki, *prep.* With.

Akiakitua, *v.* To enclose and attack from behind.

Akiha, *v.* To embowel; to eviscerate.

Akihala, *v.* To implicate.

Akilotoa, *v.* To be enclosed or surrounded.

A kimaua, *pron. du.* We two; used in speaking to a third person, but not including the person addressed.

A kimautolu, *pron. plu.* Us, we, excluding the person addressed.

A kimoua, *pron. du.* You two.

A kimoutolu, *pron. plu.* You, ye.

A kinaua, *pron. du.* They two.

A kinautolu, *pron. plu.* They.

A kitaua, *pron. du.* Us two.

A kitautolu, *pron. plu.* Us, including the person addressed.

Akitua, *v.* To walk with the hands behind.

Ako, Akonaki, Akonaki i, Akonekina, } *v.* To teach; to admonish; to discipline; to instruct; to caution.

A koe, *pron.* Thou, thee.

Akonaki, *s.* A teacher; doctrine; admonition, counsel, advice.

Akonekina, *part.* Taught, instructed.

Akoga, *s.* Disciple, learner.

Akosobe, *v.* To imitate; to try to do as superiors.

Aku, *v.* To scratch; to throw up loose earth with the hands.

Akufaki, Akuakufaki, Akufekina, } *v.* To increase; to do more than formerly.

Ala, *s.* Dear; a term of endearment.

Ala, *v.* To touch; to angle with small hooks.

Ala, *a.* Fit, suitable, eligible, congruous.

Ala, *s.* Touch; the act of touching.

Alaaga, *s.* The rendezvous of small fish.

Alaalava, *s.* The grain of wood.

Alai, *v.* To sit carelessly, and in improper places.

Alaijiaalaikologa, *a.* Useful in more work than one; as one clever at sea and on shore.

Alafaga, *s.* A place resorted to for the purpose of angling.

Alafi, *v.* To feel after with the hand.

Alafia, *v.* To be easy of accomplishment.

Alafia, *s.* A married person.

Alafia, *a.* Married.

Alafia, *a.* Suitable; middling, used of the weather.
Alafiaaga, *s.* A relative by marriage.
Alaga, *s.* The haunch; the seat of a disease.
Alaga-fale, *s.* The timber of a house.
Alaga-nima, *s.* The shoulder of an animal.
Alaga-vae, *s.* The leg of an animal.
Alaga-vaka, *s.* A term including the whole tackling and tackle of a canoe.
Alaha, *s.* A sweet scent.
Alaji, *v.* To handle; to act upon; to touch; to feel.
Alaleau, *s.* A chorus of a Tonguese song.
Alamuhu, *v.* To speak low; to depress the voice.
Alava, *s.* One species of the shark.
Alavu, *v.* To sail with only a small part of the sail.
Alea, *s.* Conversation; conference; discourse.
Alea, *v.* To converse together.
Aleale, *a.* Weak; failing.
Aleifua, *s.* The name of a fish.
Alefa, *s.* Hunger.
Alefa, *a.* Hungry.
Ali, *s.* The name of a fish; also, an indelicate term.
Aliali, *s.* A sort of mountebank play for reward.
Aliaki, } *v.* To clean the feet
Alialiaki, } by rubbing them on any thing; to stand firmly.
Aliloukabe, *s.* The name of a fish.
Alitalu, *s.* The name of a fish.
Alo, *s.* A child of rank; applied to the second person in the ever adorable Trinity; the abdomen of great personages.
Alo, *s.* Height; utmost degree, applied to the wind in a hurricane.
Aloalo, } *v.* To fan; to paddle
Aloaloa, } on the water for pleasure.
Aloi, *v.* To bring forth.
Aloifa, *a.* Small, applied to the abdomen; small bellied.
Aloofa, *v.* To compassionate, to shew mercy.
Aloofa, *s.* Compassion, mercy.
Alobaki, *v.* To sit in a row, to sit in order.
Alofaga, *s.* The rendezvous of a certain kind of fish; the distance for a paddling canoe.
Alofaki, *s.* A paddler; rowers of a canoe.
Alofaki, *v.* To paddle another to any place; to sit in a row.
Alofi, *s.* The place occupied by chiefs in a cava party.
Alofia, *v.* To paddle to any vessel to make inquiries, or in pursuit of any other object; to overtake.
Aloga, *a.* Lazy.
Aloga, *s.* An interval; the time passing between two assignable points.
Aloga, *a.* Deceitful, used in reference to one who feigns illness when work is to be done.
Alogai, *v.* To deceive, to trick.
Alomalie, *s.* Fine weather, after rain.
Alotamaki, *s.* Heavy rain; bad weather.
Alovili, *v.* To do anything determinately.
Alovili, *a.* Importunate; determined.
Alu, *s.* A creeping plant, used in making superior baskets; the gait or walk of a person.
Alu, } *v.* To go.
Alua, }
Aluga, } *s.* The course, the path,
Aluaga, } the track; footstep.
Alualuimalataukimonu, *v.* To begin badly but end well.

Alualuimonutaukimala, *v.* To begin well but end badly.

Alualumau, *v.* To go regularly and constantly.

Alui-kai, *v.* To rove in search of food.

Alu-fano, *v.* To wander, to rove.

Alu-fakaholomui, *v.* To retrograde, to go backwards.

Alu-hake, *v.* To ascend.

Alu-hifo, *v.* To descend.

Alumaki, Alualumaki, } *v.* To persist, to persevere.

Alumekina, Alumia, } *v.* To overpower and oppress; to insult the conquered; to carp over a matter already settled.

Ama, *s.* A flambeau, used by fishermen; larboard side of the canoe.

Amaamanaki, Amanaki, } *v.* To expect.

Amanaki, *s.* Expectation.

Amanaki-lelei, *v.* To hope, to expect good.

Amanaki-lelei, *s.* Hope, the extation of good.

Amanekina, *v.* To expect, to anticipate.

Ami, *s.* A part of the crab fish.

Amio, *a.* Viscous, glutinous; also twisted, crooked.

Amo, *s.* Persons who precede warriors as a look out.

Amo, *v.* To go in search of the enemy; to reconnoitre.

Amo, *a.* Unequalled, unrivalled in excellence.

Amo, *v.* To card in making ropes; to use friction upon the body.

Amoamo, *a* Unequal, not even; longer or higher than the rest.

A moua, *pron. du.* Yours, belonging to you two.

A moutolu, *pron. plu.* Yours, belonging to you all.

Amohe, *v.* To be just rousing from sleep.

Amohi, *v.* To use gentle friction in order to allay pain.

Amui, *ad.* Hereafter.

Amuji, *v.* To gather the shrub, the bark of which makes the native cloth.

Amujia, *v.* To covet, to envy.

Amujiage, *v.* To wish, to desire.

Ana, *s.* A cave, cabin, den, any snug place.

Anaana, *a.* Full of caves and dens.

Anaanaiage, Anai, Anaiage, } *ad.* Shortly, presently, by and by.

Anaini, *ad.* Instantly, immediately.

A naua, *pron. du.* Theirs, belonging to those two.

A nautolu, *pron. plu.* Theirs, belonging to them.

Anaga, *s.* A rendezvous; the central point; the source.

Ane, *s.* The moth.

Ane, *part.* Used only in composition, and refers to past time.

Aneafi, *s.* Yesterday.

Anea, Aneanea, } *a.* Moth eaten; rotten.

Ane-efiafi, *s.* Yesterday afternoon.

Ane-bo, *s.* Last night.

Ane-bogibogi, *s.* This morning or forenoon.

Anefe, *ad.* When? relating only to past time.

Ane-heafi, *s.* The day before yesterday.

Ane-heaho, *s.* Some day past.

Ane-hegihegi, *s.* This morning early, ere sun rise.

Ane-hoata, *s.* This noon past.

Anenai, *ad.* A short time past.

Anenaini, *ad.* Just this moment past.

Ane-tuaaneheafi, *s.* Two days before yesterday.

Ano, *s.* A lake, a pool, a marsh.

Anoano, *a.* Full of small pools, marshy, boggy.

Anoiha, *s.* The day after to-morrow.
Anuanu, *v.* To be frequently spitting; to wade and swim in deep water.
Anufea, *a.* Cold.
Anuhaga, *s.* A characteristic.
Anuhia, *v.* To bedawb; to spit upon.
Anusaga, *s.* See *anuhaga.*
Ata, *s.* The air; space; room.
Ata, *a.* Spacious, roomy; disengaged, free; downright.
Ata, *s.* The official name of the chief of one part of Tonga; the morning light.
Ata, *s.* A shadow.
Ata, *v.* To reflect as a mirror.
Ataata, *s.* A kind of shell fish.
Ataata, *a.* Ample, spacious, free, relieved.
Ataata, *s.* The dusk of the evening; twilight.
Ataatai, *s.* A term applied to the nights the moon is on the wane.
Ataataina, *a.* Free, exempt; alone.
Ataataina *s.* Applied to one who is friendless, none to espouse his cause.
Ataatafia, *a.* Free, without hindrance or obstructions.
A taua, *pron. du.* Ours, belonging to us two.
A tautolu, *pron. plu.* Ours, belonging to us all.
Atalea, *a.* Bare, as bones long buried.
Ataloa, } Ataataloa, } *s.* Space without bounds.
Atamai, *s.* The mind.
Atamai, *v.* To wish for, to desire.
Atanoa, *s.* See *Ataloa.*
Atanoa, *a.* Boundless.
Ate, *s.* The liver; the name of a long grass.
Ateate, *s.* A branch or shoot of the cava root.
Ateivae, *s.* The calf of the leg.
Atebili, *s.* The spleen or milt.
Atehoko, *s.* The long liver of the shark.
Atemutu, *s.* The short liver of the shark.
Atetea, *s.* Any place in the sea where the bottom is white sand and visible.
Ateteaina, *v.* To be alone, to be without company; to be exposed.
Ato, *s.* Thatch; roof of a house.
Ato, *v.* To thatch; to roof.
Atofaga, *s.* Saviour.
Ato, } Atofaki, } *v.* To build up; to work from below; to pile one thing upon another.
Ato, *a.* Fortunate, succesful.
Atofaki, } Atofekina, } *v.* To save, to deliver; to screen.
Atofaki, } Atofekina, } *s.* A saviour; one who screens another from danger.
Atofaki, *v.* To be covered over with; to be in abundance.
Atu, *s.* A kind of fish.
Atualo, *s.* A species of the above.
Atu, *v.* To give, used only when the second person follows, see *age;* to take, to throw, to fling.
Atu, *prep.* Towards, restricted as above.
Atuatu, *v.* To throw or fling.
Atuga, *s.* A characteristic.
Atugaage, See *Atugatala.*
Atugaki, *v.* To fling out of the hand, to throw at.
Atugatala, *s.* Mere talk; talk without meaning.
Atugi, *v.* To throw at; to hurl.
Atugia, *v.* To be in fear of; to cringe in subjection.
Atumooua, *v.* To waver; to be undecided.
Atumooua, *a.* Unstable; wavering.
Ava, *s.* An opening; a passage for vessels; a crevice; the

name of a fish peculiar to the lake of *Nomuka*.
Ava, *a.* Open ; hollow.
Avaava, *a.* Full of openings.
Avaavahi, *v.* To bore or perforate in many places.
Avaavanoa, *a.* Unemployed; free.
Avaia, *a.* Difficult of cure, because of remaining evil.
Avaiihu, *s.* The nostril.
Avaihua, *s.* The holes made in the canoe through which the oars are put to row along.
Avaituku, *s.* The hole through which a large rope, called the *tuku*, is passed in the canoe.
Avaga, *v.* To like ; to be in love with, to bewitch.
Avaga, *s.* Kind; general class.
Avagi, *v.* To raise up, to lift ; to make an opening.
Avaki, *a.* Useful, profitable.
Avanoa, *a.* Unemployed, not busied.
Avatahi, *s.* The name of a fish.
Ave, Avea, } *v.* To take ; to conduct ; to deprive of.
Aveaga, *s.* The taker or conveyor ; conveyance.

E

E, THE second letter in the Tonga Alphabet. Its sound is as *a* in *Day*.
E, A sign of the future tense.
E, *prep.* By.
Ee, *s.* Women catching fish.
Ei, *s.* A mark of respect and attention to the conversation of *Tuitoga*.
Eeba, A term used in reference to the position of a dead body.
Eela, *v.* To lie on the back ; to go with the face directed upwards.
Eehi, *v.* To prevent, to hinder.
Eia, *pron.* He, she, or it.
Eiki, *s.* The Divine Being ; a chief, a lord.
Eikiaga, *s.* The residence and government of a chief; also the cause to which one owes his chieftainship.
Eiki-beaoi, *s.* A quarrelsome chief.
Eiki-jia, *a.* Occupied by chiefs.
Eiki-motu, Eiki-taubotu, Eiki-toho, } *s.* A chief of the highest rank, a chief of chiefs.
Eiki-vaka, *s.* The commander of a vessel.
Eitu, *s.* A heathen feast.
Eitu, *s.* A side ; a half.
Eu, Eueu, } *s.* The corner of an axe ; corner.
Eueu, *a.* Slanting, skue.
Eutaha, *s.* The name of a felling axe.
Eba, *a.* Stately; proud.
Ebu, *v.* To drink.
Ebu, Ebuebu, } *v.* To cut up weeds ; to throw sand or earth with a spade.
Efe, *s.* The cava dust after it has been once strained.
Efeefe, *s.* A kind of food.
Efe-lolo, *s.* The dried remains after making oil.
Efe-niu, *s.* The grated cocoa nut, after the emulsion is strained out.
Efiafi, *s.* Afternoon.
Efi, Efiefi, } *v.* To carry under the arm.
Efi, Efiefi, } *a.* Crowded ; full.
Efiefi, *s.* The name of a shell fish.
Efihaki, Efihi, } *v.* To hide ; to conceal betwixt or amongst other things ; to press.

Efihia, *v.* To be entangled; to be caught; to be wedged in.
Efikona, *v.* To wear the dress in a certain way.
Efinaga, *s.* A wrapper.
Efituu, *a.* Crowded.
Efu, *s.* Dust; the name of one kind of fine mats.
Efuefu, *s.* Ashes.
Efui, *v.* To wash the hair during the process of dying it.
Efuhia, *a.* Dusty, covered with dust.
Efutoga, *s.* The name of one kind of fine mat.
Ega, *s.* Turmerick.
Egeega, *a.* Yellow, yellowish.
Eginaki, *s.* Exhortation; direction.
Eginaki, *v.* To exhort, to direct.
Eha, *pron.* What? what of it.
Eheehe, *s.* A horse laugh.
Eheehe, *v.* To laugh.
Ehi, Ehiehi, } *a.* Vain; thoughtless; proud.
Ehiehii, *v.* To take care of; to be particular about.
Eho, *a.* Putrid, fetid.
Eho, *s.* Putrefaction, putrescence.
Eji, *s.* A mound or hillock.
Eji, *v.* To raise a mound; to decorticate with the teeth; to carry fire.
Ejia, *s.* The handle of any tool.
Ejieji, *v.* To finish off with the teeth.
Eji-feilaulau, *s.* An altar.
Eke, *s.* Examination; a question or inquiry.
Eke, *v.* To inquire into, to examine, to question.
Ekeekei, *v.* To skim or brush anything from the surface of the water.
Ekei, *v.* To stir, to agitate, as water.
Ekenaki, *s.* The voice.
Ekenaki-oluga, *s.* A strong counter voice.
Ekenaki-lalo, *s.* A deep bass voice.
Eketaki, *part.* Swollen.
Ekinaki, Ekiekinaki, } See *Eginaki.*
E kimaua, *pron. du.* We, us, two, speaking to a third.
E kimautolu, *pron. plu.* We, us, excluding those addressed.
E kimoua, *pron. du.* You, two.
E kimoutolu, *pron. plu.* You.
E kinaua, *pron. du.* They two.
E kinautolu, *pron. plu.* They, them.
E kitaua, *pron. du.* We, us, two.
E kitautolu, *pron. plu.* We, us, including all addressed.
Eku, *pron.* Mine, my.
Ela, See *Eba.*
Elelo, *s.* The tongue.
Elili, *s.* The name of a shell fish.
Elito, *s.* The core or hard substance of a boil.
Elo, *v.* To stink.
Elo, *a.* Putrid; stinking.
Elomoui, *v.* To work lazily or as one all but dead.
Eluelu, *s.* A word used by the weak party when overmatched.
Eluelu, *v.* To beg quarter.
Emi, *v.* To move; to shift as the wind,
Emiemi, *v.* To make wry faces; to move; to wriggle about.
Emo, *v.* To lick.
Emo, Emoemo, } *part.* Licking or lapping, as a dog.
E na, *pron. du.* Theirs, two.
Ene, *pron.* His, hers, or its.
Ene, Eneene, } *v.* To tickle; to shew the fists or the club, as a challenge for boxing.
Enei, *v.* To report anything with the design of causing laughter; to exaggerate.
E ni, *ad.* Here; now.
E ta, *pron. du.* Ours, two.

Ete, *pron.* Mine.

Eteaki, } *v.* To be careful; to
Eteeteaki, } be cautious.

Eteete, *v.* To walk with the heel of the foot from the earth; to walk slowly.

Eva, *v.* To walk about.

Evai, } *v.* To look out; to note
Evahi, } if there be anything.

Eve, *a.* Many, much.

Eveeva, *s.* The act of walking; ambulation.

Eveeva, *v.* To walk at pleasure; to saunter; to loiter.

Eveevaaga, *s.* A walk; a sauntering place.

Eveeve, *s.* Old worn out mats.

Eveeve, *a.* Abounding in; covered with dust and bits of rotten mats.

I

I, THE third letter in the Tonga Alphabet. Its sound is that of *i* in *machine*.

I, *s.* A fan.

I, *prep.* In, within, by, through, with.

I, } *s.* The pain or sensation of
Ii, } hunger.

Ia, *pron.* He, she, or it.

Iaue, *inter.* Dear me!

Iate, *prep.* To, from, with.

Io, *s.* A part, quarter, or division.

Io, *ad.* Yes; the affirmative; even.

Ioao, *s.* The belly quarter of the fish.

Ioho, *s.* A scream, an outcry.

Ioho, *v.* To bawl aloud, to scream.

Iotua, *s.* The back quarter of the fish.

Ibiibi, *s.* The cocoa nut after the *uto* has been taken out; the white fat of fish.

Ibo, *s.* Stone blindness of the eye.

Ibu, *s.* The general name for earthenware utensils, but used with a qualifying term when particularizing, as,

[illegible], *s.* A [illegible] to drink from; [illegible]

[illegible], *s.* A frying pan.

Ibu [illegible], *s.* A [illegible]

Ibu-kai, *s.* A plate.

Ifa, *v.* To contract or draw in the belly.

Ife, *ad.* Where?

Ifi, *s.* The name of a tree, and its fruit; the act of blowing with the mouth.

Ifi, *v.* To blow; to sound an instrument of musick.

Ifiifi, *s.* The lights of the turtle.

Ifo, *s.* The taste.

Ifo-kovi, *a.* Unsavoury, disagreeable to the taste.

Ifo-lelei, *a.* Savoury, agreeable to the taste.

Igo, *s.* Displeasure.

Igo, *v.* To be vexed or displeased.

Igoigoi, *a.* Variegated; diversified in pattern and colour.

Ihu, *s.* The nose.

Ihu-baga, } *s.* A diseased nose.
Ihu-babaga, }

Ihu-bagi, *s.* A flat nose; a deformed nose.

Ihu-golo, *v.* To speak through the nose.

Ihu-vaka, *s.* A large nose.

Ihu-mene, *s.* A peak nose.

Ijiaki, } *v.* To be careful of;
Ijiijiaki, } attentive to.

Ika, *s.* Fish.

Ikai, *ad.* No; the negative.

Ikafano, *s.* Fish that migrate.

Ikamanu, *s.* The name of a fish.

Ikataane, *s.* The name of a fish.
Ike, *s.* A beater, used in beating out the *tapa.*
Ikeikaavai, *s.* The small insect in water.
Iki, *a.* Small.
Ikimoa, *v.* To tear in pieces.
Iku, *s.* The end; the tail of animals.
Iku, Ikui, } *v.* To finish; to achieve; to conquer.
Ikuga, Ikuaga, } *s.* The ending place; the termination.
Ikuiku, *s.* The ends or tail of any thing.
Ikuna, *v.* To overcome, to conquer; to accomplish.
Ikunou, *s.* A short and stumpy tail, as the *goat.*
Ikuvale, *s.* A phrase used in reference to the mortaliy of man; literally, a foolish finish.
Ila, *s.* A mark; a spot on the body.
Ilaila, *a.* Spotted; streaked.
Ilamutu, *s.* A niece, or nephew.
Ileila, *a.* Nearly ripe.
Ileile, *a.* Destitute; fearful.
Ili, *s.* What is kept or reserved for re-production.
Ilifia, *s.* Consternation, terror.
Ilifia, *v.* To be terrified.
Ilo, *s.* Knowledge, understanding.
Ilo, *v.* To know; to find; to discover; to discern; to eat.
Iloa, *v.* To be known; to be found out or discovered.
Iloaga, *s.* A knowing discerning character; the author or source of knowledge.
Iloage, *ad.* Suddenly; lo.
Iloilo, *s.* Prudence.
Iloilo, *v.* To act prudently.
Iloilo, *a.* Prudent.
Iloga, *s.* A sign; a mark.
Iloga, *ad.* Whenever, whensoever, *ke iloga ene alu;* whenever he shall go.
Ilogofua, *a.* Easy to know or understand.
Ilogataa, *a.* Difficult to understand.
Ilohele, *a.* Cunning, knowing, as a bird who knows the snare.
Ina, *v.* To expose the teeth; to laugh.
Inafo, *s.* A shoal of fish, *Atu.*
Inaga, *s.* Due; desert.
Inaji, *s.* A heathen ceremony; portion, part, share.
Ine, *s.* A fond expression, similar to *ala.*
Ineina, See *Ina.*
Ino, Inoino, } *s.* An action of the arms by which a challenge to fight is understood.
Inu, *s.* Beverage, drink.
Inu, Inua, } *v.* To drink.
Isa, Isaisa, } *v.* To hiss; to disapprove; to contemn.
Ita, *s.* Anger; displeasure.
Itaina, Iteina, Itegia, } *s.* The object of displeasure.
Iteita, *a.* Cross, peevish, ill-humoured.
Ivi, *s.* The edge of a plank or board.
Iviivi, *s.* The edges or corners of wood, as a square leg.
Iviivi, *a.* Strong, as one whose veins appear large and full.
Ivilahi, Ivimalohi, Iviivimalohi, } *a.* Strong; athletic; robust.
Ivivaivai, *a.* Small in the limbs and body.

O

O, THE fourth letter in the Tonga Alphabet. Its sound is that of *o* in *Mole*.

O, *prep.* Of; belonging to.

O, *con.* And.

O, *v.* To go, applied to two or more.

Oaoigutu, *s.* The roof of the mouth.

Oaoiniu, *s.* The outer of the cocoa nut kernal, the inner, near the shell, called *oloalo*.

Oi, *v.* To grind; to pulverize; to work or act upon; to set a going; to originate.

Oi, *s.* An expression of pain.

Oiau, *s.* An expression of surprise,

Oiaue, *inter.* Alas! alas! dear me!

Oo, *s.* The name of a fish.

Oo, *v.* To infix, to fasten.

Oo, *a.* Deep; infixt.

Oofaki, *v.* To overshadow; to nestle; to brood over.

Ooji, *a.* Perfect, complete.

Ooku, *pron.* Mine.

Oona, *pron.* His, hers, or its.

Oota, *s.* The cry of the hen when disturbed during incubation.

Ou, *pron.* I.

Oua, *v.* To desist, to cease, to give over.

Obe, } *v.* To extend; to pass
Obeobe, } the bounds.

Obeobe, *a.* Full to the brim.

Obo, *a.* Full of fat.

Oboobo, *v.* To strengthen, as by lashing a sound stick to one cracked.

Oboji, *v.* To fill up; to put on.

Obotai, *v.* To stick; to be close, as one flat surface upon another; to cleave to.

Ofa, *s.* Love, affection, esteem; a fathom, or the measure of the arms extended.

Ofa, *a.* Loving, affectionate.

Ofa, *v.* To love; to wish, as, *ofa ke behe,* O that it may be so; or, may it be so.

Ofaaga, *a.* Beloved; dear.

Ofauuuu, *v.* To love dearly, literally, biting love, love that bites the mind.

Ofafaituuga, *v.* To love in deed; to love practically.

Ofakofu, *s.* A small and trifling present, as an expression of love.

Ofamamahi, *s.* Compassion; painful sympathy.

Ofato, *s.* An insect found in old timber.

Ofatonoa, *s.* Love not reciprocated.

Ofe, } *v.* To train; to bend by
Ofei, } force.

Ofeina, } *a.* Favoured; belov-
Ofeofeina, } ed by many.

Ofefine, *s.* Daughter.

Ofi, *s.* Nearness.

Ofi, *a.* Near at hand.

Ofo, *s.* Suprise; marvel; wonder.

Ofo, } *v.* To be suprised; to
Ofoofo, } revive afresh, as any herb that appeared dead.

Ofaofaakui, *s.* Conduct unbecoming a grandfather.

Ofoofonoa, *a.* Unprepared; being taken by suprise.

Ofoofotonu, *v.* To be ready prepared for; to be in expectation of.

Ofomaumau, } *v.* To be taken by
Ofovale, } surprise.

Ofu, *a.* Overcooked; stale; withered.

Ogo, *s.* A pair, a couple; two of a sort.

Ogo, Ogo i, } *v.* To hear; to feel.

Ogo, Ogo i, } *s.* Feeling, sensibility.

Ogoogaa, *a.* Deafening.

Ogoogo, *s.* Fame, a report, rumour, reporter.

Ogoogo, *a.* Renowned, celebrated.

Ogoogo, Ogoogoa, } *v.* To report, to make known.

Ogoogo-kovi, *s.* Ill fame, disrepute.

Ogoogo-lelei, *s.* Good news, good reputation.

Ogo-fakaevaha, *s.* A wild report; an unauthenticated story.

Ogogataa, *a.* Obdurate, hard.

Ogogofua, *a.* Tender; easily affected.

Ogojia, *v.* To be wearied or overworked.

Ogojiaibe, *v.* To labour in vain.

Ogojino, *a.* Invigorating to the body; pleasing to the mind.

Ogo-noa, *v.* To hear indistinctly.

Ogo-noa, Ogo-vale, } *a.* Deaf; indistinctly to the ear.

Oha, *int.* What.

Ohi, *v.* To adopt.

Ohi, *s.* Adoption; the name given to the banana trees that have grown up from the roots of former trees.

Ohiohii, *v.* To train; to attend to.

Ohi-malaia, *s.* One who is unfortunate in adopting children; an adopted oue who does badly, notwithstanding he has been well treated.

Oho, *s.* The food of travellers or voyagers; the cramp or spasms.

Oho, *v.* To rush upon; to shoot, as spasms.

Ohoana, *s.* A wife or husband; a partner.

Ohooho, *a.* Neither full nor empty.

Ohoga, *s.* A shoal of fish.

Oho-mate, *s.* A mad desperate rush.

Oho-mohe, *s.* Supper.

Oho-noa, *v.* To rush without thought; to obtrude; to precipitate.

Oho-noa, *a.* Foolhardy, headlong.

Oho-noa, *s.* Obtruder, meddler, precipitancy.

Ohu, *s.* Smoke, soot; a spoon or ladle.

Ohu, Ohu-hake, } *v.* To lade or throw out water; to scoop.

Ohua, *v.* To be smoked.

Ohule, *s.* The name of a shell fish.

Oji, *v.* To be finished; to be done; all gone.

Oji, Ojibe, } *a.* Both.

Ojieneveneve, *a.* Endless.

Ojioji, *v.* To be consumed.

Ojiojiga-malie, *v.* To be utterly consumed.

Ojioji-loto, *a.* Without a mind; consumed by anger or grief.

Ojiki, *v.* To accomplish; to finish.

Ojikiavelega, *v.* To do with earnestness; to do till at a loss what to do.

Ojikoa, *v.* To strive or to work earnestly; to part with all.

Oka, *ad.* When (only in the future tense.)

Oko, *a.* Fat (the *Kiu.)*

Okooka, *s.* A pole bored into the sand, to which the canoe is fastened.

Okooko, *v.* To seek fire wood.

Oku, The sign of the present tense.

Ola, *v.* To scoop out with the teeth; to gnaw.

Ola, *s.* Any thing obtained after which search has been made; the fruit, the consequence.

Ola, *s.* A heathen feast; the name of a tree.

Ola, *v.* To extinguish a light; to succeed; to obtain what was sought.

Olaola, *v.* To bite off the skin of the yam; to nibble.

Oliji, *s.* The Papaw, also its fruit—pummy apple.

Olo, Oloa, Oloi, } *v.* To ensnare, to allure, to tempt; to rub, to brush, or scrub.

Oloolo, *v.* To catch sharks.

Oloolo, *s.* The bush or uncultivated land of the back part of the island.

Oloboou, *s.* The first born.

Olofakalafokoa, *v.* To allure by stratagem.

Olomea, *s.* The name of a fish.

Oma, *s.* Sponge.

Oma, *v.* To tighten; to draw up a noose; to fly.

Omai, Omi, } *v.* To bring, to fetch.

Omo, Omoomo, } *v.* To project; to shoot beyond something, above or below it. See *Amoamo.*

Omooma, Omooma-fanobe, } *v.* To walk proudly; to swagger to and fro.

Omua, See *Oua.*

One, *s.* Gunpowder.

One-iki, *s.* Fine sand.

Oneone, *s.* Sand.

Oneonea, Oneoneia, } *a.* Sandy.

One-uli, *s.* Black sand.

Onebata, *s.* Gravel.

Onó, *s.* The name of a fish.

Onó, *a.* Six; short.

Onoono, *v.* To bow down; to bend forwards.

Onogahoa, *a.* Six pairs or couples.

Onogakau, *a.* Six score.

Onogeau, *a.* Six hundred.

Onogejino, *a.* Six.

Onogofuhi, *a.* Six hundred couples.

Onogofulu, *a.* Sixty.

Ota, *a.* Raw, undressed, applied only to food.

Ota, *v.* To eat raw food.

Otai, *s.* A preparation of food.

Ota-fuifuivai, *s.* Fish washed in fresh water.

Ota-lalakoa, *v.* To eat raw and unwashed.

Ota-taefuifui, *s.* Any thing eaten raw and unwashed, used of any thing unsuitable.

Otoota, *s.* Sweepings, rubbish.

Otoota, Otootaia, } *a.* Dirty.

Otu, *s.* A row or line; a range; a rank; the sign of the plural, applying to lands.

Otua, *s.* God.

Otule, *s.* The name of a fish.

Ovava, *s.* The name of a tree.

U

U, THE fifth letter in the Tonga Alphabet. Its sound is that of *u* in *Rule.*

U, *v.* to be agreed, unanimous; to sound.

U, *s.* A bundle; a faggot, a sheaf; sound; a stick used in preparing the native oven.

Ua, *a.* Two.

Ua, *s.* The neck.

Ua, *v.* To ward off; to raise by lever.

Uaga, *s.* The maggot.

Uagaia, Uagahia, } *a.* Maggotty.

Uagofuhi, *a.* Twice two hundred.

Uagaahoa, *a.* Two pairs or couples.

20

Uagakau, *a.* Two score.
Uageau, *a.* Two hundred.
Uakai, *s.* Greediness, ravenousness.
Uakai, *v.* To crave, to long for, to raven.
Uaki, *s.* The name of a war spear.
Ualolo, *v.* To be assembled and seated, a large number.
Uamakaemaema, *v.* To be careful of his own, but trouble others for the same.
Uatei, *a.* In motion; dilation; jagging to and fro.
Ue, *int.* Similar to *Aua*.
Uei, Ueuei, } *v.* To shake; to move; to dispose; to try to set a going.
Ui, *int.* Expressive of displeasure; fy.
Ui, *s.* A call; the name of one kind of cocoa nut.
Ui, Uiui, Uiuii, } *v.* To call, to call repeatedly.
Uiui, *a.* Black.
Uimui, *v.* To speak in order to prevent.
Uo, *s.* Lobster, craw fish.
Uo, *s.* An indiscriminate assembly.
Uoua, *s.* Sinews.
Uouagakehekehe, *a.* Different opinions; not unanimous.
Uouagataha, Uouagatatau, } *a.* Unanimous; of one mind.
Uouatanu, *a.* Deep, out of sight, the veins of the arms.
Uofulu, *a.* Twenty.
Uotuu, Uouotuu, } *s.* Commotion; tumult.
Uu, *s.* The name of a shell fish.
Uu, *v.* To bite, to sting.
Uu, *s.* A bite; the act of biting.
Uua, *v.* To crow, as a cock.
Uufi, *v.* To cover, to overspread.
Uufi, *s.* A cover, an overall.
Uuku, *s.* Continuance.
Uuku, *v.* To continue; to persevere.
Uulu, *s.* Sound or noise of any thing in motion.
Uulu, *v.* To fall; to sound in falling.
Uutaki, *v.* To keep between the teeth.
Ufe, *s.* A heathen play.
Ufi, *s.* The yam; the name of a shell fish.
Ufi, *v.* To act with reverence, care, and attention.
Ufia, *v.* To be covered or hid.
Ufiufi, *v.* To cover, to conceal.
Ufiufi, *s.* A cover, a screen.
Ufikau, *s.* A covering; anything said or done to cover an offence.
Ufilei, *s.* A small kind of yam.
Ufileifieufi, *s.* One small, but very aspiring; one poor, but proud.
Ufitea, *s.* A film.
Ufivaito, *s.* A preparation of food.
Ufu, *s.* The name of a fish.
Uga, *s.* The name of a shell fish.
Uga, *v.* To whine, to cry; to beg assistance in any work.
Uga, *v.* To take shelter; to be sheltered or screened.
Uga, *a.* Rotten, decayed, as the teeth.
Ugaaga, Ugaki, } *s.* Shelter, a screen.
Ugaane, *s.* The neck, of the lobster.
Ugaki, Ugekina, Ugi, Ugia, } *v.* To shelter, to defend, to screen.
Ugakikiva, *s.* The name of a shell fish.
Uga-mate, *a.* Deadly shade.
Uga-moui, *a.* Shade favourable to life.
Ugogo, *s.* The name of an insect.
Ugouga, *a.* Full of notches and small holes.

Uha, *s.* Rain.
Uha, *v.* To rain.
Uhaia, *a.* Wet with rain.
Uha-fakahahau, *s.* A drizzling small rain.
Uha-lolo, *s.* Heavy rain.
Uha-maka, *s.* Hail.
Uha-tea, *s.* Rain that falls whilst the sun shines.
Uheina, *a.* Wet with rain.
Uhele, *v.* To prepare the oven for cooking a large quantity of food.
Uhi, *s.* The name of a shrub.
Uhi, *v.* To go or come.
Uhie, *s.* An ill omen.
Uhiuhi, *s.* The name of a tree.
Uhiuhi, *a.* Dark blue, as the deep water of the sea.
Uhiuhimau, *v.* To frequent any place.
Uhiga, *s.* Meaning, explanation, signification; the course.
Uhi, Uhiki, } *s.* The young of animals.
Uhila, *s.* Lightning.
Uhila, *v.* To lighten.
Uhinoa, Uhiuhinoa, } *a.* To go or come without any special object in view.
Uho, *s.* The umbilical chord; the root of the kava; pith.
Uhotahabe, *s.* A term applied to children of the same mother.
Uhu, *v.* To shoot, as quick pains; to go or come early in the morning.
Uhu, *s.* Morning; twilight.
Uhui, *v.* To intervene, to come between persons; to pick the teeth; to ram.
Uhui, *s.* A rammer.
Uhuihui, *v.* To pass between persons.
Uji, *s.* The buttock; the seat.
Uji, Ujia, } *v.* To bite; to be bitten.
Uka, *s.* The string of a bow; the temporary fastenings in building a canoe.
Uka, *a.* Sticky; well mixed, applied to Tonga bread.
Uke, *a.* Small.
Ukei, *s.* The challenge of a weak party to a strong one.
Uki, *v.* To inquire; to look up.
Ukiukivale, *v.* To inquire or look after in vain.
Uku, *v.* To dive.
Ukuloa, *a.* Long, applied to time.
Ukuma, *v.* To endure; to bear.
Ukuma, *a.* Patient.
Ukunaki, *a.* Persevering; industrious.
Ula, *s.* A heathen night dance; a name of office.
Ula. *a.* Quicksighted; clever.
Ula, *v.* To dance.
Ule, *s.* The penis.
Uli, *s.* Filth, contamination, nastiness.
Uli, *a.* Dirty, polluted, filthy.
Uli, *v.* To steer a vessel.
Ulia, *v.* To be terrified; to be in terror; to be lost out of sight.
Ulie, *s.* A large species of the lizard.
Uliuli, *a.* Black, dark.
Ulifofo, *a.* Very dirty, filthy.
Uligaki, Uliuligaki, } *a.* Determined, resolute, fixed.
Ulilologo, *a.* Silent, sullen, dumb.
Ulo, *s.* Flame, blaze.
Ulo, *v.* To flame, to blaze.
Uloa, *s.* One mode of catching fish.
Uloa, *v.* To catch fish by the *uloa.*
Uloulo, *a.* Flaming, blazing.
Ulotea, *s.* Faint rays of the sun.
Ulu, *s.* The head; the number ten.
Ulu, *v.* To enter; to pass through, as anything thrown or darted.
Ulu, *a.* Thick, bushy, as a dress of leaves.
Ulua, *s.* The name of a fish.
Uluaki, *a.* First.

Uluaki, *s.* First-begotten.
Uluega, *s.* The name of the tenth moon in the Tonga year.
Ului, *v.* To join; to unite with; to change the dress.
Ulua, *a.* Long-headed.
Ululu, *s.* The edge of the reef where the sea breaks; one method of taking fish.
Ulubale, *s.* The top of the mast.
Uluboko, *s.* The skull.
Ulububu, *v.* To put heads together.
Ulubububububu, *a.* Thick, close, crowded, as the hair of the head.
Ulufi, *s.* A wooly head.
Ulufia, *v.* To be connected; to come in contact.
Ulugaaga, *s.* The predominant disposition of the mind.
Ulugaue, *s.* The name of one kind of yam.
Ulugia, *v.* To be beaten; out done in any game.
Uluhika, *s.* A head the hair of which stands erect.
Uluhina, *s.* A grey head.
Ulujino *v.* To dwell in the body; to be one with man, applied to the gods.
Ulukau, *s.* The name of a fish.
Ululoa, *s.* A high or long head.
Ulumoui, *s.* Applied to the yam, or any thing set in the earth, when all its virtue is thrown out in leaves or blossoms, but no fruit.
Ulutefua, *s.* A friendless person.
Ulutukua, *v.* To be subject to another.
Ulutoke, *s.* A long head.
Uluvali, *v.* The name of a person killed at the burial of the *tuitoga.*
Uluvatu, *s.* A rendezvous; a place to which many resort.
Uma, *s.* The shoulder.
Uma, *v.* To kiss.
Umaji, *v.* To kiss by force; to pinch; to pull off the skin.
Umaki, *v.* To eat and drink alternately.
Umana, *s.* The name of a shell fish.
Umata, *s.* The rainbow.
Ume, *s.* The name of a fish.
Umea, *s.* Clay.
Umeohu, *s.* The name of a fish.
Umeumea, *s.* Rust; canker.
Umeumea, *a.* Rusty.
Umeumea, *v.* To rust; to corrode.
Umejia, *v.* To pinch; to pull the flesh.
Umelei, *s.* The name of a fish.
Umeta, *s.* The name of a fish.
Umevale, *s.* The name of a fish.
Umiji, *v.* To wish to eat fish.
Umoumo, *v.* To cork; to stop up, applied to many.
Umoji, *s.* A cork, bung, plug.
Umoji, *v.* To cork; to bung.
Umu, *s.* A basket of native food dressed; the name of a fish.
Umuumu, *s.* Small sand banks.
Umuhina, *s.* The name of a fish.
Umumoana, *s.* The name of a fish.
Umutegetega, *s.* The name of a fish.
Unaau, *s.* The name of a fish.
Unani, } *v.* To eat sparingly
Unounani, } or delicately.
Uni, *v.* To collect together, and carry in the hand.
Uno, *s.* The scales of fish; tortoise shell.
Unouno, *a.* Scaly.
Unofiiaki, *s.* A film on the eye.
Unoho, *s.* A husband or wife.
Unohoimanu, *s.* A male and female of birds or animals.
Unohoivale, *s.* A couple who are alike foolish.
Unomoa, *s.* The name of a fish.
Unu, *s.* The strainer of the kava when full.

Unu, *v.* To wet to saturate, to wash; to choose; to pass through to shed the skin, as the cockroach; to shave; to chop less, as in size, a mast; to let out the sail, to unreef; to take a knot or two from the sail.

Unu, } *a.* To draw near; to
Unuunu, } approach.

Unua, *v.* To give in; to yield.

Unufi, *s.* The caterpillar.

Unuhi, *v.* To draw out; to unsheath.

Uta, *s.* Inland; land; on shore; the cargo or freight of a vessel; applied to the *tuitoga* and persons of his, or her rank.

Uta, *a.* Fixed, habituated.

Uta, } *v.* To think over;
Utagi, } to consider; to
Utegia, } weigh over in the mind. Also, *s.* An opinion; advice.

Utaki, *v.* To carry in the mouth.

Utakikauinifo, *v.* To endure; to bear.

Utete, *s.* Jews harp.

Uto, *s.* The brains; the spongy kernel of the cocoa nut when germinating; the light sticks along the top of a fishing net.

Utotaiegamokumaokuua, *v.* To reserve food for a future time, before all are satisfied.

Utu, *s.* The name of a fish.

Utu, *v.* To fetch; to gather in; to carry.

Utu, *a.* Perpendicular, as the *Liku* at Vavau.

Utua, *a.* Used in reference to the sea at ebb tide.

Utuaki, *v.* To carry food to a distance; to supply in time of famine.

Utueuho, *a.* Dead or quite ripe, banana.

Utuutu, *v.* To glean; to seek what may remain.

Utuutufi, *v.* To run; to pour out; to flow along, as a smell in the air.

Utuutufi, *s.* A smell from a distance.

Utufata, *a.* Crowded with people.

Utufia, *v.* To pour out; to run as water from a vessel, or tears from the eyes.

Utuutugaki, *v.* To increase; to grow despite endeavour.

Utuhia, *v.* To be interrupted; stopt in the performance of any work.

Ututekaki, *v.* To fetch water in one small vessel.

B

B THE sixth letter in the Tonga Alphabet. Its sound is that of *ba* in *Bark;* and frequently its sound is that of *pa* in *Park.*

Ba, *s.* A Tonga fish hook; a shield; a report; sound; an eruption; a fence.

Ba, *v.* To be reported; to reach; to sound forth; to shoot up as plants set in the earth; to strike, to slap.

Baa, *a.* Barren.

Baa, *s.* Barrenness; indentations of trees.

Baabaa, *s.* The name of the middle rib of the banana and cocoa nut leaf.

Baabaagaua, *a.* Uncertain, undetermined.

Baaga, *s.* A flat bean pitched in gambling; a piece of money; coin; a name given to garlands, when threaded and prepared.

Bae, *s.* A dam; a sill; any thing

which prevents the rolling or moving of other matters; a leaf for catching rain.

Bae, *v.* To push or throw to a different place.

Baea, *s.* A friendless person; a pauper.

Baea, *a.* Friendless, poor, destitute.

Baea, *v.* To float on the surface of the water; to drift.

Baeaki, *a.* Full to overflowing; abundant.

Baeoa, *v.* To be ashamed; to feel confused.

Baebae, *v.* To lay logs or stones as dams or sills.

Baega, *s.* A pitching gambling place.

Baeko, *a.* Lean; wanting fat, applied to fish after spawing.

Baetaku, *v.* To sneer at.

Baetaku, *a.* Sneering contemptuous.

Bai, Baibai, } *a.* Contracted or maimed in the fingers or toes; applied also to trees stunted in the growth.

Baika, *s.* A fence built to entrap fish.

Baikea, *s.* The name of a shell fish.

Baiku, *s.* A game.

Baiku-iku, *s.* The point; the spear; the taper end of any thing.

Bao, *s.* A fringe; a flounce.

Bao, *v.* To row; to transplant the banana shoots.

Baobao, *v.* To drive forward as in pitching; to exaggerate.

Baobao-mui, *v.* To keep in the rear; to proceed warily.

Baoboji, *s.* One kind ef Tonga fish hook.

Baogataa, *s.* Obstinacy, stubbornness.

Baogataa, *a.* Obstinate, stubborn, restiff, unyielding.

Baogofua, *s.* Readiness, promptitude.

Baogofua, *a.* Ready, willing, prompt.

Bau, *a.* Confident, fixed, determined, certain, definite.

Bau, *ad.* Certainly, without, question.

Baua, *s.* The name of a fish.

Bauu, *s.* Mischief; a mischievous one; a rogue.

Bauu, *a.* Roguish, mischievous.

Bauu, *v.* To act the rogue.

Bauuji, Bauujia, } *v.* To tease; to annoy; play the rogue; to be teased or annoyed.

Bauhiuhi, *a.* Green, black, and bright.

Baulu, *v.* To fall with force or a sudden noise.

Baba, *s.* A preparation of food; the name of a fish.

Baba, *s.* A long hollow piece of wood on which the native cloth is printed; board. *Laubaba*, a board; a flat bed of stones.

Baba, *a.* Plain; even, as a road much trodden.

Baba, *v.* To break out afresh, as a wound; to crack; to shake before falling.

Babae, *s.* The name of a fish.

Babae, *a.* Slanting, oblique, bashful.

Babaea, *v.* To fall to leeward; to be driven by wind and waves.

Babai, *v.* To spread out in order; to lay upon.

Babauu, *v.* To look sullen and displeased.

Babababa, *a.* Smooth, not rough or rugged; nearly filled, applied to a wound.

Babaga, *s.* A face deformed by the *Bala*; the face or exterior of any thing that is rough.

Babagatoa, *s.* Thickly set; indistinct.

Babagatuu, *a.* See *Babagotoa*.

Babagi, *s.* A murderous blow.
Babahi, *s.* A mischief maker ; a rogue.
Babahi, *a.* Mischievous.
Babahu, *v.* To strike each other, as in *Fetaaki.*
Babaka, *v.* To flinch ; to boggle.
Babala, *v.* Diseased with the *Bala.*
Babala, *s.* See *Bala.*
Babala-amanaki, *v.* To be overtaken by the consequence of bad conduct.
Babalagi, *s.* A foreigner ; foreign manufactures, such as cloth, linen, &c.
Babale, *v.* To do at a venture ; to submit.
Babaliliki, *s.* A mat of a fine texture.
Babanaki, *v.* To presume ; to venture upon ; to fear no refusal.
Babanaki, *s.* The ends and rags of the *Fetaaki.*
Babanaki, *a.* Soft, spongy.
Babani, *v.* To forage in search of food.
Babani, *s.* Forage ; food sought abroad in time of war.
Babani, *s.* The crest or top of the *Kalae.*
Babata, *a.* Coarse in texture ; unkind, in language.
Babata, *v.* To break out, as an eruption in the skin.
Babate, *v.* To be used to ; accustomed to ; in the habit of.
Babatetele, *s.* A mat of coarse texture.
Babatoa, *a.* Threatening rain.
Babatuu, *v.* To stand withal, as a tree that cracks oft and long before it falls.
Babeva, See *Tabeva.*
Bafunoa, *v.* To talk without thought.
Babunoa, *a.* Talkative, loquacious.
Bafetaaki, *v.* To soften and smooth the *fetaaki,* ere it is made into *gatu.*
Bafua, *v.* To strike the whole surface ; to fall flat against.
Baga, *s.* A cicatrice ; a scar.
Bagia, *v.* To strike a heavy blow.
Bago, Bagovivi, } *a.* Disgusting, abominable, sad, bad, unlucky.
Bagoa, *s.* Holes or pits of water.
Bagotogoto, *a.* Abundant in flesh ; stout, large, full grown.
Baha, *s.* The name of a shrub.
Baha, *v.* To break out ; to have eruption from the body.
Bahabaha, *a.* Dark red ; blood colour.
Bahabahagi, *a.* Light, not heavy.
Bahabahagi, *s.* Lightness ; without weight.
Bahakohaka, *a.* Thin ; tall or long, but thin.
Bahakula, *a.* Red ; blood-like.
Bahi, Bahia, Bahiaoho, } *v.* To be tired of ; to be out of love with anything ; to loathe.
Bahihi, *a.* Split, riven.
Bahihi, *s.* A splinter, a thin piece of wood, used as a knife.
Bahu, *s.* A hollow tree set in water, as a filterer.
Bahu, Bahua, } *v.* To beat soundly.
Bahui, *a.* Lean, all bones.
Bahubahu, *a.* Hoarse, deep, rough, applied to sound.
Baji, *v.* To clap hands.
Bajia, Bajiejia, } *a.* Light, not burdened or laden ; clear of impediment or affliction.
Bajibaji, *v.* To continue clapping the hands.
Bajibaji, *v.* To have become incapable of exciting interest ; to weary by the same thing over and over again.
Bajika, *v.* To glide ; to skim along.

Bajilijili, *v.* To take the lead; to excel.
Bajini, *s.* An ornament for the neck, made from whale's teeth.
Bajino, *v.* To be fixed, determined, or agreed.
Bajino, *a.* Fixed, settled.
Baka, *s.* The name of a shell fish.
Baka, *v.* To flinch; to evade.
Bakau, *a.* Slender.
Bakauua, *a.* Wretchedly thin or poor in flesh.
Bakaukau, Bakabaka, Bakabakau, } *a.* Spare, slender; wanting flesh.
Bakabakaka, Bakaka, } *a.* Crisp, curled, brittle.
Bake, *v.* To challenge; to boast.
Bake, *s.* A challenge.
Bake, *a.* Boasting; exulting in one's strength.
Bakebake, Bakeke, } *v.* See *Bakabaka*.
Bakelekele, *s.* A barrier or rampart of earth.
Baki, Bakii, } *v.* To break off; to pluck; to snap.
Baki, *s.* A small paddle.
Bakia, *s.* A deathwatch; an insect that makes a ticking noise.
Bakia, *v.* To impinge; to strike against.
Bakiua, *v.* To cohabit with mother and daughter.
Bakibaki, *v.* To break bread or any brittle substance.
Bakibaki, *s.* The name of a war club.
Bakihi, *s.* A cracking noise; a shrill voice.
Bakihi, *v.* To crack; to smack.
Bakimagamaga, *v.* To break off the tails of fish, as a proof that such a quantity was caught more than could be brought to shore.
Bakimoetalaha, *v.* To gather both, when one ought to have been left.
Bakini, *v.* To whip children.
Bakitaha, *v.* To cut in two.
Bako, Bakobako, } *s.* A hollow sound; the striking of the arm, as a challenge for wrestling.
Bako, *s.* The name of a plant.
Bakoka, *v.* To use plenty of *koka* in making *gatu*.
Bakoko, *a.* Dry, shrivelled.
Bakoko, *s.* The name of the mulberry bark when dried.
Bakokoua, *a.* Double dried; twice shrivelled.
Baku, *s.* Crust; the crisp of any thing cooked; the motion of the throat of one near death.
Baku, *v.* To arrive. See *Ba*.
Baku, *a.* Unwilling, reluctant.
Bakubaku, *s.* A crust; a scab; any substance grown hard or crusty.
Bakubaku, *a.* Crimp; brittle.
Bala, *s.* The name of a disease; a sore.
Bala, *a.* Ulcerated, decayed, rotten.
Bala, *v.* To be glided along by the wind.
Bala-a, *s.* A piece of the reed fence.
Balai, *a.* Indistinct, confused, disordered.
Balau, *s.* A babbler.
Balau, *v.* To babble.
Balau, *v.* To pinch or scratch.
Bala-uli, *s.* The dark coloured cowry shell.
Balau-kovi, *a.* Not the same in works as in words.
Balabala, *s.* Dirt, mire, mud.
Balabala, *a.* Dirty, miry, soft, yielding.
Balabu, *s.* Mist.
Balabu, *a.* Misty, obscure.
Balagi, *s.* The name of a fish.

Balagia, *v.* To rot; to beat to a pulp.
Balahi, *a.* See *Balai*.
Balahia, *v.* To be deeply concerned or affected.
Balaka, *s.* The name of one kind of the sugar cane, and also of a war spear.
Balakakano, *s.* Breadth.
Balakakano, *a.* Broad.
Balalaua, *v.* To force or drive off or on, as a vessel near a reef.
Balalauatuu, *v.* To speak confusedly; to leave undecided.
Bala-kovi, *a.* Decayed; very rotten.
Balaku, *a.* Filthy, nasty.
Balala, *a.* Rough, broken sound.
Babale, *v.* To throw the net at a venture.
Balalafa, *s.* The mid rib of the cocoa nut leaf.
Balalivale, *a.* Awkward, clumsy.
Bala-taha, *a.* All on one side.
Bala-tahi, *a.* Saturated; soaked with sea water.
Bala-vale, *a.* Long; too long; longest.
Bale, *v.* To approach; to go as one weak and friendless.
Bale, *v.* To paddle; to row; to decline, as the sun when past the meridian.
Bale, *s.* A frontlet; a forked spear.
Balei, *v.* To ward or fence off; to turn aside.
Balebale, *s.* A shelf.
Balebale, *a.* Strong blowing, used when paddling canoes are the subject of conversation.
Baletuu, *v.* To go and come quickly in a small canoe.
Baleva, Baleveleva, } *a.* Tall; long; overgrown.
Balevaka, *s.* A long rod with which canoes are propelled along.
Balikiha, *s.* The name of one kind of banana.
Bali, *s.* Pubes.
Balo, *s.* The name of one kind of yam; a large kind of mouse.
Balolo, *s.* A reptile much like the earthworm, found in the sea.
Baloloa, *a.* See *Baleva.*
Balu, s. The name of a fish.
Balu, Balua, } *v.* To mix; to mingle.
Balua, *v.* To beat to a pulp.
Baluaga, *s.* Any vessel in which a mixture is made.
Balubalu, *s.* A marriageable girl.
Balufu, *s.* A shell fish.
Baluji, *s.* Paste, glue.
Baluji, *v.* To paste; to glue; to print.
Balutu, *v.* To bathe; to wash.
Balu-valea, *v.* To act out of order and character.
Ba-maka, *s.* High rocks; a wall of stone.
Bana, *a.* Slow in growth.
Bana, *v.* To stunt.
Banafunafu, *a.* Brown; snuff colour.
Banaki, *a.* Close; near at hand.
Banaki, *v.* To presume; to expect.
Banea, *a.* Old, older.
Banebanea, *a.* Dirty, filthy, applied to the head.
Banefunefu, *a.* Brown.
Bani, *v.* To anoint the head; to daub; to soil; to besmear.
Bania, *v.* To forage; to ravage.
Bani-uli, *a.* Dirty; besmeared with dirt.
Baniga, *s.* Property presented by a nephew or niece to an aunt, including every kind of Tonga treasures.
Bani-hia, *a.* Sinful; covered with sin.
Bani-tafe, *v.* To anoint profusely.
Basaga, *s.* A forked branch or tree.
Bata, *s.* Gravel or rough sand.

Bata, *v.* To break out, as an eruption in the skin.

Batailatuu, *v.* To talk and act well while all is prosperous.

Batabata, *a.* Coarse in texture; rough; large patterned.

Batabata, *a.* Too familiar; too talkative.

Bataka, *v.* To smack the mouth.

Bate-uli, *s.* A dark scar in the skin; what has become dark by keeping.

Batebate, *s.* A cicatrice; a name given to small inferior yams.

Bateto, *v.* To expose throughout; to search every part, as a wind, (the sea shore) to turn upside down.

Bato, *s.* The muscovy duck.

Bato, *s.* A noise; a stroke.

Batu, *s.* The sound of the feet in walking; the sound from any thing falling.

Batu, *s.* A scar; a cicatrice.

Batu, *v.* To dry; to harden.

Batu, *a.* Healed, sound, cicatrized.

Batua, *v.* To be at the back; to hang behind.

Batubatu, *a.* Cicatrized; marked with many scars.

Batutu, *v.* To beat; to strike repeatedly; to patter; to tread quick.

Batutu, *s.* A quick tread.

Bava, *s.* The name of a shell fish.

Be, *a.* Only or alone.

Be, *con.* Or, nor.

Bea, *con.* And, but, then.

Beau, *s.* A wave of the sea.

Beaua, *a.* Rough, boisterous, (the sea.)

Bee, *a.* Soft, spongy, (the bread fruit.)

Bee, *s.* A conquered one.

Beeatu, *s.* The name of a fish.

Beei, Beeia, Beebeei, } *v.* To beat; to thrash, in order to soften; to soften by beating.

Beebeei, *a.* Soft; not good, applied to the Tonga bread.

Beehi, *v.* To cast or throw down; to conquer, to consent unwillingly.

Beebeehi, *v.* To pitch from one; to bruise; to soften; to duck children in the water.

Beematagi, *a.* Bruised and softened by the wind (bread fruit.)

Beemoana, *s.* The name of a fish.

Bei, *ad.* Then, therefore.

Beie, *s.* A place made with stones, in which to entrap fish.

Beito, *s.* Kitchen; cook house.

Beua, *v.* To prevent; to dissuade.

Bebe, *s.* The butterfly.

Bebee, *a.* Unwilling.

Bebeu, *v.* To prevent; to hinder.

Bebelu, *v.* To fold again and again.

Bebena, *a.* Unwilling; grudging in disposition.

Bebenu, *a.* Elastic, flexible, tough.

Bebenu, *s.* Elasticity.

Behe, Behei, } *ad.* So, thus.

Behe, *v.* To say; to speak.

Beheaibe, *a.* Without change; without alteration.

Beheage, *v.* To answer; to reply.

Beheage, *v.* Used when requesting a sight of any thing present.

Beheage, Beheagea, } *v.* To wish; to desire, as, would it were so; O that.

Beji, *a.* Fat.

Beji, Bejibeji, } *s.* The claws of beasts or birds.

Bejikuku, *s.* The feet of the mast made to clip the *vugakoto.*

Bejiloa, *s.* The name of a shell fish.

Beka, *s.* The vampyre bat, or flying fox.

Beka, *v.* To change the colour of a part of the hair of the head

Beke, *s.* A sop; a mixture of several kinds of food.
Beke, *v.* To sop.
Bekebeka, *s.* A small bird.
Bekebeke, *s.* A preparation of food.
Bekebekatama, *s.* A prognostication.
Beko, *a.* Sad, sullen.
Beku, *a.* Blunt, disedged.
Bela, *s.* Pus, matter discharged from an abscess, &c.
Bela, *a.* Purulent.
Bela, *v.* To suppurate; to discharge.
Bele, *s.* A favourite, a pet, a darling.
Belebela, *s.* Mud, mire, dirt.
Belebela, *a.* Muddy, miry.
Belebelebeamele, *s.* A discarded favourite.
Belebelegeji, *a.* Friable; easily broken; weak.
Beletonoi, *s.* One discarded.
Belu, *s.* A drinking cup made from a leaf.
Belu, *v* To fold; to crease.
Belubelu, *v.* To fold repeatedly.
Belubelu, *s.* The dried husk from the young nut; the name of a fish.
Beluki, *v.* To bend; to turn over.
Bena, *v.* To mend fishing nets; to make the hair of the head black.
Benebena, *v.* To dress the head with a preparation, for the purpose of cleaning it.
Benu, *s.* A coverlet of *gatu*.
Benu, *a.* Soft, tough, yielding.
Benubenu, *s.* The refuse; the skin of any thing boiled.
Bete, *a.* Sad, mournful.
Betebete, *a.* Rough, uneven.
Biebia, *a.* Mattery, purulent, filthy.
Biala, *v.* To escape.
Bii, *v.* To wash off; to dash water into any thing.

Biu, *s.* The name of a tree; the leaf of the *Biu*, used as an envelope.
Biu, *v.* To fetch, to bring.
Biubiuaki, *a.* Zigzag.
Biutau, *v.* To fetch people to fight in war.
Bibi, *s.* The name of a tree; also, of a shell fish; the turkey
Bibi, *a.* Near, as warriors to a fort; or the flow tide to land.
Bibihele, *s.* A neck lace made from the fruit of the *Bibi*.
Bibihi, *a.* Infectious, contagious.
Bibihi, *v.* To cleave to; to hold fast.
Bibiki, *a.* Contracted, shrunk.
Bibiki, *v.* To hold by, to adhere to.
Bibiki, *s.* A young child; one with stiff contracted joints.
Bibiko, *a.* Weary, tired.
Bibine, *a.* Clotted together; covetous.
Bibito, *a.* Full, applied to more than one vessel.
Biha, *s.* A part of the ceremony at a chief's wedding.
Bihi, Bihibihi, } *v.* To fly as the spray of the sea.
Bihia, *v.* To be infected through contagion; to be influenced by example.
Bihogo, *s.* Stink, stench.
Biki, Bikibiki, } *a.* Sizy; adhesive.
Biki, Bikibiki, } *v.* To stick to, to adhere, to hold by.
Bikiaga, *s.* The person or thing held by.
Bikikulu, *v.* To cleave to.
Bikitai, *v.* To cleave to, to adhere.
Bikitauhala, *v.* To miss one's hold.
Biko, Bikobiko, } *a.* Crooked, awry, wandering.
Biko, Bikobiko, } *s.* Crookedness, equivocation, misrepresentation.

30

Bikoi, *v.* To make crooked; to mis-represent; to falsify.

Bikoua, *a.* Twisted.

Bikobikoikumai, *v.* To go from place to place, and fall again to its original owner.

Bila, *s.* Trash, used reproachingly.

Bili, *s.* A lizard.

Bilia, *v.* To go leeward in sailing.

Bilibili, *s.* The small cat fish.

Bili-lolo, *a.* Saturated with oil.

Bili-mahalo, *v.* To suspect without reason or cause.

Bilietauhala, *v.* To be exposed to danger.

Bine, Binebine, } *v.* To wedge; to fix by wedging.

Binei, *v.* To keep a sitting; to sit for a long time.

Binega, Binegaaga, } *s.* A rendezvous, reservoir.

Bitagi, *v.* To persevere through difficulties.

Bito, *s.* The navel.

Bito, *a.* Full.

Bitogutugutu, Bitomahuohua, } *a.* Brimful; full to overflowing.

Bo, *s.* Night.

Bo, *v.* To seize; to catch.

Boa, *s.* The name of a species of yam; the smell of fish.

Boa, *s.* An answer; a reply; a saying.

Boaki, *v.* To inform.

Boia, *v.* To beat soundly.

Boitonu, Boiboitonu, } *v.* To do any thing frequently and directly to one individual.

Boila, Boiboila, } *a.* Dim, obscure.

Booi, *s.* A preparation of food.

Bou, *s.* A post or pillar.

Boubou, *s.* Support, succour.

Boubou, *v.* To support; to strengthen.

Boubou-taki, *s.* The name of a rope, belonging to the sail of a canoe.

Boubou-tuu, *s.* The name of a rope, belonging to the sail of a canoe.

Bouki, *v.* To use as a support or helper.

Bouki, *s.* Food reserved till another time.

Boula, *s.* A night dance.

Bouli, *s.* Darkness.

Bouli, *a.* Dark.

Boulia, *v.* To be benighted.

Boulietoga, *a.* Dark, gloomy, sullen, angry.

Boulilolo, *a.* Thick impenetrable darkness.

Bobao, *s.* The smallest kind of paddling canoe.

Bobo, *v.* Rotten, unsound.

Bobo, *s.* Rottenness.

Boboaki, *s.* An embassy; a message.

Boboaki, *v.* To send a message.

Boboani, *v.* To eat a small portion of fish or animal food with vegetables.

Boboi, *v.* To be suspicious; to be fearful.

Bobooi, *s.* A preparation of food.

Bobobobo, *a.* Rotten.

Bobogi, *a.* Dizzy.

Bobogofua, *a.* Easily rotted; corruptible.

Boboka, *a.* Fat.

Boboki, *v.* To pat gently with the hand.

Boboko, *a.* Having the eyes covered with fat.

Bobole, *v.* To aim at more than can be done; to act clumsily.

Bobotea, *a.* Rotten and mouldy.

Boboto, *s.* To be reconciled after a quarrel.

Bobotu, *s.* The name of a shell fish.

Bobula, *s.* A slave, a prisoner; enslavement.

Bobula, *a.* Enslaved, imprisoned.

Boga, *s.* The name of tree.

Boga, Bogoboga, } *a.* Ripe before time.

31

Bogato, *a.* Having the hair longest on the back part of the head.
Bogi, *v.* To squint, to blink.
Bogia, *v.* To faint.
Bogia, *s.* Fainting.
Bogibogi, *s.* Morning, forenoon.
Bohee, *s.* The name of a fish.
Boheke, *v.* To slide over as a bad razor on the beard.
Boho, *s.* The covered part of a canoe.
Boho-mua, *s.* The fore part of the *Tafaaga.*
Boho-mui, *s.* The hind part of the *Tafaaga.*
Bohu, *s.* The name of a shell fish; a hollow sound, as the striking of any thing soft.
Bohu, *v.* To strike any thing soft; to soften by striking.
Boji, *v.* To hiss in anger.
Boka, *v.* To castrate; to emasculate.
Boka, *a.* A term used to the musquito when full of blood.
Boko, *s.* An opening; an aperture.
Bokofu, *s.* The name of a fish.
Boku, Bokua, Bokuala, } *s.* The itch.
Bokubaku, *s.* A scab.
Bokumei, *s.* The name of a fish.
Bola, *s.* The nut leaf platted for thatch, and other purposes.
Bolai, *v.* To incase fish in the platted nut leaf for roasting; to lance; to open a wound.
Bola-kuma, *s.* A pit and trap for taking rats.
Bolata, *s.* The stem of the banana tree.
Bolatulikaa, *s.* A screen made from the nut leaves.
Bolavaka, *s.* A certain kind of *bola* for covering canoes.
Bole, Bolebole, } *v.* To boast, to brag.

Bole, Bolebole } *s.* A boaster; the name of the small steering oar.
Bole, Bolebole, } *a.* Addicted to boasting.
Bolo, *s.* The name of a shrub.
Boloi, *v.* To mark, to chalk; to betroth, to be betrothed.
Bolouto, *a.* Ripe.
Bolobola, *s.* A large basket made of the nut leaf.
Bolobolo, *s.* The name of a shrub; the first fruits; the rail on the top of the canoe house.
Bolubolu, *s.* The name of a shell fish.
Bomee, *s.* A night dance.
Bone, *s.* The name of a fish.
Bonoi, *v.* To do what is most handy.
Bonobonoi, *a.* Foul; right ahead, applied to the wind.
Bonu, *s.* A worm.
Bonua, *a.* Affected with worms.
Bonutaliga, *s.* The name of a fish.
Bota, *s.* A preparation of food; a signal.
Bota, *a.* Alike, equal.
Bota, *v.* To signalize.
Botaga, *s.* Small cultivated patches; a patch.
Botea, *s.* A preparation of nut oil.
Boto, *s.* Wisdom, knowledge, skill, discretion; the name of a shell fish.
Boto, *a.* Wise, knowing, discerning.
Botoaga, *s.* The source of wisdom.
Botoaniumui, *s.* A pedant; a tyro; one whose knowledge is soon spent.
Botoboto, *a.* Globular, round.
Botobotoi, *a.* Clever.
Botu, *s.* A place, a room, a space; a passage or verse in writing.
Botubatu, *s.* The name of a shell fish.
Botubotu, *s.* A brand put out.

Botubotukehekehe, *a.* Unequal not alike in measurement.
Botubotutatau, *a.* Equal; of the same height, length, &c.
Botu-fonua, *s.* A district.
Botu-hou, *s.* A rough sea.
Botu-kai, *s.* An eating room.
Botu-lilo, *s.* A secret place; a closet.
Botu-mohe, *s.* A bed room; dormitory.
Bovai, *s.* A war weapon.
Bua, *s.* The name of a tree; a sea weed.
/Buaa, *a.* Rotten, putrid, stinking, acescent.
Buaa, *v.* To be acescent; to cherish animosity.
Buaka, *s.* A pig.
Buaka-tau. *s.* A boar pig.
Buaki, *v.* To void from the mouth; to vomit out.
Buataukanave, *s.* The name of a tree.
Bue, *v.* To win; to be first.
Bueki, *s.* The name of a shell fish.
Buekina, *v.* See *Buaki.*
Bui, *a.* Magisterial, dictatorial, dominant.
Buibui, *s.* A screen, a curtain.
Buibui, *v.* To screen, to curtain.
Buo, *s.* One kind of bread fruit.
Buobua, *s.* The name of a tree.
Buobua, *v.* To work quickly; applied to the *kabe* when too late to eat.
Buobuaga, *s.* Anger, wroth.
Buobuatahi, *s.* The salt water dried upon the body.
Bubu, *s.* An empty vessel; a nut without milk or kernel.
Bubu, *v.* To wash or rinse out the mouth, to gargle.
Bubu, *v.* To ooze out, as steam from an oven; to blow gently from any quarter after a calm.
Bubu, *s.* A long continued sound, as in blowing the *kalea,* or trumpet shell.
Bubu, *s.* A crowd of persons; steam.
Bubua, *s.* A whirl pool.
Bubububu, *a.* Closely set; crowded
Bubuga, *v.* To be taken up; to be deeply engaged.
Bubuha, *v.* To be oppressed with heat; to brawl.
Bubuhi, *v.* To spout or blow, as the whale; to blow any thing from the mouth.
Bubuke, *s.* The ague; shivering fits.
Bubuke, *v.* To be affected with the ague, or any intermittent disease; to act on the impulse of the moment.
Bubuku, *a.* Short.
Bubula, *v.* To swell; to bloat.
Bubula, *s.* A swelling; a protuberance.
Bubulu, *a.* Slimy, adhesive.
Bubuluhi, *a.* Slighty afflicted, applied to the *Tuitoga.*
Bubuni, *v.* To shut, to close.
Bubunu, *v.* To shut or close up any passage.
Bubuta, *a.* Fat, stout, plump.
Bubutamaki, *s.* A rock in the water full of holes below.
Bubuto, *v.* To be bulged out.
Bubutuu, *v.* To be confused or perplexed.
Bubutuu, *s.* Confusion, perturbation.
Buga, *s.* The name of a stone.
Buga, *a.* Diseased, applied to rats.
Bugobuga, *s.* The name of a very large fish.
Bugobuga, *v.* To be pressed down; slightly deformed, from excessive labour.
Buha, *s.* Any kind of a box or chest; heat.
Buha, *v.* To brawl; to quarrel.
Buhaga, *s.* Food or other present taken to individuals, on a visit, or at work.

Buhegia, *v.* To be suffocated with heat; to be blasted; to ferment.

Buhi, *s.* Chewed nut spread in the path, for the purpose of catching rats.

Buhi, *v.* To spit.

Buhibuhilo, *s.* The name of a shell fish.

Buhiga, *s.* Any thing into which sick persons spit.

Buho, *s.* The brain pan of fish.

Buho, *v.* To flame, to shine.

Buji, *v.* To collect; to keep together that which belongs to several.

Bujiaki, *s.* A pet; any thing petted.

Bujiaki, *v.* To pet; to feed by hand.

Buke, Bukea, } *v.* To seize, to grasp, to lay hold; to be seized by affliction.

Buke, *s.* The hillock or mound in which the yam is planted; the deck of a canoe; the outworks of a fortress; the middle length in the *kauta* and *feleano.*

Bukea, *v.* To take fish with two hooks at the same time.

Bukeaga, Bukega, } *s.* Any thing to take hold of.

Bukebuke, *v.* To hold; to restrain.

Bukebuke-tauhi, *s.* One zealous to redress the wrongs of another; one who takes hold and keeps the command of another.

Buke-mau, *v.* To grasp; to hold fast in the hand.

Buke-tanoa, *v.* To touch a sacred *kumeti,* called *tanoa* in swearing.

Bukijia, *s.* Food or *kava* taken to those employed in catching birds.

Buko, *s.* The name of a tree; a species of the banana.

Bukobuka, *a.* Soft, rotten.

Buko-fale, *s.* A very large *buko.*

Bukovili, *s.* The name of a tree.

Buku, *s.* A small kind of domestic fowl; a dwarf.

Bukubuku, *a.* Short, not tall, not long.

Bula, *s.* The name of a shrub; a Tonga game or play.

Bula, *s.* A bubble.

Bule, *s.* Reign, a governor; the name of a shell fish; the pit of the stomach.

Bule, *v.* To govern; to exact.

Buleaga, *s.* A kingdom, a government, nation.

Buleaki, Buleakii, } *v.* To take counsel, and do deeds, in order to secure a person for any purpose.

Buleekina, See *Buleakii.*

Bulei, *v.* To be governed; to be ornamented with shells.

Buleia, *v.* To be governed.

Buleoto, *s.* The name of a shell fish.

Bulebule, *a.* Spotted.

Bulebule, *s.* The name a shell fish.

Bulebulegataa, *v.* To feel a difficulty in speaking or governing to.

Bulebulegofua, *v.* To govern without any difficulty or apprehension.

Bulebuletuu, *v.* To go, and consult as you go.

Bule-fakamalohi, *v.* To govern oppressively.

Bule-kakaha, *v.* To govern with overbearing severity.

Bule-makafeke, *s.* The name of a shell fish.

Bule-malohi, *v.* To govern with rigour.

Bulematalea, *s.* The name of a shell fish.

Bulevaka, *s.* The name of a shell fish.

Buli, *a.* Secret, unseen, hidden.

Buli, *v.* To baffle; to elude.

Buloa, *s.* A mask.
Buloa, *v.* To mask.
Bulou, *s.* A veil; a cover to conceal the face.
Bulou, *v.* To veil, or cover the face.
Bulobula, *s.* Seed; the seed cuttings of yams.
Bulobulai-vae, *s.* The bottom of the toes; ankle joints.
Bulobulai-vae, *v.* To stand on the toes; tip toe.
Bulobulou, *v.* To cover over.
Buloga, *v.* To cover; to cover as with a hood.
Bulotu, *s.* The supposed residence of the gods; the unseen world.
Bulu, *s.* A kind of gum, used as pitch, in caulking canoes; shot; the husk of the cocoa nut.
Bulua, *s.* Food cooked immediately upon the death of a person.
Bului, *v.* To tie together; to tie in a heap, as a lot of cocoa nuts.
Bulubulu, *s.* A shawl, a cloak; the gummy substance from the banana.
Bulubulu, *v.* To cloak; to cover the back and shoulders.
Bulubuluaki, *v.* To take off under cover.
Buluhi, *s.* Sickness, a term used only to the *Tuitoga*, and the *Tamaha*.
Buluji, *s.* Bird lime; paste; plaister.
Buluji, *v.* To ensnare; to stick; to print; to paste; to plaister.
Buna, *v.* To fly; to rebound as an elastic body; to leap.
Buna, *s.* A leap, a bound.
Bunabunaaki, *s.* The flying of birds not full-fledged.
Buni, *a.* Closed; met together; shut.
Bunibuni, *v.* To close; to shut.
Bunou, *v.* To bow down; to bend or stoop.
Bunobuna, *v.* To go leaping along.
Bunobunou, } **Bunobunoutonu**, } *s.* A term applied to a canoe that sails right before the wind; used also to the wind when right aft, which is very difficult in Tonga canoes.
Bunubunu, *v.* See *Bunibuni.*
Bunuga, *s.* A nest.
Bunuga, *v.* To nest.
Bunuga-moui, *a.* Careful of her young, as a hen.
Bunujia, *v.* To be obstructed; to be forced back, as a canoe by a foul wind.
Bunutaki, *v.* To stop up; to close; to fill.
Buta, *s.* A wager.
Buta, *v.* To bet a wager.
Buta, *a.* Bloated, (the cheeks.)
Butaliga, *s.* One kind of banana.
Butaloto, *s.* A mind inflated with rage.
Butobuta, *a.* Fat; plump; full of flesh.
Butu, *s.* A funeral.
Butu, } **Butubutu**, } *a.* Close, near together.
Butuga, *v.* To be engaged or engrossed with in conversation.
Butuga, *s.* An assembly; a confused crowd.
Butuki, *v.* To put or place near together; to speak rapidly.

F

F, THE seventh Letter in the Tonga Alphabet. Its sound is that of *f* in *Father.*

Fa, *part.* Burst, split.
Fa, *a.* Four; hoarse.

E

Fa, } s. The name of a tree.
Fafa, }

Fa, } v. To feel after any thing, as one blind feels his way.
Fafa, }

Faa, s. A gardener; one industrious in gardening.

Faa, a. Industrious in agriculture.

Faa, s. A single tegument, roll, or layer.

Faa, a. Capable of; apt to do; skilled; ready at.

Faa-alu, v. To be capable of going; or to be frequently going.

Faa-ave, v. To be capable of taking; or to be frequently taking.

Faa-bauu, v. To be frequently in mischief.

☞ The *Faa* is prefixed to very many other words besides those given above.

Faai, v. To open.

Faai, a. Open, extended.

Faaijiji, v. To gather the leaves of the *Fi*, for making dresses.

Faao, v. To take by force, to extort, to exact.

Faao, a. Oppressive overbearing.

Faaoa, v. To be taken by force.

Faabuku, v. To take whole into the mouth.

Faahi, v. To be able to lift or carry.

Faahi, s. A side half of any thing divided.

Faahi-fefine, s. The relatives and friends of the bride.

Faahiga, s. Tribe.

Faahikehe, s. The name for all the Tonga gods.

Faahi-tagata, s. The friends of the bridegroom.

Faahi-taha, s. A house with only one side of a roof; a verandah.

Faaki, v. To lean against; to depend on; to rest upon.

Faaki, a. Dependent; leaning against.

Faala, v. To search.

Fae, s. A mother.

Faeiki, v. To apply to a chief for refuge; to interest a chief in one's behalf.

Faefine, s. The arm pit.

Faeho, } s. A stinking breath.
Faelo, }

Faele, } v. To bear; to bring forth.
Faelei, }

Faele, s. The act of bringing forth; a birth.

Fae-mate, a. Motherless.

Faeme, s. A fish.

Fai, v. To do, perform, to discharge, to execute.

Fai, s. Performance, execution; the name of a fish.

Faiaga, a. Unsettled in disposition.

Faiaga, s. Moral conduct, deportment.

Faiahu, s. The name of a shell fish.

Faiekina, v. To be overdone; to be overladen.

Faiba, v. To make the *ba* or fish hook.

Faibala, s. A fish.

Faibe, } v. To continue doing; to persevere in doing.
Faibefaibe, }

Faifaimau, v. To persevere in doing; to do without ceasing.

Faifaitaki, s. Imitation, emulation, follower.

Faifaitaki v. To imitate; to copy after; to emulate.

Faifaitaki, a. Emulous.

Faifekau, s. One who executes commands; a missionary; a delegate.

Faifoki, v. To repeat.

Faiga, v. To contend; to wrestle.

Faigamea, s. Kind, class, nature.

Faigataa, s. Difficulty.

Faigataa, a. Difficult to accomplish

Faigofua, s. Facility; freedom from difficulty.

Faigofua, *a.* Easy to perform.
Faijijili, *s.* A thunderbolt.
Faikakai, *s.* A preparation of food.
Faikakano, *a.* Larger; capable of containing more.
Faikili, *s.* A fish.
Fai-la, *v.* To set the sail of a canoe.
Fai-maea, *v.* To make ropes.
Faimanu, *s.* A fish.
Faimanava, *s.* The stomach; the receptacle of food.
Faimanava, *v.* To eat to strengthen the *manava.*
Fai-mua, *v.* To do first; to be a head; to do it at once.
Fai-mui, *v.* To be last; to do last.
Faitaki, *v.* To try; to try it on.
Faitalaigatai, *s.* The name of a fish.
Faite, *s.* The sitting posture of Tonga females.
Faiteliha, *v.* To do as one thinks right; to will; to choose.
Faiteliha, *s.* Pleasure, will, discretion, choice.
Faitoo, *s.* A surgeon, a doctor.
Faitoo, *v.* To dispense medicines.
Faitoka, *s.* A burying ground; any very rough part in the sea.
Faitoka, *v.* To do easily; to do calmly.
Faiva, *s.* Calling, occupation; any thing at which a man is clever.
Faivelega, *s.* Zeal.
Faivelega, *a.* Zealous.
Fao, *a.* Naked and fruitless, applied to the nut tree.
Fao, *s.* Spikes, nails.
Fao, } *v.* To stretch; to pull;
Faofao, } to put into; to store up; to hide in the mind.
Faoaki, *v.* To put into a store; to house.
Faoo, *v.* To be engrossed by; to be fixed in the mind.
Faofao, *s.* The name of a shell fish.
Faolaki, } *v.* To house; to
Faolekina, } store.
Faololo, *v.* To press or squeeze into.
Fau, *s.* The name of a tree; a turban; the strainer for the *kava.*
Fau, *v.* To fasten up the hair; to build or repair canoes or boxes; to pull; to lead; to teach to work.
Fau, } *ad.* Very; sign of the
Faufau, } superlative degree.
Faufau, *v.* To fasten on the outriggers of small canoes.
Faufau, *a.* Qualmish, sickly.
Faufaufua, *v.* To have in sure possession.
Faufaumao, *v.* To pull one about in anger.
Faufua, *v.* To embrace; to inclose in the arms.
Fauhia, *v.* To have possession of; to seize and keep firm hold of.
Faulalo, *s.* A string of bark used in making *gatu.*
Fauloulou, *v.* To roll the eyes as one astonished.
Fautaha, *a.* Unanimous.
Fabuku, *s.* The name of a fish.
Fafa, *v.* To carry on the back.
Fafa, *a.* Hoarse, bass.
Fafa, *v.* To grope; to feel the way.
Fafa, *s.* Name of a tree.
Fafai, *v.* To shave the head.
Fafao, *v.* To stretch; to extend out the arms; to charge as a gun; to fill up.
Fafau, *a.* Tough; elastic.
Fafau, *a.* Agreed, settled.
Fafaji, *v.* To break as waves in succession.
Fafaga, } *v.* To feed; to supply
Fafagai, } with food; to diet.
Fafagu, *v.* To awake; to rouse out of sleep.

37

Fafagu, *s.* A bell; any thing struck to collect the people.

Fafamamalua, *v.* To paddle or sail over reefs, with little depth of water.

Fafano, *a.* Tough, pliant, flexible.

Fafanoga, *s.* The name of a small bowl, idolatrously used by persons about the *Tuitoga*, and his tribe.

Fafatu, *v.* To frounce the hair in a certain way; to fold; to lay.

Fafine, *s.* Women.

Faga, *s.* That portion of the sea shore which is in a line with one's dwelling; the upper part of the sides of the head; the mouth or opening of a basket trap.

Faga, *ad.* Sign of the plural, used generally of irrational creatures.

Fagaikai, *s.* The time for eating; meal times.

Fagailube, *s.* The morning from about nine to eleven o'clock.

Fagaotaha, *s.* The principal landing place on shore.

Fagabeji, *v.* To fatten, to pamper.

Fagafaai, *v.* To stuff with food; to cram.

Fagafao, *v.* To pet; to rear by hand.

Fagafaga, *v.* To be near; to be on the point of doing.

Fagafaga, *s.* The head shaved at the top, leaving the hair on both sides.

Fagaga, *s.* A litter; the young of animals and birds.

Fagafagatatau, *a.* Equal, in a line with, strait.

Faganaki, *v.* To feed with.

Fagatua, *s.* Wrestling.

Fagatua, *v.* To wrestle.

Fagatuki, *v.* To well feed; to press to eat.

Fagogo, *v.* To pour from one vessel into another.

Fagota, *v.* To gather shell fish.

Fagu, *s.* The calabash; the scented oil.

Fagufagu, *v.* To call, in order to awake; to snort; to blow through the nose.

Fagufagu, *s.* A flute.

Faha, *v.* To drive fish into a net trap.

Faha, *s.* A mad man, fool, craziness; the name of one kind of yam.

Fahafaha, *v.* To go shouting as one foolish.

Fahi, *v.* To cleave, to split, to divide.

Fahifahi, *v.* To cleave or split up to pieces.

Fahu, *s.* One that is above law.

Faji, *v.* To break; to dislocate.

Fajia, *s.* A turning in the road; a bay or bite on the shore.

Fajia, *s.* Cunning, artifice, craft, deceit.

Fajiai, *v.* To deceive, to cheat.

Fajiabule, *v.* To cheat, to outdo.

Fajiahala, *s.* The point or turn in the road.

Faiialea, } *a.* Modifications,
Fajifajialea, } shades of meaning, &c.

Fajitua, *s.* The loins.

Fajii, *a.* Narrow, contracted.

Fajifaji, *a.* Broken up.

Fajituu, } *v.* To belie.
Fajituua, }

Faka, Used very frequently in forming compound words, being prefixed cheifly to nouns, adjectives, and verbs, signifying after the manner of; also, to cause. See the following words.

Fakaa, *v.* To awake; to open the eyes of the blind; to remind.

Fakaaau, *part.* Becoming, hastening towards, approximating.

Fakaaau, *v.* To rehearse, to explain.

Fakaaaukimua, *v.* To advance, to make proficiency.

Fakaaaukimui, *v.* To go backwards, to retrograde.

Fakaaano, *v.* To picture to the mind the doings of absent friends.

Fakaaabi, *v.* To wedge, to fasten temporally.

Fakaaafu, *v.* To heat, to make hot, as sultry weather.

Fakaaala, *a.* Any thing which looks best at a distance, or that is not what at first sight it appeared to be.

Fakaaalo, *v.* To do work gradually and in order.

Fakaaalu, *s.* Any thing given to a fisherman to engage him to catch fish for you.

Fakaaamio, *v.* To speak perversely; to misrepresent.

Fakaaata, *v.* To ripen; to shew signs of suppuration.

Fakaaeva, *v.* To allow to walk about; to let loose.

Fakaaiai, *v.* To abet; to prompt, to incite.

Fakaaitoa, *v.* To express pleasure at the misfortunes of another.

Fakaaoao, *s.* An oppressor, oppression, rebellion.

Fakaaoao, *v.* To oppress, to overpower.

Fakaaoga, *v.* To make useful or worthy.

Fakaau, } *v.* To destroy gradu-
Fakaaua, } ally, or at different times.

Fakaauau, *v.* To inflict voluntary pain, as fasting, &c. on the death of a friend; to reach to.

Fakaauaujino, *v.* To fall away, as one consumptive.

Fakaauaujino, *s.* Consumption.

Fakaauaukolo, *v.* To rattle; to rumble.

Fakaaufulia, *v.* To destroy wholesale.

Fakaaugafa, *s.* A mutual agreement on oath.

Fakaauha, *s.* Desolation, extermination.

Fakaauha, *v.* To exterminate, to destroy.

Fakaauhamalie, *v.* To make a full end; to complete any work.

Fakaauhatamaki, *v.* To persevere through difficulties.

Fakaauhe, *v.* To stroll; to walk at leisure; to cause to wander.

Fakaauhi, *v.* To famish, to starve.

Fakaauhi, *s.* Starvation.

Fakaaujia, *v.* To cause, to arrive.

Fakaaunoa, *v.* To cause to wander; to send a drift.

Fakaaunofo, *v.* To treat strangers unkindly.

Fakaaba, *v.* To cause fear; to beget reverence.

Fakaabaaba, *s.* Reverence, honour, respect.

Fakaabaaba, } *v.* To reverence,
Fakaabaabaia, } to respect, to honour, to be honoured.

Fakaabaaba, *v.* To move; to make way; to stand aside.

Fakaababagofua, *v.* To make easy; to free from restriction or prohibition.

Fakaabe, *v.* To speak doubtfully.

Fakaabe, *s.* Conjecture, guess.

Fakaabi, } *v.* To sojourn in
Fakaabiaga, } the *abi* of a friend.

Fakaabiabi, *v.* To crowd, to cumber.

Fakaafa, *v.* To raise or cause a hurricane.

Fakaafe, *v.* To turn aside; to cause to wander; to turn aside a traveller, in order to refresh.

Fakaafeitui, *a.* Serpentine, crooked.

Fakaafekafu, *v.* To cover one in sleep with his dress.

Fakaafi, *v.* To awake one asleep.

Fakafio, *v.* To place or put sacred persons or things.

Fakaafo, *v.* To put on a line to a hook.

Fakaafu, } *v.* To prepare the
Fakaafua, } oven, by heating .the stones for cooking food.

Fakaatuafu, *v.* To seek and inquire after the descendants of any one.

Fakaafuluga, *v.* To suffer to grow mouldy.

Fakaaga, } *v.* To criticise, to
Fakaagai, } remark upon the work of another.

Fakaaga, *s.* A critick, an inspector.

Fakaagaaga, *v.* To work carefully; to work to pattern; to fit.

Fakaagaagaki, } *a.* Becoming
Fakangaagatuu, } disobedient.

Fakaagaagakehe, *v.* To act differently to others; to act in opposition to the views of others.

Fakaagaitefitoniu, *v.* To give directions to others, but unable to do the work.

Fakaagaihukumamao, *v.* To remark upon any thing at a distance, and without experience.

Fakaagabauu, *v.* To make naughty or mischievous.

Fakaagahala, *v.* To cause to sin; to involve others in sin.

Fakaagaki, *v.* To air or dry by the fire.

Fakaagalelei, *v.* To make or cause a good disposition.

Fakaagamaa, *v.* To make clean or good (the disposition.)

Fakaagamakaka, *v.* To speak and act harshly; to beget or cause a like disposition.

Fakaagamolu, *v.* To soften the disposition.

Fakaagavaivai, *v.* To meeken; to make meek or humble.

Fakaagavaivai, *ad.* Meekly, humbly.

Fakaagavale, *v.* One clever at remarking upon other's work, but foolish himself.

Fakaagavale. *a.* Left handed, awkward.

Fakaageage, *a.* Great.

Fakaagi, *a.* Small, out of proportion, applied to the sail of a canoe.

Fakaagi, } *v.* To consult, to
Fakaagiagi, } meditate; to hang or place any thing in the wind to dry; to give directions; to keep the sail full.

Fakaahi, *v.* To walk as a person very weak.

Fakaahi, *a.* Weakly, poorly.

Fakaaho, *s.* A mode of fishing.

Fakaaho, *v.* To do every other day; to do on certain days.

Fakaahu, *v.* To besmoke, to smoke dry, to blote, to suffocate.

Fakaahuahu, *v.* To cause a great smoke, as a signal.

Fakaahuahu, *s.* Dark dense clouds in the horizon.

Fakaahukoua, *s.* Perseverance amidst difficulties.

Fakaaji, } *v.* To look or stare
Fakaajiaji, } into any thing; to bore, to pierce, to introduce, to open, to disclose.

Fakaajili, *v.* To cause to increase; to make to abound.

Fakaajinijini, *v.* To brighten, to make bright or shining.

Fakaaka, *v.* To cause to take root.

Fakaake, *s.* A reviver, a saviour.

Fakaake, } *v.* To re-animate,
Fakaakeake, } to quicken, to revive, to invigorate.

Fakaakeakeloto, *v.* To beget and infix in the mind.

Fakaakiakimui, *a.* Modest, unassuming.

Fakaakutaki, *v.* To increase, to grow.

Fakaala, *v.* To endeavour to please; to fall in with the views and dispositions of others; to try.

Fakaalaala, *v.* To be careful, to be gentle.

Fakaalaala, *a.* Careful, cautious.

Fakaalafia, *v.* Husband-like, wife-like.

Fakaalaga, *v.* To disjoint, to cut into joints.

Fakaaleale, *a.* Unproportionably small.

Fakaali, } *v.* To offer, to bid,
Fakaalia, } as in trading.

Fakaaliali, *v.* To exhibit, to show up.

Fakaaliali, *s.* Exhibition, show, setting forth.

Fakaaligalelei, *v.* To seek reconciliation; to make up a difference; to bring or take one thing in substitution for another.

Fakaalo, *v.* To grind edge tools.

Fakaalo, *s.* A rubbing stone.

Fakaaloalo, *ad.* Quietly, gently, slowly.

Fakaaloalo, *v.* To follow after; to do by and by.

Fakaalogaua, *a.* Uncertain, doubtful.

Fakaalogaua, *s.* Uncertainty, precariousness.

Fakaaluma, *s.* A jester, a joker.

Fakaaluma, *v.* To jest, to joke.

Fakaamio, *v.* To draw crooked.

Fakaamio, *a.* Perverse, distorted, applied to language.

Fakaamoamo, *v.* To project; to push out or forward.

Fakaamu, *v.* To wish, to desire.

Fakaamu, *s.* A wish, longing desire.

Fakaana; } *v.* To make rooms
Fakaanaana, } or berths; to partition off.

Fakaanau, *v.* To speak of the doings of absent friends.

Fakaanu, *v.* To float, to cause to float; to be in the water.

Fakaanufea, *v.* To chill; to make very cold.

Fakaata, *s.* A spy glass.

Fakaata, *v.* To take aim; to look through a glass.

Fakata, } *v.* To make room;
Fakataata, } to disencumber; to give place.

Fakaataata, *v.* To look intently; to be careful.

Fakaataataina, *a.* Exposed, unprotected, freed.

Fakaataga, *v.* To speak of a person now poor and weak as when he had plenty and was strong.

Fakaataloa, *v.* To give a wide berth; to make room.

Fakaatamai, *v.* To attend to; to give the mind to.

Fakaatanoa, *a.* To make room to no purpose.

Fakaatu, *v.* To line; to cover the inside.

Fakaatu, } *v.* To cease to trouble,
Fakaatui, } to refrain for a time.

Fakaatuatu, *v.* To express surprise, in reference to something bad.

Fakaatue, *v.* To try to discompose a fisherman when he has a bite.

Fakaava, } *v.* To open; to
Fakaavaava, } perforate; to make full of holes.

Fakaavaga, *v.* To earnestly desire, to be engrossed with.

Fakaavaki, *v.* To make useful.

Fakaea, *v.* To raise or draw up to the surface of the water.

Fakaeabi, *v.* To treat a superior as one of the *abi*.

Fakaeabi, *a.* Belonging to the *abi*.

Fakaeeiki, *a.* Chief-like.

Fakaeiki, *a.* Pert, saucy.

Fakaeonoaho, *a.* Old fashioned; antique; belonging to gone by days.

Fakaeu, Fakaeueu, } *v.* To recline; to lean sideways; to place endwise.

Fakaebu, *v.* To stir up; to agitate a liquid; to hoe small weeds.

Fakaefi, Fakaefiefi, } *v.* To press, to squeeze, to throng, to push into.

Fakaefiafi, *a.* Belonging to the afternoon.

Fakaefihi, *v.* See *Fakaefi.*

Fakaefihia, *v.* To press, to squeeze into.

Fakaefu, *v.* To raise a dust.

Fakaehiehi, *v.* To avoid contact with what is near.

Fakaeho, *v.* To corrupt; to cause to stink.

Fakaejia, *v.* To haft or handle any tool.

Fakaeke, *v.* To inquire; to institute inquiry.

Fakaeleela, *v.* To lie on the back as one on the water.

Fakaelelo, *a.* Tongued, set in.

Fakaelelouu, *v.* To stammer; to speak as one who bites his tongue.

Fakaelo, *v.* See *Fakaeho.*

Fakaeloelo, *s.* A part of a hen's eggs left unhatched.

Fakaeneene, *v.* To work cautiously and carefully.

Fakaete, *v.* To hearken secretly.

Fakaete, Fakaeteete, } *v.* To walk softly, without noise.

Fakaeve, *v.* To collect together; to gather up.

Fakaeveeva, *v.* To cause to walk; to lead astray.

Fakaeveeve, *s.* Flat cakes.

Fakai, Fakaii, } *v.* To dishearten, to discourage; to sail near a reef, or close on the wind.

Fakaioho, *v.* To set or cause one to shout.

Fakaifoifo, *v.* To taste; to try by the mouth.

Fakaigoigo, *v.* To variegate, to diversify.

Fakaigoigoi, *a.* Variegated, diversified, of many patterns and colours.

Fakaihu, *v.* To make a nose or projecting part, on the end of a canoe.

Fakaijiijiaki, *v.* To be careful; to attend to the body.

Fakaikai, *v.* To cause not to be.

Fakaika, Fakaikeika, } *v.* To be recovering from affliction; to revive.

Fakaikeikagataa, *a.* Difficult to supply, applied to a net which catches few fish.

Fakaikeikalahi, *v.* To proceed deliberately, and with an air of self importance.

Fakaikiiki, *v.* To cut into small pieces.

Fakaiku, *v.* To make an end; to point a rope.

Fakaikukovi, *v.* To make a bad finish.

Fakaikulelei, *v.* To make a good finish.

Fakaikulua, *s.* A large fish.

Fakaileila, *v.* To stay, to support; to prevent evil.

Fakaili, *s.* Seed; any thing from which its like is expected.

Fakailigataa, *a.* Difficult to keep alive.

Fakailigofua, *a.* Easy to rear.

Fakailifia, *v.* To dismay, to terrify.

Fakailo, *v.* To discover, to reveal, to promise.

Fakailoilo, *v.* To distinguish, to know, to call to mind.

Fakailoga, *s.* A sign, a mark, a proof.

Fakailoga, Fakailoiloga, } *v.* To betoken, to signify, to mark.

Fakailoloi, *s.* A lying witness.

Fakainu, Fakainumi, } *v.* To give drink; to cause to drink.

Fakaimuinu, *v.* To go along weakly, as a poisoned fish near the surface of the water.

Fakaisaisa, *v.* To hiss; to be annoyed.

Fakaita, *v.* To provoke, to rouse, to offend, to disoblige.

Fakaita, *s.* Provocation, insult.

Fakaiteita, *s.* Anger; the being angry.

Fakaiteita, *v.* To stretch.

Fakaoioi, *v.* To take part foolishly with a child; to pet.

Fakaoo, *v.* To strain, to sieve, to filtrate; to tread, as birds.

Fakaoo, *s.* A strainer, perculator.

Fakaoobo, *v.* To throw a spear in a particular manner.

Fakaoonoa, *v.* To appear careless and inattentive to what is doing.

Fakaobe, *v.* To drive or pitch on the mark in gambling.

Fakaoboobo, *v.* To fasten to; to connect with.

Fakaofa, *v.* To beget or cause love.

Fakaofi, Fakaofiofi, } *v.* To approach to bring near; to come near.

Fakaofo, *v.* To surprise, to amaze, to cause to shout out.

Fakaofoofo, *v.* To surprise only to disappoint.

Fakaofoofa, *s.* Beauty.

Fakaofoofa, *a.* Lovely, beautiful.

Fakaofu, *v.* To leave food in the oven for a long time.

Fakaogo, Fakaogoogo, } *v.* To hearken; to wait commands.

Fakaogoi, Fakaogona, } *v.* To notice, to care about.

Fakaogogataa, *v.* To make callous.

Fakaogogofua, *v.* To make susceptible; to make tender.

Fakaogojia, *v.* To trouble; to inconvenience.

Fakaogokovi, *v.* To cause an ill report; to dishonour.

Fakaogolelei, *v.* To cause a good report.

Fakaogonoa, *v.* To feign ignorance of orders.

Fakaogotuli, *v.* To feign deafness.

Fakaogovalea, *v.* See *Fakaogonoa.*

Fakaoho, *v.* To jut out; to push forward; to lengthen; to feed persons at work.

Fakaoho, *s.* Food prepared for people at work.

Fakaohooho, *v.* To abet; to push on; to fill in part. See *Ohooho.*

Fakaohomohe, *v.* To sup, to feed before sleep.

Fakaohovale, *v.* To surprise, to affright; to cause to act foolishly.

Fakaoji, Fakaojioji, } *v.* To finish; to make a complete finish.

Fakaojiojiloto, *v.* To grieve and pain to a great degree the mind of another; to relate to a third party the painful conduct of another.

Fakaojiga, *s.* The finishing point; the place of termination; the finishing cause.

Fakaojikia, *v.* To finish.

Fakaola, *v.* To extinguish; to put out a light.

Fakaola, Fakaoloola, } *v.* To reserve one's strength for expected work.

Fakaoleole, *v.* To seek to please; to gain the affection; to reconcile.

Fakaolo, Fakaololo, } *v.* To insinuate; to hint; to cheat.

Fakaolo, Fakaololo, } *s.* Insinuation, craftiness.

Fakaoluga, *v.* To pillow; to raise the head.

Fakaomooma, *v.* To strut; to walk fantastically.

Fakaomoomo, *v.* To jut or project forward.

Fakaoneone, *v.* To sand; to cover with sand.
Fakaonoaho, *s.* See *Fakaeonoaho.*
Fakaotoota, *v.* To litter; to throw things about.
Fakaotu, *v.* To range, to rank, to place in rows.
Fakaotua, *a.* Godlike, godly.
Fakaotuotumutu, *v.* To have partly done several rows, but none complete, as in planting.
Fakau, *v.* To seek help in war.
Fakau, *s.* A shield.
Fakau, *v.* To shield, to screen.
Fakaua, *v.* To repeat; to roll as a vessel at sea.
Fakauaga, *s.* A shield, a defence.
Fakaui, *v.* To call, to shout.
Fakauo, *v.* To meet together.
Fakauoua, *v.* To desire equality in rank or wealth.
Fakauouagakehekehe, *v.* To be of different opinions; to act in opposition to each other.
Fakauouagataha, *v.* To act unanimously; to be of one mind.
Fakauu, *s.* Forceps, pincers, tongs.
Fakauu, *v.* To pinch or bite from both sides; to take hold of, as with tongs.
Fakauua, *v.* To be pressed or squeezed; to be held as in the mouth; to pour scented oil on the body.
Fakauuuu, *v.* To set a dog to bite; to do to exasperate; to depend on.
Fakauuivalevale, *a.* Badly disposed, unkind.
Fakauulu, *v.* To rumble; to make a rumbling noise.
Fakauulu, Fakauulutuu, } *v.* To bluster; to make noise and confusion, but do no work.
Fakauga, *v.* To take shelter.
Fakaugaaga, *s.* Any thing used as a shelter or defence.
Fakaugouga, *v.* To notch; to cut and chop.
Fakaugouga, *v.* To secret; to hide any thing; to screen from exposure.
Fakaugi, Fakaugia, } *v.* To screen, to shelter.
Fakauha, Fakauhauha, } *v.* To expose to the rain.
Fakauhi, *v.* To finish off a canoe.
Fakauhiga, *v.* To define; to make known the meaning.
Fakauhigakehe, *v.* To misrepresent; to misconstrue.
Fakauhu, *v.* To strike, so as to cause inward pains; to excite the stomach, as the motion of a vessel.
Fakauka, *v.* To knead; to soften with the hands.
Fakaukei, Fakauketau, } *s.* The boast or challenge of a weak party, to fight with a strong one.
Fakauku, *v.* To plunge; to put under water.
Fakaukuloa, *v.* To extend, to lengthen out, to be a long time.
Fakaukunaki, *v.* To persevere; to act contrarily.
Fakaula, *a.* Clever, dexterous.
Fakauli, *v.* To steer a vessel; to make dirty, to pollute, to soil.
Fakaulia, *v.* To terrify, to dismay.
Fakauliuli, *v.* To blacken, to make black.
Fakauliuli, *s.* Dark clouds; a threatening sky.
Fakauliulilatai, *a.* Indistinct in appearance; shrowded in darkness.
Fakaulilologo, *a.* Silent, not talkative; to go to and fro without speaking.
Fakaulo, *v.* To cause to blaze.
Fakauloula, *a.* Jocose, free.
Fakaulu, *s.* A war custom of

44

carrying the slain, and placing them in order before the house of their idol; the short lengths at the end of a rope, to make it thicker in that part.
Fakaulu, *v.* To reserve the tops or heads of yams for setting; to make the head or upper part of a rope; to shout.
Fakaului, *v.* To proselyte.
Fakauluulu, *v.* To acknowledge one as head; to collect to the person so acknowledged.
Fakaulububu, *v.* To put heads together, as in conversation.
Fakaulufatu, *a.* Perverse.
Fakaulugamanu, *v.* To fail, from being too many in company.
Fakaunuunu, *v.* To cause to draw near.
Fakaulutuu, *v.* To be all confusion and uproar.
Fakausousa, *v.* To strut; to advance as a warrior.
Fakausousa, *a.* Braggart, boastful.
Fakauta, *v.* To cogitate; to ponder.
Fakauta, *s.* Cogitation, opinion, choice.
Fakautaga, *v.* To collect to; to meet at.
Fakautaga, *s.* A person or place others are fond of meeting at.
Fakautegia, See *Fakauta.*
Fakautouta, See *Fakauta.*
Fakautu, *v.* To bring or send empty vessels to be filled.
Fakautu, *a.* Greatest, most.
Fakautui, *v.* To persevere, to be determined.
Fakautuutu, } *v.* To increase,
Fakautuutugaki, } to grow.
Fakautufi, *v.* To persevere, to be fixed in purpose.
Fakautumauku, See *Fakautufi.*
Fakaba, *v.* To jostle against; to explode; to fire off a gun; to heat shell fish.
Fakabae, *v.* To throw up a mound; to pile up; to stand in rows.
Fakabaea, *v.* To make friendless.
Fakabaebae, *v.* To leave a canoe on the beach.
Fakabaebaea, *v.* To appear bashful or ashamed.
Fakabaibai, *v.* To cringe, to draw up the body.
Fakabao, *v.* To fringe, to flounce.
Fakabau, } *v.* To inquire
Fakabaubau, } particularly; to know for certain.
Fakabaubauu, *a.* Wanton, mischievous, roguish.
Fakababa, *v.* To walk awry; to insinuate; to hint.
Fakababa, *v.* To tread, to walk on; to beat out.
Fakababa, *v.* To swim in the surf on a *Laubaba.*
Fakababau, *v.* To assure, to protest, to inquire to know certainly; to be fixed.
Fakabababagatoa, *v.* To act without distinction.
Fakabababaka, *v.* To cause to flinch or cringe; to alarm.
Fakabababako, *v.* To appear very familiar; to be familiar with.
Fakabababaku, *a.* Unwilling, loath, sullen, gloomy.
Fakababalagi, *a.* Foreign fashion.
Fakabababani, *v.* To act as foragers; to destroy produce.
Fakabababata, *v.* To make coarse in texture; to be familiar.
Fakababate, *v.* See *Fakabababako.*
Fakabagai, *v.* A proverbial expression applied to small quantities of food, put into large baskets.
Fakabagobagoi, *v.* To mar, to spoil.
Fakabahabaha, *v.* To cause a redness, or glow on the skin.
Fakabahi *v.* To cause dislike.

Fakabahihi, *v.* To make like a *Bahihi.*

Fakabahubahu, *v.* To feign a hoarse or rough voice.

Fakabajika, *v.* To cause to glide or shoot along.

Fakabajikaka, *v.* To act the hypocrite; to assume; to arrogate.

Fakabajino, } *v.* To fix, to
Fakabajinojino, } determine, to settle.

Fakabakaka, *v.* To harden; to make stiff.

Fakabaki, *v.* To jostle against.

Fakabikihi, *v.* To crack the voice.

Fakabako, *v.* To make a smacking noise, as the striking of the flesh.

Fakabakohokoho, *v.* To speak bravely, but to act cowardly.

Fakabaku, *s.* A frying pan; a dish of fried meat.

Fakabaku, *v.* To fry; to broil on a gridiron.

Fakabala, *s.* A scented oil.

Fakabala, *v.* To cause rottenness.

Fakabalaku, } *a.* Dirty, slo-
Fakabalabalaku, } venly, lazy.

Fakabalaku, } *v.* To make
Fakabalabalaku, } dirty.

Fakabalatahabe, *v.* To be all on one side; to be partial.

Fakabana, } *v.* To hinder
Fakabanabana, } in growth; to stunt; to retard; to check.

Fakabanabana, } *s.* A scape goat;
Fakabanatuli, } one on whom falls the punishment designed for others.

Fakabasaga, *v.* To make forked.

Fakabatabata, *v.* To bring up a vessel to the wind.

Fakabatala, *v.* To converse about any thing, but afraid to do it at once.

Fakabatonu, *v.* To ascertain correctly; to re-assert; to corroborate.

Fakabatu, } *v.* To stamp with
Fakabatutu, } the foot; to create fear, as one stamping in anger.

Fakabe, *v.* To frighten playfully.

Fakabee, *v.* Fo cause rottenness; to make soft.

Fakabebee, *a.* Unwilling.

Fakabebee, *v.* to manifest unwillingness; to lag.

Fakabeehi, *v.* To speak as if unwilling; to speak vaguely.

Fakabebena, *v.* To do unwillingly or give grudgingly.

Fakabebenu, *v.* To make elastic or tough.

Fakabekebeka, *v.* To fasten on the outrigger of small canoes.

Fakabeko, *v.* To look sad; to look downcast.

Fakabekui, *v.* To blunt; to destroy the edge of a tool.

Fakabela, *v.* To cause an abscess to discharge.

Fakabeleavale, *v.* To pet a foolish person.

Fakabelebela, *v.* To bemire; to roll in dirt.

Fakabelebele, *v.* To pet.

Fakabenu, *v.* To put on a large dress of *gatu.*

Fakabibi, *v.* To repair and strengthen the fence of a fort; to barricade.

Fakabibi, *s.* A barricade; a place hastily made for shelter in war.

Fakabibibihi, *v.* To infect.

Fakabibihi, *a.* Infectious.

Fakabibiki, *v.* To adhere, to cleave to; to cause to stick to.

Fakabihi, *v.* To let off; to shoot from the hand; to sprinkle, to splash.

Fakabiki, *v.* To ensnare; to implicate; to fasten upon.

Fakabikibiki, *v.* To hold by; to implicate.

Fakabiko, *v.* To hinder, to interrupt.

Fakabikoi, *s.* Interrupter, hinderance.

Fakabikobiko, *s.* Idleness, an idler; a bend, a curve.

Fakabikobiko, *a.* Lazy, idle; bent, not straight.

Fakabikobiko, *v.* To be idle; to bend; to curve.

Fakabinega, *v.* To meet, to assemble.

Fakabinegaaga, *s.* A meeting place; a rendezvous.

Fakabito, *v.* To fill.

Fakabo, *s.* Murder, a murderer.

Fakabo, *v.* To murder.

Fakabo, *a.* Murderous.

Fakaboa, *s.* Food prepared and brought to a woman, by the man who wishes to marry her.

Fakaboa, *v.* To scent any thing with fish; to smell of fish.

Fakaboi, *v.* To aim a blow in jest; to excite fear; to spar; to fence.

Fakaboiavale, *v.* Accidentally to strike another in jest.

Fakabou, *v.* To set up the posts of a house.

Fakaboubouli, *a.* Dusk, gloomy, dim.

Fakaboubouli, *s.* Gloom, imperfect light.

Fakabouli, *v.* To darken, to eclipse.

Fakabouli, *a.* Dark.

Fakaboulililolilo, *s.* Gross darkness.

Fakabobo, } *v.* To make rotten,
Fakaboboi, } to rot.

Fakaboboaki, *v.* To send a message.

Fakaboboi, *v.* To stand in the way; to oppose.

Fakabobofala, *v.* To lie for a long time on the *fala;* to be contined to the bed.

Fakabobogi, *v.* To cause dizziness.

Fakaboboto, *v.* To reconcile, to quiet.

Fakaboboto, *s.* A reconciler, a peacemaker.

Fakabobotogataa, *a.* Difficult to quiet or reconcile.

Fakabobotogofua, *a.* Easy to quiet or reconcile.

Fakabobula, *v.* To make prisoners, to enslave.

Fakabogi, *s.* Murder.

Fakabogia, *v.* To murder, to kill.

Fakabogibogi, *s.* The food for the morning.

Fakabogibogi, *v.* To wink; to close the eyes as in looking at the sun.

Fakabohekeheke, *v.* To work carelessly; to be dilatory.

Fakaboloto, *ad* Secretly, privately

Fakabona, *v.* To tie a knot; to secure; to make fast.

Fakabona, *s.* A knot.

Fakaboto, *v.* To make wise, to instruct, to discipline.

Fakabotobotaga, *v.* To cultivate small patches of ground.

Fakabotoboto, *v.* To act wisely or prudently; to make round or spherical.

Fakabotoboto, *a.* Cautious, prudent, discreet.

Fakabotu, *s.* The top and bottom persons in a row.

Fakabotu, *v.* To make room; to leave a space free; to divide into rooms or spaces.

Fakabuaa, *v.* To allow to rot; to suffer the mind to become sour.

Fakabuaka, *v.* To supply the pig for an *Umu.*

Fakabuobuaka, *a.* Swinish; of filthy habits.

Fakabuebue, *s.* A race.

47

Fakabuebue, *v.* To race.
Fakabui, *v.* To dictate; to command in quick succession.
Fakabuobua, *v.* To work quickly; to act expeditiously.
Fakabubu, *v.* To make an indecent noise with the mouth.
Fakabubu, } *v.* To stand
Fakabubububu, } in a cluster.
Fakabubuha, *a.* Hot, sultry.
Fakabubuha, *v.* To make hot or sultry.
Fakabubuhi, *v.* To blow a fire to prevent its extinction; to pet in order to save.
Fakabubuke, *a.* Resembling ague.
Fakabubuke, *v.* To shiver, as one in an ague fit.
Fakabubuku, *v.* To make short, to shorten.
Fakabubula, *v.* To swell, to arrogate.
Fakabubunifo, *v.* To drivel, applied to children.
Fakabubuto, *v.* To swell out; to fill with wind.
Fakabubutuu, *v.* To cause confusion, to confuse.
Fakabuha, } *v.* To push on;
Fakabuhaa, } to urge on; to press forward; to persevere.
Fakabuhegia, *v.* To suffocate; to intercept the fresh air.
Fakabuhobuhaa, *v.* See *Fakabuha*
Fakabuhobuha, *a.* Blustering, bullying.
Fakabuke, *v.* To raise hillocks into which the seed of the yam is put; to chase in war; to make a rush upon; to cover over fore and aft of a small paddling canoe.
Fakabuke, *a.* Covered with a deck, applied to small canoes.
Fakabukua, *v.* To dash into the mouth, as the sea when one is swimming against the waves.
Fakabukubuku, *s.* *Gatu* made narrower than usual.

Fakabulamata, *v.* To hector; to assume a threatening air in jest.
Fakabule, *s.* A mode of fishing.
Fakabulebule, *v.* To spot, to print, to variegate, to fleak.
Fakabuli, } *v.* To conceal or
Fakabulibuli, } hide, so as to escape detection.
Fakabulibuli, *ad.* Slyly, secretly.
Fakabulou, *v.* To veil or cover the face.
Fakabulou, *s.* A part in a canoe; a coverall.
Fakabulobula, *v.* To encourage, to hearten.
Fakabuloga, *v.* To cover over.
Fakabulotu, *s.* A genius; a clever person; a treble voice.
Fakabulubulu, *v.* To try; to fit one thing to another.
Fakabulubuluakii, *v.* To take off under cover; to hide.
Fakabulubului, *v.* To stick upon to cause to adhere to; to cover or cloak another.
Fakabulubuluvale, *a.* Any thing the inside of which is much better than was expected from the appearance of its exterior.
Fakabuna, } *v.* To cause
Fakabunabunai, } to fly; to drive furiously.
Fakabuni, *v.* To close, to shut; to bring two ends together.
Fakabunou, *v.* To cause to bend or bow down; to bow down.
Fakabunuga, *v.* To give a woman to a man as his wife, contrary to her wish.
Fakabuta, *v.* To fill, to bulge, to bloat.
Fakabutae, *v.* To persevere, to keep doing.
Fakabutobuta, *v.* To incite, to animate, to invigorate.
Fakabutu, } *v.* To place
Fakabutubutu, } close together; to set near each other.

Fakabutuga, *v.* To assemble together to talk and make a noise.

Fakabutuga, *s.* A noisy assembly.

Fakafa, *v.* To burst or split open the nut.

Fakafaa, *v.* To act like a gardener.

Fakafaaga, *s.* The supposed shrine of the Tonga gods.

Fakafaahiga, *v.* To act in tribes; to maintain the distinction of tribes.

Fakafaahikehe, *v.* Of or concerning the gods.

Fakafaahitaha, *v.* To build a *Faahitaha.*

Fakafaaki, *v.* To cause to lean against, or rest upon.

Fakafaala, } *v.* To search;
Fakafaalaala, } to look after.

Fakafae, *v.* To take a woman for a mother; to look to.

Fakafaeho, *v.* To cause the breath to stink.

Fakafaele, *a.* Belonging to a woman in her confinement.

Fakafaemate, *v.* To treat motherless children unkindly.

Fakafai, *v.* To cause to do.

Fakafaifaitaki, *v.* To induce to imitation, to imitate.

Fakafaifoki, *v.* To command a repetition of any thing.

Fakafaigataa, *v.* To render difficult.

Fakafaigofua, *v.* To make easy, to facilitate.

Fakafaite, *v.* To teach female children how to sit.

Fakafaitoo, *a.* Doctor-like, medical; relating to a surgeon.

Fakafaitoka, *v.* To make a burying ground; to devote for a burying ground.

Fakafaiva, *v.* To do any thing like a workman.

Fakafaoa, *v.* To occupy every seat in a paddling canoe.

Fakafaufau, *v.* To cause qualm or sickness.

Fakafafa, *v.* To sling on a stick, and carry over the shoulder.

Fakafafa, *v.* To feel one's way, as one blind or in the dark; to be uncertain.

Fakafafau, *v.* To make tough and slimy, as bread fruit half cooked.

Fakafafau, *v.* To contract; to draw together; to bind close; to be of one mind.

Fakafafaga, *v.* To fill; to slacken any thing drawn through water, by which it fills.

Fakafafano, *v.* To stretch, to lengthen by pulling out.

Fakafafine, *s.* A monster.

Fakafagota, *v.* To command to get shell fish.

Fakafahufahu, *v.* To act as an outlaw.

Fakafaji, } *s.* Revenge, ma-
Fakafajifaji, } lice.

Fakafajifaji, *v.* To revenge.

Fakafajifaji, *a.* Revengeful, malicious.

Fakafajileo, *v.* To quiver the voice; to raise the voice till it breaks.

Fakafajii, *v.* To narrow; to diminish the breadth.

Fakafakau, *v.* To act unwillingly; to do in compliance with the views of another.

Fakafala, *s.* The fine mat presented with *gatu* at festivals.

Fakafalala, *v.* To cause to rest upon or trust in.

Fakafale, *v.* To make a shed over any thing springing up.

Fakafalefale, *v.* To hollow; to make with berths.

Fakafalegaua, } *a.* Doubtful,
Fakafalefalegaua, } uncertain.

Fakafalekakai, *v.* To bury a child or friend in the dwelling house.

49

Fakafalelava, *a.* Unsettled in disposition.
Fakafaletama, *a.* A term applied to the quarrelling of children by the same father, but different mothers.
Fakafana, *v.* To cook the same food more than once.
Fakafana, *a.* Mast-like, applied to one singularly courageous or strong.
Fakafanau, *v.* A term applied to a man to whom a child is born, but begotten by another.
Fakafanau, *v.* To treat children of different parents impartially.
Fakafanau, *a.* Childlike, filial.
Fakafanafana, *v.* To cook over and again the same food.
Fakafano, *v.* To stretch out.
Fakafanogo, *v.* To hearken, to listen.
Fakafanua, *s.* A name of office; a person in office.
Fakafatogia, *v.* To do work as for a tax; to do unwillingly.
Fakafatogia, *a.* Against the will, irksome, compulsory.
Fakafatogiakovi, *v.* To act unkindly and unfairly in government work.
Fakafatu, *v.* To collect; to lay up in the mind; to thicken, applied to liquids.
Fakafatuua, *v.* To wrap up or make like a *Fatuua.*
Fakafatufatu, *v.* To thicken liquids.
Fakafatuliji, *v.* To thunder heavily and in quick succession; to publish any denunciation or threat.
Fakafeao, *v.* To accompany, to guard, to escort.
Fakafeao, *s.* A guard, a companion.
Fakafeauhi, *v.* To do alike.
Fakafeauhi, *ad.* Alike, equally.
Fakafeabaabaaki, *v.* To mutually reverence and respect.

Fakafeafeafeaki, *v.* To call in at several places; to go in a zigzag course.
Fakafeagai, *v.* To act conjointly; to be connected.
Fakafealeituuaki, *v.* To talk indeterminately.
Fakafealeleaki, *v.* To converse together, to confer.
Fakafealofani, *v.* To act in concert; to confer with others, in order to act alike.
Fakafealualumi, *v.* To contend; to act in emulation.
Fakafeatugi, *a.* Oppressive.
Fakafeatugi, *v.* To oppress; to take by force.
Fakafeavagaaki, *v.* To watch a door or passage on each side, that none escape.
Fakafeavaki, *v.* To restrain, because of a superior; to be over awed; to give place to.
Fakafeeli, *v.* To harass; to annoy with work to be done.
Fakafeifeiavale, *a.* Mean, poor, or weak in appearance.
Fakafeiga, *v.* To constrain; to beget earnest desire in the mind.
Fakafeiloaki, *s.* Impudence, intrusion.
Fakafeiloaki, *a.* Impudent, intrusive.
Fakafeiloaki, *v.* To intrude; to bore into notice.
Fakafeitama, *v.* To impregnate; to bud.
Fakafeitamaloi, *v.* To feign pregnancy.
Fakafeiteitani, *v.* To cause mutual anger.
Fakafeituu, *a.* Distinct, apart.
Fakafeituulaa, *a.* At a certain time in the day
Fakafeoboji, *v.* To put things with a flat surface one upon another.
Fakafeogoogoi, *v.* To question

different parties, in order to act in concert.

Fakafeomokaki, *v.* To jut out; to push out of place.

Fakafeonofi, *v.* To look wishfully for any thing.

Fakafeuiuiaki, *v.* To call and seek after persons in order to their collecting together; to collect persons dispersed.

Fakafeufcu, *v.* To wrinkle, to crease.

Fakafeuga, *v.* To accord with; to suit one thing to another; to place in a line with.

Fakafeuga, *prep.* According to.

Fakafeumu, *v.* To cause food to be cooked.

Fakafeutaki, *v.* To press or squeeze any thing between two bodies.

Fakafeutugaki, *v.* To be in more hands than one; to be able to supply what another may lack.

Fakafefeu, *v.* To wrinkle, to crease.

Fakafebaki, *v.* To knock one against another; to go out to meet.

Fakafebakituu, *v.* To jostle one against another, as in a crowd.

Fakafebaleaki, *v.* To shuffle from one to another.

Fakafebatoji, *v.* To strike together the edges of any thing sharp.

Fakafebiubiuaki, *v.* To go in a zigzag course.

Fakafebouaki, *v.* To halt; to be in suspense.

Fakafebogaki, *s.* Slaughter, massacre.

Fakafebogaki, *v.* To kill each other.

Fakafebutagaki, *v.* To be equally determined; to emulate.

Fakafefeka, *v.* To harden.

Fakafefele, *v.* To obstruct, to put in the way.

Fakafefena, *v.* To make tough; to keep till withered.

Fakafefihitaki, *v.* To make intricate, to perplex, to entangle.

Fakafefine, *a.* Effeminate, womanish.

Fakafefine, *v.* To act like a woman.

Fakafehagahagai, *v.* To sit face to face.

Fakafehalaaki, *v.* To cause to err.

Fakafehalaaki, *s.* One who causes others to err; a deceiver.

Fakafeheaki, *v.* To pass a thing from one to another till it is lost.

Fakafehia, *v.* To cause to hate.

Fakafehiamate, *v.* To cause to hate with a deadly hatred.

Fakafehobobobokaki, *v.* To portion or divide out to others.

Fakafehokotaki, *v.* To join on to.

Fakafeholoholoi, *v.* To follow in a train

Fakafeholoholataki, *v.* To go from place to place, to avoid or shun those who seek.

Fakafehuaaki, *v.* To joke one with another.

Fakafehui, *v.* To question, to inquire.

Fakafehufaki, *v.* To place things heads and points; to lie heads and heels.

Fakafehulunaki, *v.* To fold the arms.

Fakafekau, *v.* To despatch with a message; to command.

Fakafekakei, *v.* To desire equality in rank and authority with another.

Fakafekakei, *v.* Desiring equality with a superior.

Fakafekeke, *s.* Avarice.

Fakafekeke, *a.* Avaricious.

Fakafekiki, *a.* Addicted to cheating in games.

Fakafekiki, *v,* To cheat in gaming.

Fakafekita, *v.* To pass a child, in order to be kissed by another.
Fakafekitaki, *v.* To go to meet.
Fakafekofeko, *v.* To soften; to make elastic.
Fakafekoviaki, *v.* To backbite.
Fakafekoviaki, *a.* Backbiting.
Fakafekuku, *s.* A part in the sail of a Tonga canoe.
Fakafelaitaki, *s.* A general flatterer or fawner.
Fakafelaitaki, *v.* To flatter or fawn one another.
Fakafelaulaui, *v.* Contending parties speaking of each other.
Fakafelatani, *v.* To beget a liking to a place or person.
Fakafelatogaki, *v.* To do from necessity.
Fakafelefele, *v.* To dispread, to strew; to be scattered.
Fakafelega, *s.* A practice observed at the birth of the first child.
Fakafeliaki, } Fakafeliliaki, } *v.* To be on the stretch; to work without ceasing.
Fakafeliuaki, *v.* To place or put things heads and points; to reverse the natural order.
Fakafelihaa, *v.* To litter; to scatter about.
Fakafeloiaki, *v.* To lie to different parties.
Fakafelogoi, *v.* To be mutually silent.
Fakafemataki, *v.* To look one at another in silence.
Fakafemehekataki, *v.* To envy one another.
Fakafemelekaki, *v.* To be angry one at another.
Fakafemiomioaki, *v.* To lie; to twist or prevaricate to different persons.
Fakafemouaki, *v.* To burden to and fro without advantage.
Fakafena, *v.* To make tough or withered by long keeping.

Fakafenenuaki, } Fakafenenuakina, } *v.* To speak ambiguously.
Fakafetai, *s.* Thanks, praise, gratitude.
Fakafetai, *v.* To be thankful, to praise.
Fakafetau, *v.* To contend, to argue.
Fakafetau, *a.* Contentious, controversial.
Fakafetaulaki, *v.* To go and meet in the road.
Fakafetaki, *v.* To join the hands of others.
Fakafetefete, *v.* To offend, to ruffle the mind.
Fakafetogiaki, *v.* To exchange.
Fakafetohoaki, *v.* To pull in different or opposite directions.
Fakafetokai, *v.* To contend in conversation with a chief; to speak as to an equal.
Fakafetokaki, *v.* To give each other away as slaves; also, two or more fowls to lay in one nest.
Fakafetooaki, *v.* To displace, to confuse.
Fakafetuotuakoiaki, *v.* To place things in order; to suit the voice; each to take his part in singing or chanting.
Fakafetui, *v.* To be; to appear again; to exist, though in another form.
Fakafetukuaki, *v.* To shuffle from one to another.
Fakafetulatulaki, *v.* To push one another down.
Fakafetutuki, *v.* To wish to accompany each other.
Fakafevahaanaki, *s.* The line or mark of separation, applied to any thing found in the intervening space of two or more individuals.
Fakafi, *v.* To oppose another as his foe.

Fakafieeiki, *v*. To play the chief; to assume or affect the chief.
Fakafieinu, *v*. To cause thirst.
Fakafieula, *v*. To trifle; to excite laughter and merriment by words or actions.
Fakafiefia, *v*. To cause rejoicing; to exhilirate.
Fakafiefia, *a*. Joyful, delightful.
Fakafiefieula, *v*. See *Fakafieula*.
Fakafiehua, *v*. To jest; to joke.
Fakafiekai, *v*. To cause hunger; to beget an appetite.
Fakafielahi, } *v*. To elate; to
Fakafiefielahi, } puff up; to make haughty.
Fakafiemalie, *s*. A comforter; a cause of comfort; gratification.
Fakafiemalie, *v*. To comfort, to console, to gratify, to indulge.
Fakafiemalie, *a*. Indulgent, mild, giving way to.
Fakafiefiemalie, See *Fakafiemalie*
Fakafiemua, *v*. To play the cheat; to act the deceiver.
Fakafievale, *v*. To play the fool.
Fakafiofio, *v*. To deal out a fair proportion of small and large.
Fakafiu, *v*. To weary, to tire.
Fakafiu, *a*. Tiresome, wearisome.
Fakafiufiu, *v*. To weary out; to tire out of strength and patience.
Fakafiufiu, *a*. Tyrannous, tiresome, past endurance.
Fakafifi, *v*. To hold fast, to cleave to.
Fakafifi, } *a*. Unwilling to part
Fakafifihi, } with.
Fakafifihu, *v*. To look sulky or angrily.
Fakafifiji, *v*. To feel indignation, as at the command of an inferior; to spice.
Fakafifiji, *a*. Irritable, indignant; hot with spice.
Fakafiha, *ad*. How often? how many?

Fakafihi, } *v*. To confuse, to
Fakafihituu, } entwine, to entangle, to complicate, rave.
Fakafiho, *v*. To endure, to persevere in.
Fakafiji, } *v*. To deny, to
Fakafijiga, } disown, to contradict.
Fakafijilotulotu, *v*. To deny or disown by the gods.
Fakafili, *v*. To manifest hostility; to shew enmity.
Fakafili, *s*. Hostility.
Fakafilifilimanako, *v*. To choose, to prefer one thing to another.
Fakafilo, *v*. To renew the wick of a lamp; to thread a needle.
Fakafiloha, *s*. Unwillingness, disinclination.
Fakafiloha, *a*. Unwilling, loath.
Fakafiloha, *v*. To hold fast; to disobey.
Fakafilohi, See *Fakafiloha*.
Fakafitaa, *v*. To endure.
Fakafitefitaa, *s*. Perseverance through dangers and difficulties.
Fakafitefitaa, *v*. To persevere, to persist.
Fakafitefitaa, *a*. Difficult, troublesome.
Fakafoa, *v*. To cry or sing with a loud strained voice.
Fakafoi, *v*. To beget cowardice; to affright.
Fakafoituitui, *v*. Each one to do according to his own mind.
Fakafoou, *s*. Renewal, newness, conversion.
Fakafoou, } *v*. To make new,
Fakafoofoou, } to renew.
Fakafoohake, } *v*. To lie on
Fakafoofoohake, } the back; to turn the face or front of any thing upwards.
Fakafoohifo, *v*. To turn upside down; to prostrate.
Fakafoohifo, *ad*. Prone.
Fakafou, *v*. To open; to disclose, as a secret.

Fakafofoga, *s.* A representative, an ambassador.
Fakafofoga, *v.* To represent, to speak for.
Fakafofonu, *v.* To cause cold in the head.
Fakafoha, *v.* To ripen; to make large, applied to seeds.
Fakafoki, *v.* To cause to return.
Fakafoki, *s.* One who causes others to return or go back.
Fakafokifa, *s.* Suddenness.
Fakafokifa, *a.* Sudden, unexpected.
Fakafokifa, *ad.* Suddenly, hastily.
Fakafolau, *a.* Of or belonging to a *Folau.*
Fakafolau, *s.* The name of the cat fish, when off soundings.
Fakafolo, *v.* To cause or help to swallow.
Fakafono, *v.* To acknowledge a ruler; to be subject to government.
Fakafono, *s.* The poor or governed among the people.
Fakafonoga, *v.* To go in rotation; to move in order.
Fakafonu, *v.* To fill.
Fakafonua, *a.* Belonging to the whole land.
Fakafonua, *s.* The rendezvous of the chiefs and principal warriors in times of war.
Fakafonuaau, *v.* To rise.
Fakafototehina, *a.* Belonging to the younger brothers.
Fakafotu, *s.* The family of a poorer wife than that of an *eiki.*
Fakafotufotuekina, *v.* To go towards, to approach.
Fakafua, Fakafuai, } *v.* To carry on the shoulder; to fructify, to cause to bear fruit.
Fakafuaa, *v.* To create jealousy; to serve out in equal proportion.
Fakafuahau, *v.* To do mischief under the protection of a chief.

Fakafuataga, *v.* To look at, to be aware of; to prepare the *gatu* in a certain way.
Fakafuifui, *v.* To fly in flocks; to roll in quick succession, as waves of the sea.
Fakafuofuaa, *v.* To create jealousy.
Fakafuofua, *v.* To shape.
Fakafuofuolahi, *a.* Vain, ostentatious.
Fakafuoloa, *v.* To protract, to extend.
Fakafuulau, *a.* Covered with leaves, but no fruit; simulating.
Fakafufu, *v.* To hide or conceal.
Fakafufula, *v.* To swell out; to look displeased.
Fakafufunaki, *v.* To hide, to conceal.
Fakafuga, Fakafugaahi, } *s.* A scented oil.
Fakafuhi, *v.* To hang in clusters; to tie a number of things together.
Fakafujifujiloto, *a.* Selfwilled; determined to do his own mind.
Fakafujifujiloto, *v.* To assume independence.
Fakafula, *a.* To cause disease.
Fakafuli, *s.* Overwhelming waves.
Fakafulofula, *v.* To frown or look shy upon; to be sullen.
Fakafulofula, *a.* Sulky, morose, silently sullen.
Fakafulufulu, *v.* To make rough, as a board that was smooth.
Fakafulufuluhaa, *v.* To set on end, as birds and beasts their feathers and hair, when angry; to disorder; to dress slovenly.
Fakafulutamaki, *v.* To stop the breath; to prevent free breathing.
Fakafutofuta, *v.* To act haughtily.
Fakafutofuta, *a.* Haughty, proud.
Fakafutofuta, *s.* Haughtiness, pride.

54

Fakaga, *v.* To chase out of breath; to cause to pant; to suffer a child to cry itself out of breath.

Fakagaeheehe, *a.* Spiritless, without vigour.

Fakagaeheehe, *v.* To act weakly, or without spirit.

Fakagaehu, *v.* To agitate, to disturb.

Fakagaii, *v.* To grind or gnaw with the teeth; to rub with a grinding motion.

Fakagaofe, } *v.* To bend, to
Fakagaofeofe, } curve.

Fakagaofe, } *s.* Flexion, the
Fakagaofeofe, } act of bending.

Fakagaogao, *v.* To depopulate; to send away; to desert.

Fakagaogao, *v.* To eat having only the double teeth left.

Fakagaolo, *v.* To cause to creep; to allow to crawl.

Fakagaue, *v.* To set to work; to employ.

Fakagaue, } *v.* To move, to
Fakagaueue, } cause to shift, to actuate, to excite.

Fakagaugau, *v.* To wet, to damp, to moisten.

Fakagauta, *v.* To arouse; to set in action.

Fakagafagafa, *v.* To do each his own work.

Fakagafagafa, *a.* Parcelled out, divided.

Fakagafigafi, *v.* To dress with a mat; to put a mat outside the dress of *gatu*.

Fakagafigafi, *s.* The name of the mat used as above.

Fakagagau, *v.* To make the head ache, applied to one whose conduct gives pain.

Fakagagau, *a.* Foolish, egregiously so.

Fakagagau, *v.* See *Fakagaugau.*

Fakagagake, *v.* To wet, to saturate.

Fakagagana, *a.* To cause to fall; to shake down.

Fakagagatu, *v.* To scent; to convey a scent of any thing pleasant to the smell.

Fakagahau, *v.* To obstruct; to stop up a road.

Fakagahaha, *v.* To make a rushing noise, as in passing through stubble.

Fakagahe, *v.* To induce languor.

Fakagaholo, *v.* To speed the sailing of a vessel; to loose, to relax.

Fakagahuhu, *v.* To saturate in water.

Fakagakau, *v.* To embowel.

Fakagako, *v.* To grease, to fatten.

Fakagala, *v.* To allow a child to cry till its voice is become weak; to cry.

Fakagalatoka, *v.* To feed; to make exceedingly fat.

Fakagalemulemu, *v.* to make soft or flabby.

Fakagaligali, *a.* Fitting, proper, becoming.

Fakagaligali, *v.* To gnaw; to tear with the teeth.

Fakagalo, } *v.* To forget.
Fakagalogaloi, }

Fakagalo, } *s.* Forgetful-
Fakagalogaloi, } ness.

Fakagalogalomi, } *v.* To cause
Fakagalomia, } to forget.

Fakagaloku, *v.* To wrinkle, to crease, to make uneven.

Fakagalugalu, } *v.* To go along
Fakagalugaluvai, } weakly; to waddle, as one very weak.

Fakagano, *v.* To expose the body to the sun, in order to become red or ruddy.

Fakagata, *v.* To make an end.

Fakagatagata, *v.* To circumscribe; to set bounds or land marks; to restrict.

Fakagatata, *v.* To jingle, to make a jingling noise.

Fakagavaivai, *a.* Weak, not healthy.

Fakagei, Fakageigei, *v.* To excite fear and apprehension.

Fakagei, Fakageigei, *a.* Stern, unrelenting.

Fakagehegehe, *a.* Mild, weak, applied to the sun when past meridian.

Fakagi, Fakagigi, *v.* To drizzle, as small rain; to whine, as a sick child.

Fakagigila, *v.* To polish, to gloss, to brighten.

Fakagini, *v.* To be shrivelled from exposure to cold.

Fakagofua, *v.* To annul a prohibition; to put an end to an interdict.

Fakagono, *v.* To gather the nuts from time to time before they are good.

Fakagoto, *v.* To sink; to press under water.

Fakagotoumu, *v.* To make native ovens; to devote a place to the cooking of food.

Fakagotogoto, *v.* To dive, as fish.

Fakagu, *v.* To make to speak; to induce to speak.

Fakagugu, *v.* To grumble or mutter disapprobation.

Fakagugulu, *v.* To breathe hard with a grunting noise.

Fakagutu, *v.* To make the opening or mouth of any thing.

Fakagutuhua, *v.* To jest, to joke.

Fakaha, *v.* To make known; to cause to appear; to manifest.

Fakaha, *s.* Exposure, manifestation.

Fakahaa, *v.* To scatter; to place at random.

Fakahaabulou, *v.* Each to work for before he eats or gets what he wants.

Fakahaagataha, *v.* To accomplish at once, (going or doing.)

Fakahaalavaka, *s.* The long hair worn in sign of virginity.

Fakahaamo, *v.* To order another to carry a burden; to supply the pole to carry with.

Fakahaamoga, *v.* To put in double lots, so as to *haamo.*

Fakahaea, *v.* To act foolishly; to lose by exposing.

Fakahaele, *a.* To conduct a great personage; to teach a child to walk.

Fakahao, *v.* To pilot; to direct the course of a vessel.

Fakahao, *s.* A pilot.

Fakahaoijino, Fakahaoitejino, *v.* To appear individually.

Fakahaofi, Fakahaofia, *v.* To cause to escape; to extricate from danger.

Fakahaohao, *v.* To take with care; to proceed circumspectly or cautiously.

Fakahaohaoa, *v.* To escape without fault; to free from every thing bad; to make perfect.

Fakahaohaogataa, *v.* To get through, to escape, with difficulty.

Fakahaohaogofua, *v.* To get through, to escape, with ease.

Fakahau, Fakaehau, *a.* Rigorous, tyrannical, oppressive, troublesome, annoying.

Fakahau, *v.* To put through the nose or the ear; to whine, to cry.

Fakahauhau, *v.* To bedew; to expose to the dew.

Fakahaue, Fakahauhaue, *v.* To walk or sail about for pleasure.

Fakahauhaufano, *v.* To take an airing; to sit in the breeze.

Fakahaujia, *v.* To leave exposed to the weather.

Fakahaunifo, *s.* Dentition; the act of cutting teeth.

56

Fakahabae, } v. To go as one
Fakahahabae, } crooked in the feet.

Fakahabuto, *part.* Swollen, inflated, bulged, as any thing filled with the wind.

Fakahafu, *v.* To dip the head backward into the water; to carry any thing dropping with wet.

Fakahafuhafu, *v.* To heave to; to put the head of the canoe to the wind; to drive before the wind.

Fakahafuhataha, *v.* To do orderly; to place heads and points all one way; to put alphabetically.

Fakahafuni, *v.* To cut the hair short; to be short or destitute of any thing.

Fakahaga, } *v.* To set in a
Fakahagahaga, } line with; to place exactly opposite.

Fakahagakehe, *v.* To set awry; to place obliquely.

Fakahagakehe, *s.* The name given to axes helved English fashion.

Fakahagatamaki, *v.* To cause danger; to make dangerous; to cause swellings.

Fakahagatonu, *v.* To set in a straight line; to front, to face.

Fakahago, *v.* To strew, to scatter loosely.

Fakahaha, *v.* To shew, to make known, to exhibit.

Fakahaha, *v.* To line with banana leaves the inside of the *Gotoumu.*

Fakahahae, *v.* To drag, to drawl; to speak as a foreigner.

Fakahahau, *v.* To expose to the dew.

Fakahahafu, *v.* To drop; to let fall drops of any liquid.

Fakahahaga, *v.* To sit with the legs extended.

Fakahahaka, *s.* A preparation of food.

Fakahahaka, *v.* To startle; to cause sudden terror.

Fakahahake, *a.* Easterly, towards the east.

Fakahahakonoa, *v.* To take a trip or journey of pleasure.

Fakahahatala, *v.* To tell, to talk about.

Fakahahatuu, *v.* To chastise indiscriminately; to scold all for the offence of one.

Fakahakau, *v.* To strew; to scatter about; to catch fish on the reefs.

Fakahakau, *s.* Bananas buried in the sand to ripen, but the stems in sight.

Fakahake, } *v.* To land;
Fakahakehake, } to remove things out of the water to the shore; to get out of a hole or pit.

Fakahako, *v.* To advance the growth of trees by breaking off the shoots.

Fakahako, } *s.* Seed, pro-
Fakahakohako, } geny, successors.

Fakahakohakoloto, *v.* To act according to his own mind; to indulge in obstinacy.

Fakahakolo, } *v.* To place un-
Fakahakolokolo, } suitably low or near the earth; to speak with a low rough voice.

Fakahala, *v.* To cause to err; to deceive.

Fakahala, *s.* A deceiver; one that is the occasion of error in others.

Fakahalaa, *v.* To dream of one person, what happens to another.

Fakahalai, }
Fakahalaia, } See *Fakahala.*
Fakahalahalai, }

Fakahalaua, *v.* To tear asunder.

Fakahalafaki, *v.* To take another road to avoid being seen.
Fakahalafonua, *v.* To cause a whole land trouble; to betray a whole people.
Fakahalahalaga, *v.* To crack; to make streaks or marks; to be cracked.
Fakahalakava, *v.* To leave a patch uncultivated, while all around is cultivated.
Fakahalatua, *v.* To take or bring to poor persons or relatives.
Fakahaliavale, *a.* Unkind, indolent, overgrown.
Fakahalofia, *v.* To beget hunger.
Fakahaloku, *v.* To ridge, to raise, to make uneven, to wrinkle.
Fakahalu, *v.* To order others to seek fish.
Fakahama, *v.* To put the outrigger to a canoe.
Fakahama, Fakahamahama, } *a.* Foolishly generous; indifferent.
Fakahama, Fakahamahama, } *v.* To give that to others which the party itself needs; to be indifferent about.
Fakahamanaki, *v.* To buoy up the mind; to expect.
Fakahamatefua, *a.* Like a *Hamatefua.*
Fakahamelie, *s.* A good omen; ominous of good.
Fakahamelie, *v.* To forebode good.
Fakahamuhamu, *a.* Blustrous.
Fakahamuhamu, *v.* To bluster about; to try to set others laughing.
Fakahana, *a.* Purgative.
Fakahana, *v.* To run out; to allow or cause to run out, as water from a shell.
Fakahanoku, *v.* To ridge, to bend up.
Fakahatamaki, *s.* A bad omen; ominous of evil.

Fakahatamaki, *v.* To forebode evil.
Fakahavala, Fakahavalagia, } *v.* To beget longing desire; to long after.
Fakahavilivili, *v.* To take an airing; to sit in the breeze.
Fakahe, *v.* To cause to err, to mislead, to misdirect.
Fakahe, *a.* Applied to one who leads others astray.
Fakahea, *v.* To mix a preparation for painting native cloth.
Fakahee, *v.* To drive away; to shake off.
Fakaheigofua, *a.* Easily seduced or led astray.
Fakaheihei, *v.* To look aslant or obliquely.
Fakaheihei, *a.* Oblique.
Fakahehe, *v.* To drive away, as birds.
Fakahehe, *v.* To wander; to go from place to place in search of health.
Fakahehegi, *v.* To scare; to make wild.
Fakaheheka, *a.* Granulous; a wound filling up.
Fakaheheke, *v.* To go aslant; to dive obliquely.
Fakahehema, Fakahehemai, } *v.* To excite attention; to draw away from other objects.
Fakaheheva, *a.* Foolish.
Fakaheka, *v.* To load a canoe; to freight, embark.
Fakaheke, *v.* To flatter; to slip; to cause others to slip and fall; to beguile; to ward off.
Fakaheke, *a.* Addicted to flattering.
Fakahekeheka, *v.* To accompany one about to sail to the vessel.
Fakahekelena, *a.* Deceptious, applied to a day the morning of which was beautifully fine, but afterwards very rough.
Fakahele, *a.* Tiresome, tedious.

Fakahela, *v.* To run out of breath.

Fakahele, } *v.* To cut off; to separate from.
Fakahelehele, }

Fakaheleau, } *v.* To inquire suspiciously; to take by craft.
Fakahelehele, }

Fakahelegavale, *a.* Erroneous in language; foolish; incorrect.

Fakahelegavale, *s.* Error, mistake.

Fakaheleleu, *v.* To speak or act with a different design from the apparent one.

Fakaheliaki, *v.* To insinuate, to trick.

Fakahema, *a.* Left-handed, awkward, clumsy.

Fakaheveheva, *a.* Childish, simple.

Fakaheveheva, } *v.* To act childishly.
Fakahiehiaga, }

Fakahifo, *v.* To unload; to discharge; to put down; to counteract by an offering or sacrifice.

Fakahiga, } *v.* To throw down, to cause to fall, to degrade.
Fakahigai, }

Fakahigano, *v.* To blossom, to shew fruit; a small part at the end of a canoe.

Fakahigoa, *v.* To name; to denominate.

Fakahihiaga, *v.* To act foolishly, like a child.

Fakahihiaga, *a.* Foolish, weak of intellect.

Fakahihifi, *v.* To cut out of form or shape.

Fakahihigo, *v.* To turn into another path; to go askaunt.

Fakahihili, *a.* Irritable.

Fakahikihiki, *v.* To magnify, to exalt.

Fakahila, } *v.* To look with a quick turn of the head; to look askaunt; to look as from under a hat.
Fakahilatuamata, }
Fakahilehila, }

Fakahili, *v.* To pass by; to lessen the sail in bad weather.

Fakahilihili, *v.* To speak of the progenitors of chiefs (a mortal offence,) also, to intercept; to turn into another route.

Fakahinehina, *v.* To bleach, to make white.

Fakahinohino, *v.* To lead, to guide, to direct.

Fakahinohino, *s.* Guide, guidance, direction.

Fakahinohinoi, *v.* To inform an adopted child of its real parents.

Fakahoa, *s.* Suspicion.

Fakahoa, *a.* Suspicious, inclined to suspect.

Fakahoa, *v.* To suspect, to imagine ill of another; to couple, to pair.

Fakahoata, *s.* Work done or food prepared at or about noonday.

Fakahou, *v.* To retch; to force up from the stomach; to excite to do or say.

Fakahougai, *v.* To welcome, to receive with gratitude.

Fakahouhau, *v.* To cause anger; to affront; to manifest anger.

Fakahouhau, *s.* An affront, an insult.

Fakahouhoumotua, *v.* To feel shame; to act as one ashamed.

Fakahobo, *v.* To command a person or persons from one place to another; to make one jump; to cut out, as a cancer.

Fakahoboate, *v.* To make captives; to treat as prisoners.

Fakahobohobo, *v.* To allow to hop about, as a bird from a cage.

Fakahoge, } *v.* To starve, to famish.
Fakahogea, }

Fakahogi, *v.* To seek out by the smell.

Fakahohaa, *v.* To discompose, to disquiet, to make uneasy.

Fakahohoa, *v.* To put fairly, bad and good, large and small, together.

Fakahohoko, *ad.* Singly, individually.

Fakahoholi, *v.* To domesticate; to beget a liking.

Fakahoholo, *v.* To slide; to move on any smooth surface.

Fakahoholoto, *v.* To do unwillingly; to do despairingly.

Fakahohotuu, *v.* To confuse, to cause an uproar, to be unsettled.

Fakahoko, *v.* To cause to arrive at; to apply; to join.

Fakahoko, *s.* Application.

Fakahokohoko, *v.* To bring up; to hasten towards, as a fair wind the vessel; to wish to resemble others.

Fakahola, Fakaholaki, } *v.* To unloose; to let go away; to send out of the way.

Fakaholataki, *v.* To abscond with any thing.

Fakaholo, *v.* To move in a line; to glide or run on a smooth surface.

Fakaholoholo, *v.* To move in succession, to let go; to let down; to become fair, as the wind.

Fakaholoholoi, *v.* To neglect to correct children and others who do badly.

Fakaholoki, *v.* To push down, to demolish.

Fakaholomamata, *a.* Agreeable to the sight; pleasing to look at.

Fakaholomui, *v.* To go backwards, to backslide.

Fakaholonofo, Fakaholoholonofo, } *a.* Agreeable, pleasant, applied to any thing one is pleased to sit at.

Fakahomo, *v.* To pass secretly to another, to give secretly; to untie, to loose.

Fakahomohomo, *v.* To let go, to part with.

Fakahu, *v.* To cause to go into or out of any place.

Fakahua, *v.* To banter or joke.

Fakahua, *a.* Addicted to banter or joke.

Fakahua, *v.* To tack about in sailing.

Fakahuufataha, *v.* To lay all in one direction; to lie straight and all one way.

Fakahuuhuu, Fakahuuhuufaki, } *v.* To be ashamed; to be suspicious; to have particular reference to.

Fakahuuhuuvale, *v.* To place without order; to lie down heads and heels.

Fakahufaki, *v.* To take an offender out of danger; to place another under the protection of a superior.

Fakahufi, *v.* To cause or to allow an enemy to enter a fort or any place.

Fakahufia, *v.* To chase into shelter.

Fakahuhu, *v.* To suckle, to give suck.

Fakahuhu, *v.* To search into, to examine.

Fakahuhulu, *v.* To shine, to look well, but not liked.

Fakahuki, *v.* To sit on the lap, to nurse.

Fakahukihuki, *v.* To begin to set up a child.

Fakahukovia, *v.* To chase soldiers in a state of confusion into a fort.

Fakahula, *v.* To bulge; to slacken, so as to bulge out in any part.

Fakahulu, Fakahuluhulu, } *v.* To plunge; to rush in the face of danger.

Fakahumu, *v.* To tie the fore legs of an animal; to push another to stumble.

Fakajiejia, *s.* The small eggs inside a fowl.

Fakajiijii, *v.* To lessen, to extenuate.

Fakajiijii *ad.* Sparingly, little, in a small degree.

Fakajiijii, *s.* Extenuation.

Fakajio, Fakajiojio, } *v.* To peep, to look, to stare, to pry.

Fakajiba, *v.* To throw any thing flat so as to skim along.

Fakajibi, *v.* To collect warriors.

Fakajigejigaa, *v.* To persevere through difficulties, as one who goes in the heat of noonday.

Fakajifa, *v.* To whirl round; to swing, as a vessel to the vessel.

Fakajiji, *v.* To make a beginning, to mark out.

Fakajikejike, *v.* To set a child on its heels, to teach it so to sit.

Fakajina, *v.* To be very particular in doing work.

Fakajina, *a.* Neat, particular in work.

Fakajinifa *s.* A heathen song of females only.

Fakajino, *v.* To feed, to fatten.

Fakajino, *a.* Feeding, fattening.

Fakajinonaki, *a.* Consistent in character; agreeable to.

Fakajitua, *v.* To treat unkindly on the departure or death of a parent or friend.

Fakajivejiva, Fakajivejivamea, } *a.* Unmindful, ungrateful.

Fakajivejiva, Fakajivejivamea, } *v.* To be unmindful of, to neglect, to throw away, to slight.

Fakakaekae, *v.* To use mocking language, to deride.

Fakakai, *v.* To entice with food; to pay a wager.

Fakakai, *s.* A wager won in certain games.

Fakakaibo, *v.* To eat slyly or alone; to be selfishly inclined.

Fakakaifonua, Mean, low, pauperized.

Fakakaiga, *a.* Friendly, kind, obliging.

Fakakaihaa, *v.* Thief-like, becoming a thief.

Fakakainaga, *v.* To act in tribes; to act distinctly and separately in each tribe.

Fakakainiloto, *v.* To be afflicted with the disease called *Kainiloto;* to speak through the nose.

Fakakaitamaki, *a.* Exceedingly strong, wise, or dexterous.

Fakakaivao, *a.* Mean, selfish, as one who eats in the bush.

Fakakaivale, *v.* To act selfishly; to divide unfairly.

Fakakaokaofi, *v.* To desert, to leave alone, to be all on the opposite side.

Fakakau, *v.* To implicate; to put in scores.

Fakakaufefine, *v.* To associate together (women.)

Fakakauga, *s.* The cause or origin of being implicated in any affair.

Fakakaugaabi, *a.* Neighbour-like, neigbourly.

Fakakaugagaue, *v.* To associate in the performance of any work.

Fakakaugamalie, *v.* To render easy of performance.

Fakakaugamea, *v.* To associate, to be united.

Fakakaugatamaki, *v.* To render difficult of performance.

Fakakaugoue, *v.* To garden together; to work together at gardening.

Fakakaukau, *v.* To consult; to deliberate.

Fakakaukau, *s.* Consultation, deliberation.

Fakakaukauloa, *v.* To run a vessel beyond the time and place for bringing her up.
Fakakaumea, *v.* To seek a companion or an associate.
Fakakaunaga, *v.* To treat a female as a servant.
Fakakaunaga, *a.* Female servant like; becoming a female servant.
Fakakaunifo, *v.* To scallop; to cut in the form of teeth.
Fakakaunoa, *v.* To implicate one not concerned.
Fakakauta, *v.* To come with a present though poor.
Fakakautagata, *v.* To associate together (men.)
Fakakautoutai, *v.* To associate together (fishermen or sailors.)
Fakakaba, } *v.* To leave an
Fakakabakaba, } end or corner in cutting off; to corner.
Fakakabalu, *v.* To make a flapping noise.
Fakakabataha, *v.* To refer to one end or corner or division.
Fakakabo, *v.* To bring the sail of the canoe nearer to the wind.
Fakakabu, *v.* To fill, as the sail with wind; to keep full.
Fakakafa, *v.* To supply *kafa* for any work; to make a collar with *kafa* for dogs, &c.
Fakakafaki, *v.* To go up; to be on the ascent, applied to the disposition becoming haughty.
Fakakafotahi, *v.* To dress a wound in a certain way.
Fakakafu, *v.* To cover a person when laid down or asleep.
Fakakahi, *v.* To make a scratching or flapping noise.
Fakakaho, *v.* To rib, to divide by lines.
Fakakahoa, *v.* To place a garland or ornament on the neck of another.
Fakakahokaho, *a.* Broad deep lines or ribs.
Fakajiimaaga, *v.* To eat from and make less the food provided for others.
Fakakaka, *v.* To cause to climb; to seek after forgotten friends.
Fakakaka, *v.* To impoverish the soil, as useless trees.
Fakakaka, *s.* A cheat, a deceiver.
Fakakaka, *a.* Deceitful.
Fakakaka, *ad.* Deceitfully, perfidiously.
Fakakakai, *v.* To people, to inhabit.
Fakakakau, *v.* To fasten a stick to any thing for present use; to handle.
Fakakakaha, *v.* To make very hot.
Fakakakala, *v.* To scent oil with leaves, &c.
Fakakakale, *v.* To run to and fro.
Fakakakano, *v.* To fill, to line, to put inside.
Fakakakano, *a.* Earthly, fleshly.
Fakakakata, *v.* To laugh; to titter at any trick.
Fakakakato, *v.* To make up, to complete.
Fakakakava, *a.* Causing perspiration, sudorific.
Fakakakava, *v.* To do by proxy.
Fakakake, } *v.* To peer up
Fakakakekake, } in distance, as from a hole.
Fakakala, *s.* The motions of any thing near death or dying.
Fakakalakala, *v.* To cause to smart.
Fakakalaloa, *v.* To be a long time at any thing.
Fakakalalu, *v.* See ***Fakakabalu.***
Fakakalamu, *v.* To draw a rope through the water, to drive fish into the net.
Fakakalekale, *v.* To run in confusion, as when affrighted.

62

Fakakalekaleaki, *v.* To go on without obstruction.
Fakakalia, *a.* Like a *Kalia.*
Fakakalo, *v.* To run, as betwixt showers of rain; to embrace a fair opportunity.
Fakakaloa, *a.* Not easily separated.
Fakakaloa, *v.* To remain stationary.
Fakakalokalofaki, *v.* To be careful in danger; to keep a good look out.
Fakakalu, *v.* To break up; to mash in cutting up food.
Fakakana, *v.* To prognosticate the good qualities of another; to predict.
Fakakanagataa, *v.* To be difficult to cure.
Fakakanogataa, *a.* Difficult to cure, to cook, to accomplish.
Fakakanoi, } *v.* To be full;
Fakakanokano, } to be lined, as a part of the horizon with dark clouds.
Fakakata, *v.* To excite laughter.
Fakakata, *a.* Addicted to causing laughter.
Fakakata, *s.* A name given to those who decoy persons into danger.
Fakakatakata, *v.* To try by laughing; to make others laugh.
Fakakatea, *v.* To make into a *Katea.*
Fakakatoa, *v.* To collect, to assemble; to bind together.
Fakakatoaga, *v.* To be like or similar to a *Katoaga.*
Fakakatoabo, *v.* To complete or finish any given number of nights.
Fakakatuba. *v.* To make door ways.
Fakakava, *v.* To cause a stink.
Fakakavakava, *a.* Fenced, as a road on both sides.
Fakakavealoto, *v.* To have the mind tied to any thing; to be engrossed.
Fakakavei, *v.* To sling a basket; to put slings or hanging strings to a basket.
Fakakavekavetala, *v.* To do in order to be talked about; to desire fame.
Fakake, *v.* To cause quarrelling.
Fakakeu, *a.* Dexterous, expert.
Fakakefu, *v.* To colour the hair of the head.
Fakakehe, } *v.* To change,
Fakakehekehe, } to alter, to transform, to diversify, to make distinctions.
Fakakehekeha, *v.* To scent clothes or the body; to fill with sweet odours.
Fakakeke, *v.* To cause to bleat or cry.
Fakakeke, *v.* To incite, to set on, to accept a challenge
Fakakekeva, *v.* To stiffen, to set.
Fakakele, *s.* One mode of taking fish.
Fakakelekele, *v.* To make dirty, to make unclean.
Fakakelekele, *a.* Earthy, of the earth.
Fakakemokemo, *v.* To twinkle the eyes in looking at another.
Fakakevekeva, *v.* To walk stately and erect.
Fakaki, *v.* To imitate the chirping of a bird; to trouble by frequent application.
Fakakibola, *v.* To search; to inquire after from place to place.
Fakakihi, *v.* To stunt in growth.
Fakakiki, *v.* To affright.
Fakakiki, *v.* To scream, to squeak, to make a shrill noise.
Fakakiki, *v.* To supply animal food to eat with vegetables.
Fakakikihi, *v.* To carp, to gain-

say, to parley, to argue, to debate, to wrangle.

Fakakikihi, *a.* Contentious.

Fakakikihi, *s.* Contention, altercation.

Fakakikila, *v.* To make to shine, to polish.

Fakakikina, *v.* To tease, to plague, to weary.

Fakakikina, *a.* Tiresome, teasing.

Fakakikite, *v.* To foretell, to predict.

Fakakila, Fakakilakila, } *v.* To open and shut the eyes, as one pretending to be asleep; to be seen but occasionally; to make small bald patches on the head.

Fakakili, *v.* To grow again, as the bark of trees which were stripped.

Fakakilia, *v.* To excite anger.

Fakakilikili, *v.* To spread a large kind of gravel over graves.

Fakakina, *v.* To worry, to tire out.

Fakakinatoa, *v.* To cause callousness, by teasing and worrying.

Fakakinehia, *v.* To express weariness at what does not trouble the party.

Fakakinekina, *v.* To be tired, to be wearied.

Fakakinokinoifia, *a.* Agreeable, pleasing.

Fakakita, *v.* To startle, as one ill; to cause death; to cause the death of a person ill, by exciting his passions.

Fakakite, *v.* To look anxiously and narrowly at any thing, as at what may be reported (land at sea, or a vessel in sight.)

Fakakitekite, *s.* Any thing new or strange done or said by a person just before his decease, and afterwards referred to as a prognostication.

Fakakititama, *v.* To treat as a *Kikitama*.

Fakakivi, *v.* To tease, to annoy, as salt water to the eyes; to leave the *talo* in the earth till dead.

Fakakoa, *v.* To cause foam.

Fakakofe, *v.* To call or sing out with a drawling loud voice.

Fakakofu, *v.* To dress, to clothe.

Fakakoga, *v.* To allow to squeal, as a pig; to do or speak in part only.

Fakakogakau, *a.* To act like a regiment or party of soldiers.

Fakakohi, *v.* To scratch, to make a scratching noise.

Fakakohukohu, *v.* To burn any thing, to cause a dense smoke; to move in a dense body as a shoal of fish.

Fakakoka, *v.* To work bodily at any thing, without accomplishing the object.

Fakakoko, *v.* To cause to make a noise, as in catching a fowl.

Fakakokolo, *v.* To cause to run or fall out, to guggle out.

Fakakokono, *v.* To cause pain; to strain; to make violent efforts; to grieve.

Fakakole, Fakakolekole, } *v.* To entreat, to beg kindly.

Fakakolo, *a.* Fortress-like; warlike, applied to the disposition.

Fakakoloa, *v.* To enrich; to reward; to shroud a corpse.

Fakakolokolo, *v.* To speak or sing with a feigned rough bass voice.

Fakakoloto, *v.* See *Koloto* and *Fakafelatogaki*.

Fakakolukolu, *v.* To dress with something very large and bulky.

Fakakomo, *v.* To speak but little; to utter a sentence; to know a few words of another language.

Fakakona, Fakakonahi, } *v.* To make bitter, to embitter, to intoxicate; to poison.

64

Fakakonakai, *v.* To embitter food.
Fakakonokona, *v.* To salt; to season with salt, as broth.
Fakakonokono, *v.* To tease, to annoy, to vex.
Fakakonokono, *a.* Vexatious, trying, teasing.
Fakakova, *v.* To cut the hair in front only.
Fakakovi, *v.* To make bad; to calumniate, to asperse, to derogate.
Fakakovi, *s.* Calumny, aspersion, detraction.
Fakakovi, *a.* Addicted to backbiting; calumnious.
Fakaku, *ad.* When? either past or future.
Fakakui, *v.* To blind.
Fakakuikui, *v.* To work the eye lids with a quick motion, as one *kuikui.*
Fakakubukubu, *v.* To cut up into joints or logs.
Fakakuhu, *v.* To sniff with the nose.
Fakakukafi, *v.* To persevere.
Fakakukafi, *s.* Perseverance.
Fakakukafi, *a.* Persevering.
Fakakuku, *a.* Unforgiving.
Fakakulokula, *v.* To make red.
Fakala, *a.* To supply a sail; to make a sail; to rig a canoe; to exaggerate in reporting.
Fakalaa, *v.* To expose to the sun; to bask in the sun.
Fakalaaijiamelie, *v.* The enduring inconveniences in the way of obtaining an object.
Fakalaalaa, *v.* To warm in the sun.
Fakalai, *v.* To flatter, to cajole.
Fakalai, *s.* Flattery, adulation.
Fakalaifano, *v.* To go about flattering from one to another.
Fakalailai, *v.* To break up into pieces, to mash.
Fakalaolao, *v.* To finish off work.

Fakalau, *v.* To count, to number.
Fakalaufokotuu, *v.* To talk or pile up words without determining any thing.
Fakalaujii, *v.* To narrow, to make narrow.
Fakalaukau, *ad.* Proudly, ostentatiously.
Fakalaukau, *v.* To shew off; to exhibit, to draw attention.
Fakalaulau, *v.* To talk over a thing without deciding upon it.
Fakalaulaukau, *v.* To walk at ease; to go free of restraint.
Fakalaulahi, *v.* To make broad, to widen.
Fakalauloto, *s.* Meditation, contemplation.
Fakalauloto, *v.* To meditate, to talk over the mind.
Fakalaumalie, *v.* To spiritualize.
Fakalaumalie, *a.* Spiritual.
Fakalautefuhi, *v.* To make up a *Lautefuhi.*
Fakalautelau, *v.* To bring or deal out singly one at a time.
Fakalauvale, *a.* Mean, low, like the *Lauvale.*
Fakalabalaba, *v.* To make with flat sides, as a square bottle.
Fakalabulabu, *v.* To cant, to flatter.
Fakalafalafa, *v.* To make flat, to flatten.
Fakalafi, Fakalafilafi, *v.* To hide, to shield, to take shelter under.
Fakalaga, Fakalagalaga, *v.* To transplant, to raise up, to originate, to cause, to begin, to stir up.
Fakalagilagi, *v.* To honour, to dignify; to treat with great respect.
Fakalago, *v.* To bring or entice flies.
Fakalagolago, *v.* To raise to a level; to put one thing upon or across another to raise it.

Fakalahe,
Fakalahelahe, } *v.* To strike so as to powder, but not break a stone; to neglect anointing the head with oil; to smear with lime.

Fakalahi, *v.* To increase, to augment, to enlarge.

Fakalahi, *s.* Increase, addition.

Fakalahilahi, *v.* To increase in a small degree.

Fakalaka,
Fakalakalaka, } *v.* To pass on, hand over; to cause to pass over; to pass others till you come to the right person.

Fakalakilaki, *v.* To exhibit, to make a shew of.

Fakalakaga, *v.* To do at the proper and appointed time.

Fakalala, *v.* To desert, to leave, to vacate; to cause to be deserted; to empty a place of its inhabitants; to lay waste.

Fakalalafa, *v.* To make flat, to flatten.

Fakalalafu, *v.* To set or plant the same ground for two successive years.

Fakalalaga, *v.* To beg or cause others to *lalaga.*

Fakalalago, *v.* See *Fakalagolago.*

Fakalalahi, *v.* To be on the increase.

Fakalalata, *v.* To tame, to domesticate.

Fakalalateliga, *v.* To excite expectation.

Fakalalo, *s.* An intercessor.

Fakalaloa, *v.* To intercede.

Fakalamilami, *v.* To be ashamed; to be bashful; to secret.

Fakalanu, *v.* To wash off salt water with fresh.

Fakalanu, *s.* Antidote; any thing which prevents the effects of what was designed to bring about death.

Fakalata,
Fakalatalata, } *v.* To cause a liking to a place; to make one loath to leave a place.

Fakalatajino, *a.* Agreeable to the body, but not to the mind, as a place.

Fakalava, *v.* To lie longways.

Fakalavalava, *ad.* Athwart, across.

Fakalavanoa, *v.* To get to do by chance or accident.

Fakalavanoa, *s.* Chance, accident.

Fakalave, *v.* To steer off the wind; to relieve from a confined position; to let free; to twist or insinuate.

Fakalavelave, *v.* To do at a venture; to try it on.

Fakalavekaha, *s.* One who delivers others from disgrace or destruction.

Fakalavetala, *v.* To win over to conversation; to gain upon with the tongue.

Fakalea, *v.* To cause to talk; to speak to one, to ascertain if he can speak.

Fakaleeleegu, *v.* To speak with reserve or sullenly.

Fakaleo, *s.* One appointed as overseer or watchman.

Fakaleoheu, *v.* To speak with an assumed voice.

Fakaleoleo, *v.* To look after, to watch.

Fakaleoleogu, *v.* To speak sullenly, to mutter.

Fakaleoleomalie, *v.* To be carelessly indulgent; to speak softly.

Fakaleua, *v.* To cause to trip or stumble.

Fakalebelebe, *v.* To bring and keep the vessel into the eye of the wind.

Fakaleke,
Fakalekeleke, } *v.* To divide off into apartments; to form an enclosure, to make any thing with a very uneven surface.

66

Fakalekeji, Fakalekelekeji, *v.* To be careful of and attentive to.

Fakalekeji, Fakalekelekeji, *a.* Frail, feeble, easily broken.

Fakalele, *s.* The dysentery.

Fakalele, *a.* Purging.

Fakalele, *v.* To amuse by flying birds; to fly a kite; to set others to run.

Fakalelea, *v.* To send adrift upon the sea.

Fakalelei, *s.* A peacemaker, reconciliation, pacification.

Fakalelei, *v.* To pacify, to make peace, to reconcile.

Fakalelefaa, *v.* To disencumber trees of what opposes their growth; to prune.

Fakalelehama, *v.* To sail a canoe with the outrigger out of the water.

Fakalelelelei, *ad.* Carefully, cautiously.

Fakalelemoa, Fakalelemoui, *v.* To surprise, to astound; to make one's life to run.

Fakalelemoui, *a.* Amazing, wonderful, astonishing.

Fakalelu, Fakalelui, *v.* To throw aside, to waste, to be careless about.

Fakalelulelu, *v.* To divert the mind; to withdraw the mind from any object.

Fakaleta, *v.* To put in confusion.

Fakaleveleva, *v.* To extend to all; to cover all space; to engross the whole.

Fakaleveleva, *a.* Universal, over all.

Fakali, Fakalili, *v.* To hasten; to urge others to be quick.

Fakalielia, *a.* Disgusting, filthy, detestable, abominable.

Fakalielia, *s.* An abomination.

Fakalielie, *v.* To be disgusted.

Fakaliu, *v.* To hollow out a tree, as in making paddling canoes.

Fakaliuivaka, *a.* Uneven, full of holes, as a road.

Fakalifulifu, *v.* To shiver; to shudder with cold.

Fakalika, *v.* To make known for the first time; to introduce, as a tune.

Fakalikiliki, *v.* To be advancing or progressing.

Fakalikoliko, *v.* To do by halves; to do partially.

Fakalili, *s.* A preparation of food.

Fakalili, *v.* To make to boil; to irritate; to grin at.

Fakalili, *v.* To hasten; to wish to be gone.

Fakalilia, *s.* To be sick of, to loathe, to abhor.

Fakaliliaki, *v.* To cast away, to disregard.

Fakaliliu, *v.* To put right before the wind.

Fakalilifa, *a.* Gradually descending, sloping.

Fakalilifu, *v.* To horrify; to excite fear.

Fakaliligo, *a.* Bad in appearance, suspicious.

Fakalilika, *v.* To terrify; to excite painful apprehensions.

Fakalilo, Fakalilolilo, *v.* To hide, to secrete, to conceal; to be concealed.

Fakalimu, *v.* To entice fish into a trap with the *limu*.

Fakaloia, *v.* To cause a feeling of sickness, as in eating fat.

Fakalooa, *v.* To place across. See *Looa*.

Fakaloufataha, *a.* Aspiring, ambitious.

Fakaloufujimata, *v.* To serve upon a raw leaf of the banana (a mark of distinction.)

Fakalouhiimofiji, *v.* To take hold of with one or two fingers only, as if afraid; to take hold of fantastically.

Fakalouloua, *v.* To sulk; to

appear as if displeased; to be overcast with clouds.

Fakaloba, *v.* To delay; to be a long time about.

Fakalobelobe, *v.* To mix; to cause to work.

Fakalofa, *v.* To swing round by the arm.

Fakalogoaa, *v.* To cause a noise; to make an uproar.

Fakalogo, } *v.* To cease
Fakalogologo, } making a noise, to be quiet.

Fakalogologo, *a.* Quiet, not loquacious; sullen.

Fakalogofua, *s.* The cackling of a fowl about to lay.

Fakalogonoa, *v.* To drop; to drop through; to come to nothing.

Fakalohiaki, } *v.* To belie, to
Fakalohiekina, } calumniate.

Fakaloki, *v.* See *Fakaleke.*

Fakalokubeji, *v.* To paint the *gatu* lightly.

Fakalolea, *v.* To press, to urge on; to persevere in any work.

Fakalolo, *v.* To oil, to mix with oil; to yield, to give up the contest.

Fakalolo, *a.* Used to express the state of the tide when it does not ebb as at other times.

Fakalolololo, *v.* To oil, to grease; to smear or dirt with any unction.

Fakaloloa, *v.* To lenghten out, to extend, to spare.

Fakalologo, *v.* To cease to talk; to be quiet, applied to more than one.

Fakaloloto, *v.* To deepen, to make deep.

Fakalona, *v.* To cause hiccup.

Fakaloto, *v.* To think; to act worthy a man.

Fakalotoloto, *v.* To place in the middle; to put between the first and last; to let the sail partly down.

Fakalotoloto, *a.* Difficult to appease; unforgiving.

Fakalotu, *v.* To convert; to cause to *lotu.*

Fakalotu, *ad.* Agreeably to the *lotu.*

Fakalua, *v.* To cause nausea, to sicken; to think too highly of one's self.

Fakalua, *a.* Nauseous.

Fakalue, } *v.* To jog along,
Fakalueaibe, } applied to old persons; to rock or roll as a vessel.

Fakaluo, } *v.* To make holes
Fakaluoluo, } or pits.

Fakalube, } *v.* To spring as
Fakalubelube, } any thing elastic; to shake.

Fakalusa, *v.* To relax in attention to; to disregard; to slacken.

Fakalutu, } *v.* To have a
Fakalutulutu, } different object in view to that upon which we appear bent; to assume carelessness about that which we really wish; to under value the property of another, wishing to get it.

Fakama, *v.* To shame, to make ashamed; to feel ashamed.

Fakama, *a.* Bashful, modest.

Fakama, *s.* Shame, modesty.

Fakamaa, *v.* To cleanse, to purify.

Fakamaa, *part.* Cleansed, purified.

Fakamaa, *s.* Expurgation, purification.

Fakamaau, *v.* To make known, to tell, to rehearse.

Fakamaagataha, *v.* To make one mouthful of it.

Fakamaalaala, *v.* To free from; to clear away obstructions.

Fakamaali, *v.* To shoot or flit along.

Fakamaamaa, *v.* To lighten; to lend a helping hand.

Fakamaamaanima, *s.* A feast on the completion of work.

Fakamaanu, } *v.* To cause to
Fakamaanuanu, } float; to raise from under the water, so as to float.

Fakamae, *v.* To dry or wither in the sun.

Fakamaea, *v.* To furnish ropes.

Fakamaefu, *v.* To make a dust; to cause dust to fly about.

Fakamaifa, *v.* To draw in; to contract the stomach.

Fakamaili, *v.* To flit to and fro.

Fakamaimoa, } *v.* To play,
Fakamaimaimoa, } to trifle.

Fakamaitoa, *v.* To express pleasure at other's misfortunes.

Fakamaobo, *v.* To shut, as a book.

Fakamaoboobo, *v.* To collect, to bring together.

Fakamaoluga, *v.* To make high.

Fakamaomaoganoa, *v.* To contemplate; to think seriously and alone; to cause others to be inattentive in order to fall suddenly upon them.

Fakamaomaoganoa, *v.* To seclude one's self; to prefer solitude.

Fakamaonioni, *v.* To make righteous.

Fakamau, *v.* To judge, to put in order.

Fakamau, *s.* A judge.

Fakamau, *a.* Full; up to the mark, as the tide.

Fakamau, *v.* To make firm, to establish, to fasten; to cause to stand; to marry.

Fakamauaibe, *v.* To keep on at the old thing.

Fakamauaga, } *s.* The place of
Fakamauga, } judgment, a judgment seat; the test, the touch stone.

Fakamauga, *v.* To be frequently and regularly in the same place, or doing the same thing.

Fakamaukubu, *s.* A single dress of native cloth; breadth of any thing.

Fakamaukubu, *v.* To cut up into single dresses.

Fakamaulalo, *v.* To make low.

Fakamaumau, *v.* To restrain, to repress, to keep in.

Fakamaumaugataa, *a.* Difficult to restrain or repress.

Fakamaumaugofua, *a.* Easy to repress or keep in.

Fakamaumea, *v.* To enrich, to make rich.

Fakamabee, *v.* To throw down; to bear off; to over awe.

Fakamabelu, *v.* To fold up; to draw up the legs.

Fakamabuna, *v.* To raise up; to bring again to view.

Fakamabuni, *v.* To shut up, to close.

Fakamafao, *v.* To stretch out; to extend to its full length.

Fakamafahi, } *v.* To open,
Fakamafahifahi, } to split open, to cleave.

Fakamafajia, *v.* To oppress, to overload, to encumber.

Fakamafana, *v.* To heat, to warm; to warm one's self.

Fakamafanafatu, *v.* To encourage, to excite by encouraging language.

Fakamafatua, *v.* To cause sneezing.

Fakamafi, *v.* To speak designing intimidation; to bully.

Fakamafihugamalie, *v.* To unravel, to clear, to sift.

Fakamafihugatamaki, *v.* To entangle, to confuse, to involve.

Fakamafili, *v.* To turn round; to upset.

Fakamafoki, *v.* To turn inside out, to expose.

Fakamafola, *v.* To spread out.

Fakamafu, *v.* To allow or cause to mould and smell bad.

Fakamafua, *s.* A bush or shrub made to decoy and take pigeons.

Fakamafue, *v.* To treat carelessly; to throw about as worthless.

Fakamafuke, *v.* See *Fakamafoki.*

Fakamafuli, *v.* See *Fakamafili.*

Fakamafulu, *v.* To allow the beard to grow.

Fakamaga, *v.* To open, to gape.

Fakamagamaga, } *v.* To
Fakamagamagakehe, } barb, to jag, to make forked.

Fakamagalogalo, *v.* To sink out of sight; to try to forget; to expel from the mind.

Fakamagi, *v.* To walk with the garment flowing in the breeze; to expose to a breeze.

Fakamagugu, *v.* To make a champing noise with the teeth; to exasperate.

Fakamaha, *v.* To empty, to drain, to exhaust.

Fakamahaehae, *v.* To tear, to shred.

Fakamahagaua, *a.* To extend; to jag out in opposite directions.

Fakamahaki, *v.* To cause illness, to afflict.

Fakamahalo, *v.* To cause to think; to impose upon one's own mind; to deceive one's self.

Fakamahaluhalu, *v.* To shred; to cut with a flawed instrument; to rag in cutting.

Fakamahamahaki, *v.* To cause indisposition.

Fakamahefu, *v.* To go dirty and in rags; to be careless of the body.

Fakamahekiheki, *v.* To strut along in walking.

Fakamahele, *v.* To cut in two; to stripe with lines of different colours.

Fakamaheni, *v.* To accustom, to habituate.

Fakamahi, *v.* To sour, to make acid; to dress after the Fejee style.

Fakamahiki, *v.* To go looking upwards.

Fakamahina, *a.* Monthly.

Fakamahino, *v.* To speak distinctly and intelligibly.

Fakamahu, *v.* To enrich; to cause fertility; to make fruitful; to assume abundance, but in reality poor.

Fakamahu, *v.* To speak piercing words.

Fakamahuahu, *v.* To gall, to fret, to tease, to vex, to provoke.

Fakamahui, *a.* Shy, unfriendly, austere, gruff.

Fakamahui, *v.* To coy, to despise, to estrange; to separate.

Fakamahui, *s.* Sullenness, reserve, estrangement.

Fakamahuiga, } *v.* To as-
Fakamahumahuiga, } sume, to arrogate, to take upon one's self.

Fakamahuihui, *v.* To withdraw, to separate.

Fakamahuohua, *v.* To fill to overflowing.

Fakamahuhuhuhu, *v.* To pierce; to prick with any thing pointed.

Fakamahunu, *v.* To singe, to broil, to blight.

Fakamafuke, *v.* To expose; to shew what was concealed.

Fakamajila, *v.* To sharpen, to edge.

Fakamajilijili, *v.* To flaw; to break the edge of any tool.

Fakamajiva, *v.* To impoverish, to make poor.

Fakamajivejiva, *v.* To assume poverty.

Fakamaka, *v.* To supply with stones.

Fakamakau, *a.* Lazy, indolent, dilatory.

70

Fakamakabe, *v.* To turn over; to remind of old grievances.
Fakamakaka, *v.* To harden, to stiffen.
Fakamakamaka, *v.* To make stony.
Fakamakata, *v.* To throw or sling stones.
Fakamakata, *s.* A slinger; one who uses the sling in war.
Fakamakateka, *v.* To roll to and fro, to be unstable.
Fakamakatuu, *v.* To stand firm.
Fakamakeke, *v.* To stiffen, to warp, to contract.
Fakamakoko, *v.* To indent, to press so as to cause an unequal surface.
Fakamakona, *v.* To satisfy with food.
Fakamakukaga, *a.* Careful, particular.
Fakamakukaga, *v.* To be careful; to act prudently.
Fakamakuku, *v.* To make a bustling noise, as one dressed in new *gatu*.
Fakamakulu, } *v.* To crouch;
Fakamakulukulu, } to abscond from work.
Fakamalaelae, *s.* An open space resembling a *malae*.
Fakamalaelae, *v.* To free a place from trees, &c. for a *malae*.
Fakamalaia, *v.* To curse, to anathematize, to cause a curse.
Fakamalaga, *s.* A name given to the god of a mother, supposed to be kind; an intercessor.
Fakamalaga, *v.* To intercede, to advocate; to disturb birds.
Fakamalagameitua, *v.* To originate from outside; to spring from the poor people.
Fakamalagolago, *v.* To build a canoe so as stem and stern to be above the water when sailing.
Fakamalakilaki, *v.* To preserve in health.
Fakamalala, *v.* To burn to a coke or a cinder.
Fakamalalilali, *v.* To scratch; to make rough.
Fakamalama, *v.* To cause to flame; to make to shine.
Fakamalamala, *s.* The overplus of wood in building a canoe, claimed by the carpenter.
Fakamalave, *v.* To lift into sight; to raise above the rest.
Fakamalea, *v.* To tread or beat down the grass; to allow the hair to grow downwards.
Fakamaleifua, *v.* To make comfortable by washing, &c.
Fakamalele, *s.* The finishing feast after a funeral.
Fakamalele, *v.* To set the hair of the head erect.
Fakamalelelele, *v.* To put into a dangerous position; to be in danger of falling.
Fakamaleletuu, *v.* To assemble for work, yet not do it, or do it badly, because it is the work of every body.
Fakamalena, } *v.* To make
Fakamelenelena, } smooth; to pull out of creases.
Fakamalie, *v.* To express pleasure. See *malie*.
Fakamaliga, *v.* To use every means to win the affections, as one in love.
Fakamaligakaka, *v.* To do with a design to please, but which produces the contrary effect.
Fakamaligakehe, *v.* To act inconsistent with one who desires to please the other sex.
Fakamaligi, *v.* To pour out, to empty.
Fakamalo, *v.* To praise, to applaud.
Fakamaloulau, *v.* To take food out of the oven as soon as cooked, the opposite of *Fakaafu*.

Fakamalofa, *v.* To spread out.
Fakamalohi, *v.* To strengthen, to support; to extort, to take by force.
Fakamalohi, *s.* Extortion, oppression, compulsion.
Fakamalohi, *a.* Oppressive, cruel.
Fakamalohia, *v.* To oppress, to overcome by force.
Fakamalolo, *v.* To rest, to relieve.
Fakamalolo, *v.* To bow down; to appear humble; to give in.
Fakamalolo, *s.* The act of yielding to another.
Fakamaloloaga, *s.* A resting place.
Fakamalu, *s.* A shade, an umbrella.
Fakamalu, } *v.* To screen, to
Fakamalui, } shade.
Fakamalu, *v.* To slacken; to relieve from pain.
Fakamalu, *v.* To bathe, applied to the *Tuitoga.*
Fakamalualoi, *v.* To act the hypocrite.
Fakamalualu, *v.* To tear in shreds, to shred up.
Fakamalulu, *v.* To damp, to soften in water.
Fakamalumalu, *v.* To shelter, to screen.
Fakamama, *v.* To enlighten.
Fakamama, *a.* Worldly.
Fakamama, *v.* To feel ashamed, to manifest shame.
Fakamama, } *v.* To aim at in-
Fakamamai, } timidation; to try to affright.
Fakamamaaga, *v.* To stuff the mouth with food.
Fakamamae, *v.* To like; to feel unwilling to part with.
Fakamamai, *v.* To cause to leak.
Fakamamao, *v.* To put far away; to cause distance; to stare about or yawn.
Fakamamau, *v.* To gaze, to look earnestly at.
Fakamamabu, *v.* To whistle; to make a whistling noise through the nose.
Fakamamafa, *v.* To make heavy; to treat as of vast importance.
Fakamamagia, *v.* To dazzle; to fill with light.
Fakamamafihugakehe, *v.* To act contrary to the generality; to be singular.
Fakamamaha, *v.* To catch shell fish from the rocks at low water.
Fakamamahi, *v.* To pain, to grieve.
Fakamamahi, *a.* Painful, grievous.
Fakamamaloa, *v.* To keep a light long in burning.
Fakamamalu, *v.* To feel afraid; to be overawed.
Fakamamata, *s.* Eye service.
Fakamamata, *v.* To act wishing to be observed.
Fakamamate, *v.* To swamp or upset a canoe; to benumb.
Fakamamio, *v.* To saunter about.
Fakamana, *s.* Intimidation, terror, the act of intimidating.
Fakamanaia, *v.* To use means to engage the attention of the female sex.
Fakamanako, *v.* To beget a liking to.
Fakamanamana, *v.* See *Fakamana.*
Fakamanatu, *v.* To cause to remember.
Fakamanatu, *s.* A remembrancer.
Fakamanamanatu, *v.* See *Fakamanatu.*
Fakamanava, *v.* To let air into; to allow to breathe; to be careful of.
Fakamanavafaji, *v.* To weaken; to break the *manava* by hunger.
Fakamanavahe, } *v.* To cause
Fakamanavahei, } fear, to astonish, to surprise, to awe.

Fakamanavahe, *a.* Astonishing, admirable, awful.
Fakamanavajii, *v.* To discourage, to daunt, to dispirit.
Fakamanavalahi, *v.* To encourage, to hearten.
Fakamaneke, *v.* To push or project forwards, the stomach.
Fakamanekeneke, *v.* To push or project out, the buttocks.
Fakamanifi, } *v.* To thin, to
Fakamanifinifi, } make thin; to reduce any thing thick.
Fakamanimani, *v.* To play the lover; to act with a design to gain the affections.
Fakamanimo, *v.* To take any thing secretly; to steal by the sly; to put out of sight.
Fakamaninia, *v.* To set the teeth on edge.
Fakamanoo, *v.* To tighten in the waist, or round the middle of any thing; to draw up.
Fakamanogi, *v.* To make a sweet odour.
Fakamanu, *v.* To act like a *manu.*
Fakamanuka, *s.* One kind of Tonga house.
Fakamanuki, } *v.* To deride,
Fakamanumanuki, } to treat with contempt, to taunt, to ridicule.
Fakamanumi, } *v.* To crimp,
Fakamanuminumi, } to pucker, to crease, to double up carelessly.
Fakamasanisani, *v.* To make smart or showy.
Fakamasima, *v.* To salt; to cure with salt.
Fakamata, *v.* To sharpen, to point.
Fakamataila, *v.* To harden, to make callous.
Fakamatoita, *v.* To exhibit an angry face; to look displeased.
Fakamatau, *v.* To accustom, to habituate; to do frequently; to do cleverly; to go to the right hand.
Fakamatautukehekehe, *v.* To act independently one of another; to make different statements in reference to one and the same thing.
Fakamataba, *v.* To make an entrance or door way; to put in a door or gate.
Fakamatababa, *v.* To stand close together; to arrange in rows; to front.
Fakamataboto, *v.* To look sharp; to be quick sighted.
Fakamatabule, *v.* To act the *matabule* or gentleman.
Fakamatafa, *v.* To divide into four equal numbers.
Fakamatafatu, *v.* Incorrigible, resolute.
Fakamataga, *v.* To unloose; to separate by force.
Fakamatagaa, *v.* To shame, to expose.
Fakamatagi, *v.* To wait for a fair wind.
Fakamatagigataa, *v.* To be difficult to go to or come from, owing to the position of the place with the prevailing winds.
Fakamatahoa, *v.* To shame, to put to the blush.
Fakamataka, *v.* To peel, to excoriate, to rub off.
Fakamataki, *v.* To draw out of creases; to stretch out to its full length and breadth.
Fakamatala, *v.* To rehearse, to explain, to enlarge upon, to open out.
Fakamatala, *s.* An account, an explanation.
Fakamatalea, *v.* To make the eyes sore.
Fakamatalili, *v.* To exasperate, to provoke.
Fakamatamatakubega, *s.* A play

of children; one kind of reeding.

Fakamatanikolo, *v.* To make like the front of a fort.

Fakamatatoa, *v.* To look bold and impudent.

Fakamatavalea, *v.* To act as one dull of sight.

Fakamate, *v.* To cause death, to poison.

Fakamate, *a.* Poisonous, deadly.

Fakamate, *s.* Poison; the cause of death.

Fakamateke, *v.* To push out; to draw up as a bow.

Fakamatele, }
Fakamateletele, } *v.* To cut, to shave; to skim the surface, as a swift canoe.

Fakamatemate, *v.* To make less ardent; to appear as if weakened; to subside.

Fakamatemateoji, *v.* To express the utmost surprise.

Fakamatoato, *ad.* Heartily, earnestly.

Fakamatolu, }
Fakamatolutolu, } *v.* To make thick.

Fakamatojitoji, *v.* To peck; to stock with a pointed instrument.

Fakamatua, *v.* To sit in a certain posture.

Fakamatuotua, *v.* To allow to grow ripe; to act manly.

Fakamatuutamaki, *v.* To leave any thing damp or wet, so as to occasion its rotting.

Fakamatukutuku, *v.* To desert, to leave, to separate from.

Fakamatutu, *v.* To think and speak of old grievances.

Fakamava, *v.* To separate, to cause a separation; to wean from the breast.

Fakamavaevae, *v.* To separate.

Fakamavahe, *v.* To disunite, to divorce, to extract.

Fakamavahevahe, *v.* To separate, to divide, to portion out.

Fakamaveuveu, *v.* To disturb, to disquiet, to confuse.

Fakamaveuveu, *s.* An agitator, a disturber.

Fakameaa, *a.* Ingenious, clever; the tools of such an one.

Fakameaa, *v.* To handle; to prepare what is for chiefs.

Fakameavale, *v.* To act meanly; to treat others meanly; to shame.

Fakameomeo, *v.* To look sullen and displeased.

Fakamele, *v.* To mar, to injure.

Fakamelemele, *v.* To defame, to backbite.

Fakamelemo, *v.* To drown, to expose to drowning.

Fakamelie, *v.* To sweeten, to addulce.

Fakamelino, *v.* To act in a warlike manner during a time of peace; to kill or enslave all on a sudden; to perpetuate peace.

Fakamelo, *v.* To brown by placing in the sun.

Fakamelomelo, *s.* A harbinger, a precursor, forerunner.

Fakamioi, *v.* To twist, to contort, to equivocate.

Fakamigimigi, *a.* Confused; entangled, disorderly.

Fakamiha, }
Fakamihemiha, } *v.* To dry, to scorch in the sun.

Fakamiji, *v.* To dream; to cause to dream.

Fakamiloha, }
Fakamilohi, }
Fakamimilohi, } *v.* To saunter, twist, and turn about.

Fakamoe, *s.* A friendly feast.

Fakamoemoe, *v.* To expect, to prepare for.

Fakamoi, *v.* To command others to do that which the party ordering does not like to do.

Fakamoimoi, *s.* A token of friendship; a love token to one at a distance.

Fakamoomooni, *v.* To assert, to testify.
Fakamoomooni, *s.* Affirmation, assertion.
Fakamooni, *s.* A witness, a deponent; fulfilment.
Fakamooni, *v.* To witness, to fulfil, to corroborate.
Fakamou, *v.* To overburden a vessel.
Fakamoua, *v.* To engage; to employ in any work.
Fakamoui, *s.* A saviour, a healer.
Fakamoui, *v.* To save; to give and to restore life; to heal.
Fakamouga, *v.* To raise a mound; to raise difficulties.
Fakamoulaloa, *v.* To overcome, to subject, to reduce to submission, to put down.
Fakamoumousaa, *v.* To go dirty; to appear in filth.
Fakamounu, *v.* To bait.
Fakamofi, *v.* To create fever; to make afraid.
Fakamofiji, Fakamofijifiji, } *v.* To exhibit signs of anger in the movement of the eyelids.
Fakamofutofuta, *v.* To go stately and pompously.
Fakamogumagu, *v.* To scab over; to allow to scab over.
Fakamohe, *v.* To get to sleep, to cause sleep.
Fakamohe, *a.* Narcotick, causing sleep.
Fakamohemeiulu, *v.* To impend; to be at hand, so as to cause fear.
Fakamohemohe, *v.* To get to sleep by lying by one, as a child.
Fakamoho, Fakamohomoho, } *v.* To cook thoroughly; to hasten the cooking of food.
Fakamohuga, Fakamohumohuga, } *v.* To be in detached paths; to make many of what would be best in one; to go or come many times about what might have been done at once.
Fakamoka, *v.* To slacken so as to curve.
Fakamokimokii, *v.* To separate into small divisions.
Fakamokojia, *v.* To make cold.
Fakamokomoko, *v.* To cool, to seek the cool.
Fakamokulu, *v.* To let fall, to shed; to allow to fall to pieces.
Fakamolemole, *v.* To rub out; to smooth off; to pardon.
Fakamolemole, *s.* The act of smoothing off; forgiveness, pardon.
Fakamolimolituu, *v.* To stand restless to be going.
Fakamolokau, *a.* Like a centipede.
Fakamolu, *v.* To soften.
Fakamolu, *s.* Inteneration, the act of softening.
Fakamolumalu, *v.* To cover; to put a good appearance on any thing.
Fakamomo, *v.* To crumb; to break up into crumbs.
Fakamomoa, *v.* To dry.
Fakamomoatea, *v.* To cry and mourn as for one dead who is still alive.
Fakamomoiki, *v.* To mince; to chop or cut any thing very small.
Fakamomoho, *v.* To ripen, to mature.
Fakamomoho, *s.* Bananas made ripe.
Fakamomoji, *v.* To crumb, to break small, to pulverize.
Fakamomoko, *v.* To make cold.
Fakamomomomoiki, *v.* See *Fakamomoiki.*
Fakamona, Fakamonomona, } *v.* To proceed deliberately and carefully in any work.

Fakamonu, *s.* The act of applying any present to the forehead; an act of thanksgiving.

Fakamonuia, *v.* To bless, to make a blessing.

Fakamonuka, *v.* To wound, applied to chiefs.

Fakamonumonuka, *v.* To rot, to decay; to cause decay or rottenness.

Fakamotu, *v.* To visit islands to catch fish; to cut off; to terminate.

Fakamotua, } *a.* Manly,
Fakamotumotua, } manlike, becoming an adult.

Fakamotua, } *v.* To act the
Fakamotumotua, } man; to make old; to give the appearance of age.

Fakamotuatagata, *a.* Manly.

Fakamotuatagata, *v.* To act like a man.

Fakamotuhi, *v.* See *Fakamotu.*

Fakamotumotu, *v.* To dress in sackcloth; to dress with old ragged mats; to break off connection, to separate from.

Fakamovete, } *v.* To loose,
Fakamovetevete, } to untie, to disperse.

Fakamoveve, *a.* Easily angry and angry always.

Fakamua, *v.* To act the gentleman.

Fakamuaki, *v.* To go first, to precede.

Fakamui, *a.* Last, latest.

Fakamui, *v.* To follow all the rest, to be last.

Fakamuia, *v.* To keep in view a promise; to follow, to pursue.

Fakamuiaki, *v.* To go last; to follow all the rest.

Fakamuifonua, *s.* A certain mode of making the *kava.*

Fakamuikovi, *v.* To make a bad finish.

Fakamuimui, *a.* Unmanly, youthful.

Fakamuimui, *v.* To close up; to finish off; to bring up the rear.

Fakamuitau, *a.* Whorish, applied to females.

Fakamuomua, *v.* To cause to go before; to cause to lead the way.

Fakamuomuanima, *v.* To touch or put the hand to any thing with apparent unwillingness.

Fakamuka, *v.* To cause to bud; to cause to spring and grow.

Fakamulimuli, *v.* To act as a stranger or sojourner.

Fakamulituku, *v.* To finish for the time being; to bring to an end.

Fakamulumului, *v.* To rub, to fray, to break the skin.

Fakamumu, *v.* To bring together by swarms, as flies; to entice flies.

Fakamumuhu, *v.* Rough in sound, like the howling wind.

Fakamuna, *v.* To dote.

Fakana, } *v.* To stand; to
Fakanana, } halt, as in suspense; to falter; to proceed cautiously.

Fakanaanaa, *v.* To quiet children when crying; to hush, to appease.

Fakanainai, *v.* To be over officious in exhorting; to hinder rather than forward by talking too much.

Fakanainaii, *v.* To be over careful of any one; to pet; to indulge foolishly.

Fakanaunau, *v.* To speak and hope of what is to come; to feel pleasure in expectation of something.

Fakanabikoa, *v.* To be attracted; to be influenced, to be engrossed.

76

Fakanafajia, *v.* To go to one in the character of an antagonist.
Fakanafafaki, *v.* To expect, to look out for.
Fakanamua, } *v.* To cause a
Fakanamuku, } stink; to give any thing a bad smell.
Fakananamu, *v.* To smell, to apply to the nose.
Fakananivi, *s.* Affectation.
Fakananivi, *v.* To be trifling, to be childish.
Fakanatu, *v.* To say the same thing over and over, as in kneading the motion is repeated.
Fakanavau, *s.* A distinguishing mark, fastened to any part of the animal's body.
Fakane, } *v.* See *Fakana.*
Fakanene, }
Fakaneifua, *v.* To eat fruit or something nice after a meal.
Fakaneke, *v.* To rise heavily, as one in pain.
Fakanekeneka, *v.* To cause joy and rejoicing.
Fakanenefu, *v.* To cause dimness of sight.
Fakaniu, *s.* A preparation of Tonga bread.
Fakanifo, *v.* To indent, to scoop out.
Fakanijiniji, *v.* To shew off, as a vain woman on the appearance of the other sex.
Fakanikonikoi, *v.* To variegate, to diversify.
Fakanimaboto, *v.* To work cleverly.
Fakanimavale, *v.* To work awkwardly or clumsily.
Fakaninimo, *v.* To cause giddiness.
Fakanoa, *v.* To be silent, to refrain from speaking; to dumbfound.
Fakanoaloto, *v.* To turn over in the mind.
Fakanoatuu, *s.* Mental perturbation.
Fakanonoa, *v.* To gaze vaguely, to stare about; to appear thoughtful; to be silent, not knowing what to say, as the guilty when accused; to veer about, as the wind.
Fakanoi, *v.* To press, to urge, to incite.
Fakanounou, *v.* To shorten, to abridge, to abbreviate.
Fakanofo, *v.* To appoint, to inaugurate, to espouse; to affy, to consecrate.
Fakanofo, *s.* Coronation, the act of inaugurating, nomination.
Fakanofonofo, *v.* To call persons to their proper seats in the *kava* party; to teach a baby to sit up.
Fakanoko, *v.* To bulge out as the hip. See *Noko.*
Fakanukuatea, *s.* A heathen song.
Fakanuminumi, *v.* To crease.
Fakanunu, *v.* To occasion, to be the cause of.
Fakanunumala, *v.* To provoke a curse, to cause a curse.
Fakasabi, *v.* To make wry faces.
Fakasakesake, *s.* Pride, vanity.
Fakasakesake, *a.* Vain, proud.
Fakasala, *v.* To inform, to acquaint, (a war term.)
Fakasani, } *v.* To pet, to
Fakasanisani, } make much of; to adorn, to embellish.
Fakasanisani, *a.* Smart, showy.
Fakasanisani, *s.* Embellishment, decoration.
Fakaseesee, *v.* To drive away.
Fakasesele, *v.* To act as one silly or witless.
Fakasikisiki, *v.* To call warriors out of their hiding place.
Fakasogesoge, *v.* To complain least any one should beg.

77

Fakasovini, *v.* To ooze out with a hissing noise.

Fakata, *v.* To put the ends to a Tonga house.

Fakataahine, *a.* Virgin-like; becoming young girls.

Fakataahine, *v.* To act like a maid; to do what is becoming virgins.

Fakataane, *s.* The sitting posture of the Tonga men.

Fakataane, *v.* To sit with the legs folded under the body.

Fakataataa, *v.* To stain with blood, applied to chiefs.

Fakatae, } *v.* To take off, to
Fakataetae, } carry away.

Fakatae, *v.* To cause a cough, to cause to cough.

Fakataeaoga, *v.* To render useless or unprofitable; to disqualify.

Fakataeofa, *v.* To act as one without love or natural affection.

Fakataehougai, *v.* To assume independency when presented with any thing.

Fakataelata, *v.* To cause dislike to a place.

Fakataele, *v.* To leave.

Fakataetae, *v.* To regret; to feel sorrow for what is irrecoverable.

Fakataetae, *v.* To expectorate.

Fakataetaekuha, *v.* To act at random; to treat as worthless or insignificant.

Fakatai, *v.* To season with salt or salt water.

Fakataili, *v.* To go to and fro, to go and come.

Fakataimoa, } *v.* To work
Fakataitaimoa, } carelessly; to treat as of no value.

Fakataomamao, *v.* To keep at a distance.

Fakataotao, *v.* To cover or conceal with other things.

Fakataovala, *v.* To put on another person a *Taovala.*

Fakatau, *v.* To try, to make an attempt.

Fakatau, *s.* A heathen song.

Fakatau, *s.* Barter, cost, bargain, commerce; certain pieces of wood used in the sailing canoes.

Fakatau, *v.* To barter, to trade; to bring up to the mark; to cause to fight; to lead, to conduct.

Fakatau, *v.* To act as a familiar; to assume upon an acquaintance; to presume upon kindness.

Fakatauau, *v.* To swim or stand against the current.

Fakatauagaa, *v.* To dress in sackcloth or old mats, as at funerals.

Fakatauahu, *v.* To sit in the direction the smoke is blown.

Fakatauala, *v.* To bring up a vessel to the wind; to luff.

Fakatauama, *v.* To turn the outrigger towards the shore, or another canoe, when it should be the body of the canoe.

Fakatauata, *a.* Used when the moon sets as the day is breaking.

Fakatauataina, *v.* To set free, to set at liberty.

Fakatauilea, *s.* Altercation, debate, controversy, disputation.

Fakatauilea, *v.* To contend, to dispute, to litigate, to contest.

Fakatauuta, *v.* To act like landsmen, applied to sailors.

Fakatauboou, *a.* Of or belonging to a *tauboou* or virgin.

Fakataufa, *v.* To feel after in the dark.

Fakataufaala, *v.* To trace out, to seek with care.

Fakataufua, *v.* To make a good consistence, not thin or watery.

Fakataugahele, *v.* To walk at leisure, to saunter.

Fakataugaloloa, *v.* To make long rows, as in planting.

Fakatauganonou, *v.* To make short rows, as in planting.

Fakataugataa, *a.* Costly, dear.

Fakataugataa, *v.* To be difficult of approach.

Fakatauhihi, *v.* To hint, to allude to, to speak indirectly.

Fakatauhihili, *v.* To ask more in trading than the article is worth.

Fakataukava, *v.* To serve out the *kava.*

Fakataukitua, *v,* To talk of that which is not at hand; to pledge what one does not possess.

Fakataula, *v.* To draw up the sail of a canoe; to be on the wind; to sail small paddling canoes.

Fakataulaeiki, *v.* To act becoming a *taulaeiki.*

Fakataulalo, *v.* To hang low near the earth.

Fakataumafa, *v.* To prepare the food of chiefs.

Fakataumatagi, *v.* To push through or stand in the current of air; to expose to the full force of the wind.

Fakataumataki, *v.* To embrace opportunities for doing any thing when one is like to get most by it.

Fakataumua, *a.* Of or belonging to the *taumua,* or forepart of a vessel.

Fakataumuli, *a.* Of or belonging to the *taumuli,* or stern of a vessel.

Fakatautau, *v.* To approach; to bring near; to act with moderation.

Fakatautaubo, *v.* To feel one's way; to feel after any thing, as one blind.

Fakatautaufa, *v.* See *Fakatautafa.*

Fakatautaugahele, } *v.* To go
Fakatautaugamuna, } off or get away without being noticed.

Fakataumamao, } *v.* To put
Fakatautaumamao, } at a distance; to act with reserve.

Fakatautafa, } *v.* To go side-
Fakatautautafa, } ways.

Fakatautala, } *v.* To tell any
Fakatautautala, } thing for the sake of getting information.

Fakatautotolo, *v.* To put off, to defer.

Fakatautu, *v.* To raise one so as to sit upright.

Fakatauvele, *v.* To tempt.

Fakataba, *v.* To make the border of the *gatu.*

Fakataba, } *v.* To salute or
Fakatabataba, } command suddenly; to speak rapidly.

Fakatabu, *v.* To persevere in inquiring.

Fakatabu, *v.* To prohibit, to make sacred.

Fakatabu, *s.* Consecration, dedication, anointed.

Fakatabubu, *v.* To talk rapidly; to rehearse in quick succession.

Fakatafa, } *v.* To go aside;
Fakatafatafa, } to lie on the side; to give way, to avoid coalition.

Fakatafaaga, *a.* Like a *Tafaaga.*

Fakatafaaki, *v.* To set any thing on the border of a patch of ground.

Fakatafagafaga, *v.* To clear away, to cut down trees and remove all obstructions.

Fakatafe, *s.* A certain method of catching fish.

Fakatafe, *v.* To draw or pour off, to distil, to drain.

Fakatafea, *v.* To cause a thing to be carried away by the stream.

79

Fakatafiligatamaki, *v.* To turn another awkwardly.
Fakatafoki, *v.* To turn; to cause others to turn.
Fakatafola, *v.* To scatter, to strew or spread, to overspread.
Fakatafola, *a.* Scattered, spread in every direction.
Fakatafue, Fakatafuefue, } *v.* To loose; to allow to hang loose and dangling, as ropes.
Fakatafuefue, Fakatafuefueloa, } *v.* To live in an exposed situation.
Fakatafuu, *v.* To bulge out; to raise mounds.
Fakatafuua, *v.* To excite astonishment and fear.
Fakatafugofuga, *v.* To raise with earth; to make higher.
Fakatafuli, Fakatafulifuli, } *v.* To roll.
Fakatafunaki, *v.* To blow up into a flame; to increase.
Fakataga, *v.* To persecute, to oppose, to tease; to sift, to filter; to chase.
Fakataga, *s.* Persecution, persecutor.
Fakatagakaivale, *v.* To divide unfairly; to take the best and leave the rest.
Fakatagata, *a.* Manly, becoming a man.
Fakatagata, *v.* To act the man.
Fakatagatagа, *v.* To unloose, to separate from.
Fakatagatatatau, *v.* To wish to be independent; to aim to be as those in higher rank.
Fakatagato, *a.* Loose, not tight, not fast.
Fakatagi, Fakatagihi, } *v.* To make or cause to cry; to cry for.
Fakatagitagi, *s.* To retain anger; to brood over evil.
Fakaţagikafa, *v.* To stream; to run in a narrow stream.

Fakatagutu, *v.* To set up, as a child.
Fakataha, *v.* To assemble, to meet together, to unite, to make one.
Fakataha, *s.* An assembly, a meeting, a company.
Fakataha, *v.* To reach a place in sailing without tacking.
Fakatahakehake, *s.* Acclivity.
Fakatahifohifo, *s.* Declivity.
Fakatahitahi, *v.* To wet with sea water.
Fakataji, *v.* To roll about; to be loose.
Fakatajiba, *v.* To refer directly to the party not addressed.
Fakatajilo, *v.* To make clear and lucid.
Fakataka, *v.* To twist, to roll; to turn adrift, as pigs.
Fakatakabe, *v.* To impoverish.
Fakatakafi, *v.* To cover; to bind books.
Fakaţakaga, *v.* To go as the companion of a chief.
Fakatakataka, *s.* One who accompanies a chief as a merriment maker; a doll, a play thing.
Fakatakamilo, Fakatakatakamilo, } *v.* To encircle, to revolve.
Fakatakamilo, *ad.* About.
Fakatakatakatuu, *v.* To rise and saunter about, as one tired of sitting.
Fakatakatua, *a.* Like or becoming the mean and vulgar of the people.
Fakatakatuu, *a.* Like or becoming a young man or *Takatuu.*
Fakatakavale, *a.* Unkind, foolish.
Fakatakavale, *v.* To treat unkindly; to be void of kind feeling towards others.
Fakatakitaki, *v.* To carry suspended from the hand.

Fakatakutakuleka, *v.* To act in a careless indifferent manner.

Fakatala, } *v.* To barb.
Fakatalatala, }

Fakatalagataa, *v.* To shew disobedience.

Fakatalanoa, *v.* To engage another in conversation.

Fakatalatalai, *v.* To separate from; to disentangle; to twist off.

Fakatalatubua, *v.* To act absurdly, as attempting to do something great.

Fakatalavou, *v.* To imitate young men.

Fakatalavou, *a.* Of or belonging to young men.

Fakatale, *v.* To cause a cough.

Fakatali, *v.* To hold out; to extend, as the hand to receive.

Fakatalitali, *v.* To hold in readiness, to be in waiting.

Fakataliga, *v.* To hold; to keep in suspense, and after all fail.

Fakataligavai, *s.* A place where rain water is caught in vessels.

Fakatalivai, *s.* A vessel for catching rain water.

Fakatalolo, } *v.* To subside,
Fakatalolololo, } to calm down.

Fakatalutalu, *v.* To trace downwards from time past.

Fakatama, *v.* To adopt; to take the child of another and call it one's own; to act boyish.

Fakatamaioeiki, *v.* To treat as servants; to act as servants.

Fakatamaiki, *a.* Of or belonging to children.

Fakatamaimate, *v.* To oppress or treat unkindly upon the death of a father.

Fakatamajii, } *a.* Boyish,
Fakatamatamajii, } childish, infantile.

Fakatamaki, *v.* To trouble, to annoy, to deprave.

Fakatamala, *v.* To choke; to suffocate, as a fire by putting any thing heavy or damp upon it.

Fakatamanimohe, *v.* To do by the sly; to do thinking no one knows.

Fakatamatama, *v.* To call repeatedly by the term *tama.*

Fakatamatemate, *v.* To subside, to grow less.

Fakatamulu, *v.* To do work in a careless way.

Fakatane, *v.* To wet with *kàva* the bowl in which it is made, in order that the *kava* may adhere to the bowl.

Fakatanetane, *v.* To smooth off.

Fakatanimo, *v.* To speak or act under a disguise or suspiciously.

Fakatanunu, *v.* To speak rapidly.

Fakatata, *s.* Allegory, image, portrait, parable.

Fakatata, *v.* To allegorize, to speak figuratively.

Fakatatae, *v.* To reach; to feel for with the hand.

Fakatatao, *v.* To make long.

Fakatatao, *v.* To impress upon; to lay upon as a weight.

Fakatatau, *v.* To make alike, to compare, to equalize, to contrast.

Fakatatau, *con.* According to, like as.

Fakatataba, *v.* To flutter, to speak rapidly.

Fakatatajiba, *v.* To speak indirectly or circuitously.

Fakatatagao, *v.* To go out by the sly.

Fakatatagata, *v.* To make a finish, circumscribe.

Fakatatakuane, *s.* Inattention, carelessness.

Fakatatali, *v.* To wait for.

Fakatatavaha, *s.* Any thing which shortens the time of labour or hunger.

Fakatatele, *v.* To skim along the surface of the water.

Fakatateme, } *v.* To flutter,
Fakatatemeteme, } to quiver, to shake, to hurry.

Fakatatu, *v.* To fall from side to side, as in the rolling of a vessel.

Fakatatube, *v.* To cause to swing, as any thing suspended when touched.

Fakatavaka, *v.* To act like persons who are preparing to abscond in a canoe.

Fakate, *v.* To drill, to discipline.

Fakate, } *v.* To run canoes;
Fakatete, } to cause to swim or float; to sail for pleasure; to hurry, to precipitate.

Fakatea, *v.* To shame, to affright, to turn pale.

Fakateau, *v.* To make up the hundred.

Fakateahaalai, *a.* Many in number, but of little use.

Fakateetuli, *v.* To gleam; to be nearly out, as a lamp; (from the light emitted from the *Teetuli* when killed.)

Fakateiabaa, } *v.* Askaunt;
Fakateiteiabaa, } oblique, not parallel.

Fakateiulu, *v.* To cut off the tops of the first crop of yams when taken up, and leave them with the tendrils, to produce a second crop.

Fakateiteimovai, *a.* Weakly, nearly dead.

Fakatebekia, *v.* To urge, to incite.

Fakatebi, } *ad.* Quickly.
Fakatebitebi, }

Fakatebuna, *v.* To cook much more than is necessary; to lay or throw about in a disorderly way.

Fakatefa, *v.* To act childishly; to play off the child, in order to get something.

Fakatefito, *s.* Origin, cause.

Fakatefua, *v.* To assemble together; to make up a hundred in counting nuts, &c.

Fakatefuhi, *v.* To make up a hundred couple, or two hundred.

Fakatefuli, *a.* All, applied to things not to persons.

Fakatega, *v.* To concrete, to grow hard.

Fakatehitehituu, *a.* Restless, dissatisfied, on the move.

Fakateka, *v.* To drive animals; to roll over and over; to roll upon another, as the blame of any transaction.

Fakatekau, *v.* To make up twenty.

Fakatekefili, *v.* To roll, to lie about.

Fakatekefili, } *a.* Naked, un-
Fakateketekefili, } covered, dismasted.

Fakatekefua, *v.* To shave the head.

Fakatekelili, } *v.* To shake;
Fakateketekelili, } to be strongly agitated.

Fakateketeka, *v.* To keep aloof, to avoid approach; also, as *Fakateka.*

Fakateketekefua, *a.* Bare, stript, as a vessel.

Fakateki, *v.* To cause a sudden quick motion of the body.

Fakatekiteki, *v.* To strut, to walk stately.

Fakatele, *v.* To fish by drawing the hook after the canoe; to make short excursions for the purpose of looking out in time of war; to draw out the *kafa* in lengths for making ropes.

Fakatelefua, *v.* To strip, to make naked.

Fakateletulututulu, *v.* To walk under the heaves of a house; to be near.

Fakatenetene, *s.* A nick name; a name used only occasionally.
Fakatete, *s.* A heathen feast.
Fakatetea, *a.* Whitish, applied to certain days when the weather is bad.
Fakatetee, *v.* To put or push out, as the tongue; to burst forth.
Fakateteea, *v.* To exaggerate; to cause fear by exaggeration.
Fakatetefa, *v.* To bring upon the wind in steering.
Fakatetega, *v.* To pinch, to tickle; to squeeze with the hand.
Fakateteka, *v.* To bring near the wind.
Fakatetele, *v.* To be on the increase; to assume a great deal of pain.
Fakateteki, *v.* To act modestly and cautiously; to act as one afraid.
Fakatetetete, *v.* To cause a trembling or shaking.
Fakatetetete, *a.* Frightful.
Fakato, *v.* To lay eggs; to throw down; to entrap birds by other birds of the kind; to make over; to cause to come over.
Fakatoa, *v.* To shew courage, to act courageously.
Fakatoafa, *v.* To cultivate what was once waste land.
Fakatoaki, *v.* To endure.
Fakatoatele, *v.* To act or suffer with bravery, to exhibit fortitude.
Fakatoe, *v.* To leave, to reserve; to lay up for a future time.
Fakatoi, *v.* To distil, to drop, to cause to fall in drops.
Fakatoi, *s.* Distillation.
Fakâtoitoi, *v.* To distil or drop a few drops only.
Fakatoitoi, *v.* To hide, to conceal, to cover with bed clothes.

Fakatoohema, *s.* The left side.
Fakatoohi, *v.* To move slowly; to be behind.
Fakatoohi, *a.* Slow, not quick, sluggish.
Fakatoomatau, *s.* The right side.
Fakatootoo, *v.* To make haste, to be quick.
Fakatootoo, } *s.* Haste, speed.
Fakatootooi, }
Fakatootooga, *s.* Accompaniment.
Fakatouato, *s.* A chief from both parents.
Fakatou, } *a.* Both.
Fakatouoji, }
Fakatouoloaa, *v.* To worry, to tease; to retain anger.
Fakatoubikoi, *v.* To delay; to treat with unconcern.
Fakatoubili, } *v.* To teach; to allow to follow after.
Fakatoutoubili, }
Fakatoubouli, } *v.* To go or come under cover of darkness; to keep aloof or out of sight.
Fakatoutoubouli, }
Fakatoufefine, *s.* Girls, applied to two only.
Fakatoufefine, *v.* To compare the ages of females.
Fakatoukai, *v.* To bear fruit at certain times.
Fakatoumiloha, *v.* To dally, to delay.
Fakatoumoua, *v.* To hesitate, to halt; to be engaged by two things at the same time.
Fakatoumatau, *s.* A person who can use both hands equally well.
Fakatoumatau, *a.* Clever.
Fakatoutagata, *s.* Boys, applied to two only.
Fakatoutagata, *v.* To compare the ages of men.
Fakatoutakalo, *v.* To dodge, to move to and fro.
Fakatoutama, *v.* To act as a woman still nursing children.

Fakatoutoumohala, *v.* To bring others into trouble by one's inconstancy.

Fakatoutoumokoi, *v.* To trifle; to treat as unimportant.

Fakatoutoumokoi. *a.* Trifling, not important.

Fakatoutoumoloto, *v.* To be just below the surface of the water; to be under water except the head.

Fakatoutoumua, *v.* To bespeak; to intimate a wish for any thing.

Fakatoutubulaga, *v.* To grow but slowly; to look younger than the person really is.

Fakatobe, *v.* To leave a lock or locks of hair on the head; to leave work uufinished.

Fakatobutabu, *v.* To make most sacred, as the holy of holies.

Fakatobuvae, *v.* To shoe, to cover the foot.

Fakatofu, *v.* To cease blowing; to die away, as the wind; to smooth the surface of the water, by throwing oily nut upon it; to include all.

Fakatofukaehiko, *v.* To fall calm before a strong breeze.

Fakatofutofu, *a.* Becoming calm.

Fakatoga, *s.* A heathen song; one method of casting the net into the sea.

Fakatogiaki, *a.* Like or similar to a *Togiaki.*

Fakatohala, *v.* To strike or fall in succession.

Fakatoho, *v.* To lengthen, to to drag on, to prolong.

Fakatohotoho, *v.* To drag along, as a train or trail.

Fakatoka, *v.* To run ashore, to ground.

Fakatokaga, *v.* To attend to; to cause to attend to.

Fakatokalalo, *v.* To lay down, to abase, to subjugate.

Fakatokamua, } *v.* To be
Fakatokotokamua, } first, to be before hand; to sow or plant early in the season.

Fakatokamui, *v.* To plant or sow late in the season.

Fakatoki, *v.* To throw down; to let fall; to give away.

Fakatokilala, *v.* to keep in a state of subjection.

Fakatokitala, *v.* To give good counsel, to exhort, to advise.

Fakatokitua, *v.* To get out of hand; to dispense with; to get outside.

Fakatokolahi, } *v.* To in-
Fakatokotokolahi, } crease the number of persons.

Fakatokoto, *v.* To lay down.'

Fakatokotoka, *v.* To abate the pace in walking; to smooth; to remove obstructions.

Fakatokojii, } *v.* To decrease
Fakatokotokojii, } the number of persons.

Fakatokotuu, *v.* To stake a fence; to provide the stakes for a fence.

Fakatoli, *v.* To cause others to *toli* or gather fruit or flowers.

Fakatolia, *v.* To please, to satisfy the mind.

Fakatolo, *v.* To project; to jut out longer than the rest.

Fakatologa, } *v.* To preserve,
Fakatolotologa, } to sustain, to continue.

Fakatologulu, *v.* To ruttle in the throat.

Fakatolu, *v.* To divide into three parts; (used in reference to the moon on its first appearance after a change, meaning perhaps that it is three days old.)

Fakatomabee, *v.* To prostrate, to fall down.

Fakatomo, *s.* A very large root of *kava.*

Fakatomo, Fakatomotomo, } *v.* To jut or project out; to project one so as to be higher or lower than others.

Fakatomotahabe, *v.* To make the highest or lowest of things equally long; to be out of line and order.

Fakatomotoma, *v.* To walk with affected dignity, to strut.

Fakatomutomua, *v.* To be first, or before others.

Fakatomui, Fakatotomui, } *v.* To be last or behind others.

Fakatona, *v.* To infect with the *tona;* to leave patches uncultivated.

Fakatonofefine, *v.* To cause a man to commit adultery.

Fakatonotagata, *v.* To cause a woman to commit adultery.

Fakatonu, *v.* To correct, to straighten.

Fakatonuhia, *v.* To justify, to free from charges, to clear.

Fakatonutonu, *v.* To put straight, to correct.

Fakatonutonu, *s.* Adjustment, regulation.

Fakatonumatau, *v.* To make a crooked stick straight by chipping; fitted by art, not natural.

Fakatotao, *v.* To point out, to jut forward.

Fakatotama, *v.* To cause abortion.

Fakatoto, *v.* To blood, to stain with blood.

Fakatoto, *v.* To move slyly; to go secretly.

Fakatotoafa, *s.* A wilderness looking place.

Fakatotoaki, *v.* To act with great earnestness and zeal.

Fakatotofu, *v.* To supply all present; to deal out to each his portion.

Fakatotoho, *v.* To drag along, to drawl.

Fakatotoka, *v.* To wait awhile; to act deliberately.

Fakatotoka, *a.* Gentle, deliberate.

Fakatotolo, *v.* To allow or teach a child to crawl; to train as a vine; to seek out what is unrevealed.

Fakatotomua, *v.* To precede, to go before, to be first.

Fakatotomui, *v.* To succeed; to go after; to be last.

Fakatotona, *v.* To make rough or lumpy, as when one has the *tona;* to project or push out a little; to leave, to reserve.

Fakatotonu, *v.* To adjust, to regulate, to correct, to dispose.

Fakatotonuaga, *s.* A corrector, an adjuster.

Fakatua, *v.* To expect, to anticipate.

Fakatua, *a.* Mean, vulgar, abject.

Fakatua, *v.* To act like a *tua;* to act meanly.

Fakatuai, Fakatuotuai, } *v.* To linger, to delay, to defer, to procrastinate, to protract.

Fakatuabiko, *v.* To make crooked, to bend, to elbow.

Fakatuabo, *a.* Of or belonging to midnight.

Fakatuakiato, *v.* To sit in the paddling canoe.

Fakatuakovi, *v.* To anticipate evil; to fear what is coming.

Fakatuamelie, *v.* To expect or anticipate good, to hope.

Fakatuatamaki, *v.* See *Fakatuakovi.*

Fakatui, *v.* To cause others to string flowers, beads, &c.; to inspire confidence.

Fakatui, *v.* To act like a *Tui* or ruler.

Fakatui, *a.* King-like; of or becoming a king or ruler.

Fakatuigutu, *v.* To make after the form of a *Tuigutu.*

Fakatuoiki, *v.* To plat or make of a fine texture, as *kafa* mats, &c.

Fakatuolalahi, *v.* To make of a rough or coarse texture.

Fakatuotua, *v.* To expect or anticipate.

Fakatuotuabaka, *v.* To expose or turn the back towards.

Fakatuotuakovi, Fakatuotuatamaki, } *v.* See *Fakatuatamaki.*

Fakatuotualelei, Fakatuotuamelie, } *v.* See *Fakatuamelie.*

Fakatuu, *v.* To finish, to complete according to order.

Fakatuuete, *v.* To stand on tip toe.

Fakatuugaa, Fakatuutuugaa, } *a.* Sudden, unexpected, out of time.

Fakatuuga, *v.* To pile in lots; to keep separate and distinct.

Fakatuugafulufulu, *v.* To allow to grow mouldy; to keep till mouldy.

Fakatuukimua, *v.* To place in front; to expose to view.

Fakatuumau, *v.* To fix, to establish, to settle firmly.

Fakatuumalie, Fakatuutuumalie, } *v.* To wait a favourable time; to work under favourable circumstances.

Fakatuutai, *v.* To assume qualities to which there is no right.

Fakatuutaga, *v.* To cut into square thick pieces.

Fakatuutamaki, Fakatuutuumaki, } *v.* To persevere through difficulties, opposed to *Fakatuumalie.*

Fakatuutuu, *v.* To order or command to stand still; to be recovering from an affliction.

Fakatuutuuni, *v.* To appoint, to arrange, to determine.

Fakatuba, Fakatubagi, } *v.* To open, to break open, to make openings.

Fakatube, *v.* To cause palpitation, to shake.

Fakatubu, *v.* To beget, to engender, to originate, to create.

Fakatubu, *s.* Cause, founder, generator, creator, generation.

Fakatubufoou, *v.* To regenerate, to make anew.

Fakatubufoou, *s.* Regeneration.

Fakatubuga, *v.* To originate, to be the cause of.

Fakatubulaki, Fakatubulekina, } *v.* To cause to grow, to increase.

Fakatubutamaki, *v.* To cause anger.

Fakatubutanu, *v.* To make teasing inquiries.

Fakatubutubu, *v.* See *Fakatubulaki.*

Fakatufuga, *a.* Like or becoming a *Tufuga.*

Fakatuga, Fakatugotuga, } *v.* To leave knots in trees or masts for accommodation in climbing.

Fakatuga, *v.* Hard, applied to an ulcer that does not grow better or worse.

Fakatuha, *v.* To divide out, to allot, to take aim.

Fakatuhani, *v.* To appoint.

Fakatuhotuha, *v.* To divide fairly.

Fakatuhutuhu, *v.* To point with the finger.

Fakatuki, Fakatukituki, } *v.* To use strong language in order to intimidate.

Fakatuku, *v.* To refer any case to a third party.

Fakatukuhau, *v.* To tax, to impose taxes.

Fakatukutuku, *v.* To desert, to abandon, to cast off.

Fakatula, *v.* To make bald, to cause baldness.

Fakatuli, *v.* To deafen.

Fakatuliki, *v.* To make corners, to jut.

86

Fakatulimohe, *v*. To make sleepy.
Fakatulutulu, *s*. The name of what is first put on in thatching a house.
Fakatuma, *v*. To decrease the speed of a vessel in the water.
Fakatumau, *v*. To astringe.
Fakatumu, *v*. To allow melons to grow too long.
Fakatumutumu, *v*. To express astonishment.
Fakatuta, *v*. To tire, to jade.
Fakatutu, *a*. Blustering, proud.
Fakatutue, *v*. To make lean, to emaciate.
Fakatutulu, *v*. To allow the thatch of a house to be so bad as to admit the rain.
Fakava, *s*. Play, sport.
Fakava, *v*. To play, to sport.
Fakavaa, Fakavaavaa, } *a*. Revengeful, quarrelsome.
Fakavaa, Fakavaavaa, } *v*. To revenge; to make some present trifling offence the ostensible reason for revenging a former insult.
Fakavae, *v*. To make legs or feet for any thing; to finish off nets.
Fakavaeua, *v*. To divide into two equal parts, to halve.
Fakavaevae, *v*. To prompt, to abet, to incite.
Fakavai, *v*. To soak, to wet, to liquefy.
Fakavaivai, *v*. To weaken, to debilitate, to enfeeble.
Fakavaivai, *s*. The act of weakening, enervation.
Fakavaivaiga, *v*. To trifle, to treat as of no importance.
Fakavaivaiga, *s*. Lightness, levity.
Fakavaililigi, *v*. To speak persuasively and eloquently.
Fakavaililigi, *a*. Eloquent.
Fakavao, *v*. To warm; to sit or lie round a fire; applied to chiefs. See *Talikula* and *Mumu*.
Fakavaoa, *v*. To leave ground uncultivated.
Fakavaofi, *v*. To bring near together.
Fakavagavaga, *v*. To reed or make with large interstices.
Fakavaha, *v*. To open, to thin.
Fakavahaafefine, *v*. To originate a quarrel and consequent distance among women.
Fakavahaatagata, *v*. To originate a quarrel and consequent distance among men.
Fakavahavahaa, *v*. To create discord or disagreement.
Fakavahevahe, *v*. To divide, to separate, to portion out.
Fakavaka, *v*. To handle; to cover or bind, as books; to make small pens or places for putting away yams.
Fakavaka, *s*. The binding or cover of books, &c.
Fakavakafoha, *a*. Like or similar in appearance to a *Vakafoha*.
Fakavakaga, *s*. The origin or cause of a thing.
Fakavakavaka, *v*. To turn or sit sideways.
Fakavake, *v*. To cause others to quarrel and make a noise.
Fakavala, *v*. To dress, to clothe; to supply others with clothes.
Fakavale, Fakavalea, } *v*. To make foolish.
Fakavalevale, *v*. To act as childish or foolish; to assume a level with children; to treat roughly (a child.)
Fakavalevaleloi, *v*. To feign insanity.
Fakavalu, *v*. To divide into eight parts or portions.
Fakavamamao, *v*. To separate by a long distance.
Fakavanu, *v*. To bait with the *vanu* in catching crab fish.
Fakavanuvanu, *v*. To undulate, to make uneven.

Fakavavaga, *v.* To weave reed or plait in an open careless way, not close texture.

Fakavavale, *v.* To make slippery, or difficult to hold.

Fakavavana, *v.* To cause a shuddering by alarm.

Fakavave, Fakavavevave, } *v.* To hasten, to accelerate, to expedite.

Fakaveebala, *v.* To cause ulcered feet or legs.

Fakaveebiko, *v.* To walk as one clubfooted.

Fakaveefua, *v.* To cause the legs to swell.

Fakaveema, *v.* To spread out the banana leaves in a Tonga bread pit.

Fakaveetoohi, Fakaveetuai, } *v.* To loiter, to walk slowly.

Fakaveevave, *v.* To accelerate the speed of one walking.

Fakaveeveetuia, *v.* To slacken the pace in running; to run slowly.

Fakaveeveetube, *v.* To sit askaunt; to sit in such a position as to form an angle.

Fakaveiveiua, *a.* Undetermined.

Fakaveji, *v.* To flatter in order to secure an object.

Fakavela, *v.* To heat, to make hot, to burn.

Fakavelea, *v.* See *Fakaavaga.*

Fakaveleatege, *v.* To desire death; to provoke punishment.

Fakavelekata, *a.* Laughable, ludicrous, amusing.

Fakavelekata, *v.* To excite laughter and amusement.

Fakaveli, *v.* To lessen the sail by drawing up the lower part.

Fakaveli, *s.* The term used of the above.

Fakavelii, *v.* To cause an itching.

Fakavelovelo, *v.* To jut forward; to call upon others to *velo.*

Fakavete, *s.* The name of the lower part of a canoe's mast.

Fakavevele, *v.* To tantalize; to excite pleasurable sensations but disappoint them.

Fakavikiviki, *v.* To boast, to praise, to exalt.

Fakaviku, Fakaviviku, } *v.* To wet, to moisten with water.

Fakavili, *v.* To push or bore any thing into any hole.

Fakaviligia, *v.* To expose to the wind so as to be carried away.

Fakavivi, *v.* To overwhelm or overpower, by beauty or excellence.

Fakavolu, *v.* To bruise, to soften, to beat soft.

Fakavu, *v.* To influence others to request the food or property of another, in order to be benefitted thereby.

Faki, *v.* To rely upon, to lean against. See *Faaki.*

Faki, *v.* To pluck; to break off, as bananas or nuts from the bunch; to tear off.

Fakifakia, *v.* To fall to pieces, applied to the outrigger of a canoe when the sticks give way which hold it together.

Fakifoifuji, *v.* Literally to pull off one at a time; applied to work in which all separately engage, to a case of judgment when every person is separately questioned.

Fakita, *v.* To pluck; to break off, as nuts from the branch.

Fala, *s.* A mat.

Falai, *v.* To squat down any where.

Falafala, *s.* A kind of yam.

Fale, *s.* A house.

Falea, *a.* Plentiful, many, applied to a place where there are many houses.

Falealo, *s.* The family or children of the *Tuitoga* and *Tamaha*.

Falei, *v.* To inform before, beforehand; to put one on his guard.

Falefale, *a.* Like or similar to a house, applied to a tree or rock that affords shelter.

Falefakahagatamaki, } *s.* A house
Falehagatamaki, } to which sick persons resort for medical aid.

Falefana, *s.* A small house or tent carried about in shooting certain birds.

Falefeao, *s.* The house built near the god's house for the reception of the sick.

Falega, *s.* The nest of a mouse.

Falega, *s.* Kind, class, sort.

Falelava, *a.* Diverse, variable, accommodating.

Falelo, *v.* To bore, to make a hole.

Falemanava, *s.* A house in which the parties about to be married prepare themselves.

Falemate, *s.* The origin or house of death, applied to a murderer, or to a war weapon that has killed several.

Faletao, *s.* A heathen practice on the death of a friend.

Faletolia, *s.* A small house near burying grounds, to which chiefs are brought when near death.

Faliuga, *s.* Way, manner, mode.

Faliki, *s.* The floor or pavement; a flat covering; the leaf on which food is placed before.

Faliki, *v.* To floor, to pave, to lay or spread over.

Falikiliki, *v.* To mat or floor in a temporary way.

Falo, *v.* To stretch out, to make tense, to elongate.

Faluku, } *v.* To enclose in
Falukuluku, } the arms.

Fana, *s.* A mast of a vessel; a shot, the act of shooting.

Fana, } *v.* To shoot.
Fanai, }

Fanau, *s.* Children, offspring.

Fanau, *v.* To bring forth, to give birth.

Fanaumate, *a.* Bereaved of children, stillborn.

Fanafana, *s.* Whisper.

Fanafana, *v.* To whisper.

Fanafanau, *a.* Old, aged, applied to a woman that has borne several children.

Fanafanau, *v.* To propagate, to increase, to breed from time to time.

Fanaga, *s.* A fable, a fictitious story.

Fanaga, *v.* To talk over fables; to talk without doing.

Fanifo, *s.* A game in the surf.

Fanifo, *v.* To play at the above.

Fanifokavebaba, *v.* To take for accommodation or pleasure what may prove hurtful and destructive.

Fano, *a.* Elastic, tough.

Fano, *v.* To go, used in reference to small fish going in shoals.

Fanoa, *s.* An issue, evacuation.

Fanoa, *v.* To issue, to flow out.

Fanouga, *s.* The children of a brother living or brought up by his sister.

Fanoi, *a.* Here and there one, not universal.

Fanofano, *v.* To wash the hands and mouth.

Fanogo, *v.* To hear.

Fanogo, *s.* Hearing.

Fanogonogo, *v.* To promulgate, to publish, to noise.

Fanogonogo, *s.* Promulgator, publisher.

Fanuauta, *v.* To act differently from others; to act singularly.

Fanuani, *s.* Near to shore.

Fata, *s.* A loft, a bier, or hand-barrow.
Fata, *v.* To carry, to bear on a bier.
Fatai, *v.* A shrub.
Fatafata, *s.* The breast, the chest.
Fatafataola, *a.* Large breasted; full in the chest; high in the middle of a canoe.
Fatafatalele, *s.* The name of a part in the old Tonga canoes.
Fatagogo, *s.* A hole or pit filled with fire, but open in the centre.
Fataki, *s.* A platform; a nest make of sticks crossed.
Fate, *s.* A fish.
Fatei, *v.* To wrap up, to wrap in leaves.
Fatei, *s.* A dress, covering.
Fatogia, *s.* A tax, work done for the government; compulsion, necessity.
Fatogia, *v.* To do work as a tax for government.
Fatu, *v.* To tie the rafters of a Tonga house; to commence plaiting mats; to furl, to fold.
Fatu, *a.* Raftered, denoting the stage of the work; thick, crass, applied to liquids.
Fatu, *s.* The gizzard of fowls; the abdomen.
Fatu, *v:* To complain, to murmur.
Fatuoale, *v.* To complain without just cause.
Fatuua, *s.* A piece of native cloth two stripes in length.
Fatui, *v.* To fold up, generally used for any thing large. See *Fatufatu.*
Fatufaia, *v.* To gormandize; to eat till pain ensues; to die from eating too much.
Fatufaia, *s.* Gluttony.
Fatufala, *v.* To prepare native cloth and a fine mat in a parcel as a present.
Fatufatu, *v.* To fold or wrap up.
Fatuga, *s.* The timbers to which the rafters are fastened.
Fatukala, *s.* A black pebble stone.
Fatula, *a.* Beardless.
Fatuliji, *s.* Heavy and sudden thunder.
Fatuliji, *v.* To thunder in heavy and repeated claps.
Favaka, *v.* To beg the loan of a canoe.
Fe, *ad.* Where? (abbreviation of *ife.*)
Feaaki, *a.* Awake, applied to parties watching each other.
Feaanuaki, *v.* To spit at each other.
Feao, *v.* To attend upon, to guard, to accompany as a servant.
Feao, *s.* A guard, an attendant.
Feaofi, *v.* To run; to race, applied to two or more.
Feau, *s.* Ointment; any unctuous matter smeared on wounds.
Feau, *v.* To oint, to smear with ointment.
Feauau, *v.* To contend for a prize.
Feauaki, *s.* Fornication, adultery.
Feauaki, *v.* To commit fornication or adultery; to be lost or destroyed on both sides.
Feaugani, *v.* To fix upon a time for the performance of any thing; to be agreed.
Feaugani, *s.* An engagement, a verbal agreement.
Feauhi, *v.* To strive for the mastery; to imitate each other.
Feauhimalie, *a.* Alike, equal; neither superior to the other.
Feautaki, *v.* To join from both sides.
Feabaaki, *v.* To reverence and respect mutually.
Feabeaki, *v.* To act or move in

suspense; to be held in suspense; to hesitate.

Feabiabii, *v.* To be crowded.

Feafe, *v.* To run, to race, (two or more.)

Feafeafeaki, } Feafeaki, } *v.* To go in and out; to fold over, as a coat; to come from opposite directions.

Feafeaki, *a.* Zigzag, in and out.

Feafeafekafu, *v.* Wrapt round and round the body, as a large dress.

Feafui, *v.* To smoke, applied to several fires in different places emitting smoke at the same time.

Feagai, *v.* To live together, to be of one time, to coexist.

Feagai, *a.* Opposite to; in a line with; coeval, coexistent.

Feagakoviaki, *v.* To exhibit mutual unkindness and ill will.

Feagaleleiaki, *a.* To exhibit mutual kindness and good will.

Feagamakakaaki, *v.* To exhibit mutual obstinacy.

Feaganofoaki, *v.* To exhibit mutual respect and good will.

Feagatuuaki, *v.* To exhibit mutual disrespect.

Feagiagiaki, *v.* To vary or change from point to point, as the wind when not settled.

Feahoaki, *v.* Applied to the moon when she sets at day break.

Feajiajii, } Feajiaki, } *v.* To shoot from different directions, as the lightning; to pierce through and through; to keep a look out upon each other, as contending parties.

Feaka, } Feakaaka, } *v.* To kick, to work the legs.

Feakafijii, *v.* To exhibit angry feeling, applied to two or more.

Feakahi, *v.* To kick each other.

Feakoaki, } Feakonakiaki, } *v.* To teach one another, to exhort mutually.

Feaku, *v.* To scratch the head or any part of the body, as one vexed.

Feakufaki, *v.* To be on bad terms with each other.

Fealaaki, } Fealajiaki, } *v.* To touch one another.

Fealaekina, *v.* To touch, to handle, applied to several.

Fealamuhui, *v.* To echo, to sound, as the voices of several talking together in a low tone.

Fealeaki, } Fealeleaaki, } *v.* To converse, to confer.

Fealeleaaki, *s.* Conference, oral discussion.

Fealeituuaki, *a.* Undetermined, not yet settled, still subject of debate.

Fealofaki, *v.* To paddle to and fro in a canoe.

Fealuaki, } Fealufanoaki, } *v.* To go to and fro, to wander.

Feamanakiaki, *v.* To expect, used of parties whose expectations cross each other.

Feamioaki *v.* To twist; to be contorted; to go along in a zigzag course.

Feamokaki, *v.* To jut out at both ends.

Featofaki, *v.* To thatch with speed, applied to two or more.

Featugaki, *v.* To throw at each other; to throw at any thing in succession.

Feavaaki, } Feavaavaki, } *v.* To be full of holes; to be perforated in many places.

Feaveaki, } Feaveekiha, } *v.* To take to and fro.

Feea, *s.* The affliction of a child who sucks its mother when pregnant.

Feeikivakaaki, *v.* To have command of different vessels in succession.

Feefiaki, *v.* To go to and fro carrying any thing under the arm.

Feeginakiaki, *v.* To exhort or admonish mutually.

Feekenaki, *v.* To inquire of one another.

Feeli, *v.* To come one upon the heels of another; to succeed with rapidity.

Feemiaki, *a.* Restless, unsettled.

Feemiaki, *v.* To be on the move to be uneasy.

Feemoaki, *v.* To lick each other, as cats.

Feeteakii, *v.* To be careful of and attentive to, applied to several.

Feia, *v.* To do; to wound or kill a chief.

Feiakebau, *v.* To do, to accomplish; to work at till quite done.

Feianaki, *v.* To do so; to do accordingly.

Feiohoaki, *v.* To shout one at another.

Feiumu, *s.* Baskets of food; the act of preparing the food.

Feiumu, *v.* To prepare baskets of food; to bake food in the native oven, applied to several.

Feifai, *s.* The name of a tree.

Feifeiavale, *a.* Poor, mean in appearance.

Feifeitamaki, *v.* To be worried or harassed; to be completely tired out.

Feifeilogaki, *v.* To know, to discern, to descry.

Feiga, *v.* To desire earnestly, to agonize.

Feiga, *s.* Anguish, earnest desire.

Feiji, *s.* Cohabitation.

Feilaulau, *s.* An offering, a sacrifice.

Feilaulau, *v.* To offer in sacrifice.

Feiloaki, Feilogaki, } *v.* To know each other, to have an interview, to visit, to cohabit.

Feitama, *s.* A state of pregnancy.

Feitama, *a.* Pregnant.

Feitamaloi, *v.* To feign pregnancy.

Feitatama, *a.* Pregnant; with young, applied to several.

Feiteitane, *s.* Discord, mutual anger.

Feiteitane, *v.* To be angry one with another.

Feituu, *s.* A place, situation, point.

Feituu-fonua, *s.* A place or spot of land.

Feituu-bo, *s.* The time of night.

Feituu-kakai, *s.* The place of the people; the place inhabited.

Feituu-laa, *s.* The place of the sun; the time of day.

Feitunu, *v.* To broil or roast on the fire, applied to two or more. See *Tunu.*

Feo, *s.* The coral.

Feoaki, *v.* To go to and fro, (two or more.)

Feouga, *a.* Opposite, on a line with, coeval.

Feoboji, *v.* To lie together; to join two even surfaces.

Feofaaki, Feofanaki, } *v.* To love one another.

Feofanaki, *s.* Mutual love.

Feofeo, *a.* Coralline, abounding with coral.

Feofiaki, *a.* Near, not distant.

Feofoaki, *v.* To be alarmed; to start in alarm from different directions.

Feofoofani, *v.* See *Feofaaki.*

Feogoaki, Feogoogoaki, } *a.* Mutually renowned or famous.

Feogoogoaki, *v.* To spread abroad the fame of another.

Feogoi, Feogoogoi, *v.* To converse over; to apprize of and talk over.

Feogojia, Feogojiaaki, *v.* To go and come laden.

Feohi, *s.* Union, fellowship.

Feohi, *v.* To live in union; to render offices of mutual kindness.

Feohofaki, *v.* To rush upon each other.

Feohofi, *v.* To rush forth; to press upon, applied to two or more.

Feojihaki, *v.* To be finished on both sides, as two parties contending in war; many lost on both sides, but neither victorious.

Feola, Feoloola, *v.* To gnaw with the teeth; used of pains in the joints, as if gnawing.

Feolo, *v.* To rub smooth or clean; to overcome by kind words in begging.

Feoloi, *v.* To scuffle on the earth; to rub one another against the earth; to gain and lose, to lose and gain, as vessels in sailing.

Feomokaki, *v.* Short at both ends; to meet in a place equally distant from the homes of both parties; the opposite of *Feamokaki.*

Feonofi, *v.* To sit in a crouching posture, ready to spring up, applied to several.

Feuaki, *v.* To sound as persons running in different directions.

Feuiaki, *v.* To call one to another.

Feuotuuaki, *v.* To be all commotion; to stand confused.

Feuu, *a.* Ravenous.

Feuu, *v.* To bite.

Feuuaaki, *v.* To crow in succession, as cocks.

Feuuji, Feuujiaki, Feuutaki, *v.* To bite one another; several to bite of the same piece.

Feuuluaki, *v.* To sound from different directions at the same time.

Feufeu, *a.* Wrinkled, rough, withered, as the skin of aged persons.

Feuga, *a.* Opposite, in a line with, coeval. See *Feouga.*

Feugakii, *v.* To shelter, to screen, applied to several.

Feugogai, *v.* To go away in a secret manner (two or more.)

Feuhu, Feuhuaki, *v.* To shoot or pierce in different directions, as pains in the body.

Feuhui, *v.* To leave at day break, applied to several.

Feukiukivale, *v.* To go in quest of food in times of scarcity; to be short of food when needed, applied to several.

Feukunaki, *v.* To persevere, applied to several.

Feuligaki, *v.* To tack about in different directions, applied to canoes or vessels on different tacks.

Feulofi, *v.* To shine, to flame, applied to several fires.

Feulufaki, *v.* To be placed or laid heads and tails in the same direction.

Feulugaki *a.* Prostrate, bowed down; heads in different directions.

Feulugaki, *v.* To prostrate, to bow with the head in different directions.

Feumaaki, *v.* To kiss each other.

Feunu, *s.* The piece to join in.

Feunu, *v.* To join in plaiting or weaving.

Feunui, Feunuunui, *v.* To move, to approach, applied to several.

93

Feutaaki, *v.* To take and bring, as a vessel loaded both ways.

Feutaaki, } *v.* To pay mutual
Feutagaki, } visits.

Feutaki, *v.* To hold mutually; to fasten from both sides, as dogs in fighting.

Feutani, *v.* To sail together, applied to a man and woman who are suspected.

Feutugaki, *v.* To do alike to each other; to render mutual services; to have all things common.

Febaeaki, *v.* To do work quickly and badly.

Febaetakuaki, *v.* To sneer at one another jokingly.

Febauuaki, *v.* To be mutually mischievous and roguish.

Febaubauaki, *v.* To consult others; to act in unison.

Febabaniaki, *v.* To forage; to take provisions in time of war each from the other.

Febagoaki, *v.* To act alike disgusting or disagreeable to each other.

Febakeaki, *v.* To challenge each other.

Febaki, *v.* To jostle, to jar, to clash.

Febakibaki, *v.* To crack in several places; to clash repeatedly; to crackle.

Febakihii, *v.* To sound as the breaking of sticks.

Febakituube, *v.* To jostle one against another, as when many meet in a narrow place.

Febalahaki, } *v.* To infect each
Febalahiaki, } other; to mix or muddle together.

Febaleaki, } *v.* To charge one
Febalegaki, } another; to put from one to another.

Febatakai, *v.* To smack the mouth, applied to a number.

Febatoi, *v.* To sound as the cutting of wood.

Febatoji, *v.* To strike one against another.

Febatoji, *s.* Collision, a clash.

Febatui, *v.* To sound as the striking any thing hollow.

Febatubatuji, *s.* The sound as of several running along.

Febeuaki, *a.* Undecided.

Febeuaki, *v.* To feel and speak differently upon the same subject.

Febebeeaki, *v.* To exhibit unwillingness on both sides.

Febebeuaki, *a.* See *Febeuaki.*

Febeheaki, *v.* To speak alike to each other.

Febekoaki, *v.* To look shyly at each other.

Febeluaki, } *v.* To fold in dif-
Febelukaki, } ferent parts.

Febeteaki, *v.* To make pitiful faces

Febiiaki, *v.* To dash water against; (two or more.)

Febibiaki, } *v.* To cleave one to
Febikiaki, } another; to hold each other.

Febikoaki, *v.* To go in and out; to run to and fro.

Febihiaki, *v.* To infect one another.

Feboaki, } *v.* To search fruit-
Febokaki, } lessly for any thing in different directions.

Febouaki, *v.* To halt, to be in suspense.

Feboubouki, *v.* To stand erect and firm, as two parties about to fight.

Feboboakiaki, *v.* To send messages to and fro.

Febobulaaki, *v.* To be prisoners to each other.

Febolebolei, } *v.* To brag, to
Febolegaki, } boast, to challenge (two or more.)

Febuaaki, *v.* To feel sourness of mind one to another.

Febubuhaki, *a.* Full of holes, apertures, or passages.

Febuhai, *s.* A noise in quarrelling.

Febuhai, *v.* To quarrel.

Febuhsi, *a.* Hot, as many lying together.

Febuhi, } *v.* To break out,
Febuhibuhi, } to burst forth, as sores on the body.

Febukeaki, } *v.* To hold, to
Febukei, } seize mutually.

Febulaji, } *v.* To rise as
Febulobulaji, } swellings on the body.

Febuleaki, } *v.* To govern mu-
Febulegaki, } tually, to govern one another.

Febunaaki, *v.* To fly to and fro; to go and come.

Febunabunaki, *v.* To attempt flying; to fly off in different directions.

Febunoui, *v.* To bow down (two or more.)

Febutagaki, *v.* To contend, to strive, to vie with each other.

Fefaaoaki, *v.* To take by force from each other.

Fefaaki, } *v.* To feel each
Fefafaaki, } other by the hand; to feel after any thing (two or more.)

Fefaakiaki, *v.* To lean one against another.

Fefaeikiaki, *v.* To go from chief to chief; to go the round of chiefs.

Fefaiaki, *v.* To do mutually.

Fefaifaitakiaki, *v.* To imitate each other.

Fefainoaaki, *v.* To act by mistake on both sides.

Fefaitei, *v.* To sit in state, applied to several Tonga females.

Fefaoi, *v.* To stretch out the neck as in looking, applied to two or more.

Fefaofaoaki, *v.* To put into several baskets; to deposit in several places.

Fefauaki, *v.* To pull in different directions.

Fefauhi, *v.* To embrace each other.

Fefafa, *v.* To carry on the back.

Fefafa, *s.* The name given to the second large yam from one seed, which are united from the top.

Fefafaguaki, *v.* To awake one another.

Fefakaaaki, *v.* To awake each other; to remind; to put each other in mind.

Fefakaaiaiaki, *v.* To abet; to incite from both sides.

Fefakaaogaaki, *v.* To make mutually useful or profitable.

Fefakaaauaki, *v.* To report each other.

Fefakaauhaaki, *v.* To destroy mutually.

Fefakaauhatamakiaki, *v.* To persevere through difficulties (two or more.)

Fefakaabaabaaki, *v.* To pay mutual reverence or respect.

Fefakaabeaki, *v.* To speak doubtfully on both sides.

Fefakaagaaki, *v.* To criticise and remark each other's work.

Fefakaagahalaaki, *v.* To cause each other to commit sin.

Fefakaagavaivaiaki, *v.* To exhibit mutual humility.

☞ The above words beginning *Fefaka* will serve to shew the use of the *Fe* in that numerous class of words beginning with the *Faka,* to most of which it may be prefixed, as in the above example. When thus prefixed the word is always plural, and if expressive of an action that action is always mutual.

Fefaloaki, *v.* To stretch out or pull in different directions

Fefalukuaki, *v.* To carry backwards and forwards enclosed in the arms.

95

Fefanaaki, *v.* To shoot at each other.
Fefanafanahi, *v.* To whisper one to another.
Fefanogoaki, *v.* To hear different tales at one and the same time.
Fefanogofanogoaki, *v.* To noise abroad quickly; to make known or publish one to another.
Fefataaki, *v.* To carry to and fro on a bier.
Fefatogiaaki, *v.* To work as a tax for more than one place.
Fefatuaki, *v.* To murmur or complain of each other.
Fefe, *ad.* How?
Fefejifejiaki, *v.* To act by fits and starts.
Fefejifejiaki, *a.* Fitful.
Fefehiaaki, } *v.* To hate one
Fetaufehiaaki, } another.
Fefeka, *a.* Hard.
Fefeka, *s.* Hardness, obduracy.
Fefele, *v.* To be scattered or strewed about.
Fefena, *s.* A shell fish.
Fefena, *a.* Ropy, depectible.
Fefete, *a.* Rough, lumpy.
Fefie, *s.* Fuel, fire wood.
Fefieeikiaki, *v.* To assume the chief on both sides.
Fefiefiemalieaki, *v.* To be mutually agreeable and kind.
Fefielahiaki, *v.* To shew mutual haughtiness.
Fefiemuaaki, *v.* To mutually deceive.
Fefiofi, *v.* To mix together, as persons from different places; to be near together.
Fefihiaki, *v.* To entwine; to grow one into another, as briars; entangled.
Fefiliaki, *v.* To think and talk over any subject.
Fefoakiaki, *v.* To give away each other as slaves; to give mutually.

Fefoohakei, *v.* Two or more lying with the face upwards.
Fefoohifoi, *v.* Two or more lying with the face downwards.
Fefofoai, *v.* To fracture each other's skulls.
Fefohiaki, *v.* To peel, to strip off, applied to several.
Fefokiaki, *v.* To turn again repeatedly.
Fefolauaki, *v.* To sail backwards and forwards.
Fefolatalaaki, *v.* To spread out a case in conversation, (two or more) to converse respectfully.
Fefoliaki, *v.* To take the round of a group of islands; several persons to visit a number of places in succession.
Fefolofolai, *v.* To converse. See *Folofola.*
Fefonaki, } *v.* To charge, to
Fefonotaki, } command or enjoin mutually.
Fefonogaki, *v.* To journey often.
Fefotuaki, *v.* To heave frequently in sight; to go or come frequently.
Fefuaataki, *v.* To exhibit mutual jealousy.
Fefuaabi, *v.* To contend as to whose is the prior claim to any *abi.*
Fefuakavaaki, *v.* To swear one to another.
Fefueaki, *v.* To drive in different directions. See *Fefauaki.*
Fefufuaki, *v.* To hide or conceal mutually.
Fefufulaaki, *v.* To swell, to pout at each other.
Fefufuluaki, *v.* To wash each other.
Fefuhiaki, *v.* To carry about from place to place.
Fefulifulihiaki, *v.* To roll backwards and forwards.
Fefulituaaki, *v.* To turn back to back.

96

Fefulai, Fefulufulai, } *v.* To swell; to rise in swellings on the body.

Fegaaki, *v.* To pant to and fro.

Fegaekeaki, *v.* To waddle to and fro, applied to one who goes along with difficulty.

Fegaevei, *v.* To move in a mass, applied to many children of one family.

Fegaiitaki, *v.* To grate; to make a harsh noise.

Fegaobei, Fegaofei, } *v.* To bend beneath a load or pressure (two or more.)

Fegaohiaki, *v.* To do quickly.

Fegaoloaki, *v.* To creep backwards and forwards.

Fegaueaki, *v.* To work with speed; two or more working with the same thing.

Fegautai, *v.* See *Fegaevei.*

Fegagaa, *v.* To attend; to feel concern about.

Fegagauaki, *v.* Worried; to be tired out and out.

Fegaholoaki, *v.* To fly in different directions as the clouds.

Fegalaaki, *v.* To cry to and fro.

Fegalai, *v.* To cry, as several children at the same time.

Fegali, *v.* To gnaw.

Fegalomaki, *v.* To be out of sight of each other.

Fegalului, *v.* To shake to and fro.

Feganaganai, *v.* To be impudent, applied to several.

Fegatahiaki, *v.* To be all agreed.

Fegataliaki, *v.* To work, to be loose.

Fegatatai, *v.* To sound as broken glass or earthenware.

Feginii, *a.* Cold, shrivelled with cold.

Fegugui, *v.* To talk in a low tone of voice.

Feguluaki, Fegului, } *v.* To mutter or murmur to each other.

Fegutu, *v.* To gainsay; to talk in defence of work done badly.

Fegutaki, Fegutugutuaki, } *v.* To put the mouth (to talk) in every body's business.

Fehaaki, *v.* To be in sight of each other; to kill or wound our own party in war; to know each other's minds.

Fehaamoaki, *v.* To carry between two backwards and forwards.

Fehae, Fehaehae, } *v.* To tear on all sides.

Fehaeleaki, *v.* To walk about (two or more chiefs.)

Fehaitaki, *v.* To tie; to be tied on all sides.

Fehaofaki, *v.* To surround.

Fehauaki, *v.* To tie; to lengthen by tying several together.

Fehaunamuaki, *v.* To fence; to practice the use of weapons.

Fehabaiaki, *v.* Two or more holding up any thing in the hands.

Fehabeaki, *v.* To walk as one clubfooted in both feet

Fehaboaki, *v.* Two or more striking the same thing; to hold out hands as expecting a gift.

Fehabotui, *v.* To pant; to swell and sink, as the stomach of one out of breath.

Fehafui, *v.* To drop, to fall in drops.

Fehagaaki, Fehagahagai, } *v.* To sit in a line with each other; to look each other full in the face.

Fehahaoaki, *v.* To challenge one another.

Fehakeekina, *v.* To ascend by different routes.

Fehakitekitai, *v.* To swell or bulge out; to extend to bursting.

Fehakuleaki, *v.* To rummage from place to place.

Fehalaaki, *v.* To shoot off in different directions, as fish disturbed; to fail or be disappointed from both.

Fehalotui, *v.* See *Fehabotui*.

Fehamutaki, } *v.* To snatch one
Fehamutekina, } from another; to steal.

Fehaveiaki, *v.* To destroy each other's property.

Feheaki, *v.* To go astray on both sides.

Feheuaki, *v.* To turn a paddling canoe; to steer in different directions.

Feheheaki, *v.* To stray from place to place.

Fehehekeaki, *v.* To glide to and fro, as a bird flying, or a canoe sailing to and fro in smooth water; to dance along.

Fehehemaaki, *v.* To be easily persuaded.

Fehekeaki, *v.* To work the body to and fro in a sitting position; to slip out of the proper place.

Fehele, *v.* To cut with a bad knife.

Feheleaki, } *v.* To dissemble;
Feheletaki, } to deny on both sides.

Fehehuaki, } *v.* To speak in-
Fehehuekina, } determinately.

Feheluaki, *v.* To pass to and fro near the head of one sitting.

Fehemaaki, *v.* To challenge mutually by signs.

Fehi, *s.* The name of a hard and durable wood, of which large canoes are made; the act of opening oysters.

Fehi, *v.* To open oysters.

Fehia, *s.* Hatred, disdain.

Fehia, *v.* To hate, to detest.

Fehiamate, *s.* Hatred without mixture; perfect abhorrence.

Fehianaki, } *s.* One generally
Fehianekina, } hated or disliked.

Fehibaaki, } *a.* Unequal, as-
Fehibakaki, } kant.

Fehifoaki, *v.* To descend in different directions.

Fehigaki, *v.* To fall, two or more at the same time.

Fehigaaki, *v.* To fall about as one intoxicated.

Fehigoaaki, *v.* Two persons taking each the other's name as a challenge.

Fehihiaki, *v.* To speak evil one of another.

Fehihigoaki, *v.* To take different routes in walking.

Fehikiaki, } *v.* To change fre-
Fehikitaki } quently; to move from place to place.

Fehikitagaaki, *v.* To remove the remains of deceased persons to bury in another place.

Fehilaaki, *v.* To glare from opposite directions, as lightning; to look askant one at another.

Fehiliaki, *v.* To have passed a place; to be beyond a given place.

Fehilihilii, } *v.* To pile one
Fehilihilifaki, } upon another.

Fehinoii, *v.* Two or more criticising the work of another.

Fehivaaki, *v.* To sing one to another.

Fehoanaki, *v.* To pair, to couple.

Fehoiaki, *v.* Two or more chanting *hoi*, and wishing for something. See *Hoi*.

Fehoboaki, } *v.* To jump back-
Fehobokaki, } wards and forwards.

Fehofaki, *v.* To go to and fro; to be in motion.

Fehohotai, *v.* To make a noise in eating, as pigs; to cut the water with a similar noise, as a canoe sailing.

Fehoka, *v.* To strike; to stab or pierce repeatedly.

Fehokaaki, *v.* To stab or strike each other with the end of a weapon.
Fehokotaki, *v.* To meet; to come in contact; to cohabit; to resemble, as a child its parent.
Fehokotakiaga, *s.* The place where two bodies unite.
Feholaki, *v.* Two or more running away.
Feholataki, *v.* To elope from place to place.
Feholi, *v.* To live happily together.
Feholiaki, *v.* Mutually to long after or desire.
Feholoaki, *v.* To move in different directions; to be going and coming.
Feholoi, *v.* To follow in succession.
Fehuaaki, *v.* To turn up things in quest of anything; to tack about.
Fehui, *v.* To query, to inquire, to catechise.
Fehui, *s.* A question, query.
Fehuihui, *a.* Needle-like, thorny, sharp, applied to pointed stones or coral in the road.
Fehuuhuuaki, } *v.* To lie heads
Fehuuhuufaki, } and tails, the heads of some with the feet of others.
Fehufaki, *v.* To go from one to another in supplicating pardon for any offence; to enter one opening, then another, and return the same way.
Fehufehuia, *v.* To inquire; to be very inquisitive.
Fehufekina, *v.* To intercede one for another.
Fehufekina, *s.* Mutual intercession.
Fehufi, *v.* To pass through one passage, applied to two or more.
Fehuhu, *s.* One who gives suck; a mother.
Fehuki, *v.* To nurse; to hold on the lap, used as if the act was reciprocal.
Fehukihuki, *v.* To cram into a small place; to be one upon another from want of room.
Fehulohulai, *a.* Fleshy, full of flesh.
Fehuluaki, *v.* To move about with a light.
Fehulunaki, *v.* To fold the arms; to miss each other by taking different roads in going and coming; to misunderstand each other.
Fehunukii, *v.* To stick or project out, applied to the breasts of girls at a certain age.
Fejiaki, *v.* To return to each other, as cocks fighting; to throw one at another.
Fejii, *v.* To break, to snap.
Fejii, *a.* Broken.
Fejiekina, } *v.* To relapse, to
Fejikimui, } backslide.
Fejijii, } *v.* To charge mutually;
Fejijiiki, } to lay each other under a charge.
Fejiofaki, *v.* To look one at another; to stare at each other.
Fejiojiofaki, *v.* To look in different directions.
Fejiofakamamauaki, *v.* To look intently at each other.
Fejibaaki, *v.* To reel to and fro, as a man drunk.
Fejibejibai, *a.* Bent in and out.
Fejibiaki, *v.* To slap each other with the hand; to sing challenges one to another.
Fejifaaki, *v.* To go in a zigzag course.
Fejikaki, *v.* To exhort mutually; to enter into an agreement.
Fejikejikei, *v.* To sit on the heels; to crouch (two or more.)
Fejiliaki, *v.* Two or more fishing with one net.

Fejilijili, Fejilikaki, Fejilinifoaki, } *v.* To make haste, to speed, to strive; to break each other's teeth.

Fejituaaki, *v.* To turn back to back.

Fekai, *s.* Ferocity, savageness, fierceness.

Fekai, *a.* Ravenous, ferocious.

Fekaiaki, *v.* To eat from each other's food in a friendly way.

Fekaiboaki, *v.* To eat by the sly (two or more.)

Fekaihaaaki, Fekaihaataki, } *v.* To steal one from another.

Fekailaaki, *v.* To shout one at another.

Fekainaki, *v.* To eat one another; to quarrel seriously.

Fekaivaleaki, *v.* To eat each his own without sharing it with others.

Fekau, *s.* A command, an order

Fekau, *v.* To command, to order.

Fekauivaagaaki, *v.* To interfere or meddle with parties.

Fekaumeaaki, *v.* To take each other as companions.

Fekabaaki, *v.* To extend the hands; to reach out, (two or more) to besiege each other's forts.

Fekabalui, *v.* To flap, to make a flapping noise.

Fekabeaki, Fekabei, Fekabekabeaki, } *v.* To swear one at another; to use abusive language to each other.

Fekabokaboaki, *v.* To do; to help from all sides.

Fekabuiaki, Fekabukabuaki, } *v.* To surround or enclose from all sides.

Fekabujiaki, *v.* To drive each other away.

Fekabujiekina, *v.* To drive or banish from different places; to be driven away or cast off.

Fekafoaki, *v.* To be wounded (both parties.)

Fekahoaaki, *v.* To hang about the neck, first one and then another.

Fekaka, *v.* To creep along a fence, as a vine.

Fekakaaki, *v.* To climb one thing after another.

Fekakaaki, *v.* To deceive or cheat one another.

Fekakauaki, *v.* To swim to and fro.

Fekabaaki, Fekakabaaki, } *v.* To reach out the hand in this and that direction, as a child in learning to walk.

Fekakabai, *v.* To reach towards (two or more.)

Fekakafi, *v.* To climb (two or more.)

Fekakatai, *v.* To laugh (two or more.)

Fekakamaaki, *v.* To be anxious about different things at the same time.

Fekakavaaki, *v.* To sweat, as two or more at any work; to sweat from place to place.

Fekalagaaki, *v.* To shout one to another.

Fekalagaekina, *v.* To proclaim, to shout, (two or more) to the same object; to be proclaimed by several.

Fekalalui, *v.* To make a noise like the shaking of loose papers.

Fekalamui, *v.* To buzz to and fro.

Fekalavai, *v.* To speak so as to shew the veins of the neck; to speak loud.

Fekalekalei, *v.* To run and walk fast alternately.

Fekaloaki, Fekalofaki, } *v.* To evade, to elude.

Fekalouaki, *v.* To bark one at another.

Fekamiaki, *v.* To love more than one.

Fekamoaki, *v.* To beckon one to another.
Fekamokamoji, *v.* To wink one at another.
Fekataaki, *v.* To laugh at each other.
Fekatai, } *v.* To laugh to-
Fekatakatai, } gether (several.)
Fekatakiaki, *v.* To bear one with another.
Fekatoagaaki, *v.* To feast and visit alternately.
Fekatubaaki, *a.* Open opposite to each other.
Fekaveaki, *v.* To investigate, to inquire into.
Fekavei, *v.* To swing to and fro; to draw in different directions.
Feke, *s.* The cat fish.
Fekei, } *v.* To quarrel, to
Fekeikei, } debate, to contend.
Fekeigoaki, *v.* To complain of each other.
Fekeituu, *v.* To quarrel, to be up in arms.
Fekefeka, *a.* Hard, firm.
Fekefeke, *v.* To shiver, to shake.
Fekefekelulu, *v.* To bleed at the nose.
Fekefekelotoa, *v.* To be vexed or angry; to shake mentally.
Fekekei, *v.* To bleat, as goats.
Fekekevai, *v.* To be stiffened in death (two or more.)
Fekeli, *v.* To paddle quickly.
Feketuaki, *v.* To limp to and fro.
Fekiai, *v.* To be wrinkled, to be shrivelled, to be puckered.
Fekii, } *v.* To squeak, used
Fekikii, } also in reference to vain talkative girls.
Fekioi, *v.* To chirp as chickens.
Fekika, *s.* A tree and its fruit.
Fekikavao, *s.* A tree and its fruit.
Fekiki, } *v.* To contend, to
Fekikihiaki, } debate.
Fekikilai, *v.* To stare with astonishment.
Fekikivii, *v.* To strain; to put out the whole strength (two or more.)
Fekilijiaki, *v.* To saw quickly.
Fekilofaki, } *v.* To look or
Fekilokilofaki, } stare about.
Fekinaaki, *v.* To be tired of each other; to be wearied (two or more.)
Fekiniaki, *v.* To strike moving backwards and forwards.
Fekita, *v.* To kiss.
Fekitaki, } *v.* To meet.
Fekitekina, }
Fekitegaki, *v.* To be in sight of each other.
Feko, *s.* A fish.
Feko, } *a.* Elastic, tough.
Fekofeko, }
Fekoekoei, *v.* Of one mind, happy.
Fekofei, } *a.* Pleasant in
Fekofekofe, } sound.
Fekofi, } *v.* To talk loud,
Fekofikofi, } to chatter.
Fekofuaki, *v.* To wrap up quickly.
Fekogai, *v.* To grunt together, as pigs.
Fekohiaki, *v.* To scratch each other; to scrape with speed.
Fekohii, *v.* To make a rustling noise.
Fekohuaki, *v.* To be smoking, as several fires at the same time.
Fekoji, } *a.* Discordant,
Fekojikoji, } rough.
Fekoleaki, } *v.* To beg one of
Fekolegaaki, } another.
Fekoloaki, *v.* To desire mutually.
Fekonohi, *v.* To be mutually vexed.
Fekotei, *v.* To converse in an unknown tongue.
Fekoviaki, *v.* To be evil disposed to each other.
Fekovikovi, *v.* To be at variance with each other.

Fekuihaki, *v.* To blind each other.

Fekuki, *v.* To disagree, to contend.

Fekulai, *a.* Red hot, applied to one whose face is so from work, anger, &c.

Fekului, } *v.* To hug; to
Fekulukului, } embrace closely; to huddle together.

Fekumi, *v.* To seek.

Fekunimai, *v.* To clasp the hands (two or more.)

Fela, *s.* Eyes (low term.)

Felai, *v.* To open out; to increase the opening.

Felaikiaki, *v.* To break up each other's property.

Felau, *v.* To talk much, to chatter.

Felaui, } *v.* To pinch one an-
Felauji, } other.

Felauiaki, *v.* To talk one of another.

Felaugaaki, *v.* To complain of or to each other.

Felaukauaki, *v.* To shew off before each other.

Felaulaui, *v.* To reproach one another.

Felaulauhi, *s.* A canoe race.

Felabalabaji, *v.* Chiefs to kill each other secretly.

Felabuaki, *v.* To flatter each other.

Felafii, *v.* Two or more hiding themselves.

Felagaaki, *v.* To urge each other.

Felagai, *v.* To set off before break of day, applied to two or more.

Felagaki, *v.* To be in pain.

Felagomaki, *v.* To place transversely on the ground; used also to a number who are prostrate.

Felakai, *v.* To walk quickly, to step out (two or more.)

Felalafai, *v.* To flinch, to crouch (two or more.)

Felalagai, *v.* To be marked or striped from flogging.

Felalavaaki, *v.* To wrap round quickly with *kafa.*

Felaloaki, *v.* To creep about in the sly.

Felamaaki, *v.* To watch each other.

Felami, *v.* To hide or secret themselves (two or more.)

Felamitaki, *v.* To hide or secret; to keep out of sight.

Felataaki, *v.* To feel at home in two or more places.

Felatani, *v.* To live agreeably with each other.

Felavai, *v.* To be laid down in a confused manner; to live together from different countries.

Felavajiaki, *v.* To bear with each other.

Felavakiaki, *v.* To betray each other.

Felave, *v.* To take effect.

Felaveaki, } *v.* To be dis-
Felavelaveekina, } covered in different directions.

Fele, *v.* To lay in a confused manner; to be scattered.

Feleaaki, *v.* To converse, to confer.

Felei, *v.* To stop up a road with briers; to obstruct, to belay.

Feleoaki, } *v.* To watch each
Feleohiaki, } other.

Felebaaki, } *v.* Two or more
Felebani, } vessels hove to.

Feleeleiaki, *v.* To put from one to another.

Felefele, *v.* To lay spread out.

Feleleaaki, *v.* To be driven to and fro by contrary winds.

Felelei, *v.* To run (two or more.)

Feleleifano, *v.* To run backwards and forwards, or to and fro (two or more.)

102

Felemofafo, *v.* To go out and come in at pleasure.

Feli, *v.* To succeed in rapid order.

Feliaki, *v.* To throw from one to another; to be behind alternately, as two racing.

Feliuaki, *v.* To exchange places or offices.

Feligiaki, *v.* To pour two or more liquids into the same vessel.

Felihaa, *a.* Loose, cumbersome.

Felijigaki, *v.* To stone, to throw (two or more at one object.)

Feliliaki, *v.* To rage one at another.

Feliliuaki, *a.* Changeable.

Feliliuaki, *v.* To change, to vary to and fro.

Felo, } Felofelo, } *a.* Yellow.

Feloiaki, } Felohiaki, } *v.* To lie to two or more.

Felouaki, *a.* Undecided, unsettled.

Felofai, *v.* To fly; to be scattered abroad.

Felofiaki, } Felolofiaki, } *v.* To rush and overwhelm from different directions.

Felogoaki, *v.* To have an interview with each other.

Felogoi, } Felologoi, } *v.* To be silent (two or more.)

Felogologai, *v.* To make a little noise, applied to two or more.

Felohiekina, *v.* To belie, applied to two or more.

Felohu, *v.* To knock or reach down with a stick.

Felolau, *s.* The name of a fish.

Felolouaki, *v.* To alter, to change the mind, applied to several.

Felolomaki, } Felomaki, } *v.* To veer between two points.

Felomiaki, *v.* To suppress, to put down, applied to two or more.

Felotoi, *v.* To be agreed; to feel alike towards each other.

Felotogaki, *v.* To be displeased with each other.

Felotu, } Felotuaki, } *v.* To pray for, to intercede.

Felube, *v.* To carry any thing that swags.

Feluji, } Felujiluji, } *v.* To sound as several things falling in succession.

Feluluaki, *v.* To shake, to tremble.

Felumaaki, *v.* To mock each other.

Femaaki, *v.* To be ashamed of each other.

Femaanui, *v.* To float gently on the sea (two or more objects.)

Femaeaki, *v.* To be fondly attached to each other.

Femaili, *v.* To flow gently from two or more directions.

Femaoaki, *v.* To act under mistake (two or more.)

Femaobotaki, *v.* To be closed or shut up.

Femauaki, *v.* To meet together at any given point.

Femaubui, *v.* To make a bubbling hollow sound; to talk over again what has been judged.

Femabelui, *v.* To be bent.

Femabomaboi, *v.* To babble; to talk in a bad cause, applied to two or more.

Femabuniaki, *v.* To be closed or made compact, applied to two or more openings closed up.

Femafaoi, *v.* To stretch out or extend the body.

Femafahii, *v.* To be cloven; to be split in several places; used also of two or more things cloven.

Femafilii, *v.* To lie and roll about, applied to two or more.

Femafolai, *v.* To be spread out (two or more things.)
Femafuei, *v.* To be blown to and fro, as any thing light in the wind.
Femafului, *v.* To snore, applied to two or more.
Femagaaki, *v.* To walk broad legged.
Femaguguaki, *v.* To growl at each other.
Femagugui, *s.* A noise similar to the cracking of bones.
Femahaloaki, *v.* To think about each other.
Femahikii, *v.* To move ostentatiously, applied to two or more.
Femahui, *v.* To speak suspiciously; to make a bubbling hollow sound.
Femakauaki, *v.* To twist and turn about, applied to a lazy person wandering about.
Femakaui, *v.* To twist, to contort, to writhe under a load.
Femakafilii, *v.* See *Femafilii.*
Femakakai, *a.* Stiff, unyielding.
Femakakai, *v.* To stand on end; to be raised up.
Femakamioi, *v.* To walk about, applied to two or more
Femakekei, *a.* Hard, unyielding, stiff.
Femakokoaki, *v.* To be indented in several places.
Femakukui, *v.* To make a rustling noise.
Femakulukului, *v.* To be cracked in the bones.
Femalaui, *v.* To wail, to cry mournfully, applied to several.
Femalavei, *v.* To stand head and shoulders above the rest, applied to several.
Femaleleaki, *v.* To run backwards and forwards in a body.
Femalimalii, *v.* To smile at each other.
Femalofai, *v.* To be spread out (two or more large things.)
Femaluaki, *v.* To overshade by two objects meeting overhead.
Femalualoii, *v.* To act hypocritically towards each other.
Femamaeaki, *v.* See *Femaeaki.*
Femamaoi, *v.* To stare silently and under the excitement of fear at each other.
Femamahiaki, *v.* To be pained with each other.
Femamanaaki, *v.* To be in love with each other.
Femamataaki, *v.* To see or look at each other.
Femamioaki, *v.* To be twisted; to walk backwards and forwards.
Femanakoaki, *v.* To like mutually.
Femanatuaki, *v.* To remember; to think much of each other.
Femanavaheaki, *v.* To be afraid of each other.
Femanukiaki, *v.* To mock or despise each other.
Fematagiaki, *s.* A wind to and from the same place.
Femataaki, *v.* To look each other in the face.
Fematakiaki, *v.* To spy each other.
Femataliliaki, *v.* See *Feliliaki.*
Femateaki, *v.* To be killed from both sides; to be dying here and there.
Fematematei, *v.* To hold out to the death; to maintain the fight from both sides.
Fematuaaki, *v.* To go from one to another.
Femavavaaki, *v.* To shout one to another.
Femeaaki, *v.* To converse, applied to chiefs.
Femehekaaki, } *v.* To be envious
Femehekataki, } of each other.
Femeleaki, *v.* To cough as a sign one to the other.

104

Femeleaki, Femelekaki, } *v.* To disagree.

Femioaki, Femioekina, } *v.* To equivocate; to twist and turn in conversation.

Femigimigi, *v.* To be curled, to be twisted.

Femihii, *v.* To shiver; to make a shivering noise with the mouth, as when cold (two or more.)

Femili, *v.* To rub against each other, to come into contact, to rub.

Femilihi, *v.* See *Feoloi.*

Femoiaki, *v.* To send backwards and forwards.

Femoui, *v.* To meet.

Femouekina, *v.* To be very busy with several things.

Femouluaki, *v.* To go about secretly.

Femofijii, *v.* To start, to prick; to spring up suddenly and unexpectedly.

Femofutai, *v.* To start up, to be startled, applied to two or more.

Femoheaki, *v.* To sleep in different places.

Femolimolii, *v.* To cut or break up into small pieces.

Femomoui, *v.* To shrink back, to recoil, applied to two or more.

Femomohoi, *v.* To be reddened, ripe.

Femonoiaki, *v.* To strike each other with the fist.

Femonotaki, *v.* To offer urgently.

Femuiaki, *v.* To act upon second thought.

Femuimuiakifano, *v.* To follow another from place to place.

Femuitalaaki, *v.* To follow each other's orders.

Femuhumuhui, *v.* To mutter together.

Fena, *a.* Tough, ropy.

Fena, *s.* Shrivelled yams.

Fenainaiaki, *v.* To charge each other.

Fenabaji, *v.* To be coeval with.

Fenaniviaki, *v.* To be fondling one with another.

Fenatuaki, *v.* To knead together.

Fenekai, Fenekenekai, } *v.* To rejoice together.

Feneki, *a.* Pregnant, full, bulged out.

Fenenuaki, *v.* To stammer, to faulter in rehearsing a matter.

Fenijiaki, *v.* To endeavour to entice each other by the looks.

Fenimataki, *v.* To work quickly.

Fenootaki, *v.* To tie or fasten together.

Fenokonokoi, *v.* See *Fehulohulai;* large in the hips.

Fenonoaki, *v.* To borrow one of another.

Fenujiaki, *v.* To rub together; to rub quickly, as in washing clothes.

Fenumi, *v.* To be hidden by other things.

Fenuminumiaki, *v.* To cover up or over, to conceal.

Fesabiaki, *v.* To make wry faces at each other; also, to kick one another, standing back to back.

Fesaluluaki, *v.* To feel jealousy one towards another.

Fesaniaki, *v.* To speak vainly of each other; to adorn each the other.

Fesovinii, *v.* To breathe hard through the nose when asleep; to snore (two or more.)

Fetaagaaki, *v.* To make songs of each other.

Fetaaki, *v.* To box with clubs.

Fetaaki, *s.* A club fight.

Fetaaki, *s.* The *taba* before it is printed.

Fetaakiaki, *v.* To pull up each other's plantations.

Fetaaloaki, *v.* To beckon from two or more places at the same time.

Fetaanu, *s.* The name of a tree; one kind of sugar cane.

Fetaefiaki, *v.* To swing the arm to and fro, used of one who walks idly about.

Fetaiaki, *v.* To fall in with, to meet.

Fetailiaki, *v.* To fan quickly.

Fetao, *v.* To roast human bodies for food.

Fetaoaki, *v.* To make haste in cooking food.

Fetaofiaki, *v.* To hinder, to restrain, applied to two or more; to challenge each other.

Fetaomi, } Fetaotaomi, } *v.* To crush; to press down; to follow in quick succession.

Fetau, *s.* The name of a tree.

Fetau, *s.* Contention, strife.

Fetau, *v.* To contend, to quarrel.

Fetauaki, *v.* To alter, to change the mind when too late; to express after regret about what was done with their consent, applied to two or more.

Fetauaaloaki, *v.* To paddle to and fro in sailing canoes.

Fetaubiaki, *v.* To throw water at each other; to take food quickly out of native ovens.

Fetauboaki, } Fetaufaaki, } *v.* To grope; to feel after any thing.

Fetaufehiaaki, *v.* To hate each other.

Fetauhiaki, *v.* To serve each other.

Fetauhihiaki, *v.* To wish opposite things.

Fetaukaeaki, *v.* To scorn, to deride each other.

Fetaukabaaki, } Fetautaukabaaki, } *v.* To hover as a bird on the wing; also, to go with out stretched arms as a child begining to walk.

Fetaulaki, *v.* To meet.

Fetaulakiaga, *s.* A meeting place.

Fetaumatakiaki, *v.* To bring secretly.

Fetaumuliaki, *v.* See ***Fejiitaumuliaki***; to turn stern to stern.

Fetautalaaki, } Fetautautalaaki } *v.* To inform one after another; to report to many.

Fetauteaki, } Fetauteaaki, } *v.* To chastise each other.

Fetautekai, *v.* To shrink back, applied to two or more.

Fetautotoloaki, *v.* To defer; to put off from time to time.

Fetautuaki, } Fetautui, } *v.* To sit, to squat, applied to several.

Fetaba, *s.* Salutation, greeting.

Fetaba, *v.* To salute, to greet.

Fetabaaki, *v.* To salute, to greet each other.

Fetabatabaki, *v.* To glisten, to glitter.

Fetafaaki, *v.* To cut; to lance each other; to cut up quickly.

Fetafeaki, *v.* To flow in different directions, as after heavy rains.

Fetafiaki, *v.* To sweep quickly; to clear ground for cultivation.

Fetafokiaki, *v.* To turn about; to roll from side to side.

Fetafuaki, *v.* To blow up a fire quickly.

Fetafueaki, *v.* To blow in gusts from different directions in succession.

Fetafuliaki, *v.* To roll round and round.

Fetagaaki, *v.* To surround fish with several nets.

Fetagakiaki, } Fetatagakiaki, } *v.* To look about, applied to chiefs

Fetagiaki, *v.* To cry from place to place.

106

Fetagihi, *v.* To cry or weep together.

Fetagitautaui, *v.* To deprecate punishment in the name of a third party, applied to two or more.

Fetagoaki, *v.* To go to each other in the dark.

Fetagutui, *v.* See *Fetautuaki.*

Fetajibaaki, } *v.* To reel in different directions.
Fetajibai, }

Fetajilijiliaki, *v.* To exhibit fire brands in the night as signals.

Fetakaaki, *v.* To move rapidly from place to place; to move in a zigzag course.

Fetakai, *v.* To struggle, applied to two or more.

Fetakaiaki, *v.* To roll up; to twist speedily; to roll up from both ends; to go round and round.

Fetakalofaki, *v.* See *Fekalofaki.*

Fetakatakamiloaki, *v.* To go round and round.

Fetakatuuaki, *v.* To move about; to saunter from place to place.

Fetaki, *v.* To walk arm in arm, or hand in hand.

Fetaki, *s.* Small sticks used in native cooking.

Fetakiekina, *v.* To be led from place to place.

Fetakotoi, *v.* To lie down (two or more.)

Fetalaaki, } *v.* To tell, to make known from one to another.
Fetalatalaaki, }

Fetalai, *v.* To converse, to discuss.

Fetalagataaaki, *v.* To disobey each other.

Fetalagofuaaki, *v.* To obey each other.

Fetalanoaaki, *v.* To chat, to talk (two or more.)

Fetalatagataaki, *v.* To challenge each other.

Fetaliaki, *v.* To respond; to take part, as in singing.

Fetaliaki, *v.* To take, to receive, applied to several; to wait for in several places.

Fetalifaki, } *v.* To wait or watch for in every direction.
Fetalifekina, }

Fetamateaki, } *v.* To kill each other.
Fetamateiaki, }

Fetanakiaki, *v.* To collect together from several places.

Fetanu, *v.* The name of a tree.

Fetanuaki, } *v.* To fill up from all sides.
Fetanumaki, }

Fetataeaki, *v.* To reach; to touch with the hands stretched out (two or more.)

Fetataoaki, *v.* To press; to squeeze one another; to lie in ambush against each other.

Fetatauaki, *v.* See *Fetauaki.* Also, to strain the *kava* quickly.

Fetatagi, *v.* To take revenge, one woman upon another, for illicit intercourse with her husband.

Fetatagoaki, *v.* To commit depredations and kill each other in the night.

Fetatakiaki, *v.* To lead or drive from place to place.

Fetatalaaki, *v.* To open; to unfasten the dresses; to loosen each other's dress.

Fetataliaki, *v.* To wait for each other.

Fetatekaaki, *v.* To roll or shake to and fro, applied to the walking of a young child.

Fetateleaki, *v.* To glide to and fro, as a light canoe on the surface of the water.

Fetatemeaki, } *v.* To bustle to and fro, to be over anxious.
Fetatuaki, }

Fetatube, *v.* To flop in the wind.

Fete, *v.* To swell or rise in the skin; to grow in bunches.
Feteeteenl, *a.* Wrinkled; bulged in places.
Feteuaki, } *v.* To prepare
Feteuteuaki, } each other; to adorn one the other.
Feteugatahaaki, *v.* To adorn with one and the same ornaments in succession, applied to two or more.
Fetefete, *a.* Rough, lumpy.
Fetebaaki, *v.* To turn the eyes from side to side; to look cross-eyed.
Fetebiaki, *v.* To walk or saunter to and fro.
Feteboteboi, *v.* To gabble, to prate.
Fetebutebui, *v.* Uneven, not level.
Fetekai, *v.* To roll along, applied to two or more things.
Fetekeaki, *v.* To push away; to treat as worthless.
Fetekei, } *v.* To push or
Feteketekei, } resist each other; to fix boundary lines for each other.
Fetekefilii,
Feteketekefilii, } *v.* To lie along.
Fetekefilihi,
Fetekelilii, } *v.* To shake, to
Feteketekelilii, } shiver, applied to several.
Feteleni, *v.* To clash together; to come in contact.
Fetoaki, *v.* To plant in different places.
Fetoaki, } *v.* To take the wrong
Fetooaki, } thing by mistake.
Fetoeaki, *v.* To groan; to speak moanfully to each other.
Fetooi, } *v.* To make haste,
Fetootooi, } to be quick, (two or more.)
Fetoubiliaki, *v.* To follow from place to place.
Fetoutou, *ad.* Alternately.

Fetoumouaaki, *v.* To hesitate, to pause.
Fetoumuaaki, *v.* To be on opposite sides of the same road.
Fetoutoumoliliuaki, *v.* To wander to and fro.
Fetobetobeaki, } *v.* To paddle
Fetobetobei, } quickly, applied to several.
Fetobunaaki, *v.* To fly from place to place, applied to a wanderer.
Fetofaaki, *v.* To work by turns in making a new road.
Fetofiaki, *v.* To cut and prepare each other's yams for setting.
Fetofuaaki, } *v.* To rush in dif-
Fetofuai, } ferent directions.
Fetogi, *s.* Lieu, exchange, stead, or place.
Fetogi, *v.* To exchange.
Fetogitogi, *v.* To relieve each other; to do by turns.
Fetohiaki, *v.* To correspond by writing.
Fetoho, *v.* To drag along, by several.
Fetohoaki, *v.* To pull; to drag in opposite directions.
Fetojitoji, *v.* To peck.
Fetokai, *v.* To strike each other's faces; to box.
Fetokaaki, *a.* Equal, applied to combatants.
Fetokaaki, } *v.* To attend to
Fetokagaaki, } each other, to attend to several things at the same time.
Fetokaki, *a.* Afflicted, applied to several.
Fetokaki, *v.* To miss one another in the road.
Fetoki, } *v.* Unequal, dif-
Fetokitoki, } ferent sizes.
Fetoki, *v.* To fall, applied to two or more things.
Fetokigataha, *v.* To be of the same mother.

Fetokoaki, *v.* To push a canoe to and fro with long rods.
Fetokoniaki, *v.* To help or assist each other.
Fetoliaki, *v.* To gather from the same trees, applied to two or more.
Fetoloaki, } *v.* To throw at
Fetologaki, } each other.
Fetomaaki, *v.* To challenge each other; to shew off before each other.
Fetonoiaki, *v.* To commit adultery with each other's wives or husbands.
Fetonumi, *v.* To follow in rapid succession; to press one upon another.
Fetotoakiaki, *v.* To be in earnest, applied to two or more.
Fetotoi, *a.* Bloody.
Fetotofai, *v.* To post along, applied to several.
Fetotogiaki, *v.* To pay each other.
Fetotoloaki, *v.* To defer, to put off one after another.
Fetotoloaki, } *v.* To creep about;
Fetotoloi, } to crawl, applied to two or more.
Fetotomaaki, *v.* To borrow one of another.
Fetuani, } *a.* Thick, plastered;
Fetuotuani, } layer upon layer.
Fetuukoiaki, *v.* To be near each other.
Fetui, *s.* Yams that grow wild.
Fetuiaki, *v.* To run or thrust into each other; to press through and through.
Fetuituiaki, *v.* To enter into an agreement; to club together.
Fetuoloaki, *v.* To move in different directions.
Fetuotuani, *a.* Thick one thickness upon another.
Fetuu, *s.* A star.
Fetuua, *a.* Studded with stars.
Fetuuaho, *s.* The morning star.

Fetuuaki, *v.* To be up and down in quick succession.
Fetuuejiafi, *s.* A shooting star.
Fetuuete, *v.* To stand tip toe, applied to two or more.
Fetuuji, *v.* To contend.
Fetuulutuiaki, *v.* To kneel to each other; to kneel, applied to two or more.
Fetuumalieaki, *a.* Timely, seasonable, wellplaced, applied to two or more things.
Fetuutaiaki, *a.* Well matched.
Fetuutaki, } *v.* To tie, to
Fetuutuutaki, } join together.
Fetuutamakiaki, *v.* To be in trouble, applied to two or more.
Fetuutuuniaki, *v.* To appoint, to arrange, applied to two or more.
Fetubaaki, *v.* To break holes through a fence.
Fetubeaki, *v.* To shake.
Fetubutamakiaki, *a.* Angry, applied to two chiefs.
Fetufaaki, *v.* To divide out alternately; to portion out quickly.
Fetufugaaki, *v.* To act the *tufuga* in reference to each other's doings.
Fetugaibouliaki *v.* To go in the dark.
Fetuhaniaki, *v.* To be prepared; to be ready, applied to several things.
Fetuhuaki, *v.* To point to each other with the finger.
Fetuhuluaki, *v.* To go to and fro with a lighted torch.
Fetukiaki, *v.* To strike each other with the fist; to imprecate.
Fetukiaaki, *v.* To stumble to and fro.
Fetukitokaaki, *v.* To strike each other when sitting.
Fetuku, *v.* To carry, to remove.

Fetukuaki, *v.* To take from place to place.
Fetukuaki, *v.* To accuse each other.
Fetukuafo, *v.* To take one at a time.
Fetukutuku, *v.* To remove with goods and chattels.
Fetuli, *v.* To chase, applied to several.
Fetulimohei, *v.* To seek sleep, applied to several.
Fetuloloi, *v.* To bend, to stoop, applied to several.
Fetutuaki, *v.* To beat the *taba* quickly.
Fevaaki, *v.* To make a noise in two or more places.
Fevaigaaki, *v.* To play in two or more places.
Fevauaki, *v.* To scrape quickly.
Fevaga, Fevagavaga } *v.* To desire.
Fevahaanaki, *v.* To divide, to separate.
Fevaheaki, *v.* To divide out speedily.
Fevakaiaki, *v.* To look after each other.
Fevakaivakaiaki, *v.* To look carefully about; to inspect.
Fevakiliaki, *v.* To expose; to lay open; to open out quickly, applied to two or more.
Fevakuaki, *v.* To scratch each other; to scratch quickly.
Fevalaaki, *v.* To dress with the same *gatu* (two.)
Fevalaaki, *v.* To wander to and fro in quest of property.
Fevaleaki, *a.* Debilitated in body; faint; foolish on both sides.
Fevalevalei, *s.* Incest; quarrelling amongst relatives.
Fevaloki, *v.* To cry together, applied to several children.
Fevalokiaki, Fevavaloaki, } *v.* To reprove each other.

Fevanuvanui, *a.* Abounding in ravines.
Fevavei, *v.* To go quickly, applied to two or more.
Fevekaaki, *v.* To wander from place to place.
Feveloaki, Feveloveloi, } *v.* To throw spears at each other.
Feveteaki, *v.* To unfasten quickly.
Feveveleaki, *v.* To desire two objects or things.
Fevikiaki, *v.* To boast of and to each other.
Fevilii, *v.* To speed, to go fast, applied to two or more.
Fi, *v.* To plait, to twist, to curl.
Fie, *v.* A word which has no meaning but in composition, when it answers to the verb desire, wish, feign, as
Fiea, To wish to see, as one blind.
Fieeiki, To assume or wish to be a chief.

☞ The *Fie* is prefixed to very many words in the same sense, the meaning of which may be ascertained by a reference to the simple words.

Fiealolilo, *v.* To try to conceal; to wish to be unknown.
Fieinu, *s.* Thirst.
Fieinu, *a.* Thirsty.
Fieulakovi, *v.* To act the rogue while playing the fool.
Fiefia, *v.* To exult, to rejoice.
Fiefia, *a.* Joyful, glad.
Fiefia, *s.* Joy, gladness.
Fiefiaaga, *s.* The source or spring of joy.
Fiefiatonoa, *v.* To rejoice too soon; to be disappointed in that over which we rejoiced.
Fiegutuhua, *v.* To jest, to joke.
Fiekai, Fiekaia, } *s.* Hunger,
Fiekai, Fiekaia, } *a.* Hungry.

110

Fielahi, *s.* Pride, ambition, arrogance.
Fielahi, *a.* Proud, ambitious.
Fiemalie, Fiefiemalie, } *s.* Comfort, composure, enjoyment.
Fiemalie, Fiefiemalie, } *a.* Comfortable, easy, contented.
Fiemeamalie, *v.* To do in order to secure applause or reward.
Fiemua, *s.* Deceit, cunning, deceiver.
Fiemuai, *v.* To deceive, to outwit.
Fiemaumau, *s.* Anxiety to put another in possession of something new or rare.
Fiematamua, *s.* Impudence, effrontery.
Fiematamua, *a.* Impudent, bold, intruding.
Fievaleloi, *s.* Pretended ignorance, connivance.
Fievaleloi, *v.* To pretend ignorance.
Fio, Fiofio, } *v.* To mix, to variegate, to be mixed.
Fioa, *a.* Greyheaded, variegated,
Fiu, *s.* Weariness, fatigue.
Fiu, *v.* To fag, to grow weary.
Fiuaga, *s.* Any thing by which one is tired; a part of the shell fish called *tokanoa.*
Fiugataa, *a.* Difficult to tire.
Fiugofua, *a.* Easily wearied.
Fifi, Fifihi, } *v.* To manifest great unwillingness to part with any thing.
Fifi, *s.* A term used of fish enclosed in the platted nut leaf; the nut leaf platted round trees.
Fifii, *v.* To plait the nut leaves; to enclose fish in the platted nut leaves.
Fifiikamaka, *v.* To plait the nut leaf round large fish to cook.
Fifiikavale, *v.* To plait the nut leaf round small fish to cook.

Fifihi, *s.* Applied to one who in wrestling is dexterous with his limbs, locking the limbs of his antagonist.
Fifiho, *a.* Ropy, glutinous, viscous.
Fifihu, *v.* To turn away the face in displeasure.
Fifiji, *a.* Pungent, acrid, indignant.
Fifiji, *s.* Pungency, biting heat on the palate.
Fifili, *v.* To ponder; to think over; to diliberate upon.
Fifiligataa, *a.* Difficult to deliberate upon.
Figofigo, *v.* To snort; to blow through the nose; to look angrily.
Fiha, *s.* Number.
Fihaga, *a.* Provident.
Fihaga, *v.* To provide; to collect together what will be useful.
Fihi, Fihituu, } *a.* Thick, bushy, entangled.
Fihi. *s.* Perplexity, entanglement.
Fihia, *v.* To he entangled; to feel embarrassed.
Fihifihi, *a.* Curled in the grain; linked one into another; inextricable.
Fiho, *s.* Phlegm, foam.
Fiho, *a.* Full of phlegm, as the throat in a cough.
Fihoa, *s.* The name of a shrub.
Fihofiho, *s.* The name of a fish.
Fihu, *s.* A fine kind of mat.
Fihu, *v.* To plait over; to turn back and finish off.
Fihufihu, *v.* To plait backwards and forwards; to make the hem of any platting.
Fihufihutamaki, *v.* To look about in anger.
Fiji, *s.* A flower.
Fiji, *v.* To flower, to fillip.

Fijiia, *v.* To smart; to burn as after eating any thing pungent.
Fijiba, *s.* A fillip; a jerk of the finger let go from the thumb.
Fijihina, } *a.* White; covered
Fijifijihina, } with white, as the foam or spray of the sea.
Fijifijimua, *a.* Gentlemanlike.
Fili, *s.* An enemy, choice.
Fili, *v.* To choose.
Filioi, *v.* To try; to use every expedient; to devise.
Filioi, *s.* Device, a scheme, a stratagem.
Filifili, *a.* See *Fifili.*
Filifilihi, *v.* To turn over and over; backwards and forwards.
Filifilimanako, *s.* Partiality.
Filifilimanako, *v.* To be partial; to favour; to respect persons.
Filifilimanako, *a.* Partial; inclined to favour without reason.
Filihi, *v.* To turn over, to upset.
Filimoto, *s.* The name of a tree.
Filitalabe, *v.* To choose words; to seek out suitable language.
Filitoka, *v.* To rise above that which kept one down; to overcome.
Filo, *s.* Thread or twine of any kind.
Filofilo, *v.* To twist, as thread.
Filohi, *s.* The cross reeds to which a fence is fastened in reeding.
Filu, *s.* The name of a fish.
Finagalo, *s.* The mind, applied to the *Tuitoga.*
Finaki, *s.* A cage, a net.
Fine, *s.* Women, (abbreviation of *Fefine.*)
Fitaa, *s.* Prepared or cooked food.
Fitaa, *v.* To prepare food.
Fitaa, *a.* Unsubdued, unmoved, applied to the mind.
Fitifitaa, *a.* Tired, weary.
Fitu, *a.* Seven.
Fitugeau, *a.* Seven hundred.
Fitugofulu, *a.* Seventy.
Fo, *v.* To wash clothes; to wish to eat of.
Foa, *s.* A fracture, a flaw, a crack.
Foa, } *v.* To fracture, to crack;
Foai, } to make an opening.
Foaaga, *s.* A litter, a brood; one of the same litter or brood; also, the particular place where any thing is easily cracked or broken.
Foaki, *v.* To give, to present.
Foaki, *s.* A gift, a present, liberality.
Foakiaga, *s.* The cause or person through which a gift is received.
Foi, *s.* A coward, cowardice; a single one, an individual.
Foi, *a.* Timid, cowardly, faint.
Foiakau, *s.* A pill.
Foikaiga, *s.* Near relatives, brethren.
Foikaunaga, *s.* The child of a *kaunaga* or female servant.
Foitamaioeiki, *s.* The child of a man servant.
Foimanu, *s.* An egg.
Foou, *a.* New.
Foohake, *ad.* With the face upwards.
Foohake, *v.* To lie on the back.
Foofoohake, *s.* Resupination.
Foohifo, *v.* To lie on the face, to prostrate.
Foohifo, *s.* Prostration, proneness.
Foohifo, *a.* Prostrate, prone.
Fou, *s.* To build or repair canoes.
Fou, *v.* To go.
Foui, *s.* The name of a tree.
Foufau, *s.* One kind of sugar cane.
Fofo, *v.* To rinse, to wash slightly.
Fofo, *a.* Dirty, very filthy.
Fofo, *v.* To rush, as a current of

water into deep holes; to drink up; to rub the stomach with both hands in a downward direction only.

Fofoa, *v.* To crack up into several pieces.

Fofoa, *s.* A lancer; one clever at lancing.

Fofoai, *v.* To be hatched; to be cracked, as eggs under a fowl.

Fofoou, *a.* New, renewed.

Fofou, } *v.* To bore; to push
Fofohu, } through.

Fofoga, *s.* The head; the face, applied to chiefs.

Fofoga, *v.* To be delighted with; to look greedily at, as one hungry at food.

Fofohi, *v.* To peel; to tear off the skin.

Fofola, *v.* To unfold; to spread out; to extend.

Fofonu, *s.* Cold in the head.

Fofonu, *a.* Full, applied to several wells or vessels.

Foga, *s.* False hair.

Fogia, *v.* To be engulphed; to be swallowed up.

Fogofoga, *v.* The appearance; the look; the head and face.

Fogofogaola, } *v.* To be looking
Fogofogamoui, } likely to recover.

Fogofogavale, *v.* To look foolish; to appear weak, as one afflicted.

Foha, *s.* Son.

Foha, *a.* Large, applied to yams, &c.

Fohe, *s.* A paddle.

Foheuli, *s.* A steer oar, a rudder.

Fohi, *s.* Any thing sharp used to peel or flay with.

Fohi, *v.* To peel; to strip off; to excoriate.

Fohia, *v.* To be excoriated; to be stript off.

Fohifohi, *v.* To peel; to strip off in several places.

Fohu, *s.* A sunken rock with a hole through it to which canoes are made fast.

Fohui, *v.* To bore, to perforate.

Fokai, *s.* A large species of lizard.

Foki, *v.* To turn back.

Foki, *ad.* Also, likewise.

Foki, *s.* A term of affection generally used in begging; dear.

Fokiaga, *s.* The place or thing from which one turned back.

Fokifa, *ad.* Suddenly.

Fokihi, *v.* To turn over.

Fokoutua, *v.* To lie exposed.

Fokoutua, *a.* Afflicted.

Fokololo, *v.* To dress with any old thing at sea or in rainy weather.

Fokonofo, *s.* A second wife brought by the first, generally a younger sister.

Fokotuu, *v.* To set up, to raise, to pile up, to amass; to ferry over, to set on shore.

Fokotuu, *s.* Accumulation; the act of hoarding up.

Fokotuulafoou, *s.* The first sailing of a new canoe.

Fokotuutaufale, *v.* To sweep; to clear off, applied to many.

Fokotutuu, *v.* To sit on the haunches with the knees drawn to the chin.

Fokovili, *v.* Fallen, to fall.

Fola, *v.* To spread out.

Folau, *s.* A voyage, a fleet, voyager.

Folau, *v.* To voyage, to sail.

Foloha, *s.* The hair of the *Tuitoga;* name of a tribe.

Folahi, *v.* To spread out; to publish abroad; to extend.

Folotala, *v.* To open out in language; to speak well on a subject.

Fole, *s.* A shell fish.

Folobaku, *v.* To make a noise,

in the throat when swallowing.

Folefole, *a.* Sharp, used only of a flat article, as the point of a table knife.

Foli, *v.* To walk round and round.

Foliaki, *v.* To encircle, to surround.

Folifoliauhia, *v.* To be nearly lost; to be on the eve of destruction.

Folimalo, *v.* To attempt repeatedly a different person each time.

Folo, *v.* To swallow, to engorge.

Folofola, *v.* To speak.

Folofola, *s.* Word, speech.

Folofolo, *v.* To swallow in succession.

Fono, *s.* A command, proclamation, edict; the food eaten at the drinking *kava;* a piece of wood or ivory inlaid, enamel.

Fono, *v.* To decree, to command, to harangue; to eat immediately after drinking.

Fonofono, *v.* To speak impressively, to charge; to ename; to inlay.

Fonofono, *s.* Any thing inlaid.

Fonoga, *s.* A journey, traveller.

Fonoga, *v.* To journey, to travel.

Fonoji, *v.* To charge, to inlay.

Fonu, *s.* The turtle.

Fonu, *a.* Full.

Fonu, *s.* Fullness.

Fonua, *s.* A land or country; used figuratively of a person or thing trusted in or rested upon.

Fonualoto, *s.* A vault.

Fonuamamala, *s.* A tree.

Fonuhia, *v.* To be filled.

Fonuhifo, *v.* To ebb; to flow back to the sea.

Fonukoloa, *s.* The tortoise which supplies the shell.

Fonutogotogo, *s.* A fish.

Fota, } **Fotofota**, } *v.* To press or squeeze with the hands any part in pain.

Fototehina, *s.* Younger brothers or cousins (males.)

Fotu, } **Fotui**, } **Fotuaki**, } *v.* To appear; to heave in sight; to approach.

Fotu, *a.* Unproportioned as too much of one ingredient in any preparation.

Fotu, *s.* *Kava* or some other thing taken as an introduction to a person.

Fotua, *s.* A fish.

Fotuoluo, *s.* A shell fish.

Fotuia, *v.* To fall as fruit yet unripe; to be pushed out of place, as a fruit falls by another growing in the same place.

Fotufotuekina, *v.* To go with an offender as his intercessor.

Fotugaloa, *v.* To see at a distance, as in a straight road.

Fotugataa, *a.* Difficult of approach.

Fotugofua, *a.* Easy of approach.

Fotuloua, *s.* The name of a tree.

Fu, *v.* To make a hollow noise by striking together the hands.

Fu, *s.* The noise made as above.

Fua, *s.* Produce, fruit; a measure; spawn of fish; size, bulk.

Fua, *v.* To bear fruit, to produce; to measure; to bear, to carry.

Fua, *a.* All, every one.

Fua, *ad.* Before any other, first.

Fuaa, *s.* Jealousy.

Fuaa, *a.* Jealous.

Fuaaga, *s.* The source, origin; a mother.

Fuaajivaa, *s.* A scarcity of fruit a branch here and there with a fruit.

Fuaeiki, *v.* To assume importance on account of living with a chief.

114

Fuaia, *a.* Fruitful.
Fuaiabi, *v.* To do first at home.
Fuabe, *a.* All, every one, the whole number.
Fuafekavei, *s.* A play; the rolling and tossing of a vessel at sea.
Fuafonua, } Fuafuafonua, } *v.* To be jealous of one's land.
Fuaga, *s.* A grindstone.
Fuagafuhifuhi, *v.* To bear fruit in bunches or clusters, as the nut.
Fuahau, *v.* See *Fuaeiki.*
Fuaholoholovaa, *v.* To be overloaded; bowed down with fruit.
Fuakava, *s.* An oath.
Fuakava, *v.* To take an oath, to swear.
Fuakavaaga, *s.* The place or cause of taking an oath.
Fuakavaloi, *s.* Perjury, perjurer.
Fuakavaloi, *v.* To perjure, to swear falsely.
Fuamouifia, *v.* To die suddenly.
Fuamouifia, *s.* Sudden death.
Fuatau, *s.* The name given to small yams which grow on the tendril.
Fuataukalihi, *v.* To fruit in clusters; several bunches or clusters on one stem.
Fuatautake, *s.* The fruit at the end of the stem.
Fuatabu, *s.* The first fruit.
Fuataga, *s.* A burden, a load, carried by one; a length of *gatu.*
Fuataki, *v.* Literally to carry with one, applied to persons who act improperly because they live with a chief; to commence; to set an example; to set a going.
Fuatana, *v.* To be tired; to be grieved or offended with.
Fuatekinaga, *s.* The beginning; the first acquaintance.

Fuavai, *v.* To vend medicines; to doctor.
Fue, *s.* A whisk; the name of a shrub.
Fue, } Fuefue, } *v.* To drive away flies.
Fuea, *v.* To be driven to and fro by the wind; to move the hand to and fro in despising or mocking.
Fuehega, *s.* The name of one kind of *kabe.*
Fuejia, *v.* To carry; to take in the arms.
Fuetefua, *a.* Applied to a tree that bears but little fruit.
Fuia, *a.* Afraid, terrified.
Fuifui, *s.* A flock of birds; waves of the sea.
Fuifui, *v.* To quench, to extinguish fire; to quench the thirst; to announce a flight of birds.
Fuikava, *s.* Food prepared to take off the effect of drunkenness.
Fuiva, *s.* The name of a bird.
Fuo, *s.* Size, bulk.
Fuofua, *s.* A measure, a whelk, a pimple, an eruption.
Fuofua, *v.* To measure, to carry.
Fuofua, *a.* First, earliest in time.
Fuofuaga, *s.* The pumice stone.
Fuofuonoa, *a.* Shapeless; wanting in height or width; awkward in size.
Fuofuotuu, *a.* Long, conical in shape.
Fuofuovale, *a.* Imperfect in form; wanting a part.
Fuoloa, } Fuololoa, } *a.* Long, protracted.
Fuonofo, *a.* Spherical.
Fuu, *a.* Large, great in size.
Fuulahi, *a.* Very large.
Fufu, *v.* To strike the hands together when bent or hollow.
Fufu, *a.* Hidden, secret.

Fufu, *v.* To hide, to secret, to conceal.
Fufue, *a.* Turbulent, boisterous, furious.
Fufui, *v.* To rinse, to wash, to damp, to wet.
Fufuuga, *s.* Dupes; persons involved in the doings of another.
Fufuji, *v.* To pull, to stretch out.
Fufuke, *v.* To open, to expose, to untie and lay open.
Fufula, *s.* A swelling; a gelding; any creature castrated.
Fufula, *v.* To swell.
Fufule, *v.* To rummage; to turn over and over in search.
Fufuli, *a.* Large in the limbs; fat.
Fufulu, *s.* An ablution, a washing, a cleansing.
Fufulu, *v.* To wash, to clean or cleanse.
Fufuta, *v.* To swell out; to rise as anger.
Fufute, *v.* To struggle.
Fuga, Fugofuga, } *a.* High, higher.
Fuga, *s.* The surface, the lap.
Fugavaka, *s.* The deck of a vessel.
Fugani, *s.* The topmost; the first in value.
Fugani, *a.* First in quality or rank; greatest, extreme.
Fuhega, *s.* One kind of *kabe.*
Fuhi, Fuhiga, } *s.* A bunch or cluster; a rope or any thing by which a heavy weight is carried.
Fuhi, *v.* To fasten on; to carry by.
Fuhiufi, *s.* Three large yams.
Fuhifuhi, *s.* Bunches.
Fuhifuhimokulu, *a.* Destitute of clothing.
Fuhiga, *s.* The name of a part of the yard in a canoe.
Fuhu, *s.* Boxing; the name of a shell fish.

Fuhu, *v.* To box; to fight with the fists.
Fuhuloa, *v.* To box, applied to a whole family or neighbourhood.
Fuji, *s.* The generick term for all bananas.
Fuji, Fujifuji, } *v.* To pull, to pluck; to deplume.
Fuka, *s.* A flag, a banner.
Fuka, *v.* To dress the hair in imitation of the Fejeeans.
Fukahi, *s.* The surface.
Fuke, *v.* To open; to expose to view, as the contents of an oven.
Fukefuke, *v.* To open out; to spread as a flower.
Fukofuka, *s.* The name of a tree.
Fukofuka, *v.* See *Fuka.*
Fula, *s.* A tumour, a hard swelling.
Fulai, *s.* A kind of *kabe* that is eaten.
Fulaihina, *s.* A kind of *kabe* that is eaten.
Fuleheu, *s.* A small flying bird.
Fuli, Fulibe, } *a.* All, every one.
Fuli, *v.* To be covered over with rings burnt in the skin.
Fulifulihi, *v.* To turn over and over repeatedly.
Fulihi, *v.* To turu over, to upset, to reverse.
Fulikele, *a.* Great, powerful in effect, as a hurricane that turns all upside down.
Fulilalo, *v.* To burn the lower parts.
Fulitua, *v.* To turn the back upon; to avoid.
Fulufulu, *s.* Hair, feathers.
Fulufulu, *a.* Hairy, crinigerous.
Fulufuluotua, Fulufulululu, } *a.* Coloured, as black and white feathers, &c.
Fulufuluotua, *s.* The down or

116

tender hair found on the young of birds.

Fulufuluhaa, *a.* Uncomfortable, as one not washed.

Fulufuluhia, *v.* To be tired; to be wearied.

Fulutamaki, *s.* Suffocation; death from suffocation.

Fulutamaki, *v.* To be choked or suffocated from holding the breath.

Fuluveli, *s.* A feast after a great work is accomplished.

Funa, *v.* To moult; to shed the feathers.

Funaaga, *s.* The source or origin.

Fune, *s.* The core of the bread fruit.

Funefuneimei, *s.* The *veka* while yet small.

Futa, *v.* To swell, to brag.

Fute, Futefute, } *v.* To be angry; to struggle to get free.

Futu, *s.* The name of a tree.

G

G, THE eighth Letter in the Tonga Alphabet. Its sound is that of *ng* in *hang*.

Ga, *s.* The plaintive cry of a young child.

Ga, *v.* To pant.

Gaa, *s.* The name of a fish.

Gaahi, *a.* The sign of the plural, sounded *gahi*.

Gaahoa, *s.* A couple, a pair, used only in composition.

Gaaji, *s.* A shell.

Gaajinima, *s.* The finger nails.

Gaajivae, *s.* The toe nails.

Gaaki, *v.* To cough.

Gaaki, *s.* A short asthmatic cough.

Gaehe, Gaeheehe, } *v.* To move gently along; to go weakly.

Gaehu, *a.* Muddy, turbid, applied to water.

Gaeke, *v.* To shift; to move as the wind.

Gaeke, Gaekeeke, } *v.* To waddle.

Gaeve, *a.* Many.

Gaeve, *v.* To move, to be in motion.

Gaii, *v.* To gnash the teeth; to grind one thing against another.

Gai, Gaigai, } *v.* To move at a slow pace, to hobble, to limp; to go as one lame.

Gailoa, *v.* To know.

Gaito, *s.* A shell fish.

Gaito, Gaitoito, } *a.* Tough, elastic, sticky.

Gao, *s.* The double teeth.

Gaoa, *v.* To bite with the double teeth.

Gaoi, *v.* To desire; to work, as the mind.

Gaobo, Gaoboobo, } *a.* Full, close, without aperture.

Gaobe, Gaofe, Gaofeofe, } *s.* Flexibility; a curve in wood.

Gaofe, Gaofeofe, } *a.* Flexible, yielding, bowed down, bent.

Gaogao, *a.* Partially desolate; thinly peopled.

Gaohaa, *s.* Brushwood, rubbish.

Gaohi, *s.* Creation, creator.

Gaohi, *v.* To form, to create, to make.

Gaohikai, *s.* A cook.

Gaolo, *v.* To creep, to crawl along.

Gaoloolo, *v.* To move as under a heavy load, as a vessel laden.

Gaotoota, *s.* Goods and chattels.

Gau, *v.* To chew the juice out of any thing.
Gauaga, *s.* A place where any thing has been chewed, as sugar cane.
Gaua, } *s.* Hard spots in the
Gauaia, } skin of the feet, which cause intolerable itching.
Gauafi, *s.* A firestick, a brand.
Gaue, *s.* A work, employ, business, employment, exercise; cooked food.
Gaue, *v.* To work; to be employed.
Gaue, *s.* Motion, emotion.
Gaue, *v.* To move, to shift.
Gaueue, *a.* Loose, not fast.
Gaufau, *s.* A fool; a term of reproach, as one who should chew the *Fau*
Gaugau, *a.* Moist, damp.
Gaugaue, *v.* To be in motion.
Gaugauji, *v.* To beg the *Ji*.
Gaugutuvaka, *a.* Raised fore and aft; lowest in the middle, as a canoe.
Gaumatuu, *a.* Unsuitable, out of order, unbecoming.
Gaunu, *v.* To move forward.
Gauta, *a.* Many in number.
Gauta, *v.* To be in motion, applied to a large number.
Gautouta, *v.* To move, to rouse up.
Gabulobulou, *s.* A bower, a natural arbour.
Gabulobulou, *v.* To hang over; to grow over, so as to form a hollow beneath.
Gafa, *s.* A fathom.
Gafigafi, *s.* A fine kind of mat.
Gaga, *v.* See *Gauta*.
Gaga, *v.* To pant.
Gagau, *a.* Damp, moist.
Gagau, *s.* Pain in the head.
Gagafa, *v.* To intermeddle, to trouble about what belongs to another.
Gagafu, *s.* A fish.
Gagake, *a.* Wet, damp.
Gagale, *a.* Death-like appearance of the eyes.
Gagali, *v.* To gnaw; to bite in several places.
Gagalu, *s.* The streak or mark in the water by which it is known a fish is swimming.
Gagana, *v.* To fall, to shed.
Gagato, *a.* Saturated; filled with water.
Gagatu, *a.* Pleasant; agreeable to any or all the senses.
Gahau, *s.* An arrow.
Gahaha, *s.* A rustling noise, as one rushing through brushwood.
Gahe, *s.* An epidemic languor; a tree.
Gahe, } *a.* Weak, languid,
Gagahe, } surfeited.
Gahele, } *v.* To creep, to
Gahelehele, } crawl; to go carefully, as a cat.
Gaholo, *a.* Swift, applied to vessels.
Gaholo, *s.* Swiftness in sailing.
Gaholo, *v.* To remove, as fish after being some time in a place; to move.
Gahu, *s.* The name of a tree.
Gahu, } *a.* Damp, moist.
Gahuhu, }
Gaji, *s.* A war club.
Gakau, *s.* The entrails, garbage.
Gakigakii, *s.* The small of yams and bread fruit.
Gake, *a.* See *Gagake*.
Gako, *s.* Fat, lard.
Gako, *a.* Fat, greasy.
Gakovikovi, *a.* Poor, destitute.
Gala, *v.* To cry; to raise the voice above others.
Galau, *s.* A fish.
Galatoka, *s.* A very fat pig.
Galatoka, *a.* Exceedingly fat.
Galebolebo, *a.* Weak, fragile.
Galegale, *v.* To go alone; to appear unbefriended.

Galemu, } *a.* Soft, pliable,
Galemulemu, } flabby.

Gali, *a.* Becoming, suitable, fit, agreeable to, probable.

Gali, *v.* To gnaw.

Galigali, *ad.* Likely, probably.

Galililili, *s.* The ripple caused by the fish when near the surface.

Galo, *v.* To forget; to sink; to be out of sight.

Galo, *a.* Forgetful, invariably prefixed by the noun mind, *loto*.

Galoku, } *a.* Bent by pressure;
Galokuua, } circular in form.

Galomakii, *v.* To push under or out of sight.

Galomekina, *v.* To be under water.

Galu, *v.* A sporting place in the waves of the sea; billows, waves.

Galuolua, *a.* Full of broken or separate reefs.

Galugalu, *s.* The wake of a fish swimming near the surface.

Galuhele, *v.* To swim together and chase each other in the rollers.

Galuholoholo, *s.* A disease of the eyes.

Galulu, } *v.* To shake, to
Galulululu, } tremble, to reel.

Galulutuli, *v.* To shake inside but scarcely so as to be heard.

Galutuku, *s.* The last wave or roller in which one swims on any occasion.

Galutuku, *v.* To swim in a wave or roller for the last time.

Ganagana, *s.* Impudence, forwardness.

Ganagana, *a.* Impudent, bold.

Ganogano, *a.* Red, ruddy, blowzy, sunburnt.

Gase, } *a.* Weak, languid.
Gasegase, }

Gata, *s.* The end; the snake, serpent; name of one kind of sugar cane.

Gataaga, *s.* The ending place, confine, boundary.

Gatae, *s.* The name of a tree.

Gataefekefiji, *s.* The name of a tree

Gatahi, *a.* Agreed, of one mind, unanimous.

Gatala, *s.* The name of a fish.

Gatata, *v.* To jingle, to rustle.

Gatata, *s.* A tree.

Gatetetete, *v.* To shake, to tremour.

Gatetetuu, *v.* To be all in confusion and uproar.

Gatolo, *v.* To move along in a body, as a canoe heavy laden; a sow and young.

Gatolo, *a.* Loose, not firm.

Gatu, *s.* The native cloth.

Gatu, *v.* To be in motion; on the move.

Gatu, *s.* Agitation, disturbance.

Gatugatu, *a.* Second hand; not new.

Gavaivai, *a.* Languid, weak.

Gavalea, *v.* To eat much inferior food ere better was seen.

Gaveveveve, *s.* Goods and chattels.

Ge, *v.* To cough.

Geegae, *s.* The name of a fish.

Geegee, *a.* Fat, bloated.

Geeji, *s.* A shell, a pod.

Geeji, *a.* Empty.

Geejinima, *s.* The finger nails.

Geejitaha, *s.* The name of a shell fish.

Geejitaha, *a.* Poor, destitute, as the fish who has only a single shell.

Geejivae, *s.* The toe nails.

Gei, *a.* Fearful, great, many.

Geia, *a.* Terrible, causing fear.

Gege, *a.* Small, but invariably used ironically in reference to something large.

Gegele, *v.* To wander and eat any thing that offers.

119

Gehegehe, *a.* Cool, applied to the sun when some time past meridian.
Geji, *s.* A very hard wood.
Geji, Gejigeji, } *a.* Firm, not shrivelled, applied to the skin.
Geli, *s.* The monkey.
Gene, *v.* To desire, to cry for.
Gi, *v.* To whimper.
Gigi, *v.* To drizzle, to whine.
Gigie, *s.* The name of a tree.
Gigiefau, *s.* The name of a tree.
Gigiekulu, *s.* The name of a tree.
Gigila, *s.* Polish, brightness.
Gigila, *a.* Bright, shining.
Gihi, *v.* To sob.
Gini, *a.* Shrivelled.
Goa, *s.* A shell fish.
Goe, *v.* To be tired.
Goue, *s.* Gardening; a field or garden; agriculture.
Goue, *v.* To garden; to till the ground.
Goueia, *a.* Cultivated.
Gofe, *s.* Name of a tree.
Gofua, *a.* Unprohibited, not sacred, free.
Gogo, *s.* A stout fat person whose doings bear no proportion to his or her size.
Gogo, *s.* The sea gull.
Gohe, Gohegohe, } *v.* To treat kindly; to speak affectionately.
Golo, *v.* To snuffle; to speak through the nose.
Gono, *s.* The cocoa nut while yet young.
Gono, *a.* Watery, as vegetables too long in the earth.
Goto, *v.* To sink, to swamp.
Goto, Gotogoto, } *a.* Short, thick set, applied to the body.
Gotula, *s.* The name of a fish.
Gotoumu, *s.* A native oven.
Gu, *s.* A kind of yam.
Gu, *v.* To grunt, to strain.
Guatua, *s.* The murmuring of the common people against their chiefs.
Gubuku, *s.* A kind of yam.
Gufeke, *s.* A fish.
Gugu, *s.* A hard swelling, tumour.
Gugu, *v.* To crack or break up with the teeth.
Gugugugua, *a.* Afflicted with several hard swellings.
Gugulu, *v.* To groan, to roar.
Gugulu, *s.* A groan, a deep hoarse sound.
Gugutu, *v.* To talk, to chatter.
Gugutu, *a.* Open, empty.
Guhui, Gugubui, } *v.* To break up bones with the teeth.
Gulu, *v.* To make a grunting, muttering, murmuring, noise.
Gulu, *s.* A grunter, a mutterer.
Gutu, *s.* The mouth; the opening.
Gutuava, *s.* The mouth or entrance of a passage.
Gutubabunoa, *a.* Loquacious, talkative.
Gutugutu, *s.* Openings, holes.
Gutugutuua, *a.* Double tongued.
Gutuhua, *s.* A jest, a joke, facetiousness.
Gutuhua, *a.* Addicted to, fond of jesting.
Gutuhuaia, *v.* To be pleased with or by what others do or say.
Gutukao, *s.* The name of a fish.
Gutulau, *a.* See *Gutubabunoa*.
Gutulimu, *s.* A fish.
Gutulei, *s.* The name of a bird.
Gutuloloa, *s.* The name of a fish.
Gututalatala, *s.* The name of a fish.
Guvai, *s.* A kind of yam.

H

H, THE ninth Letter in the Tonga Alphabet. Its sound is that of *h* in *hand*.

Ha, *v.* To appear in sight; to beat, to thresh.

Ha, *s.* Appearance.

Ha, *art.* A or an.

Haa, *s.* A disease of the eye.

Haa, *a.* Large; bulky, but not heavy.

Haaga, *s.* The slain in battle.

Haahaaji, *v.* To exhort; to watch over.

Haahaajia, *a.* Hard, uncomfortable, applied to the stomach.

Haaki, *v.* To throw down with violence; to overcome.

Haakina, *v.* To be thrown to the ground; to be conquered.

Haaku, *pron.* Mine.

Haamo, *v.* To carry on the shoulders, suspended from each end of a stick.

Haamo, *s.* The stick used in carrying burdens as above.

Haamoga, *s.* A burden or load carried as above.

Haanu, *v.* To come or go on an errand of kindness.

Haatuukau, *s.* A watch; one who has charge of a chief's wife.

Haatuukau, *v.* To watch; to have in charge.

Hae, *s.* A rent, a tear.

Hae, *v.* To tear; to strip off bark; to prepare the cat fish for drying.

Hae,
Haea, } *a.* Torn, riven.

Haehae, *v.* To tear into pieces; to dilacerate.

Haehae, *s.* Rents, lacerations.

Haele, *v.* To travel, to walk, to voyage, applied to chiefs; to appear, applied to the gods.

Haele, *s.* The act of walking or voyaging; the appearance of the gods.

Haeleaga, *s.* The road or path in which chiefs or gods travel.

Haeleeletuu, *v.* To walk about almost constantly.

Hai,
Haijia, } *v.* To bind; to fasten the hands or feet together.

Hai, *s.* Bonds; a kind of the banana.

Haihai, *v.* To tie up as a bundle; to fagot.

Haijia, *a.* Bound, chained.

Haituu, *v.* To fasten; to tie in an erect position.

Hao, *v.* To bring the head of the vessel into the eye of the wind.

Hao, *a.* Pleasing; agreeable to truth and justice.

Hao, *v.* To escape; to get clear; to be free; to have room; to surround; to encircle.

Hao, *pron.* Thy.

Haohao, *v.* To surround; to sit in a ring; to enclose from every side.

Haohaoa, *a.* Faultless, perfect, complete.

Haohaoa, *s.* Perfection.

Haohaoga,
Haohaogamalie, } *s.* The midst, enclosure, a circle; persons sitting to form a circle.

Haohaomua, *v.* To forestall; to tell beforehand.

Hau, *v.* To come, to arrive.

Hau, *s.* A conqueror; reigning prince; a large bone needle; ornaments for the nose or ears; the instrument used in tattooing; the rings or holes made in canoes to pass the ropes through; the *takaga* of the *Tuitoga*.

Haua, *v.* To be exposed to the wind; to blow to and fro; to wander as one insane.

Haualofaia, *v.* To fret as a weaned child.

Haue, } *v.* To go at liberty; to
Hauhaue, } act without restraint.

Hauheke, *v.* To beat at random; to strike any where and every where.

Haugaholo, *v.* To steer so as to keep the sails full.

Hauhau, *a.* Damp, elastic.

Hauhaufano, *a.* Open, airy.

Haujia, *s.* One left or abandoned by his comrades.

Haujia, *v.* To be left alone; to be deserted.

Haujia, } *a.* Damp, wet with
Hauhaujia, } dew.

Haukinima, *v.* To possess by the work of one's hands.

Haukivae, *s.* The name of a hard stone.

Hauliliki, *a.* Fine, very fair, applied to the weather.

Haumi, *s.* One kind of banana.

Haunamu, *v.* To strike at random.

Hauni, *v.* To prepare beforehand; to forecast.

Haunoa, *a.* Contented; quiet, not ravaging.

Habae, *s.* Crooked or lame in the feet.

Habai, } *v.* To hold up in
Habahabai, } the hand.

Habai, *s.* A present of food at the feast called *Tautau*.

Habatuu, *s.* The name of a fish.

Habe, *a.* Club footed.

Habetui, *a.* Near, as the knees in walking.

Habetui, *s.* One who walks as above.

Habi, *s.* A kind of fish.

Habini, *v.* To attend to, to be careful of.

Habo, *v.* To catch any thing thrown; to strike.

Habo, *s.* A blow with a stick.

Habohabo, *v.* To toss about; to throw from hand to hand.

Habu, *s.* The banana leaf tied at both ends to hold water.

Habuta, } *v.* To bulge out.
Habuto, }

Hafe, } *v.* To carry suspend-
Hafehafe, } ed by a string from the neck or shoulder.

Hafu, } *v.* To drift before
Hafuhafu, } the wind; to drop as water; to fall as ripe fruit.

Hafuhafukoka, *v.* To drop; to fall in drops.

Hafuhataha, *a.* Straight, orderly; in one line or way.

Hafule, *v.* To shell; to strip off the outside.

Hafuni, *a.* Short, cropt, applied to the hair.

Hafunoa, *a.* Free, without obstruction.

Haga, *v.* To clip; to be fast from both right and left.

Haga, *s.* A span length.

Haga, *v.* To face, to look at.

Hagahaga, *v.* To be engaged.

Hagahagai, *a.* Ahead, right opposite, as the wind.

Hagale, *s.* A tree.

Hagamalie, *a.* Free from stones; free from obstructions.

Haganaki, *v.* To persevere in work; to work with spirit.

Haganoa, *a.* Disengaged, unemployed.

Hagatamaki *s.* Any disease appearing on the surface of the body; a swelling, a sore.

Hagatamaki, *a.* Afflicted as above; rough, stony.

Hagatonu, *v.* To be in a line with any other object.

Hagavolaki, *v.* To do by constraint, not of a ready mind.

Hage, *con.* As, like as.
Hage, } *ad.* Like; the same **Hagehage**, } as; in the same manner.
Hago, *v.* To be strewed about.
Hagole, *v.* To ransack; to leave nothing unturned.
Hagulu, *a.* See *Gugulu.*
Haha, *v.* To appear; to become visible.
Haha, *s.* A kind of fish.
Haha, *a.* Fetid, bad smelling, applied to the dead.
Haha, *v.* To exhibit one's self to another.
Haha, *v.* To thresh; to beat soundly.
Hahao, *v.* To escape; to get out of danger, applied to several.
Hahao, *v.* To bring a vessel into the eye of the wind; to challenge.
Hahau, *s.* Dew, mist; a fish.
Hahau, *v.* To hang ropes to dry; to fasten to; to adze; to chip logs of wood square; to strike brandishing over the head.
Hahaba, *v.* To near, to approach.
Hahabae, *a.* Lame in the feet; club footed.
Hahabae, *v.* To walk weakly or totteringly along.
Hahabo, *s.* A kind of wood pillow; blows with a stick.
Hahabo, *v.* To strike with a weapon.
Hahafu, *v.* To drop; to fall in drops.
Hahaga, *v.* To clip; to take hold of as with tongs; to cross.
Hahaka, *v.* To flinch, to start.
Hahake, *s.* The east.
Hahake, *a.* Easterly.
Hahake, *a.* Near the shore, used of fish when they approach the shore in shoals.
Hahaki, *s.* One way of taking fish with nets.
Hahala, *v.* To cut open; to tear open.
Hahali, *v.* To scar; to slide along the surface.
Hahalu, *s.* Sugar cane that has grown after the crop has been gathered.
Hahalu, *v.* To gather the above.
Hahalulu, *v.* To work; to labour, as a vessel in cross seas.
Hahamu, *v.* To drive to and fro, as a vessel at anchor in a part that is rough; to snatch one from another.
Hahana, *v.* To be purged, applied to children.
Hahanoa, } *v.* To beat without **Hahatuu**, } care; to thresh at random.
Hahave, *a.* Broken up, smashed; beaten to a pulp.
Hajia, *v.* To be satiated, to be surfeited.
Hajia, *s.* The effect of contact with putridity.
Haka, *v.* To boil any thing; to move the hands as in dancing.
Haka, *s.* Food boiled; a hole cut into the trunk of trees for holding water.
Hakau, *s.* A sunken reef or rock.
Hakalo, *s.* A scraper for scraping old nuts.
Hakalo, *v.* To stir up, to mix.
Hakaloki, *v.* To do in secret.
Hakaluku, *v.* To mix ingredients with the hands.
Hake, *ad.* Up, upwards.
Hake, *v.* To ascend.
Hake, *s.* Flatulency.
Hake, *v.* To belch.
Hakeakii } *v.* To lift up, to **Hakeekina**, } exalt, to promote, to dignify.
Hakeakii, *s.* One who promotes, exalts, or dignifies others; exaltation.

Hakehake, *s.* A place that gradually rises.
Hakili, *v.* To desire, to long after.
Hakina, } *a.* Terrified, af-
Hakinakina, } frighted.
Hakinikini, *v.* To make a finish; to gather all; to leave none.
Hakita, } *v.* To bulge out.
Hakitekita, }
Hako, *s.* Offspring, descendant.
Hako, } *v.* To spring up;
Hakohako, } to increase, as the wind.
Hako, } *a.* Long, straight,
Hakohako, } applied to trees; strong, as the mind.
Hakoi, *s.* A long straight stick.
Haku, *s.* A kind of fish.
Haku, *pron.* My.
Hakula, *s.* The name of a fish.
Hakule, *v.* To ransack; to rummage over.
Hakuna, *v.* To do in imitation of another; to pursue the work of one dead.
Hala, *s.* Demise, applied to the *Tuitoga* and *Tamaha;* a road or path, doorway, or entrance; error, mistake: a sacred club.
Hala, *v.* To err, to miss, to fail.
Hala, *a.* Incorrect, wrong.
Halaabi, *s.* A range or a number of houses and premises.
Halaia, *s.* Sinner, convict, delinquent.
Halaia, *a.* Sinful, guilty.
Halauai, *v.* To force a passage; to tear open.
Halababa, *s.* A high road; a beaten path.
Halafaki, } *v.* To take an-
Halahalafaki, } other route to avoid individuals; to take a circuitous range, as one in conversation.
Halaga, *s.* The road of animals.
Halahalai, *v.* To force a way; to disentangle, to extricate, to disengage.
Halahalaga, *a.* Full of cracks, as glass or wood.
Halakamu, *s.* A kind of fish.
Halakamukalia, *s.* A kind of fish.
Halakava, *s.* The beard.
Halala, *s.* A kind of mat.
Halamotomoto, *v.* To gather the cocoa nuts that have kernel as well as milk.
Halatoho, *s.* A draw bridge; ponton.
Halavao, *v.* To make a way through the bush.
Halefu, *s.* A fish.
Hali, } *v.* To scar; to strike
Halia, } and pass on.
Haliaga, *s.* The place, the scar of a weapon thrown or shot.
Halifuea, *s.* Hunger at sea.
Halifuea, *a.* Hungry.
Haloba, } *a.* Drawn in, contract-
Halobe, } ed, as the stomach when very hungry.
Halofia, *s.* Hunger.
Halofia, *a.* Hungry.
Halotu, *v.* To sob in crying; to palpitate.
Halotu, *s.* Palpitation, pitapat.
Halu, *v.* To seek fish.
Halua, *v.* To be carded; to be torn or shred up.
Halu, } *v.* To card or shred
Haluhalu, } any thing.
Halulu, *v.* To exhibit displeasure at one on the look out for food.
Haluvao, *v.* To eat what may be found in the bush.
Haluvale, *v.* To eat any thing that comes to hand.
Hama, *s.* The smaller part of a double canoe; the leeward; the outrigger; a preparation for marking.
Hama, *v.* To mark, to chalk.
Hamaua, *v.* To marry two wives at one and the same time.

Hamanaki, *v.* To expect, to depend upon.
Hamatefua, *s.* The smallest sailing canoe.
Hamiha,
Hamoa, } *a.* Thoroughly dry; brittle
Hamu, *v.* To twitch or draw up the limbs as in pain; to eat food of one kind only; to snatch or tear away; to take by storm.
Hamuji, *v.* To pluck or snatch away.
Hamunoa,
Hamumunoa, } *v.* To work away careless and ignorant of what is going on.
Hana, *s.* A kind of grass, Indian corn; diarrhœa, flux.
Hana, *v.* To shoot water as through a syringe.
Hanahana, *s.* A slight diarrhœa.
Hanatoto, *s.* Bloody flux.
Hani,
Hania, } *v.* To spoil, to disleave, to strip.
Hanihani, *v.* To strip, to clean off.
Hanoku,
Hanokua,
Hanokunoku, } *v.* To set up the back, by bending forward.
Hanono, *v.* To cringe; to appear afraid.
Hanu, *v.* To murmur, to complain.
Hanuhanu, *v.* To glory in, to boast of.
Hatukaui, *s.* A person who has charge of a female chief.
Hatukaui, *v.* To watch; to accompany as a keeper.
Havei, *v.* To break, to destroy.
Havehave, *v.* To be broken up; to be smashed to pieces.
Havele, *a.* Inquisitive, importunate
Haveve, *v.* To ransack; to turn over and over.
Havili, *s.* A gale, a blast.
Havili, *v.* To blow hard.
Haviligia, *v.* To be detained or overtaken by hard blowing.
Havilivili, *s.* A gentle breeze, air.
Havilivili, *v.* To blow gently.
He, *art.* The.
He, *a.* Astray, lost; out of the way.
He, *v.* To err, to deviate.
He, *ad.* There, that place.
He, *s.* A part of the inside of certain shell fish.
Hea, *s.* The name of a tree, the fruit of which supplies one of the ingredients used in printing the native cloth.
Hea, *s.* A heathen dance.
Hee, *s.* Grasshopper.
Hee,
Heehee, } *v.* To drive fish into the net by striking the water.
Hee, *s.* The above mode of catching fish.
Heeheekina,
Heekina, } *v.* To call or repeat several times the name of another.
Heeheevao, *s.* A small black insect.
Heeki, *ad.* Not yet.
Hei,
Heihei, } *v.* To be on one side,
Heia,
Heheia, } *v.* To talk in sleep.
Heilala, *s.* The name of a tree.
Heu, *v.* To ward off; to catch birds on the wing; to turn over with a stick; to steer the paddling canoe.
Heu,
Heuheu, } *v.* To stir round and round.
Heutaha, *v.* To be of one father.
Heutala, *v.* To ward off in conversation; to give another turn.
Hebu, *s.* The rear; the last troop or party
Hefa, *s.* A kind of grass.
Hefe, *ad.* Where.
Hefu, *v.* To dress with the

same dirty thing for a long time.

Hega, *s.* A small bird; the thread tail at the end of a Tonga fish hook.

Hegi, *v.* To scar; to burn any eruption in the skin.

Hegi, *a.* Wild not tame.

Hegihegi, *s.* The dawn of day.

Hegofua, *a.* Errable; liable to error or seduction.

Hegofua, *s.* Fallibility, frailty.

Hehe, *v.* To stray; to miss the way; to wander.

Hehea, *s.* Scarcity; one here and there only; a tree and its fruit.

Hehee, *v.* To drive away.

Hehefaga, *s.* A kind of the plantain.

Hehega, *v.* To seek earnestly; to be solicitous.

Hehegi, *a.* Wild, untame.

Hehehu, } *v.* To prevaricate;
Hehu, } to shuffle in conversation.

Heheka, *v.* To heal; to fill up as a wound.

Heheke, *a.* Smooth, slippery.

Heheke, *v.* To skim or glide along the surface; to be beguiled or deceived.

Heheki, *v.* To strut; to walk proudly.

Hebele, *v.* To cut.

Hehema, *v.* To be persuaded to fall into the views of others.

Hehetuu, *v.* To reel, to stagger.

Heka, *v.* To sit upon any thing.

Hekauga, *s.* A seat, a saddle.

Hekataki, *v.* To rise from within; to swell out.

Heke, *v.* To move on the posteriors.

Hekea, *v.* To slide, to slip.

Hekeatuu, *v.* To slide; to slip, but go along.

Hekega, *s.* A perch for birds.

Hekeheke, *a.* Slippery, smooth.

Hekenoa, *v.* To go; to be where one has no business.

Heki, } *v.* To push out; to
Hekiheki, } extend to right and left.

Heku, *s.* A small bird; a proud and lazy person.

Hela, *s.* The asthma; shortness of breath.

Hela, *v.* To be tired, asthmatical, weary.

Hele, *s.* A knife; a shell fish.

Hele, *v.* To catch in a noose; to ensnare, to evade, to dissemble; to cut, to lacerate.

Helea, *v.* To cut off; to belie, to dissemble.

Hele-oboji, *s.* A butcher's knife.

Heleua, *v.* To divide, to cut in two.

Hele-unuki *s.* A shank knife.

Hele-fufu, *s.* A clasp knife.

Heleganaki, *v.* To do under a pretext of doing some other work.

Helehu, *s.* A snare for the head.

Hele-koji, *s.* Scissors.

Helema, *s.* The shell of the *Hele.*

Helemaka, *s.* The harp shell.

Heleta, *s.* A sword.

Heleveka, *s.* One kind of sugar cane.

Heli, *s.* The name of a fish.

Helu, *s.* A comb.

Helu, } *v.* To comb the
Heluhelu, } hair.

Hema, *a.* Left handed.

Hemehemalea, } *v.* To criticise
Hemehematala, } upon words or language.

Hena, *ad.* That place, there.

Heni, *ad.* This place, here.

Hi, *s.* Semen.

Hia, *s.* Sin, guilt.

Hia, *a.* Sinful, guilty.

Hiabo, } *s.* The tree the
Hiabotoga, } bark of which supplies the *Taba.*

126

Hialagamui, *v.* To stand on the defensive; to fight when driven to it by aggression.

Hia-matafaiva, *s.* An offender who gets clear of punishment.

Hia-matavalea, *s.* An offender who is not clever to get out of the way of punishment.

Hiatu, *s.* The manner of catching the *Atu*.

Hiatu, *v.* To go in search of the *Atu*.

Hiehiabo, *s.* A shrub.

Hioa, *a.* Foolish.

Hiba, *a.* Askaunt, awry, crooked; incorrect, not upright.

Hifi, } *v.* To cut, to shave;
Hifihifi, } to pare with a knife.

Hifo, *s.* A sacrifice, an oblation.

Hifo, *v.* To offer in sacrifice; to descend, to come down; to unload a vessel.

Hifo, *ad.* Down, downwards.

Hifoa, *s.* A swelling; an inflammation.

Hifoa, *a.* Swollen, inflamed.

Hifoaga, } *s.* The descending
Hifoga, } place; the landing place.

Higa, *s.* A fall, degradation.

Higa, *v.* To fall, to stumble.

Higaaga, *s.* Any thing by which one stumbles and falls.

Higano, *s.* The name of a tree.

Higavele, *s.* The name of a shell fish.

Higoa, *s.* Name, designation.

Hihe, *s.* The name of fish.

Hihi, *s.* The name of a shell fish.

Hihi, *v.* To dislodge from the shell.

Hihi, } *v.* To speak evil, to
Hihia, } backbite, to deride.

Hihia, *s.* An opening, a perforation.

Hihiaga, *s.* A place where old nuts, &c. have been got out of the shell.

Hihifi, *v.* To cut.

Hihifo, *s.* The west.

Hihigo, *v.* To start aside, to vary.

Hihiki, *v.* To raise, to lift up; to raise the eyes.

Hihiko, *v.* To snatch up, to scramble.

Hihili, *a.* Better; more valuable.

Hihili, *v.* To rob birds' nests; to to stand or sit upon a branch.

Hika, *a.* Straight, stiff on end, applied to the hair.

Hiki, *v.* To lift, to remove.

Hikiaga, *s.* The cause or reason of removing; the place to which a thing is generally lifted.

Hikiinaji, *v.* To divide out food for the gods; to devote.

Hikihake, *v.* To be lifted up, to be raised.

Hikihiki, *v.* To move by lifting.

Hikihikimaamaa, *v.* To move cheerfully.

Hikihikimamafa, *v.* To move heavily or unwillingly.

Hikijia, *v.* To lift up, to exalt, to flatter.

Hikimokulukulu, *v.* To take or remove in an unfinished state.

Hikitaga, *v.* The act of removing the bones of the dead.

Hikitaki, *v.* To exaggerate, to add to, to throw or fling.

Hikitaki, *s.* A throw or fling.

Hikiteki, *v.* To remove suddenly.

Hikituha, *v.* To work in order or in line.

Hiko, *v.* To take out of the fire or sun; to blow as in a hurricane.

Hiko, } *v.* To coil up, to
Hikohiko, } twist up; to collect together.

127

Hikohikobuku, *v.* To collect or gather up quickly.

Hiku, *v.* To go awry.

Hikui, } *v.* To turn out of
Hikuhikui, } the way; to set astray; to misrepresent.

Hikuhau, *s.* The present the remaining government.

Hiku, } *s.* The end, the
Hikuhiku, } point of a thing.

Hikuleo, *s.* Name of a Tonga god.

Hikumanunu, *s.* The name of a fish.

Hikumatagi, *s.* The end or finishing of a hurricane.

Hikuitagata, *s.* The remains of of men in former times.

Hila, *v.* To look askaunt; to turn the eyes about.

Hilatalifaki, *v.* To blow from the direction in which lightning was seen.

Hili, *v.* To put upon; to prepare arrow root.

Hili, *s.* The end or termination; the preparation of arrow root.

Hiliaga, *s.* A table, shelf; any thing on which things are laid.

Hilifaki, *v.* To lay or put upon.

Hiliga, *s.* A number of spears laid together; a place or platform on which things are laid.

Hiliga, *a.* Becoming, agreeable; what should be.

Hiligaumoji, *s.* The upper lip.

Hiligameaa, *s.* The seventh moon in the Tonga year.

Hiligakelekele, *s.* The sixth moon in the Tonga year.

Hilihili, *v.* To seek fruit when only few and scarce.

Hilo, *s.* The anus.

Hina, *s.* A bottle of any kind; the gourd; a large spider.

Hina, } *a.* White, grey.
Hinehina, }

Hinababalagi, *s.* The pumpkin; the water mellon.

Hinakaiuga, *a.* Grey headed, as a punishment for eating the *Uga*.

Hinoi, *v.* To inspect, to criticise; to direct, to give instructions.

Hiva, *s.* A song, a hymn.

Hiva, *v.* To sing.

Hiva, *a.* Nine.

Hivagofulu, *a.* Ninety.

Hivageau, *s.* Nine hundred.

Hivehiva, *v.* To chime, to sing.

Hiviivae, *s.* The shin; the forepart of the leg.

Ho, } *pron.* Thy, thine.
Hoo, }

Hoa, *s.* A second; a companion; a heathen game.

Hoa, *v.* To couple; pair with; to fellow; to accord or agree with.

Hoata, *a.* Yellow ripe, mellow.

Hoata, *s.* About mid day.

Hoata-efiafi, *s.* A little past noon day.

Hoata-bogibogi, *s.* A little before noon day.

Hoata-malie, *s.* Meridian, noon day.

Hoi, *s.* A shrub and its fruit.

Hoi, *s.* An expression, desire.

Hoifakafanogo, *v.* To sigh heavily; to excite attention.

Hoifua, *a.* Agreeable, comfortable, favourable.

Hoifua, *v.* To smile, to be gracious.

Hoihoifua, *a.* Fair, beautiful, applied to females; applied also to female chiefs when old and infirm.

Hoonamooni, *v.* To be really and truly related.

Hou, *a.* Rough, applied to the sea; qualmish, inclined to vomit.

Houa, *v.* To send; to command on an errand.

Houeiki *s.* Chiefs of rank; nobility.

Houga, *v.* To be acceptable; to be received with approbation.
Houhau, *s.* Anger, wrath; a fish.
Houhau, *a.* Angry, wrathful.
Houhauulumaka, *s.* A fish.
Houhauta, *s.* A fish.
Houmotua, *s.* The children by a former husband or wife.
Hounoa, *a.* Contented, not fretful.
Houtamaki, *a.* Masterly, imperious.
Houteliaatu, *s.* The name of a fish.
Houtoga, *v.* To oppress; to treat unkindly; to govern with rigour.
Houtuu, Houhoutuu, } *s.* Commotion, perturbation, agitation.
Houtuu, Houhoutuu, } *a.* Tumultuous, agitated.
Hoba, *s.* The banana or plantain.
Hobo, *v.* To eat unrestrained and to satiety.
Hobo, Hobohobo, } *v.* To jump, to leap.
Hobo, *s.* A jump, a spring, a leap.
Hoboagalaa, *s.* The east.
Hoboate, *s.* A captive; persons taken in war.
Hobokaga, *s.* The time for jumping or coming forward.
Hoboki, *s.* The ceremony of the first lady going on board a new canoe.
Hobokaki, *v.* To jump or leap with any thing in the hand.
Hobutu, *s.* The name of a fish.
Hofa, *s.* The name of a shell fish.
Hofa, *s.* The *Teve* when rotten and stinking very badly.
Hofagahau, *s.* The case in which arrows are kept.
Hofole, *s.* The name of a fish.
Hoge, Hogehoge, } *s.* Famine, dearth, scarcity of food.
Hogea, *v.* To be short of food.

Hogi, *v.* To smell, to sniff.
Hogo, *s.* The bladder of small animals.
Hogofulu, *a.* Ten.
Hogohago, *s.* Small sticks for fire wood.
Hogohogo, *s.* A kind of grass.
Hohaa, *a.* Uncomfortable, uneasy, restless.
Hohaa, *s.* Disquiet, uneasiness, anxiety.
Hohaaji, *v.* To arouse; to cause attention.
Hohoatamaki, *a.* Unequal in number.
Hoho, *a.* Full, as an island when many are collected together.
Hoho, *a.* Soft, yielding, as earth after rain.
Hohoia, *v.* To be pleased or satisfied.
Hohogo, *a.* Smelling like urine.
Hohoka, *s.* The name of one fishing net; the act of taking fish with the *Hohoka.*
Hohoko, *v.* To trace out the pedigree of a person.
Hohoko, *a.* Continuous, unbroken; full, applied to the tide when it does not ebb out.
Hoholi, *v.* To fawn; to play about one as a child.
Hoholo, *v.* To wipe, to rub, to slide.
Hohomo, *s.* The name of a fish.
Hohomo, *v.* To give, to slacken; to become loose.
Hohoni, *s.* The nut shell prepared and used for carrying water.
Hohoni, *v.* To lance; to make small incisions in several places.
Hohota, *v.* To make a slopping noise, as a pig eating.
Hoka, Hokai, } *v.* To pierce, to stab; to take off the husk of the nut.
Hoka, *s.* A small cross timber in a Tonga house.

129

Hokaaga, *s.* The place at which the *hoka* was performed.
Hokatuu, *s.* An upright supporter.
Hokatatua, *v.* To pierce or stab behind.
Hokituu, *a.* Full, crowded.
Hoko, *v.* To come, to come to pass, to apply; to fetch a place, to arrive at; to flow as the tide; to come next.
Hoko, *a.* Next; nearest in place or gradation.
Hoko, *s.* Image, likeness; the one who succeeds.
Hokoaga, *s.* A joint; the place of joining.
Hokoifa, *s.* The root of the tree called *Fa.*
Hokojia, *v.* To have arrived or come to pass.
Hokohoko, *v.* To splice, to join; to set in order one after another.
Hokohoko, Hokohokotuu, } *a.* Continuous, unceasing.
Hokomau, *s.* A shell fish.
Hokotaga, *s.* A joint; the place for a joint; a splice.
Hokotaki, *v.* To bring up to; to join on.
Hoku, *pron.* My, mine.
Hola, *v.* To desert, to elope, to abscond.
Hola, *s.* Departure, elopement.
Holamakifu, *v.* To abscond; to get clear and far away.
Holataki, *v.* To abscond with; to carry off; to allow to run off in steering.
Holehole, *v.* To wear as a soldiers cross belt over one shoulder and under the opposite arm.
Holi, *s.* Longing, earnest desire.
Holi, *v.* To desire, to long for.
Holiholi, *v.* To manifest anxiety or concern.
Holiji, *s.* A partition; the reeding of a Tonga house.
Holiji, *v.* To reed a house; to partition.
Holi-kovi, *s.* Concupiscence, lust, evil desire.
Holi-kovi, *a.* Lustful, lewd.
Holo, *s.* A towel; any thing used as a wiper.
Holo, *v.* To wipe, to dry; to fall, to move in quick succession.
Holo, *a.* Comfortable, refreshing
Holoa, *s.* A disease in the eyes of children.
Holoaki, Holoholoaki, } *v.* To push on in succession; to move along.
Holoi, *v.* To wipe, to rub off.
Holoi, Holoki, } *v.* To push; to knock down; to demolish.
Holoitouga, *v.* To be going and coming without intermission.
Hologa, *s.* A class, a kind, a row.
Holoholo, *s.* A pocket handkerchief; a towel.
Holoholo, *v.* To wipe, to rub, to scrape clean.
Holoki, *a.* Preferable, better.
Holotaki, *v.* To redeem.
Homi, Homihomi, } *v.* To sniff.
Homo, Homohomo, } *v.* To slacken; to become loose, to let go.
Homokula, *s.* A fish.
Honii, *v.* To lance.
Honihonii, *v.* See *Hohoni.*
Hono, *pron.* His, hers, its.
Hu, *s.* Worship, sacrifice.
Hu, *v.* To worship, to pray; to enter within.
Hua, *v.* To tack, to row, to skudd; to root or turn up the earth.
Hua, *s.* The taste.
Hua, *s.* A jest, a joke; a pre-

130

paration of food; skudding oars; juice, milk.
Hua, *a.* Comical, ludicrous, laughable.
Huaaki, *v.* To mention, to repeat, to speak of.
Huai, *v.* To turn up, to pour out, to spill.
Huaga, *s.* An entrance, threshold.
Huaaga, *s.* A place where pigs have been rooting.
Huaekina, *v.* To speak of.
Huaohei, *v.* To joke and act the familiar till punishment ensues.
Huamelie, *s.* Any thing sweet to the taste.
Huanoa, *a.* Unseasonable; out of order; overflowing.
Huanoa, *s.* Injudicious and unbecoming talk.
Huafakatua, *v.* To joke disgustingly.
Hue, *v.* To project out.
Hueekina, *v.* To repeat; to refer to or speak of some past event.
Hueina, *a.* Wet from something near.
Huelo, *s.* Rays of light.
Hui, *s.* A bone; a needle.
Hui, Huihui, } *v.* To dilute; to mix liquids; to slip over or off.
Huibalalulu, *s.* A rib bone.
Huifohe, *s.* The shoulder blade.
Huifuhi, *v.* To gather in bunches.
Huihui, *a.* Stony, thorny.
Huikouahe, *s.* The cheek bone.
Huila, *s.* A fish.
Huitutulu, *s.* A preparation of food.
Huo, *s.* A spade, a hoe.
Huo, Huohuo, } *v.* To hoe, to dig, to clear away weeds.
Huofa, *s.* The name of a fish.
Huohuai, *v.* To open up; to lift a covering.

Huui, *v.* To tread; to head towards, as in sailing or lying.
Huufataha, *a.* Parallel, straight, in one line or direction.
Huuhuu, *a.* Shamefaced; fearing to be suspected; imagining ill.
Huuhuufaki, *v.* To expect, to design.
Hufaga, *s.* A refuge, a shelter.
Hufaga, *v.* To take shelter or refuge.
Hufaki, Hufakii, } *v.* To intercede; to enter or bring into.
Hufekina, *v.* To make intercession.
Hufi, *v.* To open, applied to places for religious worship.
Hufia, *s.* Intercession.
Hufia, *v.* To intercede.
Hugalu, *s.* Any thing small that has been driven to and fro by the sea; a dead shell.
Huhu, *a.* Wet.
Huhu, *s.* The breasts; the dug or teat of animals; a fork, a skewer, a lancet.
Huhu, *v.* To suck; to bleed; to puncture; to sting.
Huhua, *s.* Milk, juice, gravy.
Huhua, *v.* To root as a pig.
Huhui, *s.* A redeemer.
Huhui, *v.* To redeem, to buy off.
Huhuhuhu, *a.* Full of knots or lumps.
Huhuhuhu, Huhuki, } *v.* To pierce, to prick.
Huhukia, *s.* A pricking sensation felt in the soles of the feet.
Huhukia, *v.* To be pricked or pierced by insects, as fruit.
Huhulu, *a.* Clear, luminous, unobstructed.
Huhumama, *v.* To doubt, to disbelieve.
Huhunu, *s.* Blight; a disease in the skin.

Huhunu, *v.* To singe, to sear, to blight.
Huhutefua, *s.* A shell fish.
Huhuvalu, *s.* A shell fish.
Huke, *v.* To sail upon the wind.
Huke, Hukehuke, } *v.* To hold or tuck up the dress.
Huki, *v.* To pierce, to puncture.
Huki, *v.* To hold on the lap; to clasp; to dandle.
Hukia, *v.* To be pierced or stung.
Hukihuki, *v.* To calk.
Hula, *a.* Bulged, distended.
Hula, *v.* To carry any thing large or bulky.
Hulaamua, *v.* To act the gentleman.
Hulali, *s.* A shell fish.
Hulamokebi, *v.* To speak sparingly, since what is complained of in others may be found at home.
Huli, *s.* The name of a fish; a plant, a sapling, a shoot.
Hulihuli, *v.* To send up many shoots or saplings.
Hulihuli, *s.* A shell fish.
Hulohula, *s.* A kind of the banana.
Hulu, *s.* Leaves dead and dried.
Hulu, *v.* To plunge; to push; to rush under water, as a canoe in a heavy sea.
Huluia, *v.* To repair mats; to light, to be enlightened.
Huluaki, *v.* To enlighten.
Hulugaki, *v.* To incline to; to be determined upon.
Huluhulu, *v.* To repair the thatch; to light, to enlighten; to be covered with dry and dead leaves.
Huluhulunaki, *v.* To persevere; to act with determination.
Hulukabe, *v.* To fasten the dress above the chest, applied to men.
Hulukebi, *v.* To fasten the dress above the chest, applied to women.
Hulumaki, *v.* To push in or through.
Hulumokebi, *v.* To adjust and fasten up the dress.
Hulumua, *v.* To go with chiefs; to become a *Mua;* to rush first.
Hulutua, *v.* To associate with the poor; to act as a *Tua.*
Humaki, *v.* To push through.
Humataniuaki, *v.* To persevere in taking any thing to another; to deliver directly to the person intended.
Humu, *v.* To stumble and fall.
Humu, *s.* The name of a fish.
Humumoana, *s.* The name of a fish.
Humuhumuki, *s.* The name of a fish.
Hune, *s.* A tree.
Hunuhunu, *v.* To toast, to singe, to broil.
Hunuhunuki, Hunuki, } *v.* To rod the yams; to stick the reed into any thing.

J

J, THE tenth Letter in the Tonga Alphabet. Its sound is that of *ch* in *cheese.*
Ji, *s.* The name of a tree.
Ji, *v.* To toss or throw along; to turn towards.
Jia, *s.* A mound or hillock raised with soil.
Jia, *v.* To net, to knit nets.
Jiaa, *a.* Good.
Jiaamalie, *a.* Easy of discernment.

Jiaatamaki, *v.* Difficult of discernment.
Jiauha, *s.* A little rain but enough to wet; a little affair but serious in its consequences.
Jiaki, *v.* To abandon; to cast away.
Jiale, *s.* A tree.
Jialetafa, *s.* A tree.
Jialetoga, *s.* A tree.
Jiana, *s.* A vagabond (used jocularly.)
Jiekina, *s.* A cast off; one deserted.
Jii, *a.* Small, little.
Jio, *v.* To look, to stare.
Jio, *s.* The name of a shell fish.
Jioata, *s.* A mirror, a glass; any thing which reflects the image.
Jioata, *v.* To look at a mirror.
Jiojio, Jiojionoa, } *v.* To gaze; to stare about.
Jiojioua, *v.* To look two ways; to try to please two opposing parties.
Jiotoofa, Jiokuofa, } The Tonga salutation.
Jiofakamamau, *v.* To look steadfastly; to fasten the eyes upon.
Jiokalojio, *v.* To be angry at another for doing what he himself is doing.
Jiu, *s.* A race with paddling canoes.
Jiu, *v.* To seek sharks.
Jiba, *v.* To stagger, to falter.
Jiba, *a.* Inaccurate, not correct.
Jibejiba, *s.* The name of a fish; the chirping of a number of birds.
Jibi, *s.* A slap or blow with the open hand; the noise by which it is known the party has killed an enemy; a felling axe.
Jibi, *v.* To smite with the flat of the hand; to cut out as garments; to chip into shreds; to sing and shout on having killed one in war.
Jibijibi, *v.* To cut into shreds or pieces.
Jifa, *s.* The mother of pearl shell; a play.
Jifa, Jijifa, } *v.* To glide; to shoot along.
Jifatafata, *v.* To smite the breast.
Jifijifi, *s.* The name of a fish.
Jifijifiloufau, *s.* The name of a fish.
Jifijifinaivatu, *s.* The name of a fish.
Jifijifitalu, *s.* The name of a fish.
Jigejiga, *a.* Difficult, as travelling at noon day.
Jiji, *s.* A dress for working in, made from the leaves of the *Ji*.
Jiji, *v.* To charge, to command.
Jijijiga, Jijijijiga, } *a.* Noon day, vertical heat
Jijigi, *v.* To strike the back when puzzled.
Jijina, *v.* To strangle; to seize by the throat; to force open. See *Jina*.
Jijina, *s.* Strangling.
Jika, *s.* A play; the upper part of the head of the pig.
Jikaamaui, *s.* Columns of smoke.
Jikaki, *v.* To exhort.
Jikakoa, *v.* To *Jika* for property.
Jikava, *s.* A fish.
Jikavi, *s.* One kind of the *Talo*.
Jike, Jikejike, } *v.* To sit on the heels.
Jike, *s.* A shell fish.
Jikijiki, *s.* The name of one of the ropes in a Tonga canoe.
Jikiviu, *s.* A small bird.
Jiko, *s.* Excrescence.
Jikota, *s.* A bird, (the king fisher;) also, a particular kind of a war club.

Jila, *s.* The yards of a canoe; the sailyard.

Jilalalo, *s.* The lower sprit or yard in a canoe.

Jilatuu, *s.* The upper sprit or yard in a canoe.

Jili, *v.* To fish with a hand net; to break the teeth.

Jilii, Jilijili, } *v.* To break any thing hard.

Jilijili, *s.* Lights from canoes sailing in the night.

Jilikekina, *v.* To chase, to pursue.

Jilita, *s.* A large fishing net.

Jilita, *v.* To fish with the above.

Jiloba, *s.* One kind of the *Ji.*

Jikula, *s.* One kind of the *Ji.*

Jilojilo, *a.* Sharp pointed.

Jimu, Jimujimu, } *s.* Heavy blowing; almost a hurricane.

Jina, *s.* A long wedge for splitting up the *kava;* a wedge.

Jina, *v.* To wedge.

Jinamanu, *s.* A breeding animal.

Jini, *v.* To be satiated; thoroughly tired.

Jinifu, *s.* Polygamy, polygamist; the wives of a polygamist.

Jino, *s.* A body; the trunk of a tree; any substance; dimension.

Jino, *a.* Stout, corpulent, large.

Jitakafalu, Jitua, } *v.* To turn the back upon.

Jitega, *v.* To appear anxious.

Jiva, *v.* To be ashamed, as one disappointed of his expectation.

K

K, THE eleventh Letter in the Tonga Alphabet. Its sounds are those of *c* in *cart*, and *g* in *gang*.

Ka, Kae, } *con.* But, if, for.

Ka, Kae, } *ad.* Although, notwithstanding, nevertheless.

Ka, *v.* To treat the gods with contempt.

Ka, *v.* To hawk; to force phlegm from the throat.

√ Kaaga, *a.* Empty, shadowy, unsubstantial.

Kaea, *v.* To deride, to mock.

Kai, *s.* Food, victuals.

Kai, *v.* To eat; to corrode; to consume gradually; to bite.

Kaiaga, *s.* A place where food has been eaten; table; manger; the time and place for eating.

Kaibo, *v.* To eat in the sly.

Kaiboji, *v.* To take food without the knowledge of its owner.

Kaifiji, *v.* To eat from different places; to depend upon others for food.

Kaifonua, *s.* A name given to the working population.

Kaiga, *s.* A relative, friend, affinity, kinsman.

Kaiga, *part.* Related.

Kaihaa, *s.* A thief, theft; depredation.

Kaihaa, Kaihaaji, } *v.* To thieve; to steal.

Kaihaajia, *v.* To be stolen.

Kaikai, *v.* To eat, applied to animals.

Kaikaifiu, *v.* To eat after being satisfied; to over work.

Kaila, *s.* The war whoop.

Kaila, *v.* To shout. √

Kailakaia, *v.* To rush past one bait to swallow another.

Kailu, *v.* To eat the fragments of a meal.

Kaimalotafoa, *v.* To eat but with bruises and bad usage.

Kaimatuu, *s.* A disease of the eyes.

Kaina *a.* Peopled; occupied by persons from different places.

Kainaga, *s.* People, tribe.

Kainiloto, *s.* A disease in the nose and throat.

Kaitaunoaia, *v.* To catch fish where it was not expected.

Kaitama, *v.* To eat a child; to cast off or neglect one's own child.

Kaivao, *v.* To live in the bush.

Kaivale, *v.* To eat alone; to eat in the sly.

Kaoinima, *s.* The fingers.

Kaokao, *s.* The sides of a vessel or canoe.

Kaokaoleleva, *s.* The name of a shell fish.

Kaokaotakai, *v.* A canoe with sides bulged out.

Kaokaotuu, *a.* A canoe with sides straight up and down.

Kau, *pron.* I.

Kau, *s.* The stem or stalk; the handle.

Kau, *v.* To interfere; to intermeddle; concern; to countenance.

Kau, *a.* Numeral seventy.

Kau, The sign of the plural, applying generally to rational beings.

Kaua, *s.* A boundary fence, generally of trees.

Kauala, *s.* A bier; a hand barrow.

Kauala, *v.* To carry on a bier.

Kauamotua, *s.* Land mark; a boundary fence.

Kauila, *v.* To fasten the sail to the yards.

Kauila, *s.* The mere remnant of a sail.

Kauimaea, *v.* To beat or flog with a rope.

Kauimaea, *s.* A short length of rope; a flogging with a rope.

Kauitalanoa, } *v.* To interfere,
Kauivaaga, } to meddle; to speak in what one is not at all concerned.

Kauga, *s.* Fellow, associate.

Kaugaabi, *s.* Neighbour; one of the same place.

Kaugagaue, } *s.* Workmen, fel-
Kaugaue, } low workmen.

Kaugamalie, *a.* Proportioned, suitable, easy.

Kaugamea, *s.* A company, a gang, accomplice.

Kaugatamaki, *a.* Disproportioned, difficult, unequal.

Kaugoue, *s.* Gardeners.

Kauhaki, *v.* To persevere.

Kauhilaua, *v.* To hold with two contending parties, a friend to neither.

Kauhiva, *s.* Singers.

Kaukau, *s.* A bath, a wash; a cutting in the male parts of generation.

Kaukau, *v.* To wash, to bathe; to preform the above operation.

Kaukaua, *a.* Athletic, strong, robust.

Kaukauola, *v.* To depend upon; to trust to as one generally useful.

Kaukauhaki, *v.* To persevere; to act determinately.

Kaukauloa, } *v.* To allow a vessel
Kauloa, } to go a head when tacking or bringing up.

Kaulalo, *s.* The lower yards of a canoe.

Kauloa, *a.* Unkind; unhealthy, as fruit that falls ere it is ripe or good.

Kaulotu, *s.* Worshippers, church.

Kaumea, *s.* A companion, an associate, a crony, a familiar.

Kaumele, *s.* One kind of yam.

Kaunaga, *s.* A female servant, handmaid.

Kaunaka, *s.* The handle of a net.

Kaunatu, *s.* A small stick rubbed on another to get fire.
Kaunoa, *s.* Officiousness, a meddler.
Kaunoa, *v.* To busy or meddle in other's concerns.
Kaunoa, *a.* Officious.
Kauta, *s.* A circular timber in a Tonga house; drumsticks.
Kautoutai, *s.* Fishermen, sailors.
Kautuu, *s.* The upper yard of a canoe.
Kauvae, *s.* The legs and feet.
Kauvaka, *s.* The crew of a vessel.
Kauvalu, *s.* One kind of the *Ji.*
Kaba, *s.* The corners and edges of any thing; a siege.
Kaba, Kabaji, } *v.* To besiege; to storm a fort; to flap the wings; to try to crawl as a child.
Kabau, *con.* If.
Kababo, *s.* A fish.
Kabafoli, *v.* To environ, to surround, to besiege.
Kabajia, *v.* To be stormed, taken, besieged.
Kabakau, *s.* Wings.
Kabakauhigano, *s.* A fish.
Kabakaba, *s.* The side fins of sharks.
Kabakaba, *v.* To flicker; to flutter; to hover on the wing.
Kabalu, *v.* To flop, to flap; to move with such a noise.
Kabatalifaki, *v.* To fly and wait near one place for the approach of fish.
Kabatoka, *v.* To begin to fly, as chickens.
Kabavale, *v.* To take what is near but belonging to another.
Kabe, *s.* A plant whose root is eaten.
Kabeuea, *s.* A plant whose root is eaten.
Kabe, Kabekabe, } *s.* Abuse, swearing.

Kabe, Kabea, Kabei, Kabekabe, } *s.* To swear; to abuse with bad language.
Kabekabe, *v.* To deepen the trenches of a fort by a second digging.
Kabea, *v.* To be sworn at.
Kabei, *v.* To pluck, to force; to take out.
Kabekabeteetuli, *v.* To pick any thing out of the ear.
Kabetefua, *v.* To lift up and throw down suddenly.
Kabetuu, *v.* To renew the *kafa* lashings of a canoe without taking the canoe to pieces.
Kabikabi, *s.* A wedge.
Kabikabi, *v.* To wedge; to fasten with a wedge.
Kabo, *s.* A self taught artisan.
Kaboga, *s.* The back fin of large fish.
Kabogatata, *s.* The water as scooped or thrown out of the canoe.
Kabokabo, *v.* To empty; to throw out all the water from the canoe hold.
Kabu, *s.* The banana leaf so formed as to hold water.
Kabui, *v.* To encircle, to surround, to wrap up.
Kabui, *s.* A wrapper, a native dress.
Kabuji, *v.* To banish, to exile, to eject.
Kabuji, *s.* Ejection, banishment.
Kafa, *s.* The cordage made from the fibres of the cocoa nut husk.
Kafai, *v.* To bind, to wrap with *kafa.*
Kafakafa, *s.* A fish.
Kafaga, *s.* A kind of strops for keeping the feet together in climbing.
Kafakafai, *v.* To make nets of *kafa* round any thing fragile.

136

Kafakala, *s.* One kind of cocoa nut.

Kafaki, *v.* To climb, to ascend; to grow, to increase.

Kafo, *s.* Wound.

Kafo, *v.* To wound.

Kafokafotamaki, *s.* Any thing barbed or very sharp that causes severe wounds in the body.

Kafu, Kafukafu, } *s.* The inner skin of seeds; a coverlet; any thing with which one covers himself to sleep.

Kafu, *v.* To cover; to wrap one in to sleep.

Kaha, *s.* The overmatched or unsuccessful in a game.

Kahi, *v.* To make a scratching noise.

Kahi, *s.* A disease common to the glands of the neck; the name of a shell fish.

Kahia, *v.* To be afflicted with the *Kahi.*

Kahikahi, *s.* The name of a fish.

Kahivae, *s.* A shrub.

Kaho, *s.* The reed; an arrow; the ribs or lines in any work.

Kahoa, *s.* A necklace; any thing round the neck.

Kahoa, *v.* To tie or hang round the neck.

Kahokaho, *s.* One kind of yam.

Kajia, *v.* To choke, to hinder, to obstruct, as weeds in a garden.

Kajigu, *s.* A motion of the arm and mouth understood as a challenge.

Kaka, *s.* A thin membraneous substance found round the young cocoa nut.

Kaka, *v.* To climb.

Kaka, *v.* To hawk; to force up from the throat.

Kaka, *s.* The name of a beautiful bird known only at *Eua.*

Kaka, *a.* Dry, barren, without moisture.

Kaka, *s.* Deceit, perfidy, imposition, delusion, treachery.

Kaka, *a.* Deceitful, perfidious, fallacious.

Kaka, *v.* To deceive, to cheat; to fob.

Kakae, *s.* Mockery, derision.

Kakae, *v.* To mock, to deride.

Kakai, *v.* To be deceived.

Kakai, *s.* People, population.

Kakai, *a.* Populous.

Kakaia, *a.* See *Kaina.*

Kakao, *s.* The legs of the crawling shell fish.

Kakao, *v.* To bore or thrust with the finger.

Kakau, *v.* To swim.

Kakau, *s.* The handle of any tool.

Kakaba, *v.* To reach out, to extend the arm to reach.

Kakabe, *v.* To raise as by a lever.

Kakabu, *s.* Mist, fog.

Kakabu, *a.* Misty, foggy.

Kakafa, *a.* Large, growing, applied to animals.

Kakaaga, *s.* A ladder; a frame for plants to creep along.

Kakafaga, *s.* The name of a tree.

Kakaha, *a.* Hot, fiery, painful.

Kakahi, *v.* To scratch.

Kakala, *s.* Any and every sweet flower; a wreath; a garland.

Kakala, *a.* Odoriferous; sweet of scent; sharp, pungent to the taste.

Kakale, *v.* To run to and fro; to run swiftly.

Kakali, *v.* To tighten; to brace up.

Kakali, *s.* The stick used in tightening ropes.

Kakalu, *s.* The cricket.

Kakama, *v.* To bustle; to drive about.

Kakamika, *s.* A herb.
Kakamo, *v.* To beckon; to give the wink.
Kakano, *s.* The kernel; the flesh; the heart or inside of any thing.
Kakata, *v.* To laugh, applied to several.
Kakato, *a.* Complete, perfect, made up.
Kakato, *s.* Fullness; the state of being perfect.
Kakava, *s.* Perspiration, sweat.
Kakava, Kakavaia, } *v.* To sweat.
Kakave, *v.* To lead out; to extend; to widen out
Kakei, *s.* The outer leaf of any thing wrapped in leaves.
Kala, *v.* To breathe and move as one dying; to die hardly.
Kalae, *s.* The name of a bird.
Kalaga, *s.* Shout, exclamation.
Kalaga, *v.* To shout, to exclaim.
Kalagaaki Kalagaekina, } *v.* To be shouted; to be proclaimed.
Kalaka, *s.* The name of a tree and its fruit.
Kalakala, Kalakalaia, } *v.* To smart.
Kalali, *v.* To scratch, to noise.
Kakalu, *s.* An insect.
Kakalu, *v.* To make a flopping noise; to crackle as dry papers.
Kalamihi, *s.* A shell fish.
Kalamu, *v.* To buzz along, as a stone from a sling.
Kalanui, *s.* Green or blue beads.
Kalava, *s.* A blood vessel; vein; the rib or stem of the cocoa nut leaf.
Kale, *v.* To run fast.
Kaleaga, *v.* To chase the fish called *Atu.*
Kaleui, *v.* To cut off; to thwart, as one hearing the complaints of another immediately gives a contrary order.
Kalekaleaki, *v.* To persevere in opposition to the views of others.
Kaleva, *s.* The name of a bird.
Kaleveleve, *s.* A large spider.
Kali, *s.* A Tonga pillow.
Kalia, *s.* The double canoe.
Kalifu, *v.* To run, to speed.
Kalihelihe, *s.* A lizard.
Kalihi, *s.* The limbs (a low term.)
Kalikau, *a.* See *Kaukaua.*
Kalo, *v.* To move the head; to avoid danger; to get out of the way of intruders.
Kaloaa, *s.* The name of a shell fish.
Kaloi, *v.* To shake the hair of the head.
Kalou, *v.* To bark, to yelp, to vociferate.
Kalofaga, *s.* A hiding place; a shelter from the storm.
Kalofi, See *Kalo.*
Kalofiama, *s.* A spark of fire.
Kalokalo, *v.* To shake the head.
Kalokalofaki, *v.* To be careful.
Kalokalotamaki, *v.* To turn about in anger.
Kalu, *v.* To cut or clean off all excrescence and dirt; to clear off the skin.
Kalu, Kalukalu, } *s.* The inside skin, next the flesh or substance.
Kalu, *v.* To be skinned over or clogged, as the throat.
Kama, *s.* A disease of the skin; eruption on the *Hiabo.*
Kama, *a.* Diseased with the *Kama.*
Kamakama, *s.* A shell fish.
Kamata, *v.* To begin; to taste.
Kamata, *s.* The tasting of any food.
Kamataaga, *s.* The beginning; the place or time of beginning any work.
Kamataga, *s.* The cause, the origin.

138

Kamakama, *a.* See *Kakama.*

Kamakamata, *v.* To begin; to appear; to be in sight.

Kami, *v.* To love, to be enamoured, used only of the fair sex.

Kamo, Kamoji, Kamokamo, } *v.* To beckon; to make signs; to give the wink.

Kamu, Kamukamu, } *v.* To cut off any thing round.

Kamunaga, *s.* A present taken by the party presenting.

Kana, *s.* A soft stone on the sea shore used for rubbing canoes.

Kanai, *v.* To rub; to clean off with the *Kana.*

Kanaefai, *ad.* To be sure, certainly, what else.

Kanaga, *s.* A cant word or saying; a proverbial expression.

Kanagataa, *a.* Incurable; difficult to heal.

Kanahe, *s.* The name of a fish.

Kanikani, *v.* To break, to spoil, to disfigure, to deface.

Kanikita, *s.* A kind of sand stone.

Kano, *s.* An abbreviation of *Kakano,* used generally in reference to the quality of the article, as *Kano kovi, Kano lelei.*

Kanoalaalava, *a.* Cross; varied in the grain.

Kanoimata, *s.* The ball of the eye.

Kanoimatauli, *s.* The pupil of the eye.

Kanofafau, *a.* Tough, ropy, applied to the flesh of animals.

Kanofihifihi, *a.* Cross; varied in the grain.

Kanogataa, *a.* Unripe, hard, ropy, applied to the bread fruit.

Kanogofua, *a.* Ripe, good, applied to the bread fruit.

Kanokano, *a.* Fat.

Kanokano, *s.* A tenor voice.

Kanokanomia, *v.* To pierce to the quick.

Kanokato, *s.* A treasure; something of first rate value.

Kanomate, *s.* The lean of flesh.

Kanotoutou, *a.* Tender, soft.

Kase, *a.* Weak.

Kasila, *v.* To sail close upon the wind.

Kata, *v.* To laugh.

Kata, *s.* A laugh; a war club; the branch of the *kava;* the pieces of the *kava* branch cut for setting.

Kataina, *v.* To be laughed at.

Kataukuma, *v.* To laugh under restraint.

Katabubunu, *v.* To laugh with the mouth closed.

Katafakamoala, *s.* A hoarse laugh.

Katakata, *v.* To smile, to laugh.

Katakataita, Katakataanifotea, } *v.* To smile or laugh though angry.

Katakatatagi, *v,* To laugh when inclined to cry.

Kataki, *s.* Patience, endurance.

Kataki, *v.* To bear, to endure.

Kataki, *a.* Patient.

Kataki, *v.* To eat the kernel of the old nut as a substitute for animal food.

Katakiofa, Katakiukuma, } *a.* Long suffering.

Katakoho, *a.* Full of wounds and putrefying sores.

Katea, *s.* The windward and largest part in a double canoe.

Kato, *s.* A basket, a packet.

Katoa, *s.* The whole, the mass.

Katoa, *v.* To assemble, to collect, to be assembled.

Katoa, *a.* Complete, full, entire.

Katoaga, *s.* A feast, banquet.

Katoaga, *v.* To feast, to banquet.

Katoato, *s.* The moon when it sets a little before break of day.

Katoi, *v.* To take full hold with the hand; to clutch or grasp.
Katotuki, *s.* A basket used in the practice of sorcery
Katuba, *s.* An opening, as a window or door.
Kava, *s.* A root; a beverage; any spirituous liquor; the beard.
Kavahaha, *s.* A shrub.
Kavahuhu, *s.* A shrub.
Kavakavaulie, *s.* A shrub.
Kavalaganoa, *v.* To drink *kava* out of time and order.
Kavatagi, *s.* The *kava* drunk immedately upon the death of a person.
Kave, *s.* The tails of the *Feke* or cat fish; the stem or stalk of fruit.
Kavea, *v.* To be drawn towards; to incline towards; to take.
Kaveaki, *v.* To persist; to persevere in.
Kavei, *s.* The hangers of baskets, pots, &c.
Kavei, *v.* To contract; to draw up.
Kaveituu, *a.* Intricate, entangled.
Kavefagota, *s.* The long tail of the *Feke*, used in collecting all within its reach.
Kavega, *s.* A burden.
Kavega, *s.* Visitor.
Kavekave, *v.* To swing to and fro; to spread abroad; to persevere.
Kavekavehoko, *v.* To act with punctuality; to do in accordance with any arrangement.
Ke, Sign of the imperative mood, *ke alu koe*, do thou go.
Ke, *s.* A quarrel, strife, dissension.
Ke, *v.* To quarrel.
Ke, *pron.* Thou.
Kea, *s.* One kind of bread fruit tree and its fruit.
Keatega, *s.* One kind of bread fruit tree and its fruit.
Keatala, *s.* One kind of bread fruit tree and its fruit.
Keamaamaa, *s.* One kind of bread fruit tree and its fruit.
Keatolo, *s.* Whitlow, hard swelling, tumour.
Kei, *ad.* Yet, whilst, during.
Keigo, *a.* Sulky, angry.
Keikeinaga, *s.* Fragments, remnants.
Keina, *v.* To eat, to be eaten; to be bitten.
Keinaga, *v.* To eat.
Keinagaaga, *s.* A place where food is eaten.
Keituai, *ad.* After a while, by and by.
Keu, *s.* A kind of yam.
Keu, *pron.* I.
Keui *v.* To ward off.
Keukeu, *s.* The toes.
Kebejiko, *s.* The name of a fish.
Kebi, Kebikebi, *v.* To tighten the dress.
Kefu, Kefukefu, *a.* Yellow, yellowish, applied to the hair; indistinct to vision.
Kefukefu, *s.* A kind of grass.
Keha, *a.* Yellow, applied to mats.
Kehe, *a.* Another; not the same; different; out of the common way.
Kehekehe, *a.* Different, mixed; all sorts and sizes.
Kehega, *a.* Similar to *Kehe.*
Kehe, Kehekehe, *s.* The convulsions preceeding death.
Keke, *v.* To bleat or cry.
Kekeu, *v.* To ward off in every direction.
Kekeho, *s.* The name of a shell fish.
Kekelo, *a.* Brown, brownish.
Kekena, *a.* Dry, withered, blighted.
Kekenu, *v.* To hoe; to cut off weeds just grown.

Kekete, *v.* To chatter, to prate, to chirp.
Kekeva, *a.* Stiff, unbending.
Kekeva, *s.* Stiffness, inflexibility.
Kele, *a.* Muddy.
Kelea, *s.* A large shell fish.
Kelebulu, *s.* Slime, mire.
Kelekele, *s.* Earth, mould, soil, dirt.
Kelekelea, } *a.* Earthy, dirty,
Kelekeleia, } miry.
Kelekeleua, *a.* Sandy; sand and soil together.
Kelemutu, *s.* A worm, grub.
Kelevai, *v.* To make water muddy.
Keli, *v.* To dig, to sink.
Keli, *s.* A dike, a trench, a ditch.
Kelikeli, *v.* To dig holes.
Kelikeliaki, *v.* To persevere; to persist in any design.
Kelitoke, *s.* The name of a shell fish.
Kelituuga, *v.* To take a stand; to resolve.
Kelo, } *a.* Brown in colour.
Kelokelo, }
Kema, *s.* The shell of the *Tokanoa.*
Kemo, *s.* The eyebrow; the wink of the eye.
Kemo, } *v.* To wink re-
Kemokemo, } peatedly.
Kena, } *a.* See *Kekena.*
Kenekena, }
Kenu, *s.* The motion of one dying.
Kete, *s.* The belly.
Ketekete, *a.* Fat, corpulent.
Ketekete, *v.* To chirp.
Keteva, *s.* A shell fish.
Ketoketo, *s.* A single spot or place of ground.
Ketu, *s.* The name of a fish.
Ketu, *v.* To hobble, to limp.
Ketu, *a.* Lame, hobbling.
Keviki, *s.* A shell fish.
Ki, *prep.* To, towards, in, at, among, against, opposite, about, concerning, for, (used before nouns common and names of places.)
Ki, *v.* To squeak.
Ki, *a.* Vain, proud; wishing to be noticed; impudent, bold.
Kia, *s.* The neck.
Kia, *prep.* To, towards, in at, among, against, opposite, about concerning, for, (used before proper names of persons.)
Kiaivae, *s.* The hollow of the leg, under the knee.
Kiate, *prep.* See *Kia,* (used before pronouns.)
Kiato, *s.* Sticks extending from the canoe to which the outrigger is fastened.
Kiatolo, *s.* See *Keatolo.*
Kie, *s.* A mat.
Kie, *v.* To make a plaintive noise.
Kiekiaua, *a.* Double throated, double tongued.
Kio, } *s.* The chirping of
Kiokio, } chicken.
Kiokio, *s.* The name of a fish.
Kiu, *s.* The name of a bird.
Kiu, *v.* To run.
Kifa, *v.* To lose in a game.
Kife, *ad.* Where?
Kifu, } *v.* To run.
Kifukifu, }
Kihi, *a.* Stunted, ill thriven.
Kihii, *a.* Small; insignificant.
Kihikihi *s.* A kind of grass; the flaps of the turtle.
Kiji, *s.* A boyish play.
Kijikijivai, *s.* An insect similar to the horse fly.
Kiki, *v.* To squeak.
Kiki, *s.* Chickens.
Kiki, *s.* Used of any thing eaten with vegetables, or in addition to ordinary food.
Kikiia, *a.* Satisfied, satiated.
Kikiu, *v.* Small bodied, thin.
Kikiuha, *s.* The squeaking noise of a bird on the approach of rain.

Kikihi, *v.* To dispute, to contend, to contest.
Kikila, *a.* Shining, dazzling.
Kikila, *v.* To shine, to glare.
Kikilo, *v.* To look from side to side.
Kikite, *s.* Divination, prophecy.
Kikite, *v.* To divine, to foretell, to augur, to prophesy.
Kikivi, *v.* To strain as in heaving heavy weights.
Kila, *a.* Shaven in one place only.
Kilekila, *a.* Shaven in patches; hoed in patches.
Kili, *s.* The skin; the bark of trees; a saw; leprosy; a file.
Kilia, *s.* A leper.
Kilia, *a.* Leprous.
Kiliata, *a.* Light in the skin.
Kiliui, *a.* Dark in the skin.
Kilifetohoaki, *s.* A cross saw.
Kiligano, *s.* Hard spots in the flesh causing intolerable itching.
Kiliji, *v.* To saw.
Kilijitahi, *s.* The bottom of the sea.
Kilikili, *s.* Small stones placed on the grave of the dead; the look or appearance; likelihood.
Kilikilia, *s.* The name of a fish; leprous.
Kilikiliua, *a.* Double barked, as certain trees.
Kilo, *v.* To look askaunt.
Kilokilo, *v.* See *Kikilo*.
Kilokiloua, *v.* To look in different directious at the same time.
Kilokiloua, *a.* Undecided.
Kilu, *a.* One hundred thousand.
Kilu, *s.* Used of large and successive waves rolling at sea.
Kilukilua, *v.* To appear at an immense distance.
Kima, *v.* To lose in a game; to be over matched.
Kimo, *s.* The glare of the sun as seen in very hot weather.

Kimokimo, *a.* Quick, fast, applied to running.
Kina, *a.* Tired, wearied.
Kinaabi, *v.* To be tired of the governor of the *Abi*.
Kinatoa, *v.* To be tired out.
Kinehia, *v.* To be tired; to be in fear of some coming trouble.
Kinekina, *v.* To be thoroughly tired.
Kini, *v.* To strike; to cut the hair short; to let blood.
Kiniji, *s.* A blow.
Kiniji, *v.* To strike with any thing light.
Kinohaa, *s.* Dung.
Kinokinoifia, *a.* Free from obstructions, clear.
Kisa, *v.* To hiss.
Kita, *pron.* I, myself.
Kita, *s.* Tetanus; a relapse; one kind of cocoa nut.
Kita, *v.* To suffer a relapse.
Kitaki, *v.* To persevere; to hold out.
Kite, *v.* To appear; to see at a distance when at sea.
Kitegamahaki, *s.* A place where sick persons are.
Kititama, *s.* A girl when married to her cousin.
Kivi, *a.* Sunk, applied to the eyes; blind.
Kivi, *s.* One kind of yam.
Kivikivi, *s.* The name of a shell fish.
Ko, A prefix, used before the proper names of persons and places, and in answer to the interrogative, who.
Ko, *s.* The name of a bird.
Ko, *s.* The croaking noise of a diseased fowl.
Koa, *s.* Foam, spume, froth, soap.
Koa, *v.* To foam, to froth.
Koaia, *a.* Foamy, frothy.
Koaga, *s.* The name of a fish.
Koe, *art.* The.

142

Koe, *pron.* Thee.
Koeuhi, *con.* Because, for.
Koeumaa, *ad.* Why so? for what purpose?
Koeha, *pron.* What? always used interrogatively.
Koena, *pron.* That.
Koeni, *pron.* This.
Koia, *pron.* That.
Koia, *con.* Therefore.
Koia, *ad.* Just so; that is it.
Kou, *a.* Uncircumcised.
Kouahe, *s.* The cheek.
Kouhaga, *s.* The groin; the inside of the thigh.
Koukouji, *s.* The name of a fish.
Kouna, *v.* To order, to command.
Koba, *s.* One kind of hair on the head.
Koboa, *s.* The name of a fish.
Kofaa, Kofaia, } *ad.* Where?
Kofe, *ad.* Which? where?
Kofe, *s.* The bamboo cane.
Kofe, *v.* To blow fair (the wind.)
Kofia, *v.* To bark, to scold.
Kofu, *s.* A garment, a covering.
Kofu, Kofua, } *v.* To clothe, to dress, to wrap up.
Kofu, *a.* Clothed.
Kofuua, *s.* The kidneys.
Kofutu, Kofutufutuga, } *s.* A short time, but always used ironically.
Koga, *s.* A piece, a plot, a joint, a fragment.
Koga, *v.* To squeal; to make a squealing noise.
Kogakau, *s.* A regiment of warriors.
Kohai, *pron.* Who?
Kohi, *s.* A scratching noise; a scratch.
Kohi, Kohikohi, } *v.* To scratch, to claw.
Koho, *a.* Scrofulous, rotten.
Kohu, *s.* Smoke.
Kohu, Kohukohu, } *v.* To smoke, to vociferate.
Koji, Kojikoji, } *v.* To cut with scissors.
Koka, *s.* The name of a tree; the juice of its bark used in painting the *gatu*.
Kokaaga, *s.* A roll of *gatu*.
Kokaaga, Kokagatu, } *v.* To make the *gatu*.
Koko, *s.* The squeaking noise of pigs and fowls.
Koko, *s.* A bend, an elbow; an inlet; the lower part of the neck of the fowl.
Koko, *v.* To squeeze, to press; to break in the hands; to get fire wood.
Kokoa, *v.* To lather, to foam.
Kokoba, *v.* To pull and haul till exhausted.
Kokofe, *v.* To make a loud drawling noise.
Kokohi, *v.* To scratch, to tear.
Kokohu, *v.* To send up smoke.
Kokoji, *v.* To make a biting chipping noise, as a rat eating.
Kokokoka, *s.* An imaginary evil or curse arising from bringing the *koka* into the house.
Kokolo, *s.* A continuous rumbling noise.
Kokolo, *v.* To make a rumbling noise.
Kokomi, *v.* To press; to squeeze between the hands.
Kokomo, *v.* To suck; to draw in with the mouth.
Kokono, *v.* To strain.
Kole, *s.* Petition, entreaty, solicitation, prayer.
Kole, *v.* To beg, to solicit.
Kolega, *v.* To entreat.
Kolekole, *v.* To entreat, to importune.
Koletaumau, *v.* To beg importunately; to supplicate.
Koletaumau, *s.* Importunity, supplication.

143

Koli, *s.* A taking fish with small hand nets; the name of a tree.
Kolili, *s.* The name of a bird.
Kolitalaaho, *v.* To fail to do in the night work appointed in the day.
Kolitoto, *s.* A tree.
Kolivai, *s.* A tree.
Kolo, *s.* The native cloth hung round a house in which a deceased person lies.
Kolo, *s.* A fortress; a bludgeon.
Kolo, *v.* To desire; to keep a look out.
Koloa, *s.* Wealth, riches, affluence.
Koloa, } *a.* Rich, wealthy.
Koloaia, }
Kolokolo, *s.* The running bubbling noise of water.
Kolokolo, *v.* To bubble, to boil.
Kolola, } *s.* A rustling noise.
Kolokolola, }
Koloto, *int.* What is to be done! how can it be helped!
Kolu, *v.* To strut with a large dress of *gatu*.
Kolu, *s.* A club split or broken in war.
Kolukalu, *s.* A substance from the sea resembling blubber.
Komaa, *ad.* Where?
Komaki, *s.* A bay; a rivulet from the sea.
Komikomi, *v.* To beat or press down as any thing bulging.
Komo, *v.* See *Kokomo*.
Komokomo, *v.* To chew any thing as a *Kiki* or relish to some other food.
Kona, *a.* Drunk, intoxicated, poisoned.
Kona, *s.* Bitterness; the lower part of the abdomen; the front of a native dress.
Kona, *a.* Bitter.
Konahia, *v.* To be poisoned or intoxicated.
Koni, *v.* To hobble, to limp.
Konohi, *v.* To strain at.
Konokona, *a.* Bitterish; inclined to bitter.
Konokonohia, *s.* The working and leaking of a vessel over freighted.
Konokono, } *a.* Bitter, sour, applied to the mind.
Konokonoloto, }
Konokonoloto, *v.* To cherish bitterness in the mind.
Koso, *s.* The nose or round end in the double canoe; a surgical operation.
Koso, *v.* To cut; to perform the above operation.
Kote, } *v.* To speak a foreign tongue.
Kotekote, }
Koto, *v.* To crop; to shorten shrubs.
Koto, *s.* A basket filled with any thing.
Kotoa, *s.* The whole mass.
Kotoa, } *a.* All, every one.
Kotoabe, }
Kotofa, *v.* To appoint, to affix.
Kotoko, *s.* The crowing noise of a fowl.
Kotokotomala, *s.* Any thing that will cause the death of a person.
Kotone, *s.* The name of a tree.
Kova, *s.* A patch of hair on the back of the head.
Kovi, *s.* Badness, corruption, fault, vice.
Kovi, } *a.* Bad, faulty, evil.
Kovia, }
Ku, *s.* The stump of the little finger.
Ku, *v.* To stink.
Kua, *a.* Foolish.
Kui, *s.* Grand parents; blindness; the name of a fish.
Kui, *a.* Blind.
Kuikui, *s.* Small eyed.
Kuikui, *s.* The name of a shell fish.

144

Kuo, The sign of the past tense, as, *Kuo alu ia*, he is gone.
Kuoga, *s.* A season, a time, an era.
Kuoloa, *ad.* Heretofore, long ago.
Kubeji, *s.* The article used for imprinting native cloth.
Kubega, *s.* A fishing net.
Kubega, *v.* To fish with a net.
Kubu, *s.* A saying, a speech; a joint.
Kubui, *s.* A sentence, a joint.
Kubukubu, *s.* Joints, logs, lengths.
Kufaho, *s.* A tree.
Kuhu, } *v.* To sniff; to
Kuhukuhu, } blow through the nose.
Kuka, *s.* The name of a shell fish.
Kuku, *v.* To clench the fist; to hold fast in the hand.
Kuku, *s.* The name of a shell fish.
Kukuuli, *s.* The name of a shell fish.
Kukukuku, *s.* The name of a shell fish.
Kukukuku, *v.* To hold and carry in the hand.
Kukutagata, *s.* A shell fish.
Kula, *s.* Beads; the name of a bird.
Kula, *a.* Red.
Kulabo, *s.* The name of a fish.
Kuli, *s.* A dog; the rail to which the large ropes of the canoe are fastened; a log of wood on which the mast rests when laid down.
Kulikuli, *s.* The smell of pork.
Kulo, *s.* A pot; any kind of pot.
Kulokula, *s.* Redness.
Kulokula, *a.* Red colour.
Kulokolo, *a.* Scooped or hollowed out.
Kulu, *s.* The name of a tree.
Kuluba, *s.* An insect.
Kulufau, *s.* A fish.
Kulufoia, *v.* To be overcome by bad smells, as of any putrid matter.
Kuluki, *v.* To press upon; to bear down the body.
Kulukia, *s.* A strain; a hurt from carrying heavy weight.
Kulukia, *v.* To strain, to wrench.
Kulukona, *s.* The name of a tree.
Kulukulu, *s.* A small kind of dove.
Kuma, *s.* The rat.
Kumala, *s.* The sweet potatoe.
Kumi, } *v.* To seek, to look
Kumikumi, } for, to investigate.
Kumikumia, *s.* A fish.
Kumuni, *v.* To hoard; to collect together.
Kumukumu, *s.* The chin; a mossy kind of substance.
Kuta, *v.* To writhe; to work as in pain.
Kutu, *s.* The louse; a shrub.
Kutua, *a.* Lousy.
Kutufiji, *s.* The flea.

L

L, THE twelfth Letter in the Tonga Alpabet. Its sound is that of *l* in *lard*.
La, *s.* A sail; the mat of which sails are made.
Laa, *s.* The sun; drought; dry weather.
Laa, *a.* Hot; intense heat from the sun.
Laaina, *a.* Sunburnt.
Laaina, *v.* To dry any thing in the sun.
Laalaa, *a.* Droughty; wanting rain.

145

Lae, *s.* The forehead, the brow.
Laea, *v.* To be ashamed, to feel confused.
Lai, *s.* The name of a fish.
Laiki, *v.* To break up; to destroy.
Laikia, *v.* To be broken to pieces.
Lailai, *a.* Soft, not hard.
Lailai, *v.* To be broken up; to be bruised.
Laofie, *a.* Dry, not raining.
Laolao, *a.* Smooth, not rough, applied to the sea; compact, closed up, applied to a canoe when the body of it is finished.
Lau, *v.* To talk, to converse; to account, to esteem; to count, to number; to read, to peruse.
Lau, } **Lalau**, } *v.* To pinch with the fingers.
Lau, *s.* A leaf, leaves; a pinch; talk; familiar discourse; perusal, the act of counting; number.
Lau, *a.* Talkative, loquacious.
Laua, *v.* To be the subject of talk; to be counted or numbered.
Lauaitu, *v.* To cry; to weep and make lamentation.
Laui, *v.* To talk of or about.
Lauikovi, *s.* Evil speaking, backbiting.
Lauikovi, *v.* To speak evil of one.
Lauikuoga, *a.* Everlasting.
Lauulu, *v.* To count or choose at random.
Laubala, *v.* To talk over old news.
Laubisi, *s.* Nonsense, useless talk.
Laubisi, *v.* To talk trash.
Laufale, *s.* A shrub.
Laufola, *s.* A dance.
Laufola, *v.* To spread out; to spread abroad what was secret.
Lauga, *s.* Complaint, murmuring.
Lauga, *v.* To murmur, to complain.
Lauga, *a.* Complaining, murmuring.
Lauga, *v.* To speak of or compare with another.
Lauji, *s.* One kind of yam.
Lauji, *v.* To pinch, to be pinched.
Laujii, *s.* Narrowness.
Laujii, *a.* Narrow, strait.
Laukau, *s.* Pride, vanity.
Laukau, *a.* Proud, vain.
Laukakai, *s.* That portion of food divided out for the god.
Laukoka, *s.* One kind of yam.
Laulau, } **Laulaui**, } *v.* To speak filthily of another; to square logs of wood; to harangue at a dance.
Laulau, *s.* A present or offering to a god, hence *Feilaulau.*
Laulau, *s.* A part of a Tonga fish hook made from the mother of pearl.
Laulau, *s.* An adress or harangue at a native dance.
Laulauakau, *v.* To smooth off boards in the Tonga style.
Laulauatea, *s.* A sand bank under water.
Laulauatea, *a.* Light, as the surface where there is a sand bank.
Laulauloto, *v.* To meditate; to deliberate.
Laulahi, *s.* Breadth, width.
Laulahi, *a.* Broad, wide.
Laulahiga, *s.* The extreme breadth; widest part.
Lauloto, *v.* To sing bass; to meditate.
Lauloto, *s.* Meditation.
Laumalie, *s.* Spirit, soul, life.
Laumalie, *a.* Alive and well, applied to chiefs.
Laumalila, *s.* A flower.
Laumata, *s.* The eyelids.
Laumea, *s.* Gills of fish.

Launoa, *s.* Nonsense, useless talk.

Launoa, *v.* To talk nonsense.

Lauta, *a.* Uniform; one in appearance though many in number.

Lautamaki, *s.* Wrath, indignation.

Lautefuhi, *s.* One hundred stripes of native cloth.

Lautoki, *v.* To relate all the particulars of any case; to disclose fully.

Lauvao, *s.* The *Ji* leaves, and the *Jiji* dress when made of the leaves.

Lauvale, *a.* Countless, inumerable.

Lauvale, *s.* Populace; the poor or working population.

Laba, *s.* Assassination, murder.

Laba, *v.* To scold; to burst suddenly upon one; to arrest unexpectedly.

Labahala, *v.* To wrap the fish in leaves after broiling, generally done before.

Labaji, Labajia, } *v.* To assassinate.

Labalaba, *a.* Square in the sides.

Labakalae, *a.* Angry, peevish.

Labavale, *s.* A mistake; a slip of the tongue.

Labavale, *v.* To blunder in speaking.

Labe, Labea, Labelabe, } *v.* To bless; to render prosperous.

Labo, *v.* To hollow out, to make hollow.

Labo, *a.* Hollow, as a gouge.

Labota, *a.* Full, bulged. See *Agina.*

Labu, *s.* Flattery, adulation, cant.

Labu, Labulabu, } *v.* To cant, to flatter.

Lafa, *s.* Ringworm, tetter.

Lafalafa, *a.* Flat, broad.

Lafi, Lafilafi, } *v.* To hide; to get into a corner.

Lafo, *s.* A game; a throw of the net.

Lafo, Lafolafo, } *v.* To throw, to pitch; to cast the net.

Lafokie, *s.* The practice of throwing good mats into the tombs of chiefs when buried.

Lafokoa, *v.* To gamble; to pitch for treasure.

Lafua, Lafulafu, } *a.* Poor, old, impoverished.

Laga, *s.* Pain; the act of turning up the soil; erection.

Laga, *v.* To pain; to be in pain; to raise up the soil; to build; to erect; to originate; to set in motion.

Laga, *s.* The pain of childbirth.

Laga, *v.* To be in labour.

Lagajino, *v.* To be plaiting or weaving the middle of a mat or the inner one of a double basket.

Lagakali, *s.* The name of a tree.

Lagalaga, Lagalagaki, } *v.* To originate; to set on foot.

Lagi, *s.* The sky; the heads of the *Tuitoga* and *Tamaha;* the burying places of the same persons.

Lagilagi, *a.* Powerful, great, applied to chiefs.

Lago, *s.* The common fly; blocks of wood on which any thing is raised.

Lago, *v.* To raise by logs or pieces of wood.

Lagoia, *v.* To be covered with flies.

Lagolago, *v.* To raise on to something else; to take part with one against another.

Lagomakii, Lagomekina, } *v.* To interfere or interest in behalf of others; to lend a helping hand.

Lagomakii, *s.* One who performs these offices of kindness.
Lagomia, *v.* To raise, to lift up.
Lagomu, *s.* A large fly.
Lagovaka, *v.* To contend with one who has conquered another.
Lagovakai, *s.* One who contends in behalf of others.
Lagotulutulu, *v.* To raise the eves of the thatch.
Lagotulutulu, *s.* The sticks used for the above purpose.
Lahe, *s.* Lime.
Lahei, *v.* To put lime upon any thing.
Lahelahe, *a.* Limy, mouldy.
Lahi, *a.* Large, many, enough, abundant.
Lahi, *s.* Abundance, plenty, greatness.
Lahiga, *s.* The place where most of any given thing may be seen.
Lahilahiage, *a.* Large, rather larger.
Lahilahigalelei, *a.* Enough; none to waste.
Lahilahihake, *a.* Larger; more in quantity.
Laho, *s.* The scrotum.
Laka, *s.* Gait, a step, a stride.
Laka, *v.* To miss; to pass by; to pass or hand along.
Lakai, *v.* To step over.
Lakaga, *s.* Appointment; the place in which to pass or hand a thing.
Lakaaga, *s.* The threshold the stepping place.
Lakahala, *v.* To step awkwardly; to be unfortunate.
Lakalaka, *v.* To step out; to step carefully.
Lakalakaimonu, *a.* Fortunate several times in succession.
Lakalakavale, *v.* To act irreverently to the god of the tribe or family.
Lakaliu, *v.* To step over the *liu*, but not scoop it out; to know that work is to be done, but pass away.
Lakatonu, *v.* To step cleverly; to be fortunate or lucky.
Lakei, *s.* Leaves made fast to the stone used in catching the cat fish as an ornament.
Lakei, *v.* To do as above.
Lakoifie, *a.* Fair, fine weather.
Lakoifua, *a.* Well in health, used of the *Tuitoga* only.
Lakofia, *v.* To fill up; to cover, as a rent in a garment.
Lakofie, *a.* Dry comparatively, used of the weather.
Lakomatuu, *v.* To speak irreverently or unbecoming the place and person addressed.
Laku, *v.* To throw.
Lakuji, *v.* To handle food; to put the hand to what others are eating.
Lakulaku, *s.* Disrespect, ill behaviour.
Lakulaku, *a.* Rude, ill bred.
Lakulakuteefeke, *s.* A play of children.
Lakulakuvale, *v.* To throw; to give away without care or concern.
Lala, *s.* The name of a tree.
Lala, *a.* Without population; deserted.
Lala, *v.* To broil slightly.
Lalaila, *s.* The name of a fish.
Lalau, *s.* A counter voice.
Lalau, *v.* To pinch.
Lalau, *v.* To pull or draw gently along.
Lalabu, See *Labu.*
Lalafa, *v.* To fall flat; to shrink under.
Lalafi, *s.* The name of a fish.
Lalafi, *v.* See *Lafi.*
Lalafo, *v.* To talk in turns or succession.
Lalafu, *a.* Poor, impoverished, applied to the soil; old.

Lalaga, *v.* To weave; to plait the mats.

Lalaga, *v.* To weave mats of small texture.

Lalaga, *s.* The streaks or marks made upon the skin by beating.

Lalago, *v.* To ward off; to withstand.

Lalago, *s.* Two of the long nut trees in a Tonga house.

Lalagolalo, *s.* Two of the long nut trees in a Tonga house.

Lalahi, *a.* Large; rather large.

Lalaka, *v.* To step; to make a noise as one walking in straw.

Lalaku, *v.* To touch any thing sacred, as food or the person of a chief.

Lalalo, *v.* To go crouching along.

Lalama, *v.* To wink, to make signs with the eyes.

Lalata, *a.* Tame, domesticated.

Lalatahi, *s.* A shrub.

Lalato, *v.* To bite a mouthful from any thing large.

Lalava, *s.* The wrapping; binding with *kafa*.

Lalava, *v.* To bind with *kafa;* to wrap.

Lalavaki, *v.* To watch; to have charge of.

Lali, *s.* The native drum.

Lalo, *ad.* Below, down, beneath.

Laloaoa, *v.* To be superseded by something better.

Lama, *v.* To watch; to shine.

Lama, *s.* The reflection or light from a distance.

Lamaji, Lamalamaji, } *v.* To watch; to keep an eye upon.

Lami, Lamii, } *v.* To conceal; to hide suddenly.

Lamilami, *v.* To cover over, as one whose dress is bad.

Lamu, Lamulamu, } *v.* To chew, to masticate.

Lamu, *s.* Mastication.

Lana, *v.* To have an eye to any thing we wish to get.

Lanu, *s.* Colour.

Lanu, *v.* To wash; to rinse in fresh water.

Lanua, *a.* Coloured; different colours; well washed in fresh water.

Lanua, Lanulanua, } *s.* Sore eyes, applied to chiefs.

Lasu, *ad.* No; not so.

Lata, *a.* Tame, domesticated; at home in a place.

Lata, *s.* A shrub.

Latajino, *v.* To feel attached to persons, not to the place.

Latakelekele, *v.* To feel attached to a place, but not to the people.

Latuu, *v.* To voyage on a sudden without preparation.

Lava, *s.* A bait for fish.

Lava, Lavai, } *v.* To accomplish, to complete, to achieve, to obtain, to conquer.

Lavai, *s.* Achievement, accomplishment, conquest.

Lavauli, *a.* White in the fore and hind parts but black in the middle.

Lavafoi, *s.* The sign or mark of a coward.

Lavaji, *v.* To endure; to put up with.

Lavahaga, *s.* A joint or splice not yet bound with *kafa*.

Lavaka, *s.* The title of the chief of *Bea*, in Tongataboo.

Lavakelo, *a.* Brown round the middle.

Lavaki, Lavakii, } *v.* To deceive; to betray.

Lavaki, *s.* A traitor.

Lavalava, *v.* To wrap; to bind in a careless manner; to accomplish.

Lavataki, *v.* To conduct or bring to a termination; to accomplish with loss.

149

Lavatea, *a.* Black and white; speckled.
Lavatoa, *s.* The sign or mark of a hero.
Lave, *v.* To hit; to strike the mark; to gain the object; to steer free; to run off.
Lave, *s.* A heathen game.
Lavea, *v.* To bite, to take, as the fish the hook.
Lavea, *s.* A cut, a wound.
Lavea, *a.* Wounded.
Lavea, *v.* To know, to see.
Laveaki, *v.* To break one stick by the aid of another.
Lavei, *v.* To knock or strike against; to know.
Lavega, *s.* The name of a fish; any part or place struck against.
Lavekovia, *a.* Unfortunate, uncomfortable.
Lavelave, *s.* A small steer oar.
Lavelave, *v.* To keep off in steering.
Lavelavea, *v.* See *Lavea.*
Lavelaveili, *a.* Unlucky; often hurt.
Lavelavemua, *v.* To take the precedence in conversation.
Laveleleia, *a.* Comfortable, fortunate.
Lavena, *s.* A fish.
Lavenoaia, *v.* To be hurt accidentally.
Lavetemutemu, *v.* To get just the end or finishing only.
Le, *v.* To drive; to affright fish into the net.
Le, *s.* The instrument used for the above purpose.
Lea, *s.* Speech, language, dialect, discourse.
Lea, *v.* To talk, to speak.
Leai, *v.* To talk to; to reprove.
Leei, *v.* To push on one side or out of the way.
Leeleegu, *v.* To speak little and sullenly.
Lei *s.* Whale's tooth.

Leia, *a.* Alive, restored.
Leo, *s.* The voice; a guard, watchman, sentinel.
Leo, *v.* To watch, to guard.
Leoaa, *s.* A rough unpleasant voice.
Leoafea, *s.* An enticing or winning voice.
Leohi, *v.* To keep watch over some particular object.
Leoleo, *v.* See *Leo.*
Leu, *a.* Ripe, soft, (the *Tava.*)
Leua, *v.* To stumble, to trip.
Leuaaga, *s.* Any thing over which one trips.
Leui, *v.* To throw on one side; to push off as any thing light.
Leuleu, *s.* An old coverlet of *gatu.*
Leuleu, *a.* Soft, worn.
Leba, *s.* A hole or pit made to contain water; a cistern; a tree.
Leba, } Lebai, } *v.* To heave to; to put the head of the canoe to the wind.
Lebatuu, *v.* To put in to an island and proceed quickly.
Lebeji, *v.* To cut up; to split into pieces.
Lebeleba, *v.* To sail close on the wind.
Lebeleba, *a.* Covered over; full.
Lebo, *s.* Leaves sewn together to keep in heat.
Leboaki, *s.* A shoal of young fish.
Leboji, } Leboleboji, } *v.* To make compact; to collect together.
Lefio, *s.* A species of butterfly.
Lefu, *s.* The smallest in a litter of pigs.
Lefulefu, *s.* The name of a bird.
Legago, *s.* The name of a shell fish.
Lehia, *s.* One kind of banana.
Lehilehi, *v.* To take care of; to pay attention to.

150

Lehilehiga, *a.* Short in duration, but always used ironically.
Leka, *a.* Short, stumpy.
Leka, *s.* One kind of pig.
Leke, *s.* A private room.
Lekeleke, *a.* Full of rooms.
Lekia, *s.* The name of a tree.
Lekileki, *s.* The name of a tree.
Lekilekimilo, *s.* The name of a tree.
Lela, *a.* Bad, disagreeable.
Lele, *s.* A run, a race; a kind of the sugar cane.
Lele, *v.* To run.
Lelea, *a.* Red, sore, applied to the eyes.
Lelea, *v.* To be driven by the wind; to go astray.
Leleaga, *s.* A course or road in which to run.
Leleaki, Leleekina, } *v.* To run with; to take off.
Lelei, *s.* Good, goodness.
Lelei, *a.* Good, pleasant, undamaged, useful.
Leleu, *s.* A cape, headland.
Lelelele, *v.* To run totteringly along; to swell; to bulge out suddenly.
Lelo, *s.* the name of a fish.
Lelu, *s.* An armlet; a large ring.
Lelu, Lelulelu, } *v.* To tire; to grow weary of; to forget.
Lemohaki, *v.* To be put under water.
Lemohekina, *v.* To be drowned by being kept under water.
Lemokaki, *v.* To put under water.
Lena, *s.* The *taba* before made into *gatu;* a sham fight.
Leta, *a.* Scattered; all on ends.
Leva, *ad.* Forthwith, at once, quickly.
Levei, *s.* A kind of yam.
Levi, *v.* To accompany, always used of something small accompanying a larger.

Levulevu, *s.* A small kind of mat.
Li, *v.* To toss; to throw; to lash together.
Li, *s.* The *kafa* which fastens the outrigger of a canoe.
Lia, *v.* To surpass; to outdo; to go ahead.
Liaki, *v.* To cast off; to discard; to abandon.
Liaki, *s.* A Tonga game with the hands.
Lialiaki, *v.* To wave; to swing to and fro.
Liekina, *s.* A castaway; one discarded.
Liekina, *v.* To throw to and fro in the arms.
Liogi, *s.* A deceased relative; one for whom it is becoming to sorrow.
Liu, *s.* The hold of a vessel.
Liu, *v.* To cease, to fail; to cease to do as formerly; to change; to appear different.
Liua, *v.* To depose; to debase; to dethrone; to degrade.
Liua, *a.* Used of canoes.
Liuua, *v.* To bale out the water of a canoe both fore and aft.
Liuga, *s.* Times, used to things and events, as *toko* is to persons.
Liutakei, *v.* To have a different appearance from being ornamented or newly dressed.
Lifio, *s.* The butterfly.
Lifulifujia, *v.* To be terrified; to be much afraid.
Ligi, Ligiligi, } *v.* To pour.
Ligoligo, *s.* A squeaking noisy insect.
Ligoligoa, *a.* Deserted, uninhabited.
Liha, *s.* A nit.
Lihamua, *s.* The name of the first lunar month.
Lihamui, *s.* The name of the twelfth lunar month.

151

Liji, *v.* To fling or throw with force.
Liji, *s.* A throw or fling.
Lijigi, } **Lijigia**, } *v.* To be thrown at.
Lika, *v.* To be advancing; growing wise.
Likamatagi, *v.* To fear tempest.
Likiliki, *s.* Small divisions of land.
Likivai, *v.* To pour a little oil into water for washing a young child.
Liko, *s.* One kind of fishing net.
Likoliko, *a.* Dirty; besmeared with dirt.
Liku, *s.* That part of an island least frequented by canoes owing to its rocky shores.
Likulikumoao, *a.* Changeable, unsettled.
Lili, *s.* Anger, fieriness.
Lili, *a.* Angry, rageful.
Lili, *v.* To be angry; to boil; to rage.
Liliu, *v.* To return; to change; to reform; to go before the wind.
Liliu, *s.* Reformation, conversion.
Lilifa, *a.* Steep, precipitous.
Liligi, *v.* To pour out.
Liligi, *s.* The act of pouring out.
Lilika, *a.* Afraid, terrified.
Liliko, *s.* The name of a fish.
Liliko, *a.* Besmeared with dirt.
Lilililі, *v.* To simmer; to boil gently.
Lilo, *a.* Hid, concealed, hidden.
Limu, *s.* The sea weed; a shell fish.
Limualako, *s.* A shell fish.
Limufuofua, *s.* A shell fish.
Limukaka, *s.* A shell fish.
Limulouago, *s.* A shell fish.
Limuteemoa, *s.* A shell fish.
Limutagau, *s.* A shell fish.
Limutuu, *s.* A kind of sea weed used in cleaning the canoes, &c.
Linoaki, *v.* To string leaves upon a rope for taking fish.
Lisalisa, *a.* Poorly, weakly; not able to work hard.
Litolito, *a.* Soft, tender, unripe.
Lo, *s.* The ant.
Loa, *s.* Any pigment used for smearing over the body.
Loa, *v.* To besmear the body.
Loa, *ad.* Some time past.
Loi, *s.* A lie, falsehood, liar.
Loi, *v.* To lie; to mix with the expressed oil of the cocoa nut.
Loi, *a.* Addicted to lying.
Loia, *v.* To be surfeited in eating.
Loio, *v.* To press; to squeeze; to break under the hands.
Loilolo, *s.* A small quantity of oil to increase a larger quantity.
Loima, *s.* A preparation of Tonga bread with the expressed oil of the cocoa nut.
Loimata, *s.* Tears.
Looa, *v.* To choke; to be choked or suffocated.
Lou, *s.* A leaf; a sheet of any thing; a single one.
Louaki, *v.* To alter, to change; to act differently on a sudden.
Louua, *a.* Bifold, double.
Louulu, *s.* The hair of the head.
Louuluotua, *s.* The hair on the head of a child when born.
Loubata, *s.* A tree.
Lougutu; *s.* The lips.
Louhiinima, *s.* Fingers.
Louhiivae, *s.* Toes.
Louloua, *s.* Anger, displeasure.
Louloua, *a.* Beclouded, overcast.
Loulouulu, *a.* Split, cracked.
Loumoa, *s.* One kind of bread fruit.
Loutoko, *s.* One kind of bread fruit.

152

Loutolu, *s.* A creeping plant.
Loba, *v.* To fasten the mast of a canoe.
Lobe, } *v.* To work; to
Lobelobe, } move, as water when shaken.
Lofa, *s.* The name of a bird (gull.)
Lofa, *v.* To fly with extended wings.
Lofai, } *v.* To spread out the
Lofeia, } hands and wings; to scatter abroad; to push down.
Lofajia, *v.* Obedient, yielding, respectful.
Lofia, } *v.* To overspread;
Lofilofia, } to cover.
Lofia, *s.* A volcano.
Lofua, *v.* To rush upon; to seize unexpectedly.
Loga, *s.* A raised bed or sleeping place.
Logauha, *v.* To rain heavily.
Logataa, *a.* Difficult to quell.
Logo, *a.* Quiet; not talkative; peaceful.
Logoa, *s.* Noise, uproar, disturbance.
Logoa, *a.* Noisy, uproarious.
Logoa, *v.* To make a noise.
Logouli, *s.* The name of a fish.
Logobee, *a.* Soft, good for eating (the bread fruit.)
Logologo, *s.* The name of a tree and its fruit.
Logologo, *a.* Prognostic, foretokening.
Logomate, *a.* Silent as death.
Logona, *v.* To inform, to report.
Logonoa, *s.* Dead silence.
Logosa, *s.* A pit; a snare for the foe.
Logotuli, *a.* Stationary; not growing.
Lohi, *s.* A falsehood, a lie.
Lohi, *v.* To lie.
Lohiaki, } *v.* To belie, to de-
Lohiakii, } fame, to libel.

Lohiekina, *v.* To belie; to be belied.
Lohofua, *s.* Large testicles.
Loholoho, *s.* The branch on which the nuts grow.
Loholohoi, *v.* To thrash with the *Loholoho.*
Loholohotaha, *s.* One kind of cocoa nut.
Lohu, *s.* A forked stick used for twisting off the bread fruit.
Lohui, } *v.* To gather fruit
Lohulohu, } with the *Lohu.*
Loka, *a.* Rough, wavy, full of waves.
Lokeia, *v.* To be dashed about by the waves.
Loki, *s.* A room, a closet.
Loki, } *a.* Dark, enclosed,
Lokiloki, } shut up.
Loko, } *ad.* Very; in a great
Lokoloko, } degree.
Lokoloka, *s.* The name of a fish, and one kind of yam.
Lokoloka, *a.* Rough, heavy, applied to the sea.
Loku, *v.* To expect, to prepare.
Loku, } *v.* To draw to-
Lokuloku, } gether; to gather in sewing; to pucker in a heap.
Lokua, *s.* The name of a fish.
Lokuafeko, *s.* The name of a fish.
Lole, *v.* To beat; to give repeated blows.
Lolea, *v.* To beat; to be beaten.
Loli, *s.* A shell fish.
Loli, *v.* To fasten; to make fast the rope of the *loba.*
Loli, *a.* Hard, lumpy, applied to Tonga bread when it does not ferment.
Loli, *s.* The squeaking of the flying fox.
Loliloli, *a.* Black.
Lolo, *s.* Oil; a disease of which many die.
Lolo, *a.* Oily, fat.
Lolo, *v.* To lower the sail in

strong wind; to rain in torrents; to descend suddenly.
Loloa, *a.* Long, tall; qualmish, sickly.
Loloa, *s.* Length.
Loloaga, *s.* The full length.
Loloi, *v.* To oil; to mix oily substance with others.
Lolou, Loloukimui, } *v.* To alter, to change, to repent.
Lolofa, *v.* To spread abroad the hands; to extend the wings.
Lolofi, *v.* To arrive unexpectedly; to press together, applied to a number of persons.
Lolofia, Lolofie, } *v.* To rejoice over; to be pleased with.
Lologa, *s.* A large fishing net.
Lologo, *a.* Quick, notloquacious.
Lologo, *s.* Sharks in a shoal; an assembly at a heathen dance.
Lolohifo, *v.* To fall; to press down; to descend; to be overwhelmed.
Lolohu, *v.* To take up or reach any thing with a forked stick.
Loloka, *a.* See *Loka.*
Loloku, *v.* To gather up or collect at once.
Loloku, *s.* Any thing done in reparation of insult to the gods or their houses.
Lolololo, *s.* Greasiness, oiliness.
Lolololo, *a.* Oily, greasy.
Lololoi, *v.* To oil, to grease.
Lolololo, *v.* To cut; to clear ground; to beat soft.
Loloma, *v.* To swell and rise as waves.
Lolomaka, *s.* A fish.
Lolomata, *s.* A preparation of food.
Lolomi, *v.* To put down; to quell; to quiet; to keep down.
Loloto, *a.* Deep.
Lolotoga, *ad.* Whilst; in the mean time; during.

Lolotu, *a.* Wild; not tame.
Lomaki, *s.* Flood, inundation, deluge.
Lomaki, Lomakii, } *v.* To drown, to deluge, to plunge.
Lomekina, *v.* To be overwhelmed by a wave; to be drowned.
Lomi, *v.* To push and keep under.
Lomia, *v.* To quell; to put down.
Lomigataa, *a.* Difficult to prevent.
Lomigofua, *a.* Easy to prevent.
Lomiloaia, *v.* To put down or quell without exception.
Lomilomi, *v.* To punish captives after war; to quell.
Lomu, *s.* The name of a shell fish.
Lomulomu, *a.* Fat; very fat.
Lona, *s.* The hiccup.
Lonuku, *v.* To sit or bow in silence.
Lotaki, *v.* To encourage, to exhort, to hearten.
Lote, Lotelote, } *v.* To stir; to mix from the bottom.
Loto, *s.* The mind; the middle, the centre; the inside, the interior; the temper.
Loto, *v.* To consent; to agree to.
Loto, *a.* Deep.
Lotoa, *s.* A fold; an enclosure; a premises enclosed.
Lotolava, *a.* Versatile; ever changing.
Lotoloto, *v.* To be in the middle.
Lotolotoua, *a.* Double minded, fickle.
Lotolotoua, *s.* Fickleness, inconstancy.
Lotolotoga, *s.* The midst, centre.
Lotofelavai, *a.* See *Lotolava.*
Lotogia, *v.* To attend to; to think of.
Lotu, *s.* Prayer, devotion, adoration, worship.
Lotu, *v.* To pray, to worship.

Lotua, *v.* To pray for; to intercede.

Lovai, *s.* Heavy and continued rain.

Louvai, *s.* The bread fruit when it falls from the tree.

Lu, *s.* The leaves of the *Talo*; the cabbage; herbs.

Lua, *v.* To vomit, to disgorge, to spew.

Lua, *s.* A sunken reef.

Luaki, *v.* To provoke another to the performance of some work.

Luaki, *v.* To be sick with.

Luabuna, } *s.* A reef with breakers on it.
Luafaji, }

Luamauku, *s.* A reef on which the waves rise but do not break.

Lue, *v.* To waddle; to move from side to side.

Luekina, *v.* To be jolted or knocked from side to side.

Luelue, *v.* To move; to roll, as a vessel in a calm.

Luo, *s.* A hole, a cavity, an excavation.

Luolua, *s.* Two small canoes lashed together.

Luoluo, *a.* Full of holes or pits; hollow.

Luomelie, *s.* A hole or cavity in sunken rocks easy to get fish from.

Luobubua, } *s.* A deep pit; abyss.
Luotaomamao, }

Luotamaki, *s.* A hole from which it is difficult to get fish.

Lube, *s.* The wild pigeon.

Lubea, *a.* Abounding in pigeons.

Lubei, *v.* To carry suspended on both sides.

Lubelube, *v.* To swag as in carrying any thing long.

Lubo, *s.* The name of a fish.

Lubolago, *s.* The name of a fish.

Lubolubo, *s.* The name of a fish.

Lubotalu, *s.* The name of a fish.

Lufa, *s.* The Navigator Island's *gatu.*

Lufilufi, *v.* To screen, to curtain; to surround.

Lufolufa, *s.* A thick kind of native cordage.

Lugekina, *v.* To suffer a relapse from exertion or motion.

Luji, *v.* To gather all, applied to nuts and bread fruit.

Lujiafa, *v.* To forage; to take where it can be found, after a hurricane.

Luki, *s.* A challenge.

Luki, } *v.* To challenge, to defy.
Lukia, }

Luku, *a.* Weak, old.

Luku, *s.* Small pieces of wood for filling up in building canoes.

Lukufua, *v.* To grasp the whole; to comprehend the whole.

Lukuluku, *v.* To wear the dress in a loose indecent manner.

Lukutaga, *s.* An armful or handful of any thing.

Lukuvaka, *s.* A disease increased or a death consequent upon a voyage.

Luli, *a.* Disgusting, disagreeable.

Lulu, *s.* The owl; the name of a fish; one kind of sugar cane; the reeding of a house.

Lulu, *v.* To shake; to reed.

Lulua, *v.* To vomit, to disgorge.

Lulua, *s.* The act of vomiting.

Luluo, *a.* Sunk, as the eyes in affliction.

Luluki, *s.* The root of the *kava.*

Luluku, *v.* To sprinkle; to baptize; to have; to hold; to keep in possession.

Lulululu, *v.* To shake hands; to cause to tremble; to shake.

Lulululu, *s.* A trembling, a shaking.

Luma, *s.* Mockery, mimickry.
Luma, Lumolumai, } *v.* To mimick, to mock, to deride.
Luma, Lumoluma, } *a.* Addicted to mockery.
Lusa, *a.* Forsaken, destitute, extinct.
Lusa, *v.* To forsake, to slacken to relax.
Lutu, *v.* To cause a sound by striking in the water.
Luvai, *v.* To wash with water, as bottles, &c. that are shaken.

M

M, THE thirteenth Letter in the Tonga Alphabet. Its sound is that of *m* in *mark*.
Ma, *s.* Shame, bashfulness; bread.
Ma, *v.* To be ashamed; to chew the *kava* root.
Ma, *a.* Bashful, modest; capable of, able.
Ma, *con.* And, used only in connecting numerals.
Maa, *prep.* For.
Maa, *a.* Clean, pure; burnt, scorched.
Maa, *s.* Cleanliness, purity.
Maau, For thee.
Maafu, *s.* A name of office; the burning of a heathen temple.
Maaga, *s.* A mouthful; a morsel.
Maagia, *a.* Scorched, burnt.
Maahi, *s.* The tail of fish.
Maahi, *v.* To taste of; to have a smack.
Maaku, For me.
Maala, *s.* Plantation of yams; a garden.
Maalaala, *a.* Clean, cleared of weeds and rubbish.
Maali, *v.* To flit across; to shoot by.
Maaliali, *v.* To sit exposed to the breeze.
Maalifekina, *v.* To see; to get a glimpse of.
Maalualu, *a.* Torn, shreded, not cut.
Maamaa, *s.* Lightness; want of weight; the lights or lungs.
Maamaa, *a.* Light, not heavy.
Maamaaikai, *s.* One light or ready to eat, but heavy or unwilling to work.
Maamaagamalie, *a.* Empty; all gone; all out.
Maamaalava, *s.* The name of a tree.
Maana, For him or her.
Maanu, Maanuanu, } *v.* To float, to swim.
Maanu, *s.* One kind of *Kolokalu*.
Maata, For me.
Maava, *s.* The name of a fish.
Mae, *a.* Withered, dried, faded.
Mae, *v.* To fade, to wither.
Mae, Maemae, } *v.* To smell mouldy and withered.
Maea, *s.* A rope, roping.
Maeakii, Maemaeakii, } *v.* To be careful of; to be particular about.
Maeatuu, *a.* Lost; overwhelmed by something sudden.
Maefu, *s.* Dust.
Maeneene, *v.* To be ticklish.
Mai, *prep.* To, towards, used before pronouns of the first person.
Mai, *v.* To make bread of.
Maiioio, *a.* Cracked; full of fissures.
Maifa, *a.* Empty.
Maifi, Maili, } *s.* A humming noise; the sensation of wind as when any thing passes near the face.
Maihi, *s.* A cut; a wound by cutting.

Maile, *s.* The name of a shrub (myrtle.)
Maikiiki, *a.* Full of cracks and splits.
Maili
Mailiili, } *v.* To blow gently.
Maimoa, *s.* A trifle, a play thing.
Maimoa, *v.* To trifle, to play.
Maina, *v.* To laugh, to titter.
Maina, *a.* White, as flesh first cut.
Maitaki, *s.* The beloved wife of a polygamist.
Maito, *s.* A shrub.
Maitoa, *int.* An expression of pleasure at the misfortunes of others.
Mao, *s.* Steam.
Mao, *a.* Clumsy, unhandy; cruel in sport.
Mao, *v.* To do without care or thought; to speak unadvisedly.
Maoa, *v.* To sound, as the breaking of cocoa nuts.
Maobo,
Maoboobo, } *a.* Shut, compact, close.
Maofa,
Maofoofa, } *v.* To smell; to send forth a smell.
Maogo, *v.* To feel; to impress.
Maogooga, *a.* Precious; great in value; important.
Maojia, *v.* To bruise; to hurt.
Maoluga, *s.* Height, elevation, eminence.
Maoluga, *a.* High, elevated.
Maomao, *a.* Dry, applied to the intervals between showers.
Maomoana, *v.* To go out far from shore.
Maomaoganoa, *a.* Silent, still.
Maomaokimua, *ad.* Beforehand.
Maoni, *v.* To continue; to do again.
Maoni, *a.* Perfect, disinterested.
Maonioni, *s.* Righteousness.
Maonioni, *a.* Righteous.
Mau, *pron.* We, us, our, excluding the person addressed.

Mau,
Mauaibe, } *ad.* Always, perpetually.
Mau, *s.* Constancy, firmness.
Mau, *a.* Constant, unwavering, fast, firm.
Mau, *v.* To obtain; to possess; to accept; to move. See *Maumau.*
Maua, *v.* To cease.
Mauaga,
Mauga, } *s.* The place for the obtaining of any thing.
Mauaki, *v.* To be so; to keep at this.
Maui, *s.* The name of that supposed being who drew up the Friendly Islands with a fish hook.
Maui, *a.* Alive, well, convalescent, applied to several.
Mauiui, *a.* Healthy; well, as a wound; flourishing.
Maubu,
Maubuubu,
Maufu, } *s.* A hollow bubbling sound.
Mauga, *v.* To frequent; to refer or have relation to.
Maukubu, *s.* A single dress of *gatu.*
Maukubu, *s.* Breadth.
Maula, *v.* Sharp, edged.
Maulalo, *s.* Depth, deepness.
Maulalo, *a.* Deep.
Mauli, *s.* A midwife.
Mauli, *v.* To practice midwifery.
Maulu, *v.* To dive; to swim under water.
Maumau, *s.* Destruction, waste, extravagance.
Maumau,
Maumaui, } *v.* To waste, to destroy, to break.
Maumau, *v.* To move, used in seeking persons, &c.
Maumauaki, *v.* To put up with; to endure.
Maumaugataa, *a.* Difficult to break; difficult to get.
Maumaugofua, *a.* Easy to demolish.

Maumaunootaga, *v.* To fill up to the place at which it is tied.

Maumautuga, *v.* To stick fast.

Maumalie, *v.* To be divided equally and fairly.

Mauna, *v.* To pain; to threaten pain.

Mauta, *v.* To have acquired; to have learnt.

Mautamaki, *v.* To be divided into portions, but not fairly or equally.

Maba, *s.* The name of a tree and its fruit; the eggs of the turtle before laid.

Mabee, *v.* To fall.

Mabeefua, *v.* To fall flat down.

Mabelu, Mabelubelu, } *v.* To bend; to fold; to bow down; to droop; to stoop.

Mabeluua, *v.* To bend double.

Maboiboi, *v.* To talk; to persist in talking.

Mabo, Mabogutu, } *s.* Vain boasting.

Mabogutu, *v.* To boast, to brag.

Mabu, *v.* To whistle; to make a whistling noise in the nose.

Mabuhi, *v.* To spout.

Mabuhoi, *v.* To sigh; to breathe hard, as one very tired.

Mabuke, *v.* To spring upon; to appear suddenly, applied to several.

Mabukebuke, *v.* To do, to accomplish.

Mabumabu, *v.* To whistle repeatedly.

Mabumabu, *s.* Space, interval, used of what is incessant.

Mabuni, Mabunibuni, } *v.* To be shut or closed; to shut or close; to coalesce.

Mabunobuna, *v.* To shoot out; to spring up, as a fountain.

Mafa, *s.* A flat or level on the side of a mountain.

Mafa, *v.* To attend to; to give the strength of the mind to any thing.

Mafa, *a.* Plenty, abundance, used in reference to things of which there lacks a corresponding proportion, as, *Mafafale* plenty of house room, but little or nothing to show in it; *Mafalau* plenty of talk, but no doings to correspond.

Mafaa, *v.* To open, to extend.

Mafaafaa, *a.* Split, cracked, choppy.

Mafai, *s.* Sufficiency, ability.

Mafai, Mafaifai, } *a.* Able to do; competent.

Mafao, Mafaofao, } *v.* To extend, to stretch out.

Mafau, Mafaufau, } *v.* To be stretched; to be drawn; to have been well worn.

Mafahi *s.* A crack or split; dissilition.

Mafahi, Mafahifahi, } *v.* To be split or cracked; to part asunder.

Mafajia, Mafamafajia, } *v.* To be tired; to be heavy laden; to be burdened.

Mafajifaji, *a.* Broken up; in pieces.

Mafaki, Mafakifaki, } *v.* To be separated; to be in joints or pieces.

Mafalo, *v.* To be drawn or stretched, as a rope.

Mafamafa, *a.* Heavier.

Mafana, *a.* Warm, zealous.

Mafana, *s.* Warmth, gentle heat.

Mafanahia, *v.* To be warmed.

Mafanafana, *a.* Warm (a little.)

Mafatua, *s.* A sneeze.

Mafatua, *v.* To sneeze.

Mafee, *a.* Open, spread out, extended.

Mafeia, *v.* To be able to do.

Mafehi, *a.* Open.

Mafeji, Mafejifeji } *v.* To be broken.

Mafela, *a.* Open, extended.
Mafelefela, *a.* Too open; too much extended.
Mafi, *s.* A conqueror, a victor.
Mafihu, } *v.* To move; to
Mafihufihu, } work.
Mafihuga, *s.* The temper, disposition, &c. including every movement of the mind.
Mafihugatamaki, *v.* To twist; to turn, so as to cause pain.
Mafili, } *v.* To turn or roll
Mafilifili, } about.
Mafimafi, *s.* Power, might.
Mafimafi, *a.* Most powerful.
Mafoa, } *v.* To be cracked or
Mafofoa, } broken; to be cracked in several places.
Mafofoa, *a.* Flawy; full of flaws.
Mafohi, } *v.* To be peeled
Mafohifohi, } or skinned in patches.
Mafohu, } *v.* To be bruised.
Mafohufohu, }
Mafoki, *v.* To be turned upside down, and inside out.
Mafola, } *v.* To be spread
Mafolofola, } out or extended; to be diffused abroad.
Mafu, *s.* The heart.
Mafu, *a.* Stale; bad in smell.
Mafua, *s.* A tree.
Mafuaatu, *s.* A tree.
Mafua, *s.* A shoal of small fish; what one is particularly fond of eating or drinking.
Mafua, } *s.* A rising ground
Mafuatanu, } formed for the purpose of bounding rods along in the game called *Jika.*
Mafue, *v.* To lie scattered and in confusion.
Mafujifuji, *v.* To pull; to jerk repeatedly.
Mafuke, *a.* Open, unfolded.
Mafuli, } *v.* To be capsized
Mafulifuli, } or turned over.
Mafulu, *v.* To snuff up the wind; to breathe through the nose.

Mafulu, *a.* Hairy.
Mafulutamaki, *s.* The sensation of one whose respiration is prevented.
Mafulufulutamaki, *a.* Angry, displeased, as one whose respiration is affected.
Mafunofuna, *a.* Ragged; not smooth on the surface.
Maga, *s.* A branch of a tree or road; a stream from a fountain; the curved part of a Tonga fish hook.
Maga, *s.* The name of a fish.
Maga, *a.* Open; forked; spreading.
Magaga, *v.* To desire; to long to do.
Magaofe, *a.* Bent, bowlike.
Magaua, *s.* A tree with two trunks at one root; a double tree.
Magalogalo, *v.* To be sinking out of sight; to be forgetting.
Magakoka, *s.* One species of *Talo.*
Magamaga, *a.* Full of branches.
Magamaga, *v.* To branch off; to take different routes; to go to more than one chief on arriving at any place.
Magamagaatai, *s.* A shell fish.
Magamaganoa, *a.* Limbed; supplied with limbs, but useless; lazy.
Magatefua, *s.* One kind of *Talo.*
Magaele, *s.* The name of a tree.
Magelei, *v.* To wash new canoes with the leaves of the *Magele.*
Magemage, *a.* Dry, shrivelled.
Magoa, *a.* Dry; without moisture, as the yam when old.
Magiji, *s.* Food prepared for strangers or persons just arrived.
Magii, } *a.* Heavy laden, as
Magiigii, } a canoe; tired.
Magoi, *v.* To impress; to make impression; to cause to feel.

159

Magoto, Magotogoto, } *a.* Deep; sunk; abundant.
Magotogoto, *s.* Abundance.
Magu, *a.* Crusted, crimp.
Magugu, *s.* One kind of sugar cane.
Magumagu, *s.* The scab of sores; dryness.
Magumagu, *v.* To scab over; to be scabbed.
Magugu, Magugugugu, } *v.* To champ; to crack up bones or any thing hard with the teeth.
Maha, *s.* Emptiness; a fish.
Maha, *a.* Empty, devoid.
Mahaamaka, *s.* Deception, as a reef which looks likely to produce shell fish, but on seeking the mistake is discovered.
Mahae, Mahaehae, } *a.* Torn; torn in several places.
Mahaihai, *a.* Bound, tied fast.
Mahau, Mahauhau, } *a.* Thin; spare; not stout.
Mahafeafea, *v.* To know; to be aware of.
Mahafu, *s.* Armour; weapons of war.
Mahaga, *s.* Twins.
Mahagaua, *a.* Double, as two trees on one root. See *Magaua.*
Mahagalei, *s.* Twins, one of each sex.
Mahagataane, *s.* Twins, both boys.
Mahahua, *a.* Dry; without moisture.
Mahake, Mahakehake, } *a.* Risen, rose up.
Mahaki, *s.* Sickness, disease; also death, when used in the past tense.
Mahaki, *a.* Sick, afflicted.
Mahaki, Mahakihaki, } *v.* To lift, to raise; to be lifted or raised.
Mahakia, *v.* To drink empty.
Mahakiia, *a.* Afflicted, unwell.
Mahakimoa, *s.* Epilepsy, convulsions, fit.
Mahala, Mahalaua, } *a.* Torn; torn in two.
Mahalahala, *a.* Torn to pieces.
Mahalo, *s.* Imagination, thought, fancy.
Mahalo, Mahalohalo, } *v.* To conjecture; to think; to suspect.
Mahamahagamalie, *a.* Empty; all out.
Mahamuhamu, *v.* To be pulled; to jerk suddenly.
Mamahalogohua, *a.* Still ebbing but near to flow, used of the tide.
Mahalu, Mahaluhalu, } *a.* Shreded; torn into shreds.
Mahamaha, *a.* Not dry nor yet deep, as reefs, &c. at ebb tide.
Mahamahaki, *a.* Subject to affliction; lightly afflicted; feeble.
Mahanihani, *a.* Clean; cloudless, as the sky; free from dirt.
Mahei, *s.* A nick name for war.
Maheiauho, *s.* The quarrelling of relatives.
Maheikau, *a.* Ripe; brown in colour.
Maheilau, *a.* Talkative; clever at talking.
Mahefu, *v.* To dress constantly with any thing dirty and ragged.
Mahehea, *s.* The sound of a voice almost lost in the distance.
Mahehei, *a.* Wrong; imprudent; bad.
Mahekiheki, *a.* Jutted out; extended.
Mahele, Mahelehele, } *a.* Cut, lacerated.
Mahelehele, *s.* A kind of grass.
Mahemu, *v.* To pass from.

Maheni, *v.* To be accustomed or in the habit of.
Mahi, *s.* Sourness, acidity.
Mahi, *a.* Sour, acid.
Mahifi, Mahihi, } *a.* Cut.
Mahihi, *v.* To be separated or dislodged from the shell.
Mahiki, Mahikihiki, } *v.* To rise; to appear higher than formerly; to rejoice; to exhibit signs of joy.
Mahili, Mahilihili, } *a.* Better, larger.
Mahimago, *a.* Hard, obdurate, callous.
Mahimahi, *s.* The name of a fish.
Mahimahi, *a.* Ascescent; rather sour.
Mahina, *s.* The moon.
Mahina, Mahinehina, } *a.* White in appearance.
Mahino, Mahinohino, } *a.* Plain, distinct, intelligible, applied to language.
Mahoaa, *s.* Arrow root; flour.
Mahofa, *v.* To be fallen; to be prostrate; to overspread.
Mahohohofa, *a.* Flat; spread out.
Mahoka, Mahokohoka, } *v.* To be speared or pierced.
Maholi, Maholiholi, } *v.* To be chipped in places.
Maholi, *s.* One kind of banana.
Maholihina, *s.* One kind of banana.
Maholo, Maholoholo, } *a.* Soft, yielding.
Mahu, *s.* Plenty, abundance.
Mahu, *a.* Fertile, fruitful.
Mahu, *s.* The hollow sound of any thing distant.
Mahua, *v.* To be spilt, poured out, lost.
Mahuamata, *v.* To see plenty but not possess.
Mahui, *v.* To leave; to separate from.
Mahuifuhi, *v.* To fall in bunches.
Mahuiga, *s.* Preciosity, value.
Mahuiga, *a.* Precious, valuable.
Mahuihui, *v.* To break from.
Mahuo, *v.* To be hoed.
Mahuohua, *a.* Brimfull.
Mahuotua, *a.* Plenty of what is becoming the poor, but no *kava*.
Mahuhu, Mahuhuhuhu, } *v.* To be pierced or pricked.
Mahuke, Mahukehuke, } *v.* To be forced or raised upwards.
Mahulafalafa, Mahutafea, } *a.* Plenty; universal plenty.
Maji, *s.* The name of a tree and its fruit.
Maji, *a.* Sour; decayed, as the nut when kept too long.
Majiata, *s.* A tree.
Majiua, *v.* To break in two any thing round.
Majiji, Majijijiji, } *v.* Cracked; chinked; full of splits.
Majikoka, *s.* The name of a tree.
Majikona, *s.* The name of a tree.
Majila, *s.* A bamboo used as a fishing rod.
Majila, *a.* Sharp, edged.
Majila, *s.* Sharpness; keenness of edge or point.
Majili, Majilijili, } *a.* Snipped; chipped, as any edged tool.
Majima, *s.* Salt.
Majitala, *s.* A tree.
Majiva, *s.* Poverty, necessity, need.
Majiva, *a.* Poor, destitute, needy.
Majivejiva, *a.* Poor in appearance; abject.
Maka, *s.* Stone or rock of any kind.
Makaafi, *s.* A fire stone; a flint.
Makai, *s.* The name of a tree.
Makaikai, *v.* To be eaten or worn into holes.

Makaone, *s.* The sand stone.
Maknu, } *v.* To coil; to twist;
Makauua, } to writhe; to walk or saunter about.
Makau, *a.* Lazy, indolent.
Makauu, *s.* A biting stone; a stone in the sea said to produce an itching on the skin.
Makabuna, *s.* Grand children.
Makafaahi, *s.* The side stones of a sepulchre.
Makafakafai, *v.* To be bound with *kafa*.
Makafala, *s.* The bottom stone of a sepulchre or vault.
Makafatu, *s.* The name of one kind of stone.
Makafeke, *v.* To catch the *Feke*.
Makafeke, *s.* A kind of marble stone.
Makafetoliaki *v.* To be of one mind; to use freely from each other's stores.
Makafokafo, *v.* To be wounded in several places.
Makahuni, *s.* The pebble.
Makakafu, *s.* The stone with which a sepulchre is covered over.
Makaka, *a.* Hard, unyielding; not pliant; clumsy, awkward.
Makaka, *v.* To stretch out the body.
Makalava, *v.* To lie along.
Makamaka, *a.* Stony; full of stones.
Makamakau, *a.* Crooked, lazy.
Makamio, *v.* To walk about.
Makamiki, *s.* A Tonga play.
Makamu, } *v.* To shoot,
Makamukamu, } to flit.
Makata, } *a.* Cut, bruised,
Makatakata, } wounded, split.
Makata, *s.* A sling for throwing stones; the head and foot stones in a vault.
Makata, *v.* To sling stones.
Makateka, *a.* Unsteady, wavering.

Makatuu. *a.* Steady, immoveable, firm.
Makeu, } *v.* To go; to ap-
Makeukeu, } pear.
Makeke, *v.* To be warped; to be raised in any direction.
Makeli, *v.* To be dug; to be in holes.
Makenu, } *s.* The sand or
Makenukenu, } earth as disturbed by one walking along.
Makii, } *v.* To laugh, to
Makiikii, } titter
Makilo, } *v.* To shew; to ap-
Makilokilo, } pear in sight.
Makini, } *v.* To smart; to
Makinikini, } tingle.
Mako, *v.* To be smeared from head to foot with black pigment.
Makoa, *v.* Wait a little; hold on.
Makoga, } *a.* Valuable.
Makogokoga, }
Makohi, } *v.* To be scratch-
Makohikohi, } ed.
Makoki, *v.* To be able, to do.
Makoko, } *a.* To be squeezed,
Makokoua, } pressed, or indented.
Makamakoaga, *a.* Variable in disposition.
Makoji, } *v.* To be eaten; to
Makojikoji, } be nibbled; bitten.
Makona, *a.* Satisfied with food; loaded, as a gun.
Makuku, *s.* A cracking noise.
Makuku, *v.* To rustle along.
Makulekule, *v.* To be ransacked.
Makulu, } *v.* To be over-
Makulukulu, } loaded and pressed out of joint.
Makulu, *v.* To drop as rain.
Mala, *s.* The name of a fish; foolishness, misfortune.
Malae, *s.* A green; a grass plat; a circus.
Malaelae, *a.* Open; free from obstructions, like a *Malae*.

162

Malaia, *a.* Dead, abandoned, accursed.
Malau, *s.* The name of a fish.
Malau, *a.* Uproarious, noisy, trifling.
Malautea, *s.* A fish.
Malauvai, *s.* A fish.
Malaga, *s.* An oration; a discourse; a sermon; preacher.
Malaga, *v.* To preach; to discourse.
Malaga, Malagalaga, } *v.* To be raised.
Malagaekina, *v.* To plead or intercede for.
Malagaifaiva, *v.* To do a work from the reported success of others.
Malagafono, *s.* The persons who attend a proclamation; one who goes to bring a report of a proclamation.
Malago, Malagolago, } *a.* Applied to a canoe that is higher fore and aft than in the centre.
Malaki, *v.* To tread; to stamp upon.
Malakilaki, *a.* Well, in health, applied to chiefs.
Malala, *s.* Charcoal, embers.
Malalaga, *v.* To execute commands; to wait upon a chief.
Malali, *s.* A feast.
Malali, Malalilali, } *v.* To be scratched, marked, or torn.
Malama, *v.* To shine.
Malamala, *s.* Chips of wood; shavings; lumps of fish.
Malamala, *a.* Sour; sourish in taste.
Malamalaatoa, *s.* A tree.
Malamalaki, *v.* To stamp upon; to tread under feet.
Malanu, *a.* Agreeable to the taste, palatable.
Malave, *v.* To be fixed or fastened.
Malave, *a.* Tall, tallest.
Male, *s.* A play.
Malea, *a.* Laid; beat or trodden down.
Malea, *s.* A track; footmarks.
Maleelea, *a.* Laid; trodden down with the feet.
Maleifua, *a.* Comfortable, clean.
Malekamoe, *s.* Blind man's buff; a play.
Malelahi, *a.* Universal, general.
Malele, Malelelele, } *v.* To incline to; to recline towards; to run, to pursue, applied to several.
Malena, Malenalena, } *a.* Smooth; free from creases.
Mali, *v.* To smile.
Maliava, *a.* Unpalatable, sour.
Malie, *v.* To be pleased or delighted; to do easily or gently.
Malie, *a.* Pleasing, fortunate.
Malie, *s.* The last drying of the native cloth ere it is used.
Malielau, *a.* Fair of speech.
Maliu, Maliuliu, } *v.* To come; to return; to be turned or exchanged.
Maligi, *v.* To be spilt.
Malimali, *v.* To smile; to appear pleased.
Malinoa, *a.* Unsettled, not fixed; here and there and every where.
Malo, *int.* Well done! fine! a word of praise and approval.
Malo, *s.* A winner in games.
Maloulau, *s.* The name of a fish.
Maloulau, *a.* New, fresh; lately cooked, as food.
Maloba, *a.* Tight; made fast; (the mast of the canoe.)
Malofa, *v.* To be spread; to be laid flat.
Malohi, *s.* Strength, power, force, energy.
Malohi, *a.* Strong, powerful, forcible.
Maloli, *v.* To be impressed; to to make impression; to affe...

Malohigutu, *s.* One stronger in words than in work.
Malolo, *s.* The flying fish; the name of a tree; rest, repose; cessation from labour.
Malolo, *v.* To rest; to cease from labour.
Malolo, *a.* Resting, quiescent.
Malolo, *v.* To bow down; to stoop; to disappear, as a swelling.
Maloloaga, *s.* A resting place.
Malomaloaa, *a.* Sore in the eyes, applied to the *Tamaha* and the *Tuitoga.*
Malomi, *v.* To be appeased; to be quelled.
Malona, *v.* To sink; to die away; to subside.
Malu, *a.* Loose, soft.
Malu, *v.* To let go; to relax.
Malu, *a.* Tight; impervious to wet.
Malu, *a.* Mild, milder, applied to the wind; easy; free from pain.
Malua, *v.* To cringe; to exhibit signs of fear.
Maluafonua, *v.* To be concealed or hidden by an island.
Malualoi, *s.* A hypocrite; hypocrisy.
Malualoi, *a.* Hypocritical.
Maluálu, *v.* To be torn or shredded.
Malui, *s.* Protection, screen, shelter.
Malui, } *v.* To protect; to
Maluia, } shelter; to screen.
Maluia, *v.* To be eclipsed or obscured by the superior excellence of another.
Malubo, *s.* A name of office in the Tonga government.
Malugia, *a.* Mild and agreeable weather during the performance of any work.
Malulu, *a.* Milder; growing mild; (the wind.)
Malulugia, *a.* Damp, wet.
Malumaea, *a.* Old and rotten, as a rope; weak, infirm.
Malumalu, *s.* Cloudy, cool, shaded.
Malumalu, *s.* Any shaded place; the cool of the day.
Malumu, *s.* A party lying in ambush; any war weapon; the sound as of striking a human being.
Malumu, *v.* To lie in ambush.
Mamaa, *a.* Thoroughly cleansed.
Mama, *s.* World; a lamp; light; fire.
Mama, *s.* A ring; a leak; a shell fish.
Mama, *v.* To leak; to chew; to masticate.
Mama, *a.* Leaky.
Mamaaga, *s.* The source of light; the sun.
Mamaaga, *s.* A very large mouthful.
Mamae, *s.* The plantain.
Mamaetuaniu, *s.* One kind of the plantain.
Mamaevai, *s.* One kind of the plantain.
Mamaehina, *s.* One kind of the plantain.
Mamae, } *v.* To value; to be
Mamaei, } careful of; unwilling to part with.
Mamae, *a.* Withered, dried.
Mamao, *v.* To yawn and stretch; to gape.
Mamao, *s.* Distance, absence.
Mamao, *a.* Distant, remote, long.
Mamao, *ad.* Afar, aloof, abroad.
Mamau, *a.* Fast, fastened, costive.
Mamau, *v.* To frequent; to visit frequently.
Mamau, } *v.* To be bitten by
Mamaua, } a shark.
Mamabu, *v.* To whistle.
Mamafa, *s.* Weight, importance.

Mamafa, *s.* Heavy, weighty, important.

Mamafi, *v.* To excite fear; to alarm, generally applied to a report.

Mamafihuga, *s.* The temper, conduct, conversation. See *Mafihuga*.

Mamaga, *v.* To stride; to extend the legs.

Mamagalo, *a.* Deep; nearly out of sight and remembrance.

Mamage, *s.* A shrub.

Mamagi, *s.* A kind of yam; a shrub.

Mamagia, *a.* Enlightened; overpowered with light.

Mamaha, *s.* Ebb tide.

Mamaha, *a.* Empty (several.)

Mamahi, *s.* Grief, pain, uneasiness.

Mamahi, *a.* Painful, sorrowful.

Mamahiia, *v.* To be in pain.

Mamahigataa, *a.* Difficult to pain; callous.

Mamahigofua, *a.* Easily pained; tender.

Mamahitaute, *s.* Pain brought on by bad conduct.

Mamaka, *a.* Rough, uncouth, blustering.

Mamala, *a.* Sourish; rather sour.

Mamali, *v.* To smile; to appear pleased.

Mamaloa, *a.* Light without intermission, as at the full moon.

Mamalu, *v.* To overshadow; to overhang.

Mamana, *s.* A lover.

Mamana, *v.* To love; to be in love.

Mamanu, *s.* A fish.

Mamata, *v.* To see.

Mamate, *v.* To be swamped or upset.

Mamate, *a.* Benumbed, steril.

Mamate, *s.* Deadness, numbedness.

Mami, *s.* One kind of banana.

Mamio, *v.* To walk.

Mamio, *a.* Twisted, strained.

Mami, } *v.* To chew; to
Mamimami, } keep biting at any thing hard.

Mamihina, *s.* One kind of the banana.

Mamili *v.* To saunter about; to idle away time.

Mamitutue, *s.* A kind of the banana.

Mamo, *s.* The name of a fish.

Mamulu, } *v.* To be rubbed
Mamulumulu, } or frayed; to fret.

Mana, *s.* Thunder; a miracle.

Mana, } *v.* To bewitch; to
Manai, } cause something to happen to another.

Manaui, *s.* A tree; the name of a fish.

Manako, *v.* To like; to approve; to prefer.

Manako, *s.* Like; the object liked.

Manamana, *a.* Showery, squally.

Manatu, *v.* To remember; to think upon.

Manatu, *a.* Anxious, as one from home.

Manava, *s.* The womb; the breath; respiration; afflation.

Manava, *v.* To breathe; to respire; to throb; to pulsate.

Manavaofa, *s.* Compassion, pity.

Manavaofa, *a.* Compassionate, pitiful.

Manavafaji, *a.* Broken winded; afflicted from being too long without food.

Manavafili, *v.* To think, to cogitate.

Manavaga, *s.* A place where all is swallowed up.

Manavahe, *s.* Fear, dread, reverence.

Manavahe, *a.* Fearful.

Manavahe, *v.* To fear.

165

Manavaheia, *a.* Fearful, awful, inspiring fear.
Manavahoko, *a.* Courageous, bold, daring.
Manavajii, *a.* Cowardly.
Manavakavakava, *a.* Zealous, eager, persevering.
Manavakavakava, *s.* Zeal, eagerness.
Manavalahi, *a.* Courageous.
Manefu, } *s.* Dawn of day.
Manefunefu,
Maneke, *v.* To bulge; to push out.
Manemanea, *a.* Weak; becoming rotten.
Manifi, } *a.* Thin.
Manifinifi,
Manimaniia, *a.* Smooth from rubbing.
Manimo, *a.* Lost; hid; out of the way.
Manini, *s.* A fish.
Maninia, *a.* Smooth, slippery.
Maninia, *v.* To be set on edge; to feel a tingling sensation through the body.
Mano, *a.* Ten thousand.
Manoa, *s.* The string with which birds are tied.
Manoo, } *a.* Small in the middle; puckered and bulged.
Manoonoo,
Manofo, *v.* To live contentedly in a place.
Manogi, *a.* Sweet scented, odoriferous.
Manonoo, *v.* To be well tied or roped.
Manonu, *s.* The name of a tree.
Manu, *s.* Animals, birds, beasts, (generic term;) the tooth ache.
Manua, *v.* To suffer from the tooth ache.
Manui, *s.* One kind of *gatu.*
Manuka, } *v.* To kill, to murder, applied to chiefs.
Manukaia,
Manuki, *s.* Derision; rude reproach; contempt.
Manuki, } *v.* To revile, to deride, to sneer; to be mocked.
Manukia,
Manuji, } *a.* Broken, smashed.
Manujinuji,
Manukiaga, *s.* One who is ridiculed or sneered at; the object of contempt.
Manumanu, *s.* A small party who commences the fighting in war; fringes or strips of any thing light hung to the canoe sail.
Manumanu, *s.* Covetousness, avarice; the name of one kind of grass.
Manumanu, *a.* Covetous.
Manumanu, *v.* To covet.
Manumanumelie, *a.* Well looking; fine in appearance, as a warrior ready for action.
Manumanutamaki, *a.* Mean; cowardly in appearance.
Manumi, } *a.* Creased; crimped, not folded.
Manuminumi,
Manutaulalo, *v.* See *Taulalo.*
Manutahi, *s.* A bird of the sea; applied to one anxious to do what is not at all becoming him, as a land bird to go to sea.
Manuvakai, *s.* The look out bird; the one that leads the way.
Masima, *s.* Salt.
Masima, *a.* Salted, pickled.
Mata, *s.* A war club.
Mata, *s.* The face; countenance; eyes; appearance; edge; boundary; mesh.
Mata, *a.* Raw, uncooked; the best state of the cocoa nut for drinking.
Mataaeva, *s.* A fish.
Mataaki, *v.* To be plucked up.
Mataali, *s.* Nuts that fall ere they are old.
Mataata, *a.* Disinterested; without view to recompense.

166

Matai, *s.* A fish; a clever one; the best one; a single one.
Matai, *a.* Clever.
Mataiika, *s.* A kind of boil.
Mataiuha, *s.* A spot or drop of rain.
Mataifale, *v.* To see and know all within.
Mataihuhu, *s.* The nipple, tug.
Mataila, *a.* Callous, hardened, obdurate, obstinate.
Mataila, *s.* Obstinacy, obduracy.
Matailagi, *s.* The horizon; the appearance of the sky.
Mataimatu, *s.* The fire fly.
Mataimoho, *s.* A shrub.
Mataitofe, *s.* The pearl.
Mataele, *s.* A fish.
Mataotao, *v.* To be pressed or kept down by a weight.
Matau, *s.* A fish hook.
Matau, *a.* Dexterous in throwing; to the right.
Matau, *s.* The right; starboard.
Mataui, *v.* To keep the eye upon any object.
Mataba, *s.* A door; gate; stile; an opening; an entrance.
Mataba-jioata, *s.* A window.
Matabogi, *a.* Twinkling; partially closed (the eyes.)
Mataboko, *a.* Sunk; deep in the head (the eyes.)
Matabolobolo, *s.* A shell fish.
Mataboto, *a.* Sharp; quick sighted.
Matabula, *s.* The name of a fish.
Matabule, *s.* A petty chief.
Matafo, *v.* To be cut; to be lacerated.
Matafao, *s.* The holes made for the *kafa* in building.
Matafaga, *s.* The sea beach opposite any dwelling.
Matafaha, *s.* The standing place of individuals in driving fish into the net.
Matafaji, *s.* The exact place where a stick or limb is cracked or broken.
Matafano, *a.* Loose; not close and hard in texture.
Matafatu, *a.* Hard; not easily made to cry.
Matafi, Matafitafi, } *v.* Swept, clean.
Matafui, *s.* A shrub.
Mataga, *s.* A regiment; a body of men standing.
Mataga, *s.* An observatory; a place from whence objects may be best viewed.
Mataga, Matagataga, } *v.* To be peeled or excoriated.
Matagaki, *a.* Open.
Matagi, *s.* The wind.
Matagia, Matagiia, } *v.* To be favoured with a fair wind.
Matagimalie, *s.* A wind to go and come.
Matahaa, *s.* Red inflamed eyes.
Matahafu, *s.* Sore eyes.
Matahekeheka, *s.* A shell fish.
Matahele, *s.* The name of a shell fish.
Matahema, *s.* The upper mark of the tattooing on the left side.
Matahilaaho, *a.* Unobserving though close at hand.
Matahoa, *v.* To be ashamed, as one badly dressed at a feast
Matahua, *a.* Comely, beautiful.
Matahuakuku, *s.* Sore eyes.
Matajili, *s.* The germ or sprout of the old nut.
Mataka, Matakataka, } *a.* Peeled off, excoriated.
Matakakamo, *s.* The choice, the best.
Mataki, *s.* A traitor, a betrayer, a spy.
Mataki, *v.* To spy.
Mataki, Matakitaki, } *a.* Well spread out; stretched.
Matakubega, *s.* The instrument used in the meshes in making nets.

Matala, *a.* Open, expanded, as a flower; free from restraint; ready, applied to the mind.
Matala, *v.* To burst away; to get free.
Matalai, *s.* Sore eyes; a blossom or flower.
Matalafi, *s.* Small wedges used in tightening the *kafa.*
Matalaga, *s.* The spot where the earth is raised for digging and setting the yams.
Matalala, *a.* Like a deserted place.
Matalava, *s.* A kind of boil.
Matalavea, *a.* Literally, knowing with the eyes, but invariably used ironically of one who is irreverent and ill behaved, who acts as if he knew no one.
Matalea, *s.* A kind of *Ji;* sore eyes.
Mataliki, *s.* A constellation of stars.
Mataliki, *v.* To appear in sight, used of many.
Matalili, *s.* Anger.
Matalili, *v.* To exhibit anger.
Matama, *s.* Shame, shame facedness, modesty.
Matama, *a.* Shame faced, modest.
Matamau, *a.* Fixed; tearless, applied to the eyes.
Matamata, *s.* A shell fish; the appearance or resemblance.
Matamata, *v.* To seem, to resemble.
Matamata, *a.* New, applied to a canoe.
Matamataga, *s.* A cause assigned for not inflicting punishment.
Matamatakubega, *s.* The cobweb.
Matamatakubega, *a.* Membraneous, resembling cobwebs.
Matamatamanu, *s.* The flower and seeds of the grass called *Mujie.*
Matamea, *s.* A fish.
Matani, *s.* One kind of the *Ji.*
Mataniji, Matanijiniji, } *a.* Proud, vain.
Matanikolo, *s.* The gates or entrances into a fort.
Matata, *s.* The mark or impression from a blow.
Matata, *s.* The sound as of something being torn asunder.
Matata, *v.* To be inclined or disposed to.
Matata, *a.* Clear; free from filth; fixed, determined.
Matatau, *s.* A straight or sure eye.
Matatafa, *s.* A cut; a surgical opening.
Matatagi, *a.* Fretful; often crying.
Matatahi, *s.* Shore, beach.
Matateteka, *s.* A fish.
Matateve, *s.* A shell fish.
Matavai, *s.* A spring, a fountain.
Matavalea, *a.* Dull of sight; not sharp in looking out.
Mate, *s.* Death; the dead; guess.
Mate, *v.* To die; to upset; to turn over, as a canoe.
Mate, *a.* Dead, deadly, extinct, benumbed.
Matea, *a.* Deadly, mortal, capital.
Matea, *v.* To guess.
Mateaga, Mategа, } *s.* The place or cause of one's death.
Matei, *s.* Funnel.
Matei, *s.* A small straight stick used in catching fish.
Matebu, *v.* To bulge out; to jet.
Mategu, *a.* Palatable; agreeable to the taste.
Mateke, *a.* Bulged; pushed out; extended.
Matele, Mateletele, } *v.* To glide along; to cut through, as in the water.
Matemate, *a.* Comparatively smooth (the sea;) becoming smooth.

168

Matemate, *a.* Perfect, complete, fixed, settled.
Matematetaha, *v.* To die one after another; to follow in succession.
Matemutukia, *v.* To die in the prime of life.
Mato, *s.* The edge or boundary of a high perpendicular rock.
Matoo, *a.* Open.
Matoo, *v.* To disunite; to fall asunder.
Matofa, *a.* Marked out; beaten, as a path.
Matofi, Matofitofi, } *a.* Cut into sets or pieces.
Matohi, Matohitohi, } *a.* Marked, scratched, shreded.
Matoji, Matojitoji, } *a.* Pecked; bit in holes; snipped.
Matoli, Matolitoli, } *v.* To break; to fall in pieces; to be broken; to be chipped.
Matolo, Matolotolo, } *a.* Scraped, scratched.
Matolu, *s.* Thickness; a shrub.
Matolu, Matolutolu, } *a.* Thick.
Matu, *s.* The name of a fish.
Matu, Matua, } *v.* To be poured out; to be shaken off.
Matua, *s.* Parents; old people.
Matua, *s.* A play with the hands.
Matua, *v.* To frequent.
Matuaki, *ad.* Very; superlatively.
Matuo, Matuotuo, } *v.* To pull by a sudden jerk, as a fish at the hook or in the net; to be pulled.
Matuotuo, *a.* Ripe, mature.
Matuu, *v.* To stop; to cease to flow; to be cut.
Matuu, *a.* Dry.
Matuutamaki, *a.* Mildewed; rotten from being wet.
Matuutuu, *a.* Cut and lacerated in different directions.
Matuutuumalie, *a.* Seasonable, suitable, becoming.
Matuutuutamaki, *a.* Unseasonable, unsuitable.
Matugaki, *v.* To bend or yield to a superior force.
Matuke, Matuketuke, } *a.* Shrivelled, wrinkled.
Matuku, Matukutuku, } *v.* To subside; to sink; to grow less.
Matula, *s.* A fish.
Matulafulafu, *s.* A fish.
Matule, *v.* To recline; to lie; to bend.
Matuvelo, *s.* A fish.
Mavae, *v.* To be weaned.
Mavae, *v.* To separate; to leave each other.
Mavae, *s.* Separation, divorce.
Mavaeoluga, *v.* To decide by contest.
Mavaevae, *v.* To be separated; to be in divisions.
Mavahe, Mavahevahe, } *v.* To be divided; to be separated into portions.
Mavava, *s.* A general shout; acclamation.
Mavava, *v.* To shout.
Maveu, Maveuveu, } *s.* Confusion, disorder, commotion.
Maveu, Maveuveu, } *a.* Confused; jumbled together; without order.
Mavivi, *v.* To accomplish; to do.
Meaa, *a.* Good, clean, generally used ironically of what is filthy.
Mea, *v.* To do; to look; to attend to.
Mea, *s.* Things in general; matters; property; affairs.
Meai, *v.* To know; to be acquainted with.
Meai, *s.* A fish.
Meaiaka, *s.* A fish.
Meaiule, *s.* A fish.
Meaituoua, *s.* A fish.
Meau, *s.* A fish.

169

Meavale, *s.* The poor; populace.
Mee, *s.* A dance; a feast at which there is dancing.
Mee, *v.* To dance; to rejoice.
Meemeavale, *a.* Poor; like the populace.
Meemee, *v.* To dance; to try to dance.
Meemee, *a.* Glad, joyful.
Mei, *s.* The bread fruit and its tree.
Mei, *prep.* From.
Meigutuveka, *s.* A fish.
Meihe, *v.* Hush, be still (to a child.)
Meimei, *ad.* Nearly, almost.
Meitauajila, *s.* A fish.
Meite, See *Meihe*.
Meo, } *v.* To look displeased.
Meomeo, }
Meheka, *s.* Envy.
Meheka, *a.* Envious, jealous.
Meheka, *v.* To envy, to grudge.
Mehekitaga, *s.* An aunt.
Mehigo, A shell fish.
Mejimaji, *a.* Neither green nor dry; partially dry.
Mele, *s.* A defect, a blemish.
Mele, } *v.* To feign a cough;
Melemele, } to cough lightly.
Melefo, *s.* A fish.
Meleketu, } *v.* To limp, to
Melemeleketu, } hop.
Melemo, *v.* To be drowned.
Melie, *s.* Sweetness.
Melie, *a.* Sweet, delicious.
Melino, *s.* Peace; freedom from war.
Melino, *a.* Peaceable.
Melinoaga, *s.* The origin or the cause of peace.
Melo, } *a.* Brown, ripe.
Melomelo, }
Memea, *s.* A fish.
Menega, *s.* A fish.
Menumenu, *s.* A trifle; a light insignificant thing.
Mioi, *s.* A misrepresentation; contortion; falsehood.

170

Mioi, *v.* To misrepresent; to equivocate; to contort; to twist.
Mioia, *v.* To be twisted; to be belied.
Miomioaki, *v.* To twist and turn; to go in a serpentine path.
Migao, *a.* Ashamed, bashful.
Migi, } *a.* Wooly; thick;
Migimigi, } mixed; twisted.
Miha, } *a.* Dry; hard in
Mihemiha, } the sun.
Mihi, } *v.* To sob; to draw
Mihimihi, } up into the nostrils.
Miji, *s.* A bird; a dream.
Miji, *v.* To dream; to chirp.
Mijikia, *v.* To be sucked or drawn into; to be engulphed.
Mijimiji, *v.* To make a chirping noise with the mouth.
Milemila, *s.* A small thin stick or twig used as a comb.
Milihi, } *v.* To handle; to
Milimilihi, } turn about in the hands.
Mili, } *v.* To rub; to em-
Milimili, } brocate.
Milimili, *s.* An embrocation; the act of rubbing.
Milimilina, *a.* Poorly; lightly afflicted.
Milimilina, *s.* A light or trifling affliction.
Milo, *s.* The name of a tree.
Miloha, *v.* To saunter and idle to and fro.
Milohi, } *v.* To twist; to
Milomilohi, } wrench off.
Milolua, *s.* One method of straining out the *kava*.
Mimi, *s.* Urine.
Mimi, *v.* To make water.
Mimio, *v.* To twist; to contort.
Mimio, *s.* Dissembling.
Mimiji, *v.* To suck; to draw towards.
Mo, *con.* And.
Mo, *pron.* You (dual number.)

Mo, *prep*. With, besides.
Mo, *s*. A short and fat kind of pig.
Moa, *s*. The domestic fowl.
Moa, *a*. Dry, dried.
Moauli, *s*. A bawd.
Moauli, *v*. To bawd.
Moafefine, *s*. A hen; a female fowl.
Moala, *s*. One kind of yam.
Moana, *s*. The deep sea, ocean.
Moataane, *s*. The male fowl, the cock.
Moanahauhau, Moanavavale, } *s*. The deep; the sea far from soundings.
Moeaki, *v*. To sleep at a place expecting to do some work on the morrow.
Moei, Moemaia, } *v*. To trample; to tread upon.
Moegalo, *s*. A shrub.
Moejila, *ad*. Near at hand.
Moemoe, *v*. To feel for with the feet.
Moemoei, *v*. To touch the soles of a chief's feet as a mark of reverence.
Moemoebo, *v*. To assassinate; to murder by the sly, as one asleep.
Moemoegamalie, Moemoegatonu, } *v*. To be ready; to be prepared for.
Moemoegatamaki, *v*. To be unprepared; to want preparation.
Moi, Moimoi, Moimoii, } *v*. To accompany a short distance; to see another off; to escort.
Moifi, *s*. A buzzing, as wind caused by something in quick motion.
Moifua, *v*. To take or bring, go or come, altogether.
Moihu, *s*. A priest; a meditator; one who offers sacrifice.
Moihula, *s*. A present.
Moo, *prep*. For.
Moou, For thee.
Moojibo, *s*. A shrub.
Moomao, *s*. A fish.
Mooni, *s*. Truth, reality, fact.
Mooni, *a*. True, real.
Mooni, *ad*. Truly, verily, really.
Moonia, *s*. A tree.
Moota, *s*. A tree.
Mou, *pron*. You.
Mou, *a*. Heavy laden, as a vessel.
Moua, *a*. Very busy; entangled; overtaken,
Moua, *pron*. Your (dual number.)
Moui, *s*. Life.
Moui, *a*. Alive.
Moui, *v*. To live.
Mouiaga, *s*. The source of life.
Mouifa, *s*. A tree or log that burns for a long time.
Mouimomanava, *a*. Precarious, uncertain, as one often poorly.
Mouga, *s*. A mountain.
Mouga, *a*. Mountainous.
Mougia, *v*. To be sheltered or hid by another.
Moulaloa, *s*. Subjection.
Moulaloa, *v*. To be subjugated; to be governed.
Moulu, *v*. To bore; to push under; to work away underneath.
Moumau, *a*. Fast; not moveable, as stains.
Moumoua, *a*. Rich, wealthy.
Moumoui, *a*. Recovering; getting better.
Mounu, *s*. A bait.
Mounufakalele, *s*. A bird tied by the leg and set to fly to entice others.
Mounufujifuji, *s*. Similar to the above, but not allowed to fly.
Mousaa, *a*. Afflicted with many diseases.
Mofi, *s*. Fever.
Mofi, *v*. To astonish; to cause fear.
Mofi, *a*. Feverish.
Mofia, *a*. Burnt, scorched.
Mofiji, *s*. The shrimp.

Mofiji, } v. To shoot as sparks; to get unexpectedly; to exhibit bad feelings upon being reproved.
Mofijifiji, }

Mofimofi, *a.* Rather feverish.

Mofuike, *s.* Earthquake.

Mofuta } *v.* To assume a proud and daring gait.
Mofutofuta, }

Moga, *s.* The throat, gorge, swallow.

Mogea, *a.* Satisfied, satiated.

Mogomoga, *s.* The cockroach, beetle.

Mogumagu, *s.* A scab.

Mohe, *s.* Sleep.

Mohe, *v.* To sleep; to congeal; to concrete by cold.

Mohea, *v.* To be slipt in; to be frequented, as a place by fish.

Mohealio, *s.* The name of a fish.

Moheaga, } *s.* A bed; a sleeping place.
Mohega, }

Mohefiji, *v.* To keep in motion when asleep.

Mohega, *v.* To cohabit.

Mohemohe, *s.* The name of a tree.

Mohi, *s.* The name of a fish; also, a shell fish.

Moho, *s.* The name of a bird.

Moho, *a.* Cooked; ready to be eaten; rotten.

Mohoota, *a.* Cooked, but not well dressed.

Mohobala, *a.* Cooked to rottenness.

Mohogia, *a.* Scorched, cooked.

Mohokoi, *s.* The name of a tree.

Mohomoho, *s.* The ends and pieces of yams prepared for sets which prove to be rotten.

Mohu, *a.* Plentiful, abundant.

Mohuku, *s.* Grass.

Mohumea, } *a.* Plentiful; abundant; in quick succession.
Mohumohumea, }

Mohumohu, *v.* To happen frequently or in succession.

Moji, *v.* To do now and again.

Moji, } *v.* To chirp as the *veka;* to drop as rain.
Mojimoji, }

Mojimoji, *s.* A light shower.

Mojikaka, *s.* A particular kind of basket.

Moka, *a.* Bent; not tight and straight.

Moka, } *a.* Light; clear in the skin.
Mokomoka, }

Mokau, *a.* Conquered, subdued.

Mokimokii, *a.* Very small; diminutive.

Moko, *v.* To fasten the thatch to certain nuts.

Moko, *s.* A kind of lizard.

Mokoa, *v.* Wait awhile; hold on.

Mokoi, } *a.* Cold; very cold.
Mokoii, }

Mokobuna, *s.* A grand child.

Mokofiji, *v.* To writhe; to twist and kick about.

Mokofute, *s.* The sticks of the *Hiabo,* when stripped of its bark.

Mokohula, *s.* A small black biting insect.

Mokohunu, *s.* A shell fish.

Mokojia, *a.* Cold.

Mokojia, *s.* Coldness, frigidity.

Mokolooa, *v.* To stretch out the neck; to look towards.

Mokomoka, *a.* Brown in the skin; neither light nor dark.

Mokomoko, *a.* Cool.

Mokomoko, *s.* Coldness.

Mokomokoaho, *s.* The cold about day break.

Mokomokotuaniu, *s.* An insect found in the nut leaves.

Mokotola, *s.* The name of a shell fish.

Mokulu, } *v.* To fall, as tears; to run out; to fall to pieces.
Mokulukulu, }

Mola, *a.* Without meaning; without cause or reason.

Mole, *a.* Lost; out of sight; taken; gone.

Mole,
Molemole, } *a.* Smooth, even.

Moleaga,
Mòlega, } *s.* The place or cause of being lost.

Molekamoe, *s.* Blind man's buff.

Mòlemolè, *s.* Evenness, smoothness.

Molemolegamalie, *v.* To be quite finished or exhausted; all done.

Moli, *s.* The shaddock; the orange.

Moli, *v.* To move; to progress or regress.

Moliuku, *s.* One kind of the shaddock.

Molimoli, *v.* To cut off; to cut into small pieces.

Molimolituu, *v.* To stand restless to be gone.

Molou, *s.* The name of a fish.

Molokau, *s.* The centipede.

Moloki,
Molomolo,
Molomoloki, } *v.* To tread; to stamp upon.

Molomolomuivae, *v.* To tread upon the heels; to trip up.

Molu, *s.* Softness.

Molu, *a.* Soft, yielding.

Molumalu, *a.* Genteel; chief-like in appearance.

Molumalufakafono, *a.* Chief-like in appearance but governed.

Molulu,
Molumolu, } *a.* Becoming soft.

Momea, *s.* A shrub.

Momi, *v.* To beg; frequently to make known wants.

Momi, *a.* Indented; fallen in, as the mouth without teeth.

Momiki, *v.* To break up.

Momo, *s.* Crumbs.

Momo, *a.* Broken up, crumbled.

Momoa, *s.* Dryness; the name of a fish.

Momoa, *a.* Dry.

Momoa, *v.* To become dry.

Momoi, *v.* To return a present or a portion divided out; to twist the article with which ropes are made.

Momoi, *a.* Small, insignificant.

Momoi, *v.* To take; to present an offering or sacrifice; to return, to give back.

Momoiki, *a.* Small pieces.

Momou, *v.* To shrink back; to recoil; to turn away.

Momofi, *s.* Heat from fire.

Momohe, *v.* To cohabit.

Momoho, *a.* Ripe; brown in colour; ready to burst.

Momoji, *v.* To rub, grind to powder.

Momoke, *s.* Confusion, uproar; a ding; clatter and noise.

Momoko, *a.* Cold.

Momole, *a.* Smooth on the surface.

Momoli, *v.* To cut from; to break off.

Momomomo, *a.* Broken; dashed to pieces.

Momoto, *v.* To strike with the fists.

Momotu, *a.* Drawn; contracted in different places.

Mona, *v.* To do, to dispose or arrange orderly.

Monimonu,
Monitonu, } *a.* Prosperous, blessed.

Mono, *v.* To squeeze; to press in; to fill.

Mono, *s.* The article used in filling up the lashing holes of a canoe.

Monoi, *s.* A side blow with the fist.

Monoi, *v.* To take the first chance; to wish to be first; to strike with the fist.

Monoji, *v.* To cork; to play.

Monojivai, *s.* One kind of the *Ifi.*

Monomono, *s.* A tree; a patch.

Monomono,
Monomonoji, } *v.* To patch, to mend.

Monu, } s. A blessing, felicity.
Monuia, }

Monuia, a. Blessed, happy, felicitous.

Monuka, s. A wound.

Monuka, } a. Wounded; cut; moth eaten, applied to sacred things and chiefs; rotten; decomposed.
Monumonuka, }

Moto, s. Bud, buds.

Moto, } v. To bud.
Motoiakau, }

Motou, s. A tree.

Motohiko, s. A heavy blow with the fist.

Motohiko, v. To strike another with the fist.

Motolu, s. The name of a fish.

Motomoto, a. The cocoa nut when strong through age, and unpleasant drinking.

Mototo, s. A fish.

Motu, s. An island; one kind of banana.

Motu, a. Broken; snapt asunder.

Motua, s. An old man; a married man.

Motua, a. Old; ripe; fit to eat.

Motualea, s. Alphabet.

Motui, a. Old and torn.

Motuu, a. Old, applied to the nut only.

Motuu, s. Native cloth presented to voyagers on their arrival.

Motuu, v. To exchange a wet and dirty dress for a dry one.

Motufau, a. Distant; out of reach.

Motuhi, v. To cut through; to separate; to break.

Motuhia, v. To be loosed; to be broken away.

Motukaenavei, v. To break away though bound; to fail despite every means.

Motukafa, v. To break away from restraint or confinement.

Motuku, s. A sea gull.

Motulau, s. A fish.

Motuloutou, a. Broken short off; decisive.

Motuloutou, v. To break short; to decide; to settle a dispute by force of arms.

Motumotu, s. A rag; a torn tattered dress.

Motumotu, a. Ragged; torn in tatters.

Movete, } v. To be scattered; to fall to pieces; to be loose.
Movetevete, }

Moveve, a. Credulous in reference to evil reports; suspicious.

Moveveveve, s. Small pieces; remnants of something large.

Mu, s. A kind of butterfly; a fish.

Mua, ad. Aforetime, formerly.

Mua, prep. Before; further onward in place; in front of.

Muagutu, s. The lips; the part near the lips; the beak of birds.

Muagututaha, v. To speak one and the same thing, applied to several.

Muajino, a. Forward to present the body, but implying that the mind is left behind.

Muaki, a. First.

Muaki, s. The first; the first in a number of baskets of food.

Muaki, v. To precede; to take the precedence.

Muanima, s. The ends of the fingers.

Muavae, s. The toes and fore part of the feet.

Muabaka, s. A present taken by the party presenting.

Mui, s. the tails of birds; the end; the hind part.

Mui, a. Unripe, immature; last, behind.

Muia, v. To pursue, to chase, to follow.

174

Muiaki, *s.* The last; the latest; the youngest.
Muifonua, *s.* A point of land, a cape.
Muiga, *s.* The corner or end of a net or basket.
Muiku, *s.* One kind of Tonga comb.
Muimui, *a.* Unripe, soft.
Muimui, *v.* To follow.
Muimomua, *a.* Neither first nor last; neither this nor that but between the two.
Muitau, *s.* A harlot, a whore.
Muitaga, *s.* A part in the entrails of swine and large fish.
Muitala, *s.* Obedience.
Muitala, *v.* To obey; to follow directions.
Muitala, *a.* Obedient.
Muivae, *s.* The heel.
Muomua, *v.* To go before; to precede; to lead.
Muomuaki, See *Muaki*.
Mugaki, *v.* To warm or dry by the fire.
Muhu, } **Muhumuhu**, } *v.* To speak quietly together.
Muhu, *s.* The sound as of persons talking together.
Mujiakovi, *v.* To take as a wife a young growing girl.
Mujie, *s.* One kind of grass.
Muka, *s.* The young leaves of the nut and other trees; the name of a whitish hard stone.
Muka, } **Mukomuka**, } *v.* To put forth leaves; to spring, to grow.
Mukaia, *a.* Abounding in buds or young leaves.
Mula, } **Mulomula**, } *v.* Soft, unripe.
Mula, *s.* The bottom part of an unripe yam; the name of a shell fish.
Muli, *s.* A foreigner, a stranger.
Muli, *s.* See *Muiga*.
Mulione, *s.* A shell fish.
Mulimalo, *s.* An ornament; a set off; a plume of feathers.
Mulu, } **Mului**, } *v.* To work slightly or carelessly; to wear the dress in an indecent manner; to draw along as a curtain.
Mulumulu, } **Mulumului**, } *v.* To rub or peel off.
Mumu, *v.* To warm by a fire.
Mumu, *v.* To collect together.
Mumu, *s.* One kind of the *Talo*.
Mumui, *v.* To imitate, to follow.
Mumuhu, *s.* The roar of the sea or wind.
Mumutau, *v.* To meet and quarrel or fight, as waves meet and dash against each other.
Muna, *v.* To talk nonsense; to act as one insane.
Muna, *s.* The sayings and doings of one foolish.
Munoa, *v.* To be unacquainted with what is going on.
Munomuna, *s.* One kind of banana.
Munua, *s.* The name of a fish.
Mutu, *v.* To tear across the warp.
Mutu, *s.* The name of a sharp shell used in cutting the *Fetaaki*.
Mutumutu, *v.* To prepare the *Fetaaki* to make native cloth.
Mutumutu, *s.* The name of a fish.
Mutuki, *v.* To break; to tear with the hands.

N

N, THE fourteenth Letter in the Tonga Alphabet. Its sound is that of *nah* in English.

Na, *pron.* They, their, (dual number.)
Na, *a.* Respectful.

Na, *s.* Fear, respect.
Naa, A sign of the past tense.
Naa, *con.* Lest.
Naa, *v.* Hush! be still! used to children.
Naa, *s.* Used of broken food brought from a distance for friends.
Nae, A sign of the past tense.
Nai, *ad.* Perhaps.
Nai, A term of endearment or affection.
Nai, *v.* To collect, to scrape together, as broken food.
Naijia, *v.* To do in season; to strike while the iron is hot.
Nainai, *v.* To attend to; to be careful of; to exhort.
Nainai, *s.* Exhortation.
Nau, *pron.* They, their (plural.)
Naunau, *s.* The materials for any work; ornaments, accoutrements.
Nautolu, *pron.* Them.
Nabanabagamalie, *a.* Prepared, ready for.
Nabanabagatamaki, *a.* Unprepared.
Nabe, *s.* One method of plaiting *kafa*.
Nafa, *s.* A native drum.
Nafui, *v.* To repeat; to do again and again.
Nafunafua, *a.* Limy; scaly; rough, as the skin not oiled.
Nafaki, } *v.* To expect; to
Nanafaki, } wait for.
Nanafaki, *s.* Expectation, hope.
Nahu, *s.* The name of a tree.
Nahunahui, *v.* To take care of.
Naji, } *v.* To be on the look
Najinaji, } out; to watch; to attend to.
Namo, *s.* A bay enclosed with a reef.
Namu, *s.* The musquito; scent, odour.
Namu, *v.* To smell.
Namua, *a.* Abounding in musquitoes.
Namuaa, } *a.* Bad in smell; dis-
Namuku, } agreeable odour.
Namuhaha, *v.* To smell of decomposition.
Nanamu, *v.* To smell.
Nanamu, *s.* Odour, smell.
Nani, } *v.* To act fondly.
Nanivi, }
Nanuga, *s.* The character; the conduct.
Natu, *v.* To knead, to mix.
Navalalo, *v.* To push off a canoe when hanging in the wind.
Navei, } *v.* To bind, to
Navenavei, } handcuff.
Navu, *s.* A preparation of lime for cleaning the head.
Navu, *v.* To dress the head for cleaning.
Navunavua, *a.* Limy; whitish; dirty, applied to the head.
Ne, A sign of the past tense.
Ne, *pron.* He, she, it.
Neinei, No wonder; no marvel.
Neu, *pron.* I (always in the past tense.)
Neufi, *s.* A fish.
Nebi, } *v.* To tighten; to
Nebinebi, } straighten the dress.
Nefu, *s.* A fish.
Neka, *v.* To rejoice, to joy.
Nekejia, *v.* To prompt, to incite.
Nekeneka, *s.* Joy, rejoicing, delight.
Nekeneka, *v.* To rejoice; to exhibit signs of rejoicing.
Nenefu, *s.* Twilight, dimness.
Nenefu, *a.* Dim, dull, uncertain.
Neneke, *v.* To rise; to swell; to bulge.
Nenenu, } *v.* To stammer; to
Nenu, } faulter in speech.
Neveneve, *s.* The nest and young of the *Kalevelеve*.
Niihi, *a.* Some.

Niu, *a.* Old, hard, as the skin of an old person.
Niu, *s.* The cocoa nut tree and its fruit.
Niukafa, Niuui, Niuleka, Niumea, Niumeaalava, Niumeatoto, Niuvale, Niubulufufula, } *s.* Different kinds of the cocoa nut.
Nifi, *a.* Little, but generally used ironically.
Nifo, *s.* A tooth, teeth, horn.
Niji, Nijiniji, } *s.* Vanity.
Niji, Nijiniji, } *a.* Vain.
Niko, Nikonikoi, } *a.* Variegated; of divers colours and patterns.
Nima, *s.* The hand.
Nima, *a.* Five.
Nimafua, *s.* Thick or swollen arms.
Nimageau, *a.* Five hundred.
Nimagofulu, *a.* Fifty.
Nimakovi, Nimalami, } *a.* Light fingered.
Nimaji, Nimajia, Nimenima, } *v.* To work quickly; to handle quickly.
Nimameaa, *a.* Clever, ingenious.
Nimoitalafau, Not to be found yet there.
Nini, *v.* To rub the head with the finger ends.
Ninifo, *a.* Large, full grown.
Ninika, *v.* To make ado.
Ninima, *v.* To work with both hands; to work quickly.
Ninimo, *s.* Giddiness, dizziness.
Ninimo, *a.* Dizzy, giddy.
Ninimo, *v.* To become dizzy or giddy.
Noa, *s.* Dumbness.
Noa, *a.* Dumb, random, trivial, worthless, undesigned, disengaged.
Noe, Noenoe, } *a.* Fretful, peevish.
Noi, Noinoi, } *v.* To limp; to hobble along.
Noo, *s.* A belt, a waistband.
Noo, Noonoo, } *v.* To bind together.
Noona, *s.* Strangling.
Nooua, *v.* To strangle.
Nootagavala, *s.* The loins.
Nootaki, *v.* To tie up, to fasten.
Nou, *v.* To tie together.
Nou, Nounou, } *a.* Short, contracted.
Nofatu, *v.* To use a girth round the stomach when pinched by hunger.
Nofatu, *a.* Hungry.
Nofo, *v.* To dwell; to abide; to sit.
Nofoa, *s.* A seat.
Nofoaga, *s.* A dwelling place; a habitation.
Nofoi *s.* A shoal of fish.
Nofoi, *v.* To wait for on bended knees; to catch between the knees when kneeling down; to sit upon; to cover.
Nofoia, *v.* To dwell with; to inhabit.
Nofoia, *v.* To endanger the steer oar in tacking a canoe.
Nofu, *s.* The name of a fish.
Noga, Nogonoga, } *a.* Sheltered; not exposed; peaceful.
Nogia, *v.* To borrow.
Noko, *s.* The hip.
Nokonoko, *s.* A bread fruit.
Nokonoko, *a.* Large in the hips.
Noku, Nokunoku, } *v.* To jerk; to pull suddenly; to try to break by suddenly jerking.
Nomu, *s.* Food made for infants.
Nono, *s.* An insect.
Nono, *v.* To borrow.
Nonoo, *v.* To gird; to tie up.

177

Nonofo, *s.* The state or circumstances of persons living together.

Nonofo, *v.* To dwell together.

Nonu, *s.* A tree.

Nota, *v.* To act differently on a sudden.

Nue, *s.* A fish.

Nuha, *v.* To extract a shot or piece of an arrow from the body.

Nuji, *s.* A garland; a wreath of flowers.

Nuji, Nujinuji, } *v.* To rub in the hands.

Nukonuka, *s.* The name of a shrub.

Nunu, *v.* To assemble; to gather together.

Nunua, *s.* Demerit, retribution.

Nunutuu, See *Bubutuu.*

Numi, Numinumi, } *v.* To gather in sewing; to plait; to pucker; to crease.

Nunuji, *v.* To be all on an uproar and tumult.

S

S, THE fifteenth Letter in the Tonga Alphabet. Its sound is that of *s* in *sarcasm.*

Sa, *s.* An expression of disgust and disapproval.

Sai, Saisai, } *a.* Good.

Sao, *a.* Pleasing; agreeing with what is right and just.

Sauni, *v.* To reward.

Sausau, *a.* Half-dressed; badly clothed.

Sabi, *s.* A kick from the foot thrown behind.

Sabi, *v.* To kick as above; to wry the mouth.

Sago, *s.* A reproachful term for arms and legs.

Saka, *a.* Good.

Sakiki, *s.* The *biu* leaf stretched and sewn to a stick, used as a sun screen.

Sala, *s.* A cope, a hood.

Sala, *v.* To cope; to wrap round the head.

Salulu, *v.* To be angry with one who is on the look out for food.

Sani, Sanisani, } *v.* To be particular about; to decorate; to pet.

Sasuli, *v.* To talk vainly and at random.

See, Sesee, } *v.* To drive; to fright away, as birds, &c.

Seuke, Seukele, } *int.* Dear me! alas!

Sekisekia, *v.* To assume superiority in the presence of strangers.

Sesele, *a.* Eccentric; odd; approaching insanity.

Sikisiki, *s.* A rope belonging to a canoe.

Soki, *s.* Spikes; pointed sticks.

Sokii, *v.* To place spikes to wound the feet.

Sosaa, See *Hohaa.*

Sove, Sovesove, } *v.* To beat; to beat to softness.

Sovini, Sovinivini, } *v.* To hiss; to bubble up.

T

T, THE sixteenth Letter in the Tonga Alphabet. Its sound is that of *t* in *tar.*

Ta, *s.* The circular end of a Tonga house; a blow; a row of bananas; the tattooing of the body.

Ta, *v.* To strike; to beat; to hew; to tattoo.
Taa, *s.* The name of a fish.
Taau, *s.* The coalition of the water in the wake of a vessel.
Taabaa, *s.* The blows of one childless.
Taaga, *s.* The cutting down of wood; wood cut down; a song.
Taaga, *v.* To cut wood for mechanical purposes; to sing, to chant.
Taagi, *v.* To chant the excellencies or defects of others.
Taagalava, *s.* Any place that is free for the operation of all; a place from which many are served.
Taahine, *s.* A virgin, a maid.
Taaki, } *v.* To eradicate; to
Taakii, } tear up; to bring to light what was hid or forgotten.
Taaki, *s.* Eradication; the act of tearing up by the roots.
Taakifuu, *v.* To tear up root and branch; to eradicate.
Taalo, *v.* To beckon at sea.
Taalo, } *v.* To fan another.
Taaloalo, }
Taalofaki, *v.* To bathe and clean the head with clay, applied to the *Tuitoga.*
Taane, *s.* The marriage of a chief.
Taane, *v.* To celebrate a marriage feast.
Taataa, *s.* Blood, applied to chiefs.
Tae, A deprivative particle, used to form compound words, like the English deprivative in *un*, *less*, &c.; and is always prefixed to the word, as, *taeofa*—without love; *taeaoga*—useless.
Tae, } *v.* To reach; to stretch
Tatae, } out the arm to any object.
Tae, *s.* A cough; excrement; feces.
Tae, *v.* To cough.
Taefaivae, *a.* Footless; lame; not able to use the feet.
Taefi, *v.* To throw the arm backwards and forwards.
Taegolo, *v.* To cough with a ruttling hoarse sound.
Taehaoota, *v.* To be destitute of one who will act the friend in all things.
Taele, } *s.* Sediment, remains.
Taelele, }
Taemi, } *v.* To caper and
Taemiemi, } jump along.
Taemo, *v.* To exhibit the tongue in eating.
Taemoa, *s.* One kind of the *Ifi.*
Taene, *v.* To work the fists or the club in challenge.
Taeneleke, *a.* Free from restraint; at liberty.
Tai, *s.* A small dust bag.
Tai, *v.* To powder, to dust.
Tai, *v.* To strike, to beat.
Tai, *s.* A round, a circular, a row.
Taibaga, *v.* To fall; to bruise; to break.
Taifiifi, *a.* Light, not weighty.
Taiga, } *a.* Small, invariably
Taitaiga, } used ironically of something large.
Taiki, *v.* To give it a salt taste; to remain immoveable.
Taikiiki, *a.* Clear, lucid.
Taili, } *v.* To fan; to dread;
Tailiili, } to fear.
Taili, } *s.* Dread, horror.
Tailiili, }
Tailoilo, *a.* Very cold.
Tailoilo, *v.* To feel the cold.
Taimalie, *a.* Fortunate; just in time.
Tainamu, *s.* A screen or curtain to keep off the musquitto.
Taino, *v.* To work the fists as a challenge to box.
Taiseni, *s.* The name of a bird.
Taitai, *a.* Hungry, brackish.

Tao, *s.* A spear.
Tao, *v.* To cook food in an oven; to bake; to be baked.
Taofi, *s.* A restraint, an obstacle, a hindrance.
Taofi, *v.* To impede, to obstruct, to hinder; to choose; to refrain, to restrain; to challenge; to swing the arm in walking.
Taofia, *v.* To be hindered or prevented; to be selected; to be challenged.
Taokave, *s.* A superior kind of nut.
Taokete, *s.* An elder brother or sister.
Taomaga, *s.* A stick used in wringing out the oil of the nut.
Taomagamalie, *a.* Fortunate, well timed.
Taomaki *s.* A presage, prognostic.
Taomi, Taomia, } *v.* To crush; to lie upon; to squeeze; to be covered.
Taomifonua, *s.* One who keeps the people under; the wood pillow of the *Tuitoga* and *Tamaha*.
Taonatagata, *s.* The death of chiefs of rank.
Taotao, *s.* Logs or sticks used for keeping *gatu* on the earth when spread out; any thing to make up a barter.
Taotao, Taotaomi, } *v.* To bear upon; to lie or press upon; to cover with something heavy.
Taotoka, *v.* To keep down by a weight; to sit upon the outrigger in bad weather to keep it down.
Taovao, *s.* One kind of the *Kie*.
Taovala, *s.* The mat worn over the *gatu*.
Taovala, *v.* To put on, to wear the mat over the *gatu*.

Tau, *s.* A season; a crop; a year.
Tau, *v.* To arrive; to fit; to hit or strike against; to squeeze or wring out.
Tau, *pron.* We, us.
Tau, *s.* War, fighting.
Tau, *v.* To fight, to war.
Tau, *a.* Immoveable, as a stain, &c.
Tau, *a.* Becoming, fit, proper, agreeable.
Taua, *v.* To build two canoes at the same time.
Tauagaa, *s.* Old torn mats worn as a sign of mourning.
Tauabe, *v.* To waver; to stand undetermined whether to go on or return.
Tauaalo, *v.* To paddle in a sailing canoe.
Tauaalo, *s.* The song or chant in paddling or in doing any work.
Tauage, Used generally in begging importunately, by which the person addressed considers his love to the person begging put to the test.
Tauagea, *v.* To wish or desire earnestly.
Tauaki, *s.* The state of one near death; the food which such an one still takes.
Tauaki, *v.* To dry in the sun; to be alike or equal on both sides.
Tauala, *v.* To feel in different directions with the hand; to luff; to bring the vessel to the wind.
Tauala, *a.* Used of a canoe that sails close to the wind.
Tauama, *s.* A rope of a canoe.
Tauataina, *s.* Liberty, freedom.
Tauataina, *a.* Free, at liberty.
Tauatevalu, *v.* To have many children.
Tauene, *v.* To desire, to long.

180

Taueneuluboko, *a.* Used of one who has borne many children.

Taui, *v.* To fight; to war against; to surpass; to excel; to engender.

Tauia, *v.* To criticise; to remark upon; to wring the juice from any thing.

Tauia, *s.* A present or offering, only used when many make presents together.

Tauifaiva, Tauifeiva, } *v.* To aim to out do another in sports.

Tauivi, *v.* To work with all his strength.

Tauoi, *a.* Restless; at work; on the move.

Tauoko, *v.* To fasten the sail yard standing to the canoe.

Tauoluga, *s.* A long timber in the upper part of a Tonga house.

Tauomoomo, *v.* To place; to sit on the edge in jeopardy.

Tauua, Tauuai, } *s.* A pair, a couple, (nuts, &c.)

Tauufi, *v.* To bring every man a yam.

Tauuka, *v.* To fasten in a temporary way in building canoes.

Tauukei, *v.* To challenge a stronger than oneself.

Tauuta, *a.* High and dry (a canoe not sailable.)

Tauuto, *v.* To gather up a fishing net by the sticks called *uto*.

Taubau, *v.* To keep in view; to mark with the eye in chasing; to cleave to old things.

Taube, *v.* To hang upon; to bear down.

Taubi, *v.* To splash water; to throw dirt, as from a spade.

Taubibito, *v.* To fill; to take or bring well filled.

Taubiki, Tautaubiki, } *v.* To take hold of; to feel the way as one blind.

Taubiko, *v.* To go and come; to run to and fro.

Taubo, Tautaubo, } *v.* To grope; to feel the way.

Tauboa, *v.* To scent the water with fish to catch others.

Tauboou, *s.* A virgin.

Taubobo, *a.* High and dry; laid up, as a canoe out of repair.

Tauboboaki, *v.* To send messages in succession.

Taubola, *v.* To thatch in a temporary way with the *bola*.

Taubota, *v.* To hoist a signal.

Taubotu, *s.* The extreme each way; the first; the last; the nearest and farthest.

Taubuga, *s.* The stone with which any creature is sunk in the water.

Taubugai, *v.* To fasten a heavy weight for the purpose of sinking any creature.

Taufa, *s.* A squall.

Taufa, *a.* Squally.

Taufa, *v.* To smell any thing brought by the wind; to be carried by the wind.

Taufa, Tautaufa, } *v.* To grope; to feel after with the hand.

Taufaao, *s.* A scuffle.

Taufaao, *v.* To scuffle.

Taufaala, *v.* To search out; to trace up.

Taufaia, *v.* Squally; overtaken with a squall.

Taufaoo, *v.* To stoop in walking; to bend forward.

Taufau, Taufaui, } *v.* To mend a sail; to fasten; to tie; to look after; to attend to.

Taufakamau, *a.* Full up to high tide mark.

Taufale, *s.* A hand broom; a besom; banana ripened in the house.

Taufale, *v.* To sweep with the above.

Taufehia, *s.* Hatred, abhorrence.

181

Taufehia, *v.* To hate, to abhor.

Taufeji, } *v.* To go and come;
Taufejiaki, } to be here and there; to run to and fro.

Taufetuku, } *v.* To carry;
Taufetukutuku, } to take or bring.

Taufoe, *s.* A rope belonging to the steer oar.

Taufoe, *v.* To make fast the steer oar with the *Taufoe.*

Taufonua, *s.* One of the place or land.

Taufua, *v.* To wring out the simple juice without the addition of water.

Taufui, *v.* To besprinkle; to throw water or dust.

Taufuji, *v.* To pull; to draw towards.

Tauga, *s.* Cooked food reserved for eating at another time; a row; a roost of the flying fox.

Taugalau, *a.* Out of reach, distant.

Taugalea, *v.* To speak often of or about; to speak to one as a confidant.

Taugaloloa, *a.* Long, as rows of yams.

Tauganonou, *a.* Short, as rows of yams.

Taugatabu, *s.* The nut tree upon which the *tabu* or prohibition was hung.

Taugatamaki, *a.* Unprovided; short of certain essentials.

Taugavaka, *s.* The anchorage of canoes.

Tauhaaki, *a.* Full, as the tide.

Tauheua, *v.* To turn aside, as one who intercedes.

Taugatualega, *v.* To dress with what is bad while in possession of good.

Tauhele, *s.* A snare, a gin.

Tauhele, *v.* To ensnare; to entrap; to decoy.

Tauhi, *s.* A nurse; a protector; steward, guardian; service.

Tauhi, } *v.* To protect; to
Tauhii, } provide for; to keep; to serve; to take food.

Tauhihi, } *v.* Similar to the
Tauhihii, } above but perhaps more expressive.

Tauhia, *v.* To be served; to be attended to.

Tauhihi, *v.* To angle; to fish with hooks.

Tauhiku, *v.* To finish off; to be finishing.

Tauhikuhiku, *v.* To hang on the top branches, as fruit.

Tauhila, *v.* To turn up the eyes; to look suspicious.

Tauhili, *v.* To sit or stand upon any thing very high, as a mast head.

Tauji, *v.* To catch rain water by hanging out the *Hohoni.*

Taujijikabu, *s.* A *Jiji* or leaf dress that surrounds the body, used of a chief that includes all authority within himself.

Taukae, *s.* Scorn, contempt, abuse, reproach.

Taukae, *v.* To scoff, contemn, to reproach, to flout.

Taukaba, *v.* To flap the wings; to strike the hands as one sinking.

Taukabo, } *v.* To pull over hand,
Taukaboi, } as in pulling fish in the water.

Taukajikaji, *v.* To speak contemptuously.

Taukajikaji, *s.* Contempt, scorn.

Taukakaba, *a.* Distant; out of reach.

Taukalihi, *s.* A large bunch; a bunch with very many fruit.

Taukamo, *v.* To beckon with the hand.

Taukatea, *s.* The name of a rope belonging to a canoe; a part of the canoe.

Taukava, *s.* The man who wrings out the *kava.*

Taukava, *v.* To wring the *kava* into cups for drinking.

Taukave, *v.* To persevere; to worry on.

Taukave, *s.* A rope used in the *Fekejike.*

Tauki, *a.* Loquacious, vain; joyous, merry.

Taukavekave, *v.* To inform by shouting from one another.

Taukoka, *v.* To persevere in; to maintain.

Taula, *s.* An anchor.

Taula, } *s.* The name given
Taulaeiki, } to heathen priests.

Taulaga, *s.* Anchorage, a harbour.

Taulagi, *v.* To superintend; to give directions in any work.

Taulaka, *s.* The step; the gait in walking.

Taulaki, *s.* The washing off; a preparation put on the hair for cleaning it.

Taulaki, *v.* To stay, to wait, applied to canoes at sea; to wash the head.

Taulaki, *v.* To stay, to wait, applied to persons.

Taulalo, *v.* To speak in behalf of; to intercede for; to do the hardest or most menial of the work.

Taulalo, *s.* The fruit of a tree nearest the ground.

Taulalo, *a.* Near; within reach.

Taulama, *v.* To watch and keep down the outrigger of a canoe in bad weather.

Taulamua, *s.* A name for heathen gods.

Taulani, *v.* To take in tow.

Tauleleka, *a.* Beautiful, applied to several (males only.)

Taulelu, *v.* To cause, to care about.

Taulofu, *a.* Full; up to the mark.

Tauloto, *v.* To carry a load suspended behind and before from a stick across the shoulders.

Tauloto, *s.* The load or burden so carried.

Taulu, *v.* To make fast the ropes in a canoe.

Taumaa, *s.* The last straining of any preparation.

Taumaia, *v.* To wish or desire earnestly.

Taumau, *v.* To remain stationary.

Taumau, *v.* To repeat; to say over and over again.

Taumauga, *v.* To frequent; to be often at one place.

Taumafa, *v.* To eat, applied to the *Tuitoga.*

Taumafa, *s.* The food of great personages.

Taumafafonua, *s.* The last of several feasts and ceremonies.

Taumagaga, *v.* To desire earnestly.

Taumahua, *a.* Full to overflowing.

Taumaka, *v.* To fasten small stones on the edge of a fishing net.

Taumakeke, } *v.* To appear anx-
Taumalaga, } ious to get away; to be on the move.

Taumalaga, *v.* To be too near the wind.

Taumalie, *a.* Full.

Taumama, *a.* Leaky; not fit to sail.

Taumamao, *a.* Deep, distant, afar off.

Taumatau, *v.* To angle.

Taumataki, *v.* To do because an individual is present.

Taumounu, *v.* To bait; to entice by shewing favours.

Taumoji, *s.* A light rain; a sprinkling.

Taumotumotu, *v.* To dress in

rags; to fight till one is broken or conquered.

Taumua, *s.* The head or fore part of a vessel; prow.

Taumua, *v.* To be on a line with; to point; to sail towards.

Taumuli, *s.* The stern; the hind part of a canoe or vessel; the person who sits behind in paddling canoes.

Taumuli, *v.* To sit behind and steer paddling canoes.

Tauta, *v.* To touch; to put out the hand to touch; to angle for the *Ta.*

Tautaa, *s.* Perspiration.

Tautaa, *v.* To perspire.

Tautau, *v.* To hang.

Tautau, *s.* A heathen feast.

Tautauafega, *v.* To yield; to come near.

Tautauaga, *s.* Any thing or place where a thing is hung.

Tautauamanu, *s.* A tree.

Tautauamanu, *v.* To hang from a rope in a canoe as a signal that land is in sight.

Taufetogi, } *v.* To relieve;
Tautaufetogi, } to do by turns.

Tautaufetuku, *v.* To go and come repeatedly with a load.

Tautaukatefo, *v.* To reserve food while some present are hungry.

Tautaumoliliu, *v.* To go backwards and forwards; to run to and fro.

Tautaba, *s.* The calling of one in imminent danger; the first and largest in a bunch of bananas.

Tautaba, *v.* To beg; to call upon when in trouble.

Tautafa, *v.* To squeeze through an opening.

Tautaha, *a.* One, single, alone.

Tautahi, *v.* To be still in the water; to wash with or use sea water regularly.

Tautake, *s.* The lowest nut in a bunch.

Tautala, } *v.* To inform an-
Tautautala, } other of our designs in order to know his mind.

Tautalagauli, *v.* To converse and sail along, as two canoes; to do quickly without form and ceremony.

Tautata, *a.* Near, not distant.

Taute, } *v.* The result, the
Tautei, } consequence.

Taute, }
Tautei, } *s.* Punishment, chas-
Tautea, } tisement.

Taute, } *v.* To punish; to
Tautei, } correct; to chastise;
Tautea, } to beat roughly.

Tautefua, *v.* To hang singly, one and only one.

Tauteka, *v.* To move in fear; to flinch; to wear a kind of sandal on the soles of the feet.

Tautekovi, *v.* To treat unkindly.

Tautekovi, *s.* Inattention, unkindness.

Tautokai, *v.* To go; to hit against any thing projecting out as one blind.

Tautoko, } *v.* To walk with
Tautautoko, } the help of a stick.

Tautolu, *pron.* Us.

Tautotolo, *v.* To defer; to put off from time to time.

Tautonu, *v.* To hit the precise place and time.

Tautu, *v.* To sit.

Tautua, } *v.* To strike the
Tautuafaga, } back; to speak to no advantage.

Tautuloba, *a.* Full, high, (the tide.)

Tauvae, *v.* To gather nuts and fasten them to the *kafaga* on the feet.

Tauvao, *s.* An acknowledgment

for the loan of a patch of ground.
Tauvaka, *s.* One who goes in a borrowed canoe to look after it.
Tauvele, *s.* Temptation.
Tauvele, *v.* To tempt.
Taba, *s.* The border of the native cloth; the border or edge of any thing; a reserve in war.
Taba, *v.* To glitter in the sun.
Tababa, *v.* To beat a drum.
Tababaku, *a.* Well baked, crimp, crisp.
Tabafua, *v.* To call upon, to address.
Tabafuaia, *v.* To call upon by name.
Tabahu, *v.* To do; to be doing.
Tabaji, *v.* To strike or clap the hands together.
Tabakau, *s.* The coarse mats for flooring.
Tabaki, Tabakia, } *v.* To pluck; to break off.
Tabala, *a.* Blotched; not clear and distinct.
Tabale, *s.* A game or play in the water.
Tabale, Tabalea, } *v.* To break up; to destroy; to strike from every side.
Tabamanava, *v.* To eat; to support by eating.
Tabanu, *v.* To do; to be doing.
Tabataba, *s.* A crab fish.
Tabataba, *v.* To glitter; to shine.
Tabeva, *s.* A sprain.
Tabeva, *v.* To sprain, to twist.
Tabi, *v.* To wipe across.
Tabi, Tabibi, } *v.* To dash along; to send the spray flying.
Tabigaafeituukau, Tabigaifeituukau, } *v.* To boast; to maintain the right in a matter not yet judged.
Tabigaamama, *a.* Worldly; like the world.
Tabili, *s.* Bellows, a fan.
Tabili, *v.* To blow; to fan the fire.
Tabo, *s.* A certain kind of fishing net.
Tabo, *v.* To fish with the above.
Tabou, *v.* To exhort; to put upon guard.
Tabotu, *a.* Short.
Tabotu, *v.* To work as a short vessel in a rough sea.
Tabu, *s.* Prohibition, embargo; the sign of prohibition.
Tabu, *a.* Forbidden, consecrated, sacred.
Tabua, *s.* A term of reverence to a chief when speaking meaning of himself.
Tabua, *s.* The mouth or opening of a cage or fowl net.
Tabuaki, *v.* To bless; to intercede for.
Tabuaki, *s.* A blessing; the act of blessing.
Tabuani, *s.* The name of one kind of yam.
Tabuekina, *a.* Blessed.
Tabuekina, *v.* To bless.
Tabui, Tabuia, } *v.* To prohibit.
Tabuofe, *v.* To bend under a load.
Tabubu, *a.* Rapid, ceaseless.
Tabubu, *v.* To keep up; to flow in a rapid succession.
Tabuha, *v.* To be hallowed; to be consecrated.
Tabukitea, *s.* A planet, the evening star.
Tabuku, Tabukubuku, } *a.* Short, stumpy, thick set.
Tabulu, *s.* One way of tattooing.
Tabuni, *s.* A lid.
Tabuni, *v.* To shut; to embar; to stop up.
Tabuta, *s.* Pools of water in rocks, &c.
Tabutabui, *v.* To prohibit.
Tabutano, *s.* An article from a burying ground used as a sign of prohibition.

185

Tafa, *s*. A gash; an open wound made by something sharp; the act of cutting up.

Tafa, } *v*. To cut, to carve, to
Tafai, } gash.

Tafaaga, *s*. The fishing canoe.

Tafaaki, *s*. The side; the right or left.

Tafaakilagi, *s*. The horizon.

Tafaga, } *a*. Cleared; free
Tafagafaga, } from trees

Tafagafaga, *s*. A spot free from trees, &c.

Tafagaloa, *a*. Open, free, wilderness-like; without trees.

Tafale, *s*. A canoe built out of an old one.

Tafani, *v*. To widen; to join on to increase its width.

Tafano *s*. One kind of fishing net.

Tafano, *v*. To fish with the above.

Tafanogo, *v*. To strike native drums for the amusement of others.

Tafatafai, *v*. To cut; to lance in several places.

Tafataha, *a*. Independent; free of others.

Tafatua, *v*. To swim in the surf with the hand on the back.

Tafe, *v*. To run, to flow, to pour, to drop.

Tafea, *v*. To be carried away by the stream.

Tafeaga, *s*. A conduit; a drain; a channel for water.

Tafejinoivai *a*. Unmixed, pure, distinct.

Tafetafe, *v*. To run; to flow gently; to drop.

Tafi, *v*. To sweep; to clean with a besom.

Tafia, *v*. To sweep off; to carry away with violence.

Tafie, *s*. Small supporters in a canoe.

Tafihu, *v*. To look on one side; to turn the face from.

Tafihufihutamaki, *v*. To look from side to side in displeasure.

Tafiji, *v*. To fillip; to strike with the finger to know whether or not it is ripe, cooked, full, &c.

Tafilala, *v*. To be swept off.

Tafili, } *v*. To roll over; to
Tafilifili, } turn from side to side.

Tafiligatamaki, *v*. To roll or turn and hurt oneself.

Tafitafi, *v*. To wash or wipe with any thing wet; to clear away.

Tafitoga, *a*. Cloudless, clear, applied to the sky.

Tafoa, *v*. To break, to crack.

Tafoe, *v*. To luff; to bring near the wind.

Tafofo, *v*. To sip; to swallow with greediness.

Tafoki, } *v*. To turn over,
Tafokifoki, } to turn round.

Tafola, *v*. To be scattered; to be strewed in different directions.

Tafoli, *v*. To walk round; to go the circumference of a place.

Tafu, *s*. A hole, a burrow.

Tafu, } *v*. To blow; to fan
Tafutafu, } up a fire.

Tafua, *s*. A canoe made by hollowing out a single tree.

Tafua, *v*. To strike a rolled up mat as a drum.

Tafuc, *v*. To blow strong and boisterous; to speak strong and angry words.

Tafue, *v*. To skip with a cord.

Tafuefue, *v*. To be the sport of the wind; to be blown in every direction.

Tafuu, } *v*. To bulge out.
Tafuufuu, }

Tafuua, *v*. To be astounded.

Tafuua, *s*. Affright, terror.

Tafuga, } *s*. A mound, a
Tafugofuga, } hillock, rising ground.

Tafugofuga, *a.* High, hilly, uneven.
Tafuli, } *v.* To move round;
Tafulifuli, } to roll along.
Tafulu, *s.* Anger; noisy talk.
Tafulu, *v.* To speak angrily.
Tafulufulutamaki, *v.* To exhibit signs of anger in the eyes.
Tafuna, *s.* A pile of *kava.*
Tafunaki, } *v.* To feed with
Tafutafunaki, } fire wood; to increase.
Tafute, *v.* To be angry with.
Taga, *s.* The large gut.
Tagai, *s.* A narrow bag, a sack.
Tagau, *s.* A fish; flesh or fish that is eaten with vegetables.
Tagaba, *s.* A small bladder found in fish and animals.
Tagabula, *s.* A swelling.
Tagafa, *s.* The name of a fish.
Tagakaho, *s.* A quiver; the bamboo for holding arrows.
Tagakakai, *s.* The crop, the gizzard.
Tagaki, *v.* To open, to lift up; to regard; to look towards.
Tagamimi, *s.* The bladder.
Tagata, *s.* Man.
Tagatagа, *s.* A cup made of the nut shell from which to drink *gkava.*
Tagato, } *a.* Loose, not firm.
Tagatagato, }
Tagato, *s.* The name of a tree.
Tagege, See *Nifi.*
Tagi, *s.* A cry.
Tagi, *v.* To cry, to weep.
Tagifetuki, *v.* To cry and beat the face with the fists.
Tagilaulau, *s.* A mourning, a lamentation.
Tagilaulau, *v.* To mourn, to lament.
Tagita, *s.* A lock of hair.
Tagitautau, *v.* To cry and lay the blame on another; to cry in the name of another.
Tagitagi, *s.* Flowers partially open; the sound of the war whoop.
Tagitagi, *a.* Stretched to the utmost.
Tagitofuhia, *s.* The oozing of blood from the ears and nose caused by diving.
Tagituvae, *v.* To cry and strike the foot against the earth.
Tagivale, *v.* To wish or desire what is not in character or becoming.
Tago, *s.* The visiting of females under cover of night.
Tago, } *v.* To visit in the
Tagofia, } night; to go to a female in the dark.
Tagotago, *v.* To find out the way in the night.
Tagulu, *s.* A rattling in the throat; a snoring.
Tagulu, *v.* To snore.
Tagutu, *v.* To sit.
Tagutugutu, *s.* The stump or root of a tree above ground.
Taha, *a.* Numeral one.
Tahake, } *s.* Acclivity.
Tahakehake, }
Tahatahaana, *s.* A single one, but important.
Tahehu, *v.* To prevaricate.
Tahele, *v.* To strike with rapidity the native drum.
Tahi, *s.* The sea; the heart of wood.
Tahi, *a.* Red; sound; with little or no sap.
Tahifi, *v.* To cut, to cut off.
Tahifo, } *s.* Descent, de-
Tahifohifo, } clivity.
Tahifo, } *a.* Gradually de-
Tahifohifo, } scending.
Tahihina, *a.* Sound, but light in colour, as wood.
Tahikia, *a.* Wet with sea water.
Tahina, *s.* Native cloth.
Tahuli, *s.* Shoots, suckers.
Taji, } *a.* Small; not befitting;
Tajiji, } unsuitable in size.

Tajiba, *v.* To reel to and fro.
Tajibi, *v.* To strike several times with the open hand.
Tajifa, *v.* To shoot or glide along.
Tajifi, *s.* The name of a fish.
Tajika, See *Bajika.*
Tajili, Tajilijili, } *v.* To hold up lights from different canoes at sea in the dark.
Tajilo, Tajilojilo, } *a.* Clear, transparent, limpid.
Tajilo, Tajilojilo, } *s.* Clearness, limpidness.
Tajinoivai, *a.* Free, pure, unmixed.
Taka, *v.* To go about and do, as, *Takaloi*—to go about telling lies, &c.; to look at; to witness; to see; to move as the wind.
Taka, *s.* The short line attached to Tonga fish hooks.
Takaaki, *v.* To accompany; to conduct from place to place.
Takaaki, *s.* A thing done or got up to engage the affection of a chief.
Takaea, *a.* Lost in fear, agast.
Takai, *v.* To anoint; to oil the body, to wrap round with *kafa.*
Takai, *s.* Anointing.
Takai, *v.* To roll up; to coil; surround.
Takao, *v.* To make any thing round in the hands, as pills; to make balls.
Takaoa, *v.* To surround, to be on all sides.
Takaoaga, *s.* A kneading trough.
Takabau, *s.* The rough mat for flooring, called also *Tabakau.*
Takabe, *a.* Unmarried, single.
Takabe, *v.* To be short or destitute of clothing.
Takafalu, *s.* The back of chiefs; the name of a tree; a shell fish.
Takafi, *v.* To cover, as a book.
Takafi, *s.* A cover; the article with which a book is covered.
Takafia, *v.* To operate, as medicine in the system.
Takafiji, Takafute, } *v.* To caper; to act as one in convulsions.
Takaga, *s.* The attendant or attendants of a chief.
Takagaika, *s.* A shoal of fish.
Takahi, *v.* To scratch as a cat; to make a scratching noise.
Takajia, *a.* Light, not laden, applied to a canoe.
Takale, *s.* A term of reproach for the head.
Takalekale, *s.* An empty nut, but not broken.
Takalo, *v.* To evade; to get out of work.
Takamilo, *v.* To turn round and round; to surround.
Takamo, *v.* To beckon; to make signs with the eyes.
Takaniko, *v.* See *Takamilo.*
Takaniko, *s.* A shell fish; circles round the moon.
Takaneva, *s.* A fish.
Takanoa, *v.* To be free; to be at liberty; to walk at large.
Takatau, *v.* To fight; to war with places in succession.
Takatau, *s.* A chief who has fallen in war.
Takataha, *v.* To go alone.
Takatahiaveka, *v.* To be at sea, and yet dirty.
Takataka, *v.* To walk about.
Takatakaaleala, *s.* One kind of grass.
Takatakai, *s.* A shoal of large fish.
Takatakai, *v.* To roll round and round; to make into a roll.
Takatakao, *v.* To round as pills.
Takatakamilo, *s.* To encircle; to whirl round; to turn round and round.

188

Takatakaniko, *s.* Circles round the moon.
Takatakaniko, *v.* To be encircled, as the moon.
Takatakata, *v.* To walk about and strike others.
Takatakatuu, *v.* To stand or walk as a relief from sitting; to walk after an affliction.
Takatata, *a.* Pugnacious; fond of striking others.
Takatene, *v.* To struggle; to kick and knock about.
Takatofu, *s.* A light shifting wind.
Takatua, *v.* To absent oneself from chiefs.
Takatuu, *s.* Young men.
Takatuu, *v.* To rise; to stand for work.
Takavao, *v.* To live in the bush.
Takavao, *s.* Bushranger.
Takavale, *a.* Short of food; famishing; thin of flesh, applied to a chief.
Take, *s.* The top of the nut shell when prepared for drinking; the original root of a tree.
Takeba, *s.* The nut when at the best for drinking.
Takeha, *a.* Burnt, dried up.
Takele, *s.* The keel of a canoe; the bottom of any box, basket, &c.
Takele, *v.* To bathe, to wash.
Takemo, *v.* To move the eyelids up and down repeatedly.
Tahenu, *v.* To strike with the fins; to kick up dust; to throw dirt in every direction.
Taketu, *v.* To limp, to hobble along.
Taki, *v.* To lead; to barter; to hold.
Taki, *a.* Each.
Takiaki, *v.* To prevaricate.
Takiekina, *v.* To be led or drawn.
Takibo, *v.* To hold a light through the night.
Takiboubou, *v.* To assist by a rope in getting the sail of a canoe to the opposite end of the canoe when tacking.
Takifu, *v.* To scamper off.
Takimalie, *s.* The last spreading out of *gatu*.
Takimua, *s.* A leader.
Takimua, *v.* To lead the way.
Takina, *v.* To drive away; to lead off forcibly; to lead away.
Takinaga, *s.* The place where *gatu* is spread out and dried; a leader.
Takitaki, *v.* To hang suspended; to draw fishing nets through the water; to straighten by drawing out.
Takitala, *v.* To strike with words; to reprove; to admonish.
Takituu, *v.* To lead along a canoe in shallow water.
Takituu, *v.* To paddle slowly.
Takohi, *v.* To make a scratching noise.
Takoji, *a.* Confused; out of time and order.
Takomo, *v.* To sip up; to swallow greedily.
Takoto, *v.* To lie down (two or more.)
Taku, *v.* To call by, to designate.
Takua, *v.* To mention, to call by name.
Takuo, *s.* The name of a fish.
Takuhali, *s.* The name of a fish.
Tala, *v.* To tell, to reply, to speak of.
Tala, *s.* A bird; a thorn; the pricking fin on the back of fish; an answer.
Tala, *a.* Thorny, prickly.
Talaa, *v.* To turn over in the mind; to feel dissatisfied with a decision.
Talaa, *a.* Unsettled, undetermined.
Talai, *v.* To instruct; to admo-

nish children; to report, to make known; to smooth off rough edges.

Talaihagamai, *v.* To speak so and so because the party is present.

Talaia, *v.* To be pricked with thorns; to rase along a reef.

Talauhuaki, *v.* To speak incitingly; to induce by constant talk.

Talauhui, *a.* Irreverent, disrespectful, applied to children.

Talauhui, *v.* To speak out of order; to speak interferingly.

Talabau, *v.* To speak or tell decidedly.

Talafaikitano, *v.* To speak to the dead.

Talafaituuga, *v.* To speak having a foundation; to be free from that for which we reprove others.

Talafau, *s.* The name of a double basket.

Talafakahaha, *v.* To speak insinuatingly or indirectly.

Talafefine, *v.* To be much in the company of females.

Talafekau, *s.* Envoy, messenger.

Talafekau, *v.* To deliver a message.

Talafi, *v.* To investigate a case; to tell one of another in a clandestine way.

Talafili, *v.* To act in a haughty restless manner, as a conquered but proud enemy.

Talafu, *s.* The cooking place on board a canoe.

Talafua, *v.* To let go the rope that holds the sail of the canoe.

Talaga, *v.* To converse over.

Talagaua, *a.* Uncertain, undecided.

Talagataa, *s.* Disobedience.

Talagataa, *a.* Disobedient.

Talagataa, *v.* To disobey.

Talagofua, *s.* Obedience.

Talagofua, *a.* Obedient.

Talagofua, *v.* To obey.

Talaha, *s.* The remains of the bread fruit after gathering.

Talahaga, *v.* To tell of *gatu* to be made; to act overseer in the making of *gatu.*

Talahoka, *v.* To speak without reserve or fear; to speak words that pierce.

Talahoko, *v.* To speak to; to bring the words to the person concerned.

Talahua, *a.* Jocose, waggish.

Talahua, *v.* To speak jocosely or merrily.

Talaka, *v.* To speak contemptuously of the gods.

Talakakau, *v.* To take off the handle.

Talakeikaba, *s.* Precaution, premonition.

Talakeikaba, *v.* To forewarn, to premonish.

Talaki, *s.* One kind of fishing net.

Talaki, *v.* To fish with the *Talaki.*

Talaki, *v.* To report; to spread abroad.

Talalakulaku, *v.* To speak irreverently and disrespectfully.

Talalo, *s.* The level land at the foot of a hill; a valley.

Talaloa, *v.* To rip open; to cut open, (any thing long.)

Talalotofale, *v.* To speak evil; to speak to incite to evil.

Talamokabui, *v.* To speak guardedly.

Talamu, *v.* To work the jaws as in chewing.

Talamuka, Talatalamuka, } *v.* To bud.

Talatalamuka, *a.* Full of buds; abounding in young leaves.

Talanoa, *s.* A conversation.

Talanoa, *v.* To converse.

Talanumaga, *s.* A dance at the burial of a chief.

Talata, *s.* The name of a bird.
Talatagata, *v.* To challenge, to boast.
Talataha, *v.* To do at a word; to do freely.
Talataha, *s.* The name of a fish.
Talatala, *v.* To tell of.
Talatala, *a.* Thorny, prickly.
Talatalaaki, *v.* To accuse.
Talatalaaki, *s.* Accusation, an accuser.
Talatala, } *v.* To extricate, to
Talatalai, } disentangle.
Talatalaamoa, *s.* A shrub.
Talatalaamoamaka, *s.* A shrub.
Talatalavale, *v.* To tell all; as a child.
Talato, *v.* To speak evil of what one has sought but cannot obtain.
Talatuu, *v.* To speak with energy, applied to one whom the king hears and obeys.
Talatubua, *s.* Tradition, fable.
Talatubua, *v.* To relate fables and traditionary tales.
Talatuki, *v.* To aver; to declare with emphasis.
Talatuki, *s.* Asseveration, affirmation.
Talatuku, *s.* The last, the parting advice or commands of a friend.
Talatuku, *v.* To give the last directions or commands to others.
Talaveka, *s.* The name of a bird.
Talavou, *s.* A young man, a youth.
Tale, *s.* A cough.
Tale, *v.* To cough.
Talele, } *a.* Used of children
Talelelele, } beginning to run about.
Taleta, *a.* Strewed about as old nuts when plentiful.
Taleta, *a.* Scarce, few; only one here and there.

Tali, *s.* Food prepared for visitors.
Tali, } *v.* To prepare food for
Talia, } visitors; to wait for; to respond; to receive.
Talia, *v.* To knock against something; to be hit or hindered by something.
Taliuli, *v.* To sail and not heave too when overtaken by a squall.
Taliaonomui, *v.* To wait until the thing or person shall be brought.
Talifaki }
Talitalifaki, } *v.* To wait for; to be in readiness.
Talifekina, }
Talifiji, *v.* To wait for what may accidentally come.
Talikilagi, *v.* To wait upon the clouds, applied to swamps and places only full when it rains.
Talimahaga, *s.* The noose in large ropes.
Talituu, } *v.* To resent; to
Talitalituu, } treat with contempt the words of another.
Talitalinoa, *v.* To wait, to hope without reason or foundation.
Talituu, *s.* One manner of plaiting the *kafa*.
Talo, *s.* A vegetable root, smaller than the yam.
Talokula, *s.* A vegetable root, smaller than the yam.
Talolo, *v.* To make a sudden appearance, applied to a number.
Talolo, *v.* To be hushed; to be calmed down.
Talomonu, *v.* To solicit by actions the blessing of the gods.
Talotalo, *s.* The casting lots.
Talotalo, *v.* To cast lots.
Talu, *s.* A lock or bush of hair.
Talu, *ad.* Since.
Taluaibe, } *ad.* Ever since;
Talutaluaibe, } just as then; no alteration.
Tama, *s.* A boy.

Tama, *v.* To grate, to scrape.
Tamai, *s.* A father.
Tamaioeiki, *s.* A male servant.
Tamaiki, *s.* Children.
Tamaimate, *a.* Fatherless.
Tamaimate, *s.* A fatherless one.
Tamabua, *s.* An idol, a doll.
Tamajii, *s.* A little boy.
Tamaki, *s.* Sore eyes.
Tamaki, *a.* Bruised, rotten.
Tamakitagatai, *a.* Bad, disagreeable, because of the people.
Tamala, Tamalamala, } *a.* Bitter in taste.
Tamamahi, *s.* A blow or reproof that causes pain.
Tamanu, *s.* The name of a tree.
Tamate, Tamatei, } *v.* To kill, to extinguish, erase, to destroy, to blot out.
Tamate, *s.* Extinction; the act of extinguishing.
Tamate, Tamatemate, } *v.* To subside, sink; to die away.
Tamate, Tamatemate, } *a.* Dry, healing; dying as a wound; smoother.
Tamato, *s.* A miscarriage, an abortion.
Tamule, *v.* To handle; to turn over and over in the hands.
Tana, *s.* One kind of yam.
Tana, *v.* To be offended; to be tired.
Tanafa, *s.* The name of a fish.
Tanaki, *s.* Gleaning, gleaner.
Tanaki, *v.* To collect; to glean; to bring together.
Tane, *s.* A disease in the skin.
Taniu, *s.* A casting lots to know the origin of a disease.
Tano, *s.* A burying place of the dead.
Tanoa, *s.* A *kava* bowl.
Tanoa, *v.* To ward, to forewarn.
Tanu, Tanua, } *v.* To bury, to conceal, to hide.
Tanuaun, *v.* To hide; to secret oneself in a favourite place.
Tanuaga, *s.* A burying place.
Tanubobo, *v.* To fill full and pressed.
Tanuga, *s.* See *Tanuaga*.
Tanuma, *v.* To bury the dead by numbers, as burying bananas for *ma*.
Tanumaga, *s.* The name of the eleventh moon.
Tanumaki, Tanutanumaki, } *v.* To earth up any plant or tree; to hoe; to cover; to bury and cover in the mind.
Tanunu, *v.* To follow in quick succession; to flow with rapidity.
Tanutanu, *s.* The name of a fish.
Tanutanu, *v.* To bury; to cover over with earth.
Tata, *s.* The scoop for bailing water out of canoes; a covering for the top of the thatch of a house; any covering for the head; a dabber used in making *gatu*.
Tata, *v.* To cover, to dab.
Tata, *a.* Near, not distant.
Tata, *v.* To collect up; to clean out as a well; to wipe, to rub.
Tataalagovaka, *s.* The anger of a foe who has obtained the mastery.
Tataatuanima, *a.* Near, as the back of the hand to the palm, used figuratively of those who are near but get nothing; also of what is near, but difficult to do.
Tatae, *v.* To reach; to extend the arm to collect; to gather up.
Tatao, *v.* To press, to squeeze; to put under a weight; to lie in wait.
Tatao, *s.* A party lying in ambush.
Tatau, *s.* Resemblance, likeness,

similarity; a screen made of the *Takabau*.
Tatau, *a*. Similar, equal, express.
Tatau, Tataua, } *v*. To wring, to strain.
Tatau, *v*. To criticise, to remark upon.
Tataba, *v*. To flutter, as a fowl in the hands; to flurry.
Tatabi, *v*. To wipe.
Tatafa, *v*. To shoot; to pass along with speed.
Tatafe, *v*. To flow; to run as a current.
Tatafefie, *s*. A shell fish.
Tatafi, *v*. To clean and sweep off.
Tatagata, *v*. To silence; to make a finish.
Tatagi, *v*. To ring; to tinkle.
Tatagia, *s*. A tree.
Tatago, *v*. To seize; to attack suddenly.
Tataha, *s*. A sudden gush or blow.
Tatajino, *a*. Near, but only the body.
Tataka, *a*. Unsettled; at work, used of the mind.
Tataki, *s*. A leader or guide; one manner of catching fish.
Tataki, *v*. To lead or guide; to stretch out; to take fish as above.
Tataku, *v*. To call several names together in succession.
Tatala, *v*. To tear off; to open, to rend; to separate what adheres.
Tatali, *v*. To wait, to tarry.
Tatali, *s*. Waiting, tarrying.
Tatali, *v*. To make a perfect riddance or clear out; to take all.
Tatanu, *a*. Cloggy, soft, as soil after rain; yielding.
Tatatau, *v*. To tattoo.
Tatatau, *s*. The tattooing.
Tatava, *a*. Sour, inclined to sourness.
Tateau, *s*. One kind of banana.
Tateua, *v*. To work the mouth as in eating
Tatebi, *v*. To walk, to step.
Tatebi, *v*. To work with a quick and repeated stroke, as beating *taba*.
Tatebo, *s*. A gabbler.
Tateka, Tateketeka, } *v*. To run, as a child; to roll along.
Tatele, Tateletele, } *v*. To slip along; to plane; to slide on an even surface.
Tateme, Tatemeteme, } *v*. To flutter, to bustle.
Tatoka, *v*. To sleep two or more together.
Tatokaabuaka, *v*. To fall together as wrestlers.
Tatu, *v*. To work about; to be in motion.
Tatu, *a*. Loose, not fixed.
Tatube, Tatubetube, } *v*. To shake, to flop.
Tava, *s*. The name of a tree.
Tava, See *Tatava*.
Tavaamanu, *s*. The name of a shell fish.
Tavae, *v*. To trip up the heels.
Tavai, *v*. To drink and eat together.
Tavai, *v*. To clean out a pond, well, &c.
Tavao, *v*. To hoe; to clear of weeds grown large.
Tavahe, *v*. To strike with a quick repeated stroke.
Tavahi, *s*. The name of a tree.
Tavaka, *v*. To abscond in a canoe.
Tavi, *s*. The work or occupation of an individual.
Taviki, *s*. The name of a bird; one kind of yam.
Tavikitoto, *s*. The name of a bird.
Tavaku, *v*. To scratch; to get up earth with the hands.
Tavale, Tavalea, } *v*. To work or order at random; to act

without thought; to eat any thing and every thing.
Tavatava, *s.* The name of a shell fish.
Tavava, *a.* Open, applied to badly set teeth.
Tavave, *a.* Quick.
Tavilovilo, *v.* To be blown by the wind.
Te, *pron.* I.
Te, A sign of the future tense.
Te, *v.* To float; to sit on the surface of the water.
Tea, *a.* Whitish; light in colour.
Teau, *a.* A hundred.
Teavai, *a.* White in the skin.
Teato, *s.* A shell fish.
Tee, *s.* The dung of animals.
Teefo, *s.* The name of a fish.
Teefoulumaka, *s.* The name of a fish.
Teenifo, *s.* Gums.
Teetee, *s.* A poisonous fish.
Teeteebuaka, *s.* A grass.
Teeteemanu, *s.* The name of a tree.
Teetuli, *s.* An insect.
Teiulu, *s.* The second crop of yams raised from the tendrils of the first.
Tei, Teitei, } *ad.* Nearly, almost.
Teu, Teui, Teuteu, } *v.* To prepare, to deck; to qualify; to make ready.
Teu, Teui, Teuteu, } *s.* Qualification, preparation.
Teuaga, *s.* A place for dressing and adorning.
Teuga, *s.* Preparation, adorning, ornament.
Teuga, *v.* To adorn, to decorate, to garnish.
Teugataha, *v.* To dress or adorn with one and the same thing, applied to several.
Teuteuaga, *s.* See *Teuaga.*
Teba, *a.* Cross eyed.

Teba, *v.* To look across or askaunt.
Tebekia, *v.* To hurry; to precipitate others.
Tebi, Tebitebi, } *v.* To walk; to go or come; to do with a quick repeated motion, as plaiting.
Tebotebo, *v.* To gabble; to garble in speaking.
Tebu, *s.* A knot in wood.
Tebutebu, *a.* Full of knots and protuberances.
Tefa, *a.* Fondling.
Tefau, *s.* The name of a yam.
Tefito, *s.* The root, the origin.
Tefitoihala, *s.* The entrance into a path.
Tefitoua, *a.* Nice, particular as to food.
Tefua, *v.* To be collected or assembled together.
Tefua, *a.* Two hundred, in counting nuts only.
Tefuhi, *a.* One hundred couples.
Tega, *s.* The thigh; a swelling, a tumour.
Tega, Tegai, } *s.* The seeds of trees and plants.
Tegage, *s.* A shell fish.
Tege, *s.* A hard swelling.
Tege, *v.* To swell up.
Tegehaga, *v.* To cry; to weep.
Tegetega, *s.* The name of a bird.
Tegihia, *v.* To cry or mourn after.
Tegitage, *a.* Afflicted, applied to chiefs.
Tegitage, *s.* Affliction, applied to chiefs.
Tegitegi, *s.* The nut leaf plaited in a certain way.
Tehaga, *s.* A span length, used of a short length.
Tehitehituu, *v.* To stand; to be restless; to saunter.
Teka, *s.* A play; a kind of sandal; a piece of wood fastened

194

to the mast to wrap the rope upon.

Teka, } v. To roll.
Tekai, }

Tekau, *a.* Twenty.

Tekakai, *v.* To roll upon others what ought to be done by himself.

Tekanoa, *s.* An odd one; one by himself.

Tekanoa, *v.* To occur accidentally; to come or go by chance.

Teke, *s.* A bracket, a supporter, resistance.

Teke, } *v.* To push out; to resist; to refuse.
Tekea, }
Tekei, }

Tekefiho, *s.* The nut when past the best for drinking.

Tekefili, } *v.* To lie exposed.
Teketekefili, }

Tekefua, *v.* To cut off the hair; to shave the head.

Tekefua, } *a.* Naked, stript, as a vessel of her masts, &c.
Teketekefua, }

Tekela, *s.* A pole that keeps out the sail.

Tekelei, } *a.* Bare, exposed, stript, as after a hurricane.
Teketekelei, }

Teketekai, *v.* To roll along, as casks.

Teketeke, } *v.* To resist; to drive off; to push.
Teketekei, }

Tekelili, } *v.* To shiver, to quake, to shake, to tremble.
Teketekelili, }

Tekena, } *v.* See *Teketeke.*
Teketekena, }

Teketeketuakoi, *v.* To push away or remove the land mark of another to increase his own.

Teki, } *v.* To start, as in a fright; to set up the shoulders in walking; to strut.
Tekia, }
Tekiteki, }

Tekehi, *s.* A Tonga pillow.

Tekina, *v.* To be carried away by the sea.

Tekivale, } *a.* Easily persuaded or entreated.
Tekitekivale, }

Tekoga, *a.* Peacemeal, in pieces.

Tekoni, *v.* To hobble; to be lame in one leg.

Tela, *v.* The flat of the shark's head.

Telae, *s.* The name of a fish.

Tele, *s.* A razor; a shaver; any instrument used in shaving, planing, &c.

Tele, *v.* To shave; to plane; to smooth off.

Telea, *s.* A dreary passage.

Teleaga, *s.* The place of planing wood.

Telefua, *s.* Nakedness.

Telefua, *a.* Naked, bare.

Telegehe, *s.* Stars.

Telehea, *s.* A shell fish.

Telekihi, *s.* The name of a fish.

Teletele, *v.* To plane, to scrape.

Telia, *con.* Lest, because.

Telie, *s.* A tree and its fruit, (almond.)

Telieamanu, *s.* The name of a tree.

Teliteliuli, *s.* A small fish which accompanies the shark; used of one who is ever at the heels of another.

Temomo, *s.* Relative, acquaintance.

Tene, *v.* To prepare the body.

Teneaka, *s.* A shell fish.

Tenifa, *s.* A large kind of shark.

Tete, *v.* To tremble.

Tete, *v.* To float, to swim.

Tetea, *s.* The name of a fish.

Tetea, *a.* Whitish, pale, pallid.

Tetee, *v.* To hang; to suspend; to burst forth.

Teteba, *v.* To stare askaunt or across.

Tetebu, *s.* A small part; an outskirt.

Tetebu, *v.* To be apart or separated from the main body.
Tetefa, *s.* A tree.
Tetega, *a.* Hard, swollen.
Teteka, *v.* To glance to and fro; to separate from; to be leaving; to go towards, as a canoe to a reef.
Teteke, *v.* To draw the bow in shooting; to draw back.
Teteki, *s.* Fear, fright, cautiousness.
Teteki, *a.* Fearful, cautious.
Tetetete, *s.* Trembling, quaking.
Tetetete, *v.* To tremble, to quake, to quiver.
Teteve, *a.* Sandy, gritty.
Teve, *s.* A shrub whose root is eaten in famine.
Tevehaamoa, *s.* A kind of the above.
Tevela, *s.* A fish.
To, *v.* To fall; to set; to give over to another; to be absent; to forget another.
To, *s.* A fall, the act of falling; the sugar cane; the act of planting.
Toa, *s.* The name of a tree.
Toa, *s.* Courage.
Toa, *a.* Courageous.
Toafa, *s.* Wilderness, a desert.
Toaga, *s.* The place where one has fallen.
Toaki, *ad.* Unwillingly.
Toatebe, *s.* A tree.
Toe, *v.* To groan; to remain.
Toe, *ad.* Again, a second time.
Toe, *s.* The remnant, the remainder; the youngest child in a family; a groan.
Toeu, *v.* To hobble along in walking.
Toega, *s.* The remnant, the remainder.
Toegafiliga, *s.* The remains after all have had their choice.
Toemi, *v.* To move quickly; to move from side to side.

Toetoe, *v.* To moan; to groan repeatedly.
Toetoe, *s.* The remains.
Toi, *s.* The name of a tree; the gum of trees; a drop.
Toi, *v.* To drop, to extil.
Toi, *v.* To lurk; to hide; to keep out of sight.
Toitoi, *v.* To lurk; to hide oneself; to drop.
Toitoiaga, *s.* A lurking place.
Too, *s.* The name of a shell fish.
Too, *v.* To take; to carry in the hand; to open.
Tooa, *v.* To be opened; to act as one possessed with a devil.
Tooiio, *v.* To divide a fish int four parts.
Toouli, *v.* To cook yams with the skin and dirt.
Tooga, *s.* Fine mats; waiting men and maidens.
Toohema, *a.* Left, on the left side.
Toohi, *a.* Slow; behind in work.
Tookie, *v.* To give general orders to plait the mat called *kie.*
Toola, *v.* To give general order to plait mats for sails.
Tooliu, *v.* To flute; to hollow out; to cut a channel in a tree.
Toomau, *v.* To hold, to keep possession of.
Toomatau, *a.* Right, on the right side.
Toomotafi, *a.* Good, very good.
Toona, *v.* To be stolen, taken off.
Toonaki, *v.* To cook large quantities of food.
Tootoo, *a.* Quick.
Tootoo, *v.* To be quick.
Tootooa, *a.* Vain, boasting.
Tootooga, *s.* The entrails; the appurtenances of any work.
Tootoonoa, *v.* To take any thing that one meets with; to be light fingered.
Tootoovalea, *a.* Easily moved

or persuaded, invariably used of one who is difficult to move or persuade.

Tou, *s.* The name of a tree and its berries, which are used as a paste.

Toua, *s.* A rope to climb by.

Toua, *s.* The place occupied in a kava party by the people, as opposed to the *Alofi.*

Touaki, *v.* To put the stones on the fire in cooking; to complain when lazy persons are fed.

Toui, *v.* To do more or better than another.

Touia, *a.* Wounded; pierced as by a spear.

Touia, *v.* To let down the net at a venture; to hang up; to excel, to surpass.

Toube, *a.* Free, without children.

Toubili, *v.* To follow, to pursue, to go after.

Toubuna, *v.* To hem, to darn.

Toufefine, *s.* Women of one age or generation.

Toufefine, *s.* A sister, used only by a brother; one kind of the tree called *Tou.*

Toufo, *v.* To scoop out water; to drink up.

Touhala, *v.* To neglect the proper time and place for any work.

Touhuhu, *s.* A play.

Touhuhu, Toutouhuhu, } *a.* Full of knobs or lumps, knotty.

Toukai, *s.* The time for fruit trees bearing.

Toukubu, *s.* A limb; the limb from one joint to another.

Toulekeleka, *s.* A beauty; a handsome man.

Toulekeleka, *a.* Goodly, fine, well proportioned.

Touliki, Toutouliki, } *a.* Water into which oil has been introduced; oiled while yet wet with water.

Touloku, *s.* A shrub.

Toulu, *a.* Full of leaves; covered with tendrils and leaves, as a plantation.

Toumaga, *s.* The branch of the yam vines or tendrils.

Toumama, *s.* The people or worshippers of any given god.

Toumanu, *s.* The season in which birds lay.

Toumata, *s.* A shade for the eyes.

Toume, *s.* The cover of the nut branch as it fruits from the tree, used when dry as a torch.

Toumoua, *v.* To hesitate.

Toumoua, *s.* Hesitation.

Toumohomoho, *s.* The banana leaves baked with the food.

Toumua, *s.* The road belonging to an *abi* or premises.

Toumui, *s.* The end of the rows of yams.

Toutai, *s.* The person who gives directions in sailing canoes; a sailing master.

Toutai, *v.* To fish, to take fish.

Toutai, *s.* Fish caught from the sea.

Toutai, Toutaiika, } *s.* A fisherman.

Toutaba, *s.* Woman or women who paste the *taba* together in making *gatu.*

Toutaba, *v.* To paste together the *fetaaki* in making *gatu.*

Toutagata, *s.* A race; a generation; one kind of the tree called *tou;* a man who takes care of women in an *abi;* a brother, used by a sister only.

Toutagata, *a.* Equal; alike in age; of one generation.

Toutakao, *v.* To box; to fight with the fists.

Toutakao, *s.* A boxing match.

Toutali, *s.* The second in number of baskets of food.

Toutama, *a.* Giving suck or suckling.
Toutama, *s.* A suckling woman.
Toutou, *a.* Tender, not tough.
Toutou, *v.* To be in fear; to reciprocate.
Toutoui, *v.* To paste together small pieces in making *gatu.*
Toutouia, *v.* To hang up; to suspend from above.
Toutonu, *v.* To do at the proper time and place.
Toutoubili, *v.* To follow close.
Toutouhiko, *s.* A play of chief girls.
Toutouhua, *v.* To cover as with a shawl.
Toutu, *s.* The name of a fish.
Toutui, *v.* To push through the wind; to sail with the wind right ahead.
Toutuu, *v.* To go and come repeatedly.
Toutuu, *s.* A large plantation of yams belonging to several.
Toutufala, *s.* Fish.
Toba, *s.* A sore mouth.
Tobala, *v.* To fall rotten ripe from the trees.
Tobe, *s.* A lock of hair; a fleak.
Tobe, Tobetobe, } *v.* To paddle with a quick stroke.
Tobetobe, *v.* To remain here and there one.
Tobihi, *v.* To fall soft ripe.
Toboli, *s.* The noise of the *Moho.*
Tobono, *a.* Satisfied, filled.
Tobui, *v.* To prohibit; to make sacred.
Tobuuno, *s.* A shrub that invariably grows upon other trees, applied to one who appears afraid to sit on the earth.
Tobuga, Tobugobuga, } *v.* To sit as a dead weight on the surface of the water, applied to a canoe that sails badly.
Tobukie, *s.* A shining substance on the bark of trees seen in the dark.
Tobulagi, *s.* The name of a shell fish.
Tobulaka, *s.* A frame to throw spears over *ata* mark.
Tobulaka, *v.* To spear, to throw spears over any thing.
Tobuna, *v.* To leap, to run along.
Tobuvae, *s.* Shoes, footstep, sandals.
Tobuvaetaha, *v.* To walk in one and the same footstep.
Tofa, *v.* To lay out, to make, as a road.
Tofa, Tofafa, } *s.* Sleep, only used to chiefs.
Tofai, *v.* To cut through the midst.
Tofaaki, Totofaaki, } *v.* To sleep with; to awake to do, as work in the morning.
Tofaga, *v.* To arrive suddenly, as a canoe.
Tofaki, *a.* Deep.
Tofale, *v.* To make small houses.
Tofatakavale, *v.* To die as one poor and friendless yet a chief.
Tofe, *s.* The name of a shell fish.
Tofeloa, *s.* The name of a shell fish.
Tofelouifi, *s.* The name of a shell fish.
Tofetofe, *s.* The name of a shell fish.
Tofi, *s.* A knife made with hard wood.
Tofi, *v.* To cut in small pieces.
Tofia, *s.* An inheritance, a patrimony.
Tofifatafata, *s.* A yard, half fathom, measuring from the end of the fingers to the middle of the chest.
Tofiga, *s.* The time for cutting yams into sets.
Tofiholoaki, *v.* To cut sets of yams at different times.

Tofiji, *s.* One kind of sugar cane.
Tofitofi, *v.* To cut into pieces.
Tofo, } *a.* Out of the ordinary
Tofoi, } order of things.
Tofogi, *v.* To take off a prohibition.
Tofoto, *s.* A payment for medicine.
Tofu, *s.* A calm.
Tofu, *a.* Calm.
Tofu, *v.* To be all supplied.
Tofua, *v.* To bake the yams whole; to rush in upon.
Tofuaa, *s.* The whale.
Tofue, *s.* The name of a shell fish.
Tofuhi, *a.* Covered with fruit (trees.)
Tofuhia, *v.* To be becalmed; to be all served.
Tofuji, *v.* To run, to go, to come, (a low word used to a superior.)
Tofuki, *s.* A dead calm.
Tofunaga, *s.* A spot where food has been cooked, a cooking place.
Tofutofu, *a.* Nearly calm, light winds.
Tofutofu, *s.* A smooth part in the sea.
Tofutuu, *v.* To take a spring in diving in the water.
Toga, *v.* To arrive panting for breath.
Togabuleia, *v.* To be governed, to be under law.
Togafiji, *s.* One clever at sea.
Togi, *v.* To carve, to engrave.
Togi, *s.* Carved work, engraving.
Togia, *v.* To relieve for a time.
Togiaki, *s.* A sailing canoe; the former double canoes of Toga.
Togitogi, *v.* To carve.
Togo, *s.* The name of a tree; a preparation for turning the hair red.
Togo, *v.* To dress the head with the above.

Togoi, *s.* A kind of butterfly.
Togolei, *s.* A tree.
Togotogo, *s.* One kind of the *Ji.*
Tohala, *v.* To be too late; to be out of the way at the proper time.
Tohi, *s.* A book, a writing, a letter; a small sharp shell used in splitting leaves.
Tohi, *v.* To write, to enrol.
Tohi, } *v.* To score, to streak,
Tohitohi, } to split.
Tohitohi, *s.* The name of a shell fish.
Toho, *v.* To drag, to tow along.
Tohoa, *v.* To take off.
Tohoga, *s.* The mark in the road where any thing has been dragged.
Tohotoho, *v.* To drag by force; to abuse a female.
Tohumu, } *v.* To stumble
Tohumuhumu, } along.
Tohuni, *s.* The name of a tree.
Toji, } *v.* To peck, to nibble,
Tojitoji, } to jagg.
Toka, *v.* To bespeak a particular article at any festival.
Toka, *s.* The particular article bespoken.
Toka, *a.* Aground, asleep, submissive, conquered.
Toka, *v.* To sleep; to lie down, as one afflicted; to be, to exist, as in a given state.
Toka, *s.* Sleep; one kind of the *Kolokalù;* a sediment.
Tokaaga, *s.* The bed or sleeping place of chiefs.
Tokaage, Think, imagine.
Tokai, *v.* To add to, to mix with.
Tokai, *a.* Right ahead, (the wind.)
Tokai, *s.* A blow with the fist.
Tokai, *v.* To go direct to.
Tokaimaanaga, *a.* Open, exposed, without a covering.
Tokafa, *v.* To fall ripe (the *Ifi.*)

Tokafo, *v.* To fall, to die from a spear or shot.
Tokaga, *s.* Attention, advertency, care.
Tokaga, *a.* Attentive, careful.
Tokaga, *v.* To attend, to care for.
Tokaga, *s.* A place where many birds lay their eggs; a patch of ground often planted with yams; a point from which the wind blew.
Tokagai, *v.* To take care of, to attend to.
Tokagaiteita, *a.* To be hated.
Tokagagoue, *s.* Land under cultivation, divided out into gardens.
Tokagalaa, *s.* The west; the place of sun setting.
Tokagamahaki, *s.* A place where several sick persons lie.
Tokageegaea, *v.* To lie overdone with fatigue.
Tokaki, *v.* To take to a place.
Tokakovi, *a.* Qualmish, sickly inclined.
Tokalaelae, *v.* To lie with the face upwards, as one laid out.
Tokalali, *s.* The name of a shell fish.
Tokalalo, *s.* The lowest in any situation; subjection.
Tokalalo, *v.* To submit, to yield to.
Tokalosi, *s.* A surgical operation.
Tokaluta, *v.* To stand or lie firm.
Tokamea, *v.* To have charge of; to look after.
Tokamua, *a.* Early.
Tokamua, *ad.* Beforehand, previously.
Tokamui, *a.* Late.
Tokamui, *ad.* Behind, too late.
Tokanoa, *s.* The name of a shell fish.
Tokanoa, *a.* Unfrequented, solitary.
Toke, *s.* The sea eel.
Toke, *v.* To cut up the whale.
Tokebokulu, *s.* A fish.
Tokegatala, *s.* A fish.
Tokehe, *v.* To break or fall from.
Tokehe, *v.* To go aside; to stray to the right or left.
Toketanu, *s.* A fish.
Toketea, *s.* A fish.
Toki, *s.* An axe, hatchet; the name of a shell fish.
Toki, *ad.* Then, lately, just past.
Toki, } *v.* To ravish; to be
Tokia, } ravished.
Tokilalo, *v.* To be subdued, to fall under.
Toko, *s.* Long rods used for pushing along canoes in shallow water.
Toko, *v.* To work as above; to make preparations on a large scale.
Toko, A particle used before numerals and in asking a question, meaning person or individual, applied also to irrational animals.
Tokoua, *s.* A brother, a sister.
Tokofeke, *v.* To go in search of the *Feke*.
Tokomataba, *s.* A bar; a stick used to fasten doors.
Tokomohu, *s.* Hiccup.
Tokonaki, *s.* Preparation; food prepared for any special occasion.
Tokonaki, *v.* To prepare; to collect together; to rest the hand upon any thing.
Tokoni, *s.* Help, assistance, support.
Tokoni, *v.* To help, to assist, to encourage.
Tokonifuji, *s.* The name of a fish.
Tokoto, *v.* To lie down.
Tokoto, *v.* To be lying down.
Tokotoko, *s.* A walking stick.
Tokotokoi, *v.* To rub; to stroke the flesh and limbs of young children.

Tokotokonaki, *v.* To be preparing.

Tokotuu, *s.* The stakes used in the reed fencing.

Toku, *s.* A kind of knife made from the common tortoise shell.

Toku, *v.* To chop; to smack the mouth in eating.

Tokua, Used when addressing another, but without any definite meaning.

Tokulu, *v.* To crouch.

Tokutoku, *v.* To eat as rabbits or mice.

Tola, *s.* The snout, the mouth; the native drum; a play of children; the top part of the nut tree.

Toleka, *s.* One kind of sugar cane.

Tolele, *a.* Purged; afflicted with a purging.

Toli, *v.* To gather, to pluck, to take off.

Toli, *s.* The gathering of flowers for garlands.

Tolia, *a.* Satisfied, pleased (the mind.)

Tolii, *v.* To chip, to break off.

Tolifili, *v.* To pick and choose.

Tolilo, *v.* To hide; to put out of sight of others.

Tolitoli, *s.* The name of a shell fish.

Tolo, *s.* The name of a fish; a game; a way of taking fish; a throw; the throwing overboard to lighthen the vessel.

Tolo, *v.* To rub; to ignite; to throw; to cast goods overboard.

Tolo, *a.* Half grown (the yam.)

Toloa, *s.* The duck.

Toloa, *v.* To cast overboard.

Toloaki, *s.* A breed, a hatch.

Toloaki, Toloekina, } *v.* To move; to place in a different situation; to draw along.

Toloi, *v.* To increase; to extend; to lenghten out; to crush; to force.

Tolouoji, *a.* Destitute; neither in the house nor outside.

Tolounua, *v.* To run a splinter or thorn into the foot.

Tolounua, *s.* A sore caused by a splinter.

Tolobi, *v.* To turn up, to disrupt.

Tolofa, *a.* Wide, broad, spread out.

Tolofa, *v.* To wear a dress long and spreading.

Tolofia, *v.* To creep towards; to get at by the sly.

Tologa, *a.* Durable, long lived, lasting, permanent.

Tologa, *s.* Duration, permanency; the large stick used in getting fire.

Tologaki, *v.* To throw at, to pelt.

Tologalu, *a.* Heavily freighted.

Tologalu, *v.* To rattle in the throat.

Tologulu, *s.* A ruttling in the throat.

Tologulu, *v.* To ruttle in the throat.

Tolokakanoa, *v.* To pierce to the quick.

Tolomoana, *s.* A fish.

Tolona, *v.* To move off in another direction, as a squall.

Tolotalo, *s.* A shrub.

Toloto, *v.* To get entangled; to get within a net.

Tolotolo, *v.* To throw repeatedly and at random.

Tolotolo, *s.* A cape; a projecting part of land.

Tolotolofaki, *v.* To creep along; to crawl with something in the hand.

Tolotologa, See *Tologa*.

Tolotologulu, See *Tologulu*.

Tolovaia, *v.* To near, to approach, as one canoe chasing another.

Toloveu, *s.* Light rubbish.
Tolu, *a.* Three.
Tolutolu, *s.* The name of a shell fish.
Tolutoluhama, *s.* A small stick fastened to the outrigger; a stand by.
Toma, *s.* Pride, vanity.
Toma, *a.* Proud, vain.
Toma, *v.* To expect to do.
Tomabee, *v.* To fall or bow down.
Tomaga, *v.* To walk with extended legs.
Tomo, *a.* Longer, taller.
Tomo, *v.* To project, to jet out.
Tomoi, *s.* Sodomy.
Tomohobo, *v.* To fall and rise, as a vessel in a heavy sea.
Tomokulu, *v.* To come together one after another; to come at different times
Tomotahabe, *a.* Longest, tallest.
Tomotoma, *v.* To swagger, to boast.
Tomotomo, *s.* The top of the canoe mast.
Tomua, *a.* First, earliest.
Tomua, *ad.* Early, too early.
Tomui, *a.* Last, latest.
Tomui, *ad.* Late, too late.
Tomuhu, *v.* To speak; to converse in a low tone of voice.
Tona, *s.* A native disease resembling small pox; the lumpy or rough part of the *Feke.*
Tono, *s.* A kind of grass.
Tono, Tonoi, } *s.* Adultery.
Tonoa, *v.* To part with foolishly.
Tonoa, *a.* Vain, fruitless.
Tonoa, *v.* To be adulterated, to commit adultery.
Tonoi, *v.* To commit adultery.
Tonofefine, *s.* An adulterer.
Tonotagata, *s.* An adulteress.
Tonotama, *v.* To adopt a child already adopted by another.
Tonu, *s.* The name of a fish.

Tonu, *a.* Straight, correct, free from error, fixed.
Tonuuli, *s.* A fish.
Tonufagamea, *s.* A fish.
Tonuga, *a.* Faithful, upright and downright.
Tonuhia, *s.* Justice, equity.
Tonuhia, *a.* Just, righteous.
Tonuhia, *v.* To be justified; to be clear from charges.
Tonukuli, *s.* A fish.
Tonumaga, *s.* Any thing buried for a time, as yams for setting.
Tonumaki, *v.* To say and do unkind things to another repeatedly. See *Tanumaki.*
Tonumekina, *v.* To be buried or covered over by accident.
Tonutea, *s.* A fish.
Totao, *s.* The name of a fish.
Totao, *a.* Sharp, long, pointed.
Totahi, *v.* To be lost at sea.
Totakutaku, *v.* To blow in gusts strong and sudden.
Toteia, *v.* To fall; to die by a blow.
Totebe, *v.* To move quickly; to bustle about.
Toto, *s.* Blood; the name of a tree.
Toto, *v.* To bleed.
Toto, *v.* To bend or stoop in walking.
Toto, *v.* To give the mind to; to be absorbed with.
Totoa, Totoia, } *a.* Bloody.
Totoafa, *s.* A waste uncultivated spot.
Totoaki, *s.* Earnestness, zeal.
Totoaki, *a.* Earnest, zealous.
Totoaki, *v.* To do earnestly.
Totoe, *v.* To groan, to mourn.
Totoi, *v.* To leave a remnant.
Totoogakehe, *v.* To act differently from former times.
Totou, *v.* To paste together the *Fetaaki* with the *Tou.*
Totofa, *v.* To walk as through a thicket.

202

Totofaaki, *a.* Near; at hand, as to-morrow.
Totofi, *v.* To cut; to cut a second time.
Totofia, *a.* Maggotty.
Totofo, *v.* To seek medicine.
Totofu, *v.* To be supplied; all to have a portion.
Totogi, *s.* Payment, wages, fee, expiation.
Totogi, *v.* To pay, to reward, to expiate, to fee; to nibble, as a fish at the bait; to change; to relieve another by taking his place.
Totogo, *v.* To spring up; to be growing, as the beard.
Totoho, *a.* Streaked, plaided.
Totoho, *v.* To drawl out, to lengthen out.
Totoji, *v.* To nibble, to eat slowly.
Totoka, *v.* To sink as a sediment.
Totoka, *s.* Any sediment.
Totoka, *ad.* Slowly, gently, gradually.
Totoka, *a.* Slow, gentle.
Totokalihi, Totokalihilihi, } *s.* A dead calm.
Totoke, *v.* To trip along, as one pleased with his errand.
Totoko, *v.* To walk with the help of a long stick; to push out.
Totoko, *s.* A smoothing instrument.
Totoko, *v.* To smoothen, to make even.
Totoku, *v.* To eat eagerly.
Totokula, *s.* A tree.
Totola, *a.* Hard; too fresh or new.
Totolo, *v.* To crawl, to creep.
Totoma, *v.* To borrow adornings for the body.
Totomotuabaaga, *v.* To be all in earnest; to do with all one's might.
Totona, *a.* Lumpy.
Totonu, *a.* Straight, correct, upright, equitable, real.
Totonu, *s.* Equity, justice, uprightness, reality.
Totototo, *a.* Red.
Totutubu, *v.* To set when sprouted.
Totutuli, *v.* To set before sprouted.
Tovale, *a.* Lost.
Tu, *s.* The name of a bird.
Tua, *s.* The back.
Tua, *s.* One species of the yam; the outside of any thing; the common people.
Tua, *a.* External, outward, exterior.
Tua, *v.* To push; to drive against.
Tuaa, *s.* The outside of the fence.
Tuaata, *s.* A kind of yam.
Tuaeitu, *s.* A Tonga feast.
Tuai, *v.* To push, to knock against.
Tuai, *s.* A push.
Tuai, *s.* Delay, procrastination; the back.
Tuai, *a.* Slow, dilatory.
Tuai, *v.* To be long, to defer.
Tuaimeiuta, *v.* To be long or delayed but on shore.
Tuaofo, *s.* The bend or curve in the end of Tonga houses.
Tuaba, *v.* To bury on the cover stone of a vault; to bury temporarily.
Tuababa, *s.* A broad surface of sand stone at the sea side.
Tuabeukai, *s.* A person of inferior rank who interferes to prevent the preparing food for a chief.
Tuabiko, *a.* Humpbacked.
Tuabiko, *s.* A humpbacked person.
Tuafehuiua, *a.* Inquisitive, fond of inquiring.
Tuahaa, *v.* To forebode evil.

Tuahi, *s.* The name of a shell fish.
Tuahuoa, *a.* Injured by the back of the *huo,* applied to the yam in getting up.
Tuajina, *s.* An uncle.
Tuakatoaga, *s.* A second or after feast.
Tuaki, *s.* Breeding sickness.
Tuakia, *s.* The back of the neck.
Tuakie, *s.* An inferior mat made from the outside of the *Kieuli.*
Tuakofe, *v.* To clean the entrails of animals with any thing sharp.
Tuakolo, *s.* The least frequented side of a fort; that side of a fort which is defended by the sea or a forest, &c.
Tuamafa, *s.* One kind of wild pigeon.
Tuamata, *s.* The outside of the eye lash.
Tuamataaki, *v.* To close the eyes, to rest.
Tuamea, *s.* The name of a tree.
Tuamelie, *v.* To anticipate good, to hope.
Tuanaki, *v.* To depend on, to confide in.
Tuatalaeiki, *s.* A poor person who talks much of his relationship with chiefs.
Tuatalamatagi, *s.* One forward with his opinion of the wind though among sailors.
Tuatamaki, *v.* To apprehend evil.
Tue, *s.* The name of a shell fish.
Tue, *v.* To shout, to triumph over.
Tueina, *v.* To attend to; to make much of.
Tuenoa, *a.* Disconsolate, bereft.
Tui, *s.* A king, a governor; one who governs of either sex.
Tui, *s.* Faith, belief, credence; the knee; the name of a shell fish.
Tui, *a.* Believing, credulous.
Tui, *v.* To believe, to credit; to file; to string as beads, &c.; to thread a needle; to pierce; to perform an operation on the eye.
Tuia, *v.* To be pierced or wounded by any thing sharp; to be seized by affliction.
Tuia, *s.* The attack or seizure of any disease.
Tuiafala, *v.* To lie afflicted on a *fala* or mat.
Tuiaki, *v.* To rush through the midst; to divide asunder an opposing army; to tow a vessel.
Tuiaki, *s.* The individual who acts as above; a rope in a canoe.
Tuiekina, *v.* To rush through.
Tuiinima, *s.* The elbow.
Tuifakafakau, *v.* To yield an unwilling assent.
Tuiga, *s.* A string of beads, flowers, &c.; a wig.
Tuigataa, *a.* Unbelieving; difficult to pierce.
Tuigofua, *a.* Credulous, unsuspecting.
Tuigutu, *v.* To pierce the cheeks on the death of a chief
Tuigutu, *s.* The one side of a double canoe used as a paddling canoe.
Tuikata, *s.* The name of a shell fish.
Tuila, *v.* To make or mend sails.
Tuitala, *a.* Believing, obedient.
Tuitui, *s.* The name of a tree and its fruit; needle work.
Tuitui, *v.* To sew.
Tuituia, *s.* Conception.
Tuituia, *v.* To conceive.
Tuituu, *s.* Wreaths of scented flowers.
Tuo, *s.* Times, used similarly to *Liuga.*
Tuo, *s.* A sudden jerk; a strong and sudden pull.
Tuo, *v.* To pluck, to jerk.

Tuoua, *s.* The very fine mats from Samoa.

Tuofefine, *s.* A sister (used only by a brother.)

Tuoni, *s.* A single hair, thread, or fibre; a gust of wind.

Tuotua, *v.* To raise up with the back.

Tuotua, *a.* Strong, too strong; not fine, as thread, &c.

Tuotua, *a.* Dirty; without a floor or covering, as a house.

Tuotuai, *v.* To be long, used as *Tuai.*

Tuotuabolata, *v.* To bulge out.

Tuotuamelie, See *Tuamelie.*

Tuotuatamaki, See *Tuatamaki.*

Tuotuo, *v.* To jerk; to snatch or pluck suddenly.

Tuu, *v.* To stand, to rise; to void the fæces; to finish; to be lit.

Tuu, *s.* A white mattery substance in the eye; one kind of the *Kabe.*

Tuua, *v.* To cut through; to grow double; to be in two parts.

Tuuau, *v.* To stand; to tread down the rope to which leaves are fastened; to take fish.

Tuuabo, *s.* About midnight.

Tuuabolilolilo, *a.* Dark, thick darkness.

Tuuabomalie, *s.* Midnight.

Tuuabotakiaho, *s.* Past midnight, approaching day.

Tuuaki, *s.* The lower part of the sail yards; also of the *Feleano.*

Tuuaki, *v.* To carry a child about; to hawk for sale; to prepare food; to stand with something in the hand.

Tuualialiaki, *v.* To stand firmly.

Tuualialiaki, *s.* Steadfastness.

Tuuava, *v.* To stand in the passage to seize the canoe on entering.

Tuuekina, *v.* To break; to tear by pressure.

Tuuete, *v.* To stand on tip toe.

Tuui, *s.* The name of a large fishing net; a present of food to the friends of a deceased person.

Tuui, *v.* To speed, to hasten.

Tuuika, *s.* A present in return for fish.

Tuuihonima, *v.* To turn out of the hand; to desert; to give up.

Tuuola, *v.* To walk and appear here and there as ghosts.

Tuubou, Tuuboubou, } *v.* To stand as a post.

Tuububu, *v.* To grow thick in clusters.

Tuubuku, *v.* To appear, as fruit on the tree.

Tuufue, *a.* Without meaning; unexpected.

Tuuga, *s.* A foundation, a site; a ladder; a pulpit; a pile.

Tuuga, Sign of the plural.

Tuugaa, *a.* Sudden, unexpected; out of time and order.

Tuugaiku, *s.* The seat, rump, buttocks.

Tuugafana, *s.* The step upon which the mast stands.

Tuugafulufulu, *s.* Mould.

Tuugafulufulu, *a.* Mouldy.

Tuugutufaga, *v.* To stand at the mouth of a trap.

Tuugutugutu, *v.* To stand in the entrance.

Tuuhiuhi, *s.* A preparation of food.

Tuuhuluni, *v.* To stand in the shade of another; to be hid by another.

Tuuji, *v.* To cut off, to reap, to defalcate.

Tuujiuho, *v.* To cut the unbilical chord.

Tuujiuho, *s.* The work for which any one is noted.

Tuukauoi, *v.* To be at hand while another is distressed for the same.

Tuukauga, *s.* The resting place of birds, a roost; the shelter of rogues.

Tuukauga, *v.* To perch as birds; to rendezvous near at hand.

Tuukaumamafa, *a.* Not quite fledged; without feathers; not full feathered.

Tuukata, *v.* To cut short lengths of the *kava* branch for setting.

Tuukinga, *v.* To stand in one's proper place; to stand out of the way.

Tuukimua, *a.* Foremost, first in dignity.

Tuukina, *v.* To stand on end, as the hair of the body in fright, &c.

Tuukofe, *v.* To erect the fishing rods in the canoe as a sign that fish have been caught.

Tuula, *s.* A stick upon which birds are carried about; a bird roost.

Tuulaua, *v.* To be spoken or talked of.

Tuulavae, *v.* To appear in the person of another, used of the gods.

Tuulea, See *Tuugaa.*

Tuulili, *s.* One kind of the *Kabe.*

Tuulomia, *a.* Subject, submissive.

Tuulu, *v.* To fall headlong; to bow down the head; to lop off the branches.

Tuului, *v.* To change the dress often.

Tuulutui, *v.* To kneel, to bend the knee.

Tuumau, *v.* To stand fast, to continue.

Tuumau, *a.* Steadfast, constant, costive.

Tuumalie, *a.* Timely, seasonable.

Tuumaleafi, *v.* To do without consulting the proper parties.

Tuumee, *s.* One who attends a dance to take a part therein.

Tuumilu, *v.* To cut into short lengths.

Tuumua, *s.* The front teeth; a principal person with a chief; the first or foremost.

Tuunoa, *v.* To relieve nature.

Tuuta, *s.* Rows, one upon another.

Tuuta, *v.* To step; to go on shore after a voyage.

Tuutai, *a.* Goodly, comely.

Tuutaifakakava, *a.* Good in appearance only.

Tuutaubeube, *v.* To stand in danger.

Tuutauhoa, *a.* Opposite, in a line with.

Tuutaga, *s.* The neck of a pig; a lump, a log, a clod.

Tuutagamalie, *a.* Good in size, neither too large nor too small.

Tuutajiba, *v.* To stand crooked or slanting.

Tuutamaki, *a.* Untimely, unseasonable.

Tuutamaki, *v.* To slant, not level; to be in danger; to be in trouble.

Tuutata, *v.* To make water; to repeat after a short interval.

Tuuteitei, *v.* To stand ready for a flight.

Tuuteketekenaki, *v.* To raise by bearing upon the hands.

Tuutui, *v.* To bend the knees; to stand upon the knees.

Tuutuu, *v.* To cut in pieces, to hack, to revive.

Tuutuuaa, *v.* To do; to do without intermission.

Tuutuuata, *s.* One by himself; one without a defender.

Tuutuuata, *v.* To stand exposed.

Tuutuui, *v.* To speed another, to hasten.

Tuutuugataa, *v.* To rise or stand unwillingly or with difficulty.
Tuutuuhola, *v.* To stand ready to abscond.
Tuutuukautala, *s.* One kind of the banana.
Tuutuulele, *v.* To stand ready to run.
Tuutuumamao, *v.* To keep a respectful distance.
Tuutuumouga, *v.* To be out of reach, as one on a mountain, applied to one who is screened by a chief.
Tuutuuni, *s.* An appointment, an ordinance.
Tuutuuni, *v.* To appoint.
Tuutuutaufa, *a.* Squally.
Tuuvaka, *v.* To sail in quest of any object.
Tuuvala, *v.* To exchange the dress repeatedly (a custom at Tonga weddings.)
Tuba, *s.* A hole or opening; an entrance; the name of a shell fish.
Tubaba, *v.* To beat with a quick stroke.
Tubagi, *v.* To make a hole; to tear open.
Tubaku, *v.* To be burnt to a cinder, as food.
Tube, *s.* A thin piece of nut shell used in pitching; a play of children; pitapat, palpitation.
Tubei, } *v.* To shake off, to
Tubetubei, } shake.
Tubekina, *v.* To be shaken away.
Tuboko, *v.* To apply fire to parts in pain.
Tubotubagi, *v.* To make many holes or passages.
Tubu, *v.* To spring, to grow, to accrue, to arise from; to be caused to sprout.
Tubu, *s.* Growth, produce, proceeds, increase; the groin; the odd numbers in counting.

Tubua, *s.* Any thing new or wonderful.
Tubuaga, *s.* The origin, source, cause, author, creator.
Tubuiotua, *s.* A self existent god; a god whose origin is unknown.
Tubufakabolo, } *v.* To grow,
Tubufakaholoholo, } to arise in succession.
Tubuga, See *Tubuaga*.
Tubulaki, } *v.* To increase,
Tubulekina, } to advance, to grow.
Tubunoa, *v.* To be without any apparent cause.
Tubutamaki, *s.* Anger, displeasure, applied to chiefs.
Tubutamaki, *a.* Angry.
Tubutomua, *v.* To be or exist too early.
Tubutomui, *v.* To be or exist too late.
Tubutubu, *s.* Clouds that have a land-like appearance from the sea.
Tubutubua, *a.* Endless, for ever.
Tubutubulua, *v.* To make a drivelling noise as children.
Tufa, *v.* To divide, to portion out, to allot, to deal, to distribute.
Tufakautufa, *v.* To pay off in the same way.
Tufakaga, *s.* A portion, a lot, a dividend.
Tufafakama, *v.* To divide out as balls of bread.
Tufaki, *v.* To divide into small portions.
Tufaki, *s.* Distribution; the act of portioning out.
Tufatuha, *v.* To divide or separate to persons as they may sit.
Tufekina, See *Tufaki*.
Tufi, } *v.* To collect together;
Tufitufi, } to pick up small things.

207

Tufotufa, *v.* To divide out.
Tufotufaulunima, *v.* To give out from hand to hand.
Tufu, *s.* The name of a fish; water that is brackish.
Tufuga, *s.* An artificer, a carpenter.
Tuga, *s.* A knot in wood; the joint in cane; an insect.
Tuga, *a.* Destitute; without; not possessing.
Tugai, *v.* To hobble in walking.
Tugaivae, *s.* The ankle.
Tugage, *s.* One kind of turtle.
Tugaki, *v.* To light a fire for guidance of a canoe nearing shore.
Tugia, *v.* To set on fire, to burn.
Tugotuga, *a.* Knotty, full of knots.
Tuha, *a.* Alike, equal, opposite, in a line with.
Tuhani, *v.* To appoint, to prearrange.
Tuhi, *s.* A fish.
Tuhituhi, *a.* Striped.
Tuhu, *s.* The finger.
Tuhu, } *v.* To point with
Tuhutuhu, } the finger.
Tuhulu, *s.* A torch or flambeau.
Tuhulu, *v.* To light with a torch.
Tuka, *v.* To stand on a sudden.
Tukau, *s.* A handle for the fishing rod.
Tukaba, *a.* Distant, far off.
Tuke, *s.* The knuckles.
Tuketuke, *v.* To speak amorously of gentlemen.
Tuke, } *v.* To be stript or
Tuketuke, } made bare, as a tree of its branches.
Tuki, *s.* A superstitious practice by which thieves, &c. are said to be accursed.
Tuki, *s.* A blow, a thump, a striker.
Tuki, *v.* To strike, to drive, to drub; to make a present at a funeral.

Tukia, *v.* To strike against; to wreck.
Tukia, *a.* Soft, bruised.
Tukia, *v.* To stumble.
Tukiaaga, *s.* A stumbling block.
Tukibalagia, *v.* To beat soundly.
Tukifakaaugafa, *v.* To imprecate extinction in case of guilt.
Tukifulei, *s.* Onanism.
Tukiga, *s.* The place or point to which a thing is struck or driven.
Tukihau, *s.* One kind of reeding.
Tukikalava, *v.* To beat the body with the shreaded *Kalava* bound round the fists.
Tukitala, *v.* To warn; to beat with words.
Tukitalai, *v.* To doom, to execrate.
Tukitoka, *v.* To strike while lying.
Tukituki, *v.* To strike; to wrap gently.
Tukituki, *s.* Short sticks driven into the outrigger, and fastened to rails from the body of the canoe; a pin, a peg, a stopper.
Tukitukifao, *v.* To nail, to fasten with nails.
Tukolokalo, *s.* A preparation of food.
Tuku, *s.* A rope in the canoe.
Tuku, *v.* To cease, to desist, to adjourn; to let, to suffer or allow; to bequeath; to slacken, to let go; to dye or stain.
Tukua, *v.* To excommunicate, to put away.
Tukua, *v.* To cease, to give over.
Tukuaga, *s.* Any place for stores; the end or finishing.
Tukuagakoloa, *s.* A store.
Tukuage, } *v.* To deliver up, to
Tukuatu, } give, to yield; to disenthral, to release.

Tukuage, } *s.* Release, dismis-
Tukuatu, } sion.
Tukuaki, } *v.* To accuse unjust-
Tukuakii, } ly.
Tukuaki, *s.* Crimination, unjust accusation.
Tukuekina, *v.* To be accused; to accuse wrongfully.
Tukui, *s.* A bale of *gatu* or any treasure.
Tukuigata, *v.* To work or do with all the strength.
Tukuituba, *v.* To place in a line with; to put opposite.
Tukuumu, *v.* To take presents of cooked food to a female as an expression of wishing her in marriage.
Tukuba, *s.* The Tonga manner of declaring allegiance when war is expected.
Tukubala, *v.* To let go or slacken suddenly or too much.
Tukubalu, *s.* A particular manner of taking fish.
Tukufakaholo, *v.* To possess or inherit in succession.
Tukufakakai, *v.* To do any thing trifling as a payment of a lost game.
Tukufakalele, *v.* To let go by the run.
Tukufala, *v.* To make presents to a relative near death.
Tukufatogia, *s.* A general making of presents to a chief.
Tukuga, See *Tukuaga.*
Tukugakovi, *s.* One to whom roguery is generally imputed.
Tukugamea, See *Tukuagakoloa.*
Tukugoue, *v.* To atone for, to redeem.
Tukuhau, *s.* Tribute, finance, revenue.
Tukuhau, *v.* To pay tribute.
Tukuhaujia, *v.* To be deserted, exposed, left alone.
Tukuhali, *s.* A kind of sea serpent or eel.
Tukuhua, *v.* To make each other laugh; to joke.
Tukukatei, *v.* To reserve food while some present are hungry.
Tukuku, *s.* The name of a fish.
Tukulalo, *v.* To speak low, to whisper.
Tukuleia, *s.* A fish.
Tukumamao, *v.* To leave behind in the rear.
Tukumiji, *s.* The name of a shell fish.
Tukutau, *v.* To follow all; to see all before.
Tukutautalaga, *v.* To converse; to arrange and leave it.
Tukutavahi, *v.* To prepare the *kafa* for a black dye.
Tukutuku, *v.* To let go gradually; to sink in the sea.
Tukutukubau, *v.* To fix; to determine.
Tukutukutaumuli, *s.* A superstitious custom observed on the finishing a new canoe regarded as making it a lucky canoe.
Tukutukutonu, *v.* To let, to drive right upon.
Tula, *a.* Bald, uncovered.
Tulaki, *v.* To push down; to cut the hair of the *Tuitoga.*
Tulalia, *a.* Disgusting, useless.
Tule, *v.* To nod as one drowsy; to jog along as one old and weak.
Tulei, *v.* To leave shore or anchorage, applied to vessels.
Tulikina, *v.* To push or be pushed forward.
Tulelu, *v.* To be tired in waiting.
Tulemohe, *a.* Sleepy, dozy.
Tuletule, *s.* The name of a shell fish.
Tuletule, See *Tule.*
Tuli, *a.* Deaf.
Tuli, *s.* Deafness.

209

Tuli, *v.* To chase, to pursue.
Tulia, *v.* To be chased, to chase.
Tuliimui, *v.* To follow in succession.
Tuliki, *s.* The corner of a place.
Tulitulihega, *v.* To follow close to the hook (a fish.)
Tulitulita, *v.* To strike while chasing.
Tuloaloa, *a.* Dull, dark, showery (day.)
Tuloia, *s.* A sore.
Tulolo, *v.* To stoop, to crouch; to boil oil and other ingredients in making *Faikakai.*
Tulotula, *s.* A war weapon.
Tului, *v.* To drop into the eyes or any wound.
Tulubeka, *s.* A shell fish.
Tulugahehe, *s.* A shell fish.
Tuluki, *a.* Crowded.
Tuluta, *s.* A drop; a single drop or tear.
Tulutulu, *s.* The eaves of a house.
Tulutulu, *v.* To drop; to let in water.
Tuluveelei, *s.* A shell fish.
Tuma, *a.* Slow, dull, applied to a vessel.
Tuma, *s.* The louse.
Tumomoji, *v.* To burn beauty marks on the body.
Tumohokohoka, *v.* To cook food several times a day.
Tumolele, *v.* To take up and begone in a moment.
Tumu, *s.* An expression of surprise.
Tumu, *a.* Soft, rotten.
Tumuaki, *s.* The crown of the head.
Tumuakiua, *s.* Double crowned head.
Tumutumu, *s.* Peak, summit, top.
Tumutumu, *v.* To express surprise.

Tuna, *s.* The eel.
Tuna, *a.* Great; large in quantity.
Tunu, *v.* To toast, to broil.
Tunu, *s.* Food broiled or roasted on the fire.
Tunuku, *a.* Dark, thick, as the horizon threatening rain.
Tusa, *a.* Equal, on a par.
Tuta, *v.* To be tired of.
Tutaki, *v.* To cut with.
Tutolo, *s.* A film on the eye.
Tutolo, *a.* Growing, half grown, (yam.)
Tutu, *s.* The bark of the Chinese Mulberry of which the *gatu* is made; a shrub.
Tutu, *v.* To beat the *Tutu* in making native cloth; to burn; to set on fire.
Tutue, *a.* Lean, meagre.
Tutue, *s.* Leanness, emaciation.
Tutui, *v.* To sow seeds.
Tutu, Tutuu, } *s.* The porpoise.
Tutuu, *v.* To stand, applied to many; to cut off, to lop off.
Tutuuli, *s.* A shrub.
Tutubu, *v.* To sprout, to grow.
Tutugia, *a.* Shrivelled, withered.
Tutuha, *a.* Equal, on a par.
Tutuhina, *s.* A shrub.
Tutuhu, *v.* To point out; to speak suspiciously of another.
Tutuki, *v.* To drive, to strike.
Tutuki, See *Tukituki.*
Tutuku, *v.* To finish; to separate, to disperse.
Tutukua, *v.* To doom, to execrate.
Tutuli, *v.* To make speed, to haste.
Tutuli, *a.* Without sprouts.
Tutulu, *a.* Not water tight.
Tutulu, *v.* To drop; to fall in drops.
Tutuna, *s.* The name of a tree.
Tutuna, *a.* Hard, lumpy.

210

V

V, THE seventeenth Letter in the Tonga Alphapet. Its sound is that of *v* in *varnish*.

Va, *s.* A laughing noise.

Va, *v.* To laugh and make a noise.

Va, *s.* The space or distance between two given objects.

Vaa, *s.* A branch, a bough.

Vaamei, *s.* One kind of banana.

Vaata, *a.* Open.

Vaavaa, *a.* Branchy; full of branches; open, large in the meshes.

Vaavaakaka, *a.* Poorly, not well, (the *Tamaha.*)

Vaavaaki, } *v.* To incite, to
Vaavaakina, } abet, to encourage.

Vae, *s.* The foot; the legs of tables, &c.

Vae, *v.* To divide a fish longways.

Vaeuamalie, *v.* To divide into two equal parts; to halve.

Vaeuamalie, *s.* Half.

Vaefi, *a.* Close, no intervening space.

Vaevae, *v.* To divide out.

Vaevae, *v.* To run, to go quickly.

Vai, *s.* Water, medicine, a liquid.

Vaiata, *s.* Soup without fish or fowl.

Vaiola, *s.* A supposed fountain in *Bulotu* where wondrous things are said to be effected.

Vaiga, *s.* Play, sport, frivolity, vanity.

Vaiga, *a.* Frivolous, vain, trifling.

Vaiga, *v.* To play, to trifle.

Vaihu, *s.* Soups cooked in the native ovens.

Vaihutagutu, *s.* Soup made of a large fish.

Vaiji, *s.* A warm drink made of *Ji.*

Vailau, *v.* To talk; to chatter away.

Vaitafe, *s.* A brook, a river.

Vaivai, *s.* A kind of banana.

Vaivai, *s.* Weakness, frailty, debility, imbecility.

Vaivai, *a.* Weak, frail, faint, feeble, helpless.

Vaivaiaga, *s.* The cause or place of weakness.

Vaivaiatai, *a.* Feigned weakness.

Vaivaiga, See *Vaiga.*

Vaivaima, *s.* A preparation of food.

Vaivao, *s.* Mist, dew.

Vao, *s.* The bush.

Vao, } *a.* Covered with bush;
Vaoa, } fallow.

Vaofi, *v.* To be separated by a narrow space.

Vau, } *v.* To scrape.
Vauvau, }

Vagavaga, *a.* Open, net-like, spaced.

Vagi, }
Vagia, } *v.* To swear at.
Vagituga, }

Vago, *v.* To talk and chatter on whilst none care about it.

Vaha, *s.* Space at sea.

Vahaa, *s.* Space; short distances between islands.

Vahaateua, *v.* To be surrounded by those who are ornamented and prepared while you are destitute.

Vahai, *v.* To separate by getting between the parties; to set between.

Vahavaha, *s.* A fish.

Vahavahai, *v.* To intermix; to cause variety.

Vahe, *s.* A chapter, a section, a division.

Vahe, } v. To separate, to di-
Vahei, } vide out, to portion; to deduct, to abstract.

Vahega, s. A portion, lot.

Vahevahe, v. To divide; to portion out.

Vahivahi, s. A fish.

Vajia, v. To keep about the persons of chiefs; to act the sycophant.

Vajia, s. A preparation of food.

Vaka, s. The general name for all vessels that sail.

Vakai, v. To discern, to look, to behold, to take care.

Vakai, a. Vigilant, aware.

Vakafoha, s. A boil.

Vakafokotuu, s. A boat.

Vakavaka, s. The side.

Vakavakaahina, v. To be carried on the shoulders of another.

Vakavakaamei, s. A bread fruit tree used as a canoe.

Vakavakai, See *Vakai*.

Vakavakamua, v. To speak first; to be always ready with the tongue.

Vake, s. An uproarious noise.

Vake, v. To make such a noise.

Vake, a. Grey headed, very grey.

Vakili, v. To lay open, to dislodge from a box or basket.

Vaku, } v. To scratch, to
Vakuvaku, } claw.

Vala, s. A dress, clothes, covering.

Vala, v. To dress, to clothe.

Valau, s. Noise, uproar.

Valau, v. To noise, to make confusion.

Valavala, s. The dress; the disposition.

Vale, s. A fool, folly, ignorance, fondness.

Vale, a. Foolish, absurd, ignorant.

Valea, s. The skin of the *Feke*; a game or play.

Valea, a. Abundant, plentiful.

Valeiatama, v. To act foolishly from affection to a child.

Valebeaita, v. To be in the wrong yet angry with others.

Valefakaaga, s. A fool yet fond of criticising.

Valehakau, s. Used of a day the *Hakau* does not yield any fish.

Valetalavale, s. A foolish one speaking of others as foolish.

Valevale, a. Young, tender, applied to babes.

Vali, s. Paint.

Vali, v. To paint, to smear.

Valii, v. To work at several things but finish none.

Valo, s. The name of a shell fish.

Valo, v. To talk or shout at random.

Valoa, s. A sea weed.

Valoki, s. A reproof.

Valoki, v. To reprove, to warn.

Valovalo, v. To cry as children in pain.

Valu, v. To scrape.

Valu, s. The name of a fish.

Valu, a. Eight.

Valugeau, a. Eight hundred.

Valugofulu, a. Eighty.

Valulouniu, s. A fish.

Valumaka, s. A fish.

Vamamao, a. Distant; separated by a wide space.

Vana, s. The name of a shell fish.

Vanani, s. The name of a shell fish.

Vanahuhu, s. The name of a shell fish.

Vanakao, s. The name of a shell fish.

Vanamea, s. The name of a shell fish.

Vanevane, v. To make a little less; to take a little off.

Vanu, s. A deep headlong steep.

Vanuto, *a.* Full of pits.
Vanuvanu, *a.* Full of holes or pits.
Vatau, *s.* A quarrelling noise.
Vatuke, *s.* The name of a shell fish.
Vava, *s.* The distance or space between any two bodies.
Vava, *s.* One kind of the banana.
Vavae, *s.* The cotton tree, cotton.
Vavae, *v.* To divide, to portion out; to bring together the two canoes in building a *Kalia*.
Vavaga, *a.* Open, not close.
Vavahea, *s.* A game or dance of chiefs.
Vavala, *a.* Old, worn.
Vavale, *a.* Slimy, soapy.
Vavalo, *s.* The note of alarm from old fowls.
Vavatu, *s.* A shrub.
Vavana, *v.* To shudder, to tingle.
Vave, *s.* Expedition, haste.
Vave, *a.* Quick, expeditious.
Vavevave, } *a.* Quick.
Vavevavea, }
Vee, *s.* The feet, when used with an adjective: as, *vee kovi*, bad feet; also, the side: as, *vee hala*, the side of the road.
Veefua, *s.* The elephantiasis.
Veehala, *v.* To step wrong.
Veemoji, *v.* To go about, to saunter.'
Veetonu, *v.* To step right.
Veetuai, *a.* Slow in walking.
Veevave, *a.* Quick in walking.
Veevee, *s.* A wreath of flowers.
Veia, *a.* Dead fish supposed to die from the heat of the sun.
Veiba, *v.* To contend.
Veiba, *v.* To wash the hands with the *bolata* warmed, to relieve them from further *tabu*.
Veifua, *s.* Nuts warmed for drinking.
Veikaji, *v.* To contend for.

Veuki, } *v.* To confuse, to
Veuveuki, } jumble together.
Vehoveho, *v.* To appear glad; to express affection.
Vejiveji, *s.* One kind of yam.
Veka, *s.* The name of a bird and of a fish.
Vekeveke, *v.* To be more ready with the tongue than the hands.
Vekeveke, } *v.* To be first
Vekevekemua, } and foremost to speak or do.
Vela, *s.* A burn or scald, a burning.
Vela, *v.* To burn, to scald.
Vela, *a.* Hot.
Velevela, *a.* Hot from the sun; burning; annoying (disposition.)
Velevele, *v.* To long for; to take pleasure in.
Veli, } *v.* To itch.
Velia, }
Veli, *s.* An insect in the water like the centipede; the down-like substance on the reeds.
Veliveliava, *s.* One kind of the stone for *Makafeke*.
Velo, *v.* To launch, to dart.
Velo, *s.* A launch, a throw.
Veloaki, *s.* The first of animals.
Vesa, *s.* A bracelet.
Vesa, *v.* To ornament the arms and legs.
Vete, *s.* The name of a fish.
Vete, } *v.* To seize the spoil of
Vetea, } a conquered foe; to untie; to loose; to disburden; to confess.
Veteki, *v.* To take to pieces; to scatter abroad.
Vetevala, *v.* To beg the dress of another.
Vetevete, *v.* To untie, to loose.
Veve, *s.* Rubbish.
Vevea, *a.* Full of rubbish.
Veveu, *a.* Bad, confused.
Veveho, See *Vehoveho*.
Vevehu, *v.* To cover with *Veve*.

Veveke, See *Vekeveke*.
Vevela, *a.* Burnt, hot.
Vevele, *v.* To long for; to exhibit gladness.
Vi, *s.* The name of a tree and its fruit.
Via, *s.* A tree.
Vio, } Vigo, } *a.* Dead, stinking.
Viki, } Vikiviki, } *v.* To boast, to brag of, to glory in.
Viki, } Vikiviki, } *s.* Boasting.
Viku, *s.* Wetness.
Viku, *a.* Wet.
Vikuviku, *a.* Rather wet, damp.
Vili, *s.* A gimblet, an augre.
Vili, *v.* To perforate, to drill; to persevere; to go quickly.
Viligahua, *s.* The hole through which the *hua* is passed when rowing the canoe.
Viligia, *v.* To be blown away; to be blown.
Viligataa, *a.* Hard to bore.
Viligofua *a.* Easy to bore.
Vilihola, *v.* To bore the way out.
Vilitaki, *v.* To bore; to work in order to sink; to persevere.
Vilivili, *s.* The tail of fish.
Vilivili, *v.* To wag; to move the tail.
Vilo, } Vilovilo, } *v.* To dart from the hands with a twist; to twirl.
Vivao, *s.* A tree.
Vivi, See *Vio*.
Vivi, *s.* A grass.
Viviku, *a.* Wet.
Vivili, *v.* To feel; to be conscious of.
Vivini, *v.* To increase; to be more.
Voivoi, *v.* To wrap; to adorn war weapons.
Volaki, *v.* To endure because of others.
Volo, *s.* A fish.
Volovalo, *s.* A tree.
Vovo, *a.* Palatable.
Vovonu, *s.* The name of a bird.
Vu, *s.* The narrow end of a canoe sail.
Vugakoto, *s.* The step upon which the mast of the canoe stands.
Vuguvugu, *v.* To dress the hair; to make the hair black.

214

A LIST OF IDIOMATICAL PHRASES, &c.

Aoaokimajijiva, Kind; thoughtful to the poor.

Auhiaamotuafanifo, A phrase, one in trouble but expert at extricating himself.

Abifaatoetuuaieteve, An *Abi* that have plenty from their work, with the addition of fruit trees.

Alaijiaalaikologa, Useful in more work than one, as one clever at sea and on shore.

Alualuimalataukimonu, To begin badly but end well.

Alualuimonutaukimala, To begin well but end badly.

Umuboulikaeaihoota, A phrase, divided in the dark, but not forgotten, having a friend present.

Utotaugamokumaokuua, To reserve food for a future time, before all are satisfied.

Bibikomoenifo, A phrase, meaning lazy in work; lazy with the teeth.

Bikobikoikumai, To go from place to place, and fall again to its original owner.

Faalafakataukihemuiulu, To seek through every place till we arrive at the right.

Faimaietemeimeitagi, Generally repeated, used when two persons report their cases, and the one hearing is alike affected by both.

Fagotafaikihekatoava, Literally, to gather shell fish into a basket with holes, used in reference to what is done with trouble, but in vain.

Fakaitafaikitahi, A figurative expression, to be revenged on another by punishing oneself.

Fakauameamelie, To wish to eat sweet or superior food only.

Fakabikoiatohovaka, To be lazy in that which must be done, and done by those who are lazy.

Fakalaaijiamelie, The enduring inconveniences in the way of obtaining an object.

Fakatatamalafaikihala, To be careless in not making suitable provision for the future.

Fakatovakaakubolu, To give and again take back by force.

Fetauiakubegatutui, The contest of two persons or parties equally strong and courageous.

Fetoutoumoliliuaki, To wander to and fro.

Fieuokaekaibo, To covet society but eat alone and by the sly.

Fiemuaetuakimua, To attempt a trick upon one clever at tricks.

Filihiamoeelili, To gain the object, though with difficulty and pain.

Fouinefai, A phrase, tantamount to, he has what he ought to have expected.

Fokotuutuuafefiehu, Abundance, but nothing useful.

Haihaijiakaeheia, To possess at home, yet go about as one destitute.

Halaitagataia, To be destitute of a man for the purpose.

Hiaifanakava, Sin or offence committed where it is not lawful to punish.

Hiligamotolukoemotutokanoa, A phrase like this, if not there where all was favourable surely not here where all is adverse.

215

Hinaaetoumohomoho, A jocose phrase, meaning that it is long since food was cooked.

Hogeamohoueiki, To be short of food, but enjoying the benefit of living with a chief.

Holobetuuhekoegaluefaji, Tantamount to, be easy it will come to pass.

Holikieutuutuihemaalautu, Any thing got by mere accident, or without care, yet better than what has cost much trouble.

Jioaematakaehokaaetala, To talk of an absent person while a child or near relative is present.

Jinamutaefeogoogoi, To do, to take, without consultation or intimation.

Kaihaatagitauloto, A thief who not content with a little and escape, waits to get a full load and is hurt or killed.

Kailufahetuugau, To be eating crumbs and accidentally find a large portion; to be in search of small things and find a large and valuable one.

Kanakanafaikitahi, To trifle or act carelessly with what may be serious in its consequences, as going to sea unprepared.

Kiamataealomua, To assume, to take the place or work of the proper person

Kovijikogaoi, One lame or afflicted, and yet wishful to do difficult work.

Kubegaetautaukaefagota, Literally the net is hung up, but it will be used again, applied to what there will be an opportun-of proving.

Laukaufalelava, Proud; vain in more ways than one.

Lautamafaikihefatu, To speak, to boast, of what is yet uncertain.

Loligaamotu, What is common or usual at the islands.

Lujiakitaulaga, Safe though in trouble, as a vessel at anchor in bad weather.

Lukiakafaikifiji, To challenge a superior in every respect.

Mauetukukuoavemaatalanuku, to have but little, and yet take that little to one who has abundance.

Maumauaeelilimoeloka, A phrase similar in meaning to, no rose without a thorn.

Mafitokihaatuele, To challenge when and where there is no prospect of an antagonist.

Malafaietagata, One who dies from his own misconduct.

Malagafaiiheate, To speak or discourse when it is too late, having neglected the proper opportunity.

Malakinaamoojibo, To tread down but grow again.

Mamaoafolau, Distant, but on a voyage, meaning there is a possibility of again meeting.

Mamaoahikuhikujila, A phrase, used in reference to persons or things distant but easy to come at.

Mamahiitabukakuoilo, The painful prohibition of what one knows the advantage of.

Mamahinoaagutuofuiva, To be concerned about that from which no advantage can arise to the individual; as the *Fuiva* chatters on the approach of the bread fruit season but eats not thereof.

Manakoseamanakosau, To be in love with two opposite parties or things.

Mataikafaikihebubua, To see and desire what canot be obtained.

Matagileleitokilamahaehae, Good but useless, as a good wind in a torn sail.

Matakovikanaefiliekita, Unhandsome, but one of my own choice.

Mataliuaifinekehe, To be enamoured with strange women.

Mategaivaokaka, To work to death upon barren soil, unprofitable work.

Matematealiku, The calm or stillness of the sea at the *Liku* where, though it may appear calm, there is always rollers and waves.

Mohemohekulifafaga, A phrase, literally to awake a dog to be bit by him, used in reference to any thing one sets a going to his own hurt.

Neiakomaileekakau, A phrase meaning, do it, shall I be the only sufferer.

Nifienikaenafaamui, Little now, but great after awhile.

Nofoiheabimolikaefuhala, To live where a thing is taught, and yet not know it.

Nonofononofoiloaaetaeoenonofo, To live together for a length of time, and then find out the evil of so doing.

Sosaaatagatabuli, To trouble for a short time and then begone.

Taelagokeimamao, To prepare in time, to forecast.

Taieokoatu, A phrase tantamount to, you will know here after it will come upon you.

Taimalieatagatavale, To be where there is plenty but get nothing.

Taufegogofaifuakiheulu, To aim, to desire one and all to gain the prize.

Tagikevikiakaeauaekaiga, To be anxious for applause, though at the expense of other's property and lives.

Takailalohakaga, To be so impoverished as to eat filth.

Takagaabibimokahi, To make a pet or comrade of one who will cause trouble and pain.

Takagaatogiaki, To have as a companion, but to desert in time of need.

Takitahaukuenefonu, A phrase meaning, let each do as he thinks best and take the consequences.

Talaafinejiikaikaimavivi, The report of one who tells what is right, but treated with contempt.

Talabouliabuko, To backbite and be overheard by the party.

Talabeituamamao, The talk or report outside.

Talataefakaejia, To say and do not; to say one thing but do the contrary.

Taliaaumukabe, To wait for what when obtained is of no service.

Tamajiiukeikiamaui, A child who dares to challenge a man.

Teutokakakoetue, To yield to fate but to fear derision.

Tefuaavakalautala, Clever hands collected together at any work.

Tegetegautuakimamiji, A small bird carrying food to feed a large one; the poor feeding the rich.

Tofujiakivahaaufi, A part of the heathen ceremony at the *Inaji*.

Toleleiaeataata, The sun setting in a clear sky.

Tonuhiaaefaiekina, The innocence of an oppressed or friendless person.

Tuakoeaofato, Near or related, but not so as to visit or converse with each other.

Tubuatalakiatamaiki, To tell that to children you would wish kept secret or be forgotten.

Vakakiua, Literally, to make a canoe of the shoulders, used of things carried inland on the shoulders.

A VOCABULARY OF THE PARNKALLA LANGUAGE.

SPOKEN BY THE NATIVES

INHABITING THE WESTERN SHORES OF SPENCER'S GULF.

TO WHICH IS PREFIXED A COLLECTION OF

GRAMMATICAL RULES,

HITHERTO ASCERTAINED.

BY C. W. SHÜRMANN,

OF THE LUTHERAN MISSIONARY SOCIETY, DRESDEN.

ADELAIDE:
PRINTED AND PUBLISHED BY GEORGE DEHANE, MORPHETT-STREET.

1844.

TO

HIS EXCELLENCY G. GREY, ESQ.

GOVERNOR OF SOUTH AUSTRALIA, &c., &c.

THE FOLLOWING PAGES ARE RESPECTFULLY DEDICATED

BY HIS OBEDIENT AND HUMBLE SERVANT,

C. W. SCHÜRMANN.

PREFACE.

The following Vocabulary owes its appearance to the liberality of His Excellency, Governor Grey, at whose wish and expense it has been printed.

Although the Vocabulary, and still more the collection of grammatical rules, would have gained [illegible]

PREFACE.

The following Vocabulary owes its appearance to the liberality of His Excellency, Governor Grey, at whose wish and expense it has been printed.

Although the Vocabulary, and still more the collection of grammatical rules would have gained, both in extent and accuracy, by a farther intercourse with the natives, yet it was deemed advisable to print the collected materials in their present shape, for these reasons.

First:—that they might be placed on permanent record.

Secondly:—to assist those settlers in Port Lincoln who may feel disposed to acquire the native language. In the more thickly populated districts around Adelaide, the colonists have less occasion to learn the language of the Aborigines, since the latter can speak the English intelligibly. But in Port Lincoln where the white population bears so small a proportion to that of the black, quite the reverse obtains, so that to establish and maintain an easy intercourse with the natives there, it seems almost necessary that the Settlers should endeavour to make themselves acquainted with their language. It would no doubt have answered the purpose better if an English-Aboriginal part had been added to the Vocabulary, but this plan could not be adopted on account of the encreased expense.

On comparing this Vocabulary with the one published at Adelaide in 1840, a great resemblance will be found to exist between the two, many words used by both tribes are identical: but by far a greater number undergo a slight alteration, subject to the following rules :—

1.—The verbs which end with the Adelaide tribe in the syllables—*andi, endi, ondi,* assume in the Parnkalla, the terminations—*ata, iti, uti*; for instance :—

Adelaide.	Parnkalla.
Kundandi	*Kundata,* to strike
Kattendi	*Kattiti,* to bring
Padlondi	*Padlutu,* to die

2.—In many words that in Adelaide begin with a T., this letter is either dropped altogether; as :—

Adelaide.	Parnkalla.
Tidna	*Idna,* foot
Titta	*Itta,* string
Tikkandi	*Ikkata,* to sit down

Or it is changed into the softer consonant Y; as :—

Adelaide.	Parnkalla.
Ta,	*Ya,* mouth
Toka,	*Yoka,* mud
Turti,	*Yurti,* arm
&c.	*&c.*

In forming however an opinion on the affinity of languages or dialects, one has to look not only to the number of similar words, but still more to the grammatical structure and idiom. In this respect the similarity between the Adelaide and Parnkalla dialect is very striking, as a glance at the grammatical part will show, and to this fact, it is no doubt to be attributed, that the Port Lincoln natives who have come over to Adelaide, learn to speak the Adelaide dialect in so short a time, notwithstanding that many words in either dialect are radically different. Under this point of view it may indeed be asserted, that the dialects of all New Holland, so far at least as they have been collected, from New South Wales to Swan River, constitute only one language, as may be seen by comparing the different grammars and vocabularies, of New South Wales, by Mr Threlkeld; of Swan River, by Capt. Grey; of Adelaide, by Messrs. Teichelmann and Schürmann; and of Encounter Bay, by Mr Meyer.

Doubts have been expressed with regard to the artificial and complex nature of the grammar of the Aboriginal dialects, and it has been thought unlikely that so rude and ignorant a nation, as the natives of this continent are admitted to be, should possess a regular grammatical system.* This argument however is evidently untenable, for else it would follow on the other hand, that the most civilized nation or the most cultivated language must have the most artificial and complex grammar, which is by no means the case. The English language for instance, highly cultivated as it is in all branches of literature, has the simplest grammar imaginable, so that one might infer with as much reason the very opposite, viz: that the more a language is cultivated, the more its grammar will be simplified, and *vice versa.* Languages are in my opinion not the product of human art, but the gift of God, subject to a certain extent, to the influence of time and events. This influence seems to me exemplified in an interesting manner by the Aboriginal dialects. If we suppose what appears to be very probable, that the scattered native tribes of this Continent started from one point and were originally one tribe; they would of course speak one language. As they spread over the face of the country they would naturally in the course of time more or less corrupt the pronunciation and change the signification of many words; would

* See Moore's Descriptive Vocabulary of the Aboriginal language of Western Australia.

forget old and invent new terms for many things; till at last the most distant tribes seemed to speak almost radically different languages. Hundreds and perhaps thousands of years may have elapsed during that process; but no invasion of, or amalgamation with a foreign nation having taken place, consequently no fresh element introduced into their social life: their minds retained the impressions of the original stamp, they could not divest themselves of the forms of their mental intercourse inherited from their forefathers, or what is the same thing, of the grammatical laws of their language. Hence the surprising uniformity and regularity of grammatical structure amidst a Babylonic confusion of dialects.

To those who may undertake to study the Australian dialects from curiosity or philological interest, I should recommend to divest their minds as much as possible of preconceived ideas, particularly of those grammatical forms which they may have acquired by the study of ancient or modern European languages. In which case, I have no doubt it will be found, that the grammatical system of the Aboriginal dialects of New Holland is less artificial than novel, and less complex than admirably regular and consequently simple.

C. W. S.

ERRATA.

PART I.

p. 2, l. 24, *for* accentation *read* accentuation
,, 4, ,, 24, ,, contain ,, contains
,, 5, ,, 16, 26, genetive ,, genitive

p. 7, l. 4, *for* peng *read* pengi
,, 9, ,, 11, ,, coalesses ,, coalesces
,, 10, ,, 19, ,, genetive ,, genitive
,, 16, ,, 4, ,, cengugation ,, conjugation

PART II.

p. 1, l. 12 *for* williti *read* wittiti
,, 1, ,, 17, ,, bakbata ,, bakkata
,, 1, ,, 23, ,, pastfix ,, postfix
,, 2, ,, 35, ,, kano ,, kano
,, 3, ,, 7, ,, kallkarridni ,, kalkarridni
,, 5, ,, 24, ,, 6nina ,, niona
,, 6, ,, 33, ,, pitraarri ,, Pitararri
,, 7, ,, 15, ,, innulli ,, innelli
,, 7, ,, 31, ,, iratann ,, iratanna
,, 8, ,, 1, ,, irangutannn ,, irangutanne
,, 8, ,, 12, ,, iringtutarru ,, iringutarru
,, 8, ,, 34, ,, murlu ,, murtu
,, 9, ,, 14 ,, father ,, farther
,, 11, ,, 6&7 ,, kalkalkarrimatta *read* kalkarrimatta
,, 12, ,, 3, ,, kaltirrtao ,, kaltirritao
,, 12, ,, 9, ,, ngkatao ,, ngukatao
,, 13, ,, 27, ,, kairko ,, karnko
,, 14, ,, 28, ,, ngnkanao ,, ngukanao
,, 14, ,, 32, ,, muyn ,, muyu
,, 15, ,, 7, *dele* or
,, 15, ,, 9, ,, karkorarkora ,, karkurarkuru
,, 16, ,, 19, ,, wvorniti ,, worniti
,, 19, ,, 3, ,, ngangkella ,, ngangkalla
,, 19, ,, 18, ,, kodlalyiti, ,, kulalyiti
,, 22, ,, 4, ,, *dele* not
,, 23, ,, 34, ,, kattadla ,, kuttadla
,, 25, ,, 26, ,, malta ,, malla
,, 25, ,, 29, ,, mabingo ,, mabinye
,, 26, ,, 1, ,, ngia ,, ngai
,, 26, ,, 3, ,, top ,, lap
,, 27, ,, 4, *dele* have
,, 27, ,, 16, ,, mallanga ,, madlanga
,, 27, ,, 22, ,, yurramata ,, yuwamatta
,, 27, ,, 24, ,, *dele* (e.g.)
,, 27, ,, 27, ,, an an egg ,, as, an egg
,, 28, ,, 25, ,, marrakatu ,, marra kattu
,, 29, ,, 32, ,, kartati ,, karteti
,, 30, ,, 18, ,, mekkalla ,, mekalla
,, 30, ,, 18, ,, as ,, *i e*
,, 30, ,, 19, ,, ilkannu ,, ilkanna
,, 31, ,, 28, ,, metullu pira ,, metullu pirra

p 32, l 11, *for* millari,yarnu ,, millari yarnu
,, 32, ,, 22 ,, mingkarriti ,, mingkarniti
,, 32, ,, 28, ,, the words : it jumps far, belong to the preceding line
,, 32, ,, 32, ,, menku ,, menka
,, 33, ,, 9, ,, parobi nunkurnura *read* pardni nunkurnuru
,, 33, ,, 18, ,, miririki ,, mirriki
,, 33, ,, 30, ,, mai makalla mai worna *read* mai mokalla=mai worna
,, 33, ,, 32, ,, mokayna ,, mokanya
,, 35, ,, 12, ,, pinnare bairi mai *read* pinnara bidni mai
,, 35, ,, 21, ,, *read* to be enraged from jealousy
,, 35, ,, 31, ,, did ,, dig
,, 36, ,, 7, ,, karungunga ,, karnkunga
,, 36, ,, 15, ,, murkunkiti ,, murkurkiti
,, 37, ,, 11, ,, nungkakka ,, nungkukka
,, 37, ,, 19, ,, marroba..mirriye *read* maraba...mirrinye
,, 37, ,, 35, ,, wiliti ,, wiiti
,, 38, ,, 18, ,, wabmaoya ,, wabmanga
,, 38, ,, 19, ,, wabna ,, wabma
,, 38, ,, 25, ,, ngeirtye ,, ngaitye
,, 39, ,, 19, ninmilye ,, nimmilye
,, 39, ,, 23, ,, nunkapalliti ,, ninkapalliti
,, 39, ,, 25, ,, warnitao ,, wornitao
,, 39, ,, 33, ,, nirkiriti ,, nirkiti
,, 39, ,, 35, ,, nitakayu ,, nitakano
,, 40, ,, 4, ,, woman ,, women
,, 40, ,, 11, ,, puru kungkukku *read* paru nungkukka
,, 40, ,, 24, ,, ngungkurninyingo ,, ngang kurninyinge
,, 43, ,, 4, ,, aoter ,, oyster
,, 43, ,, 19, ,, ngailka ,, ngallaka
,, 43, ,, 28, ,, ngallikurikariti *read* ngallikurikuriti
,, 43, ,, 30, ,, parnkato ,, parnkata
,, 43, ,, 35, ,, dele strong, able
,, 44, ,, 5, ,, ngammama ,, ngammanna

p 44, *l.* 24, *for* ngangunge *read* ngangunye
„ 44, „ 26, „ nganinganinguta *read* nganinganinguku
„ 45, „ 34, „ ngappiriti „ ngappirti
„ 45, „ 36, „ ngarkabakko *read* ngarkabukko
„ 46, „ 7, „ paita „ paiata
„ 46, „ 22, „ ngarrarrita „ ngarrarta
„ 46, „ 37, „ ngarrinyelburninye, *read* ngarrinyelburninge
„ 47, „ 3, „ ngarrinyinyi ngakannao bebe *read* ngarrinyingi ngukannao bebi
„ 47, „ 6, „ willitanna „ wittitanna
„ 47, „ 30, „ pullinye „ pullinge
„ 48, „ 3, „ nguetu „ ngulta
„ 48, „ 12, „ bullorki „ bullocki
„ 48, „ 14, „ you „ yon
„ 49, „ 11, „ yataranga „ yutaranga
„ 50, „ 4, „ padluyunu „ padluyunu
„ 50, „ 7, „ yurreyappu „ yurreyappa
„ 51, „ 1, „ extend, remarks *read* extends, remark
„ 51, „ 22, „ murniti „ marniti
„ 52, „ 3, „ pulta „ palta
„ 52, „ 22, „ florted „ fluted
„ 53, „ 5, „ worra „ warra
„ 53, „ 12, „ pappiranye „ pappirünye

p 54, *l.* 1, *for* ngauralla *read* ngauwalla
„ 54, „ 17, „ murdlirinvi *read* murdliringe
„ 54, „ 28, „ madla partutyunu *read* kadla partütyuru
„ 54, „ 34, „ nudluo'atto „ nudlut'atto
„ 55, „ 1, „ pathar „ pathara
„ 55, „ 5, „ kauanno „ kauanna
„ 56, „ 35, „ padnato „ padnata
„ 56, „ 36, „ pinba „ pinda
„ 59, „ 32, „ ninni „ ninna
„ 60, „ 12, „ wayandatarra *read* wayandatarra
„ 61, „ 27, „ mulitated „ mutilated
„ 62, „ 20, „ kavo „ kauo
„ 62, „ 32, „ tarkulla „ tarkalla
„ 63, „ 33, „ pilla „ pilla
„ 65, „ 23, „ lovely „ lonely
„ 66, „ 12, „ wortanuga „ wortannanga
„ 68, „ 19, „ wanginia „ wangini wangini
„ 72, „ 24, „ wallulla „ willullu
„ 76, „ 35, „ yabmauna „ yabmanna
„ 80, „ 12, „ yapurrunganga *read* yapurrunga
„ 84, „ 2, „ yuwaaityao „ yuwaintyao

PART I.

GRAMMAR.

GRAMMAR.

1.—ON LETTERS.

The following letters are required to express the sounds and write the words of this dialect, viz.

CONSONANTS.

b, d, g, k, l, m, n, ng, p, r, t, th, ty, w, & y.

Most of these letters have exactly the same power as in English, the only ones deviating are :

G. which is always hard as in the English words, *good, god ;* sometimes it is still harder, so as to approach the letter *k,* as in *wang-gata,* where the second *g* has this hard sound; yet it would be incorrect to spell the word with a *k, wang-kata.*

Ng, this nasal letter has exactly the same power as the English *ng,* in the words *king, wing,* and the only difference is, that the Australian *ng* mostly commences syllables, while in English it is alway final.

R, has generally the same power as in English, but sometimes it has a very capricious sound which it is difficult to imitate. To approach the native pronunciation, put the tip of the tongue to the roof of the mouth and then pronounce *r* dwelling some time upon it. By reason of this peculiarity, many words, spelled alike in the Vocabulary, differ as well in pronunciation as in meaning, as :

yurra, man	*yurra,* earth
wirra, scrub	*wirra,* air or rain
karra, high	*karra,* grass

The words in the right column have the peculiar sound described above.

Sometimes a subdued *d* is heard behind the *r*, as :

yurdne instead of *yurne* throat
ngappardni *ngapparni.*

VOWELS.

a sounds in most cases as *a* in *are, far,* but when preceded by the letter *w* it sounds as *a* in *fall, ball.*
e sounds as *e* in *when, men*
i " *i* " *will, skill*
o " *o* " *for, come*
u " *u* " *full, pull*

DIPHTHONGS.

ai sounds as *i* in *white, quite* ; if preceded by *w,* it sounds nearly as *oi* in *oil, spoil.*
au sounds as *ow* in *vow, now,*
ü sounds like the French *u* or German *ü.*

. The accentation of words is subject to nearly the same rules as in the English language ; dissyllables have the accent on *penultima,* in words of three or more syllables, it rests on *antipenultima* ; as : *kátta,* club, *márniti,* good, *wayándata.* The latter of these rules however is not observed in the conjugation of verbs which are apt to retain the accent on the first or second syllable of the root, even when followed by more than two syllables; as *ngúkain-tyanna, ngukáintyaranna.*

2.—ON NOUNS.

The parts of speech in this language do not appear to be kept so distinct as in other languages, many words being used *ad libitum* either as a substantive, adjective or adverb. Thus for instance, the word *paitya* may be employed in these three capacities:

Paitya karata, to pick or commence a fight or quarrel
Paitya yura, a hostile man
Paitya palkata, to jump or run in a hostile manner, make warlike gestures.

Nor has this language so many parts of speech as the English, the prepositions and conjunctions being expressed by small particles at the end of words in the shape of terminations or suffixes. *In general and through all parts of speech, the Australian Idiom has a tendency to express all secondary relations of a proposition or sentence, for which the English language has distinct words such as prepositions, conjunctions, interjections, auxiliary verbs, etc. by suffixes, as will appear in the sequel.*

SUBSTANTIVES.

In accordance with the other Australian dialects no distinctions on account of gender have been discovered in the *Parnkalla* language; but it is characterized by a high degree of distinctness and accuracy with regard to number and cases.

For the singular number, there is no particular form or termination, except that it always ends in a vowel.

The dual number ends invariably in the syllables—*lbelli* which are an abbreviation of the numeral *kalbelli*, two; the letters *k* and *a* being dropped; and the termination for the plural number is : *rri*. These two terminations are affixed to the simple singular, the final vowel of which is always retained, as :—

Sing.	*Dual.*	*Plur.*
Yurra, man.	*yurralbelli*, two men.	*yurrarri*, men.

There is another form for the plural number which may be properly called the *intensive plural*, as it is only used when a great number or quantity is to be expressed. It is formed by affixing the syllables, *ilyaranna* to the singular, as :

Yurrailyaranna, a great number of people.
Kauiilyaranna, a great quantity of water.

NOTE.—Observe that the vowel *i* coalesces with the final vowel of the singular number.

This language has no declension of substantives in the common acceptation of the word, but there is a variety of terminations which supply the place of cases and prepositions, conjunctions and adverbs and which may be affixed to the substantive, either in the singular, dual or plural number. The following list which is probably far from being complete, contain those affixes hitherto met with :—

1.a—*nga* forms what has been termed by other writers upon the idiom of Australia, the "*active nominative case*," indicating that the person or object is acting upon another; wherefore it is always followed by an active or transitive verb; as : *tyilkellinga ngai kúndanárru, i·e. Tyilkelli* me did beat.

b.—*nga* stands also for the ablative case, when it has to be rendered English by a preposition; as: *marrály-inga ngai píttanarrù kányanga,* the boy me did hit with a stone.

c.—*nga* very commonly indicates the locality of a thing or person; as: *wortannanga,* in the sea; *karnkunga,* in the house.

d.—by the termination, *nga* is further expressed the time of an event, in which case it must be translated by the adverb, *when*; as: *panna ngultapanga mundulturri babmantinanna,* when he (was) a young man the Europeans arrived.

e.—*nga* very frequently denotes the reason of an action; as: *ngukatia maii madlanga,* I shall go away because I have no food.

2.a—*ru* forms the genetive or possessive case; as: *inna ngankuru palta? Wingaltaru,* this whose cloak? *Wingalta's*

b.—it indicates the place or object to which a person is moving; as: *ngai ngukata karnkuru,* I shall go to the house, or home.

c.—*ru* denotes the purpose for which anything is done; as: *kalalta mankut'atto kuyaru,* dry bark, I shall take to fish, *i.e.* for the purpose of fishing, *maiiru ngukat ai,* for food I shall go, *i.e.* look out for it.

3.—*dni* or *rdni* } this suffix forms another genetive case; but seems to differ from the preceding one by indicating the origin of a thing rather than the possession of it, hence it will have to be translated by the prepositions *of* or *from*; as: *paru kattika ngappardni,* fetch meat of *Ngappa.*

4.—*bidni* has the same meaning as the former, which seems in fact to be only an abbreviation from this; as: *ngadli kubmanna ngamnmibidni,* we two are of one mother; *ngai warra bidni,* I am from far, *i.e.* my country is far off.

5.—*dninga* or *rdninge* } expresses the place or locality where a person or thing is to be found; it seems however to be only applicable to proper names and pronouns; as *Yutalta yarridninga, Yutalta* is with *Yarri; kapmarra nunkurdninga ikkat'ai,* always with thee I shall stop.

6.—*dnuru* *rdnuru* } to, towards: as: *mulyadnuru ngukat'ai,* I shall go to *Mulya; ngaityidnuru ninna ngannaru kutta babmantini, i.e.* why did you not come to me?

This termination is also confined to proper names and pronouns.

7.—*ngunne* denotes a motion away from an object; as: *karnko ngunne,* from the house; *warra ngunne,* from far

8.—*tarri* indicates a direction, and must be rendered by over, by way of, in the direction of; as: *tallallatarri ngukat'arrinyelbo,* by way of *Tallalla* we shall go *yarto yuwatao yurre, mudla tarri,* yonder stands the hill over the point.

9.—*mba,* the meaning of this suffix seems to correspond with the English *ward*; as: *Kayallamba,* northward, to the north of. *Wailbimba,* westward or to the west of.

10.—*dla, dlu, dli,* the terminating vowel of this suffix always corresponds with the final vowel of the word it is affixed to. The meaning of it resembles that of the preceding suffix:—

Iatadla, north eastward, or farther to the north east.

Wortattidli, farther south east.

11.—*nta,* expresses instrumentality; as: *midlanta wittiti,* to throw spears with the wommara

12.—*pengi,* means for, for the value of; as: *gadla peng mai nungkunanna,* for fire wood they gave the food.

13.—*yallani,* on account of, about; as: *warru yallani paitya ngutarritanna,* about a kangaroo they quarrel.

Besides the above suffixes, partaking of the nature or meaning of prepositions in English, several others have been noticed that appear to have an adverbial signification. These are the following:—

14.—*ngkalli,* denotes a question; as: *padluntyao wibmangkalli?* has he died already?

15.—*ndi,* has an affirmative or corrobarative meaning; as: *maitya Kungka nunko yunga? ngaitye yungandi,* is Kungka your brother then? my brother certainly

16.—*ko,* signifies nearly the same as the former; as:—*Ngulga ngaitye ngammana, ngannako,* Ngulga is my uncle, what else (should he be)

17.—*itye,* the meaning of this suffix which is in frequent use it is difficult to describe: *Mai ngaitye pulyo kulakaitye,* cut me a little bread pray. *Ngatta yurringutu ngattuitye,* I understand well enough.

18.—*anni* / *inni* / *unni* } is of an entreating nature; as: *ngai inni ngai inni nungkuka pappi,* to me, to me give (it) father. *Innanni nungkukka, innanni,* give it to this person, to this. This suffix may perhaps denote the dative case.

19.—*nda.* expresses satisfaction or joy; as: *ngaitye*

ngammannanda, my uncle (viz is kind or some such word is to be understood) *palta ngaityinda,* my cloak.

20.—*lbo,* means *for* or upon, *maiilbo kanaturru,* he waits for food. *Paltalbo kanatarru,* he expects clothing.

21.—*lla lli llu,* expresses a comparison; *as, like, as if;* as *yuralla pony yerbatunno,* like a man you command the pony, *i.e.* you speak to him as if he were a man, able to understand you; or: *warru yantyinilli yarraityalla ngammatinni,* you run so fast as if hunting a kangaroo.

22.—*indi* or *indo,* likewise, also, with; as: *ngai Munni indo* I and Munni, or I (am) also (called) Munni.

23.—*nganna* / *nginni* / *ngunnu* } this suffix consists properly of two, namely *nga* (which occurred under *nro.* 1,) and the syllables *anna, inni, unnu,* which latter answer in meaning to the English adverb along; as: *kaityarri widlanganna mankukka, i.e.* take the children along in the path, *wambiringinni ngukatia,* along the coast I shall go

24.—*kuntu,* corresponds with the English final syllable *ly* as: *yalturru kuntu wanggakka,*speak boldly. *Parnkalla kuntu wanggakka,* speak Parnkalla.

It is not necessary that the above suffixes from number 14 downwards, should always be attached to a substantive, they are as often connected with other parts of speech, generally with the last word in a sentence,

NOTE.—Those cases of substantitives for which there are no terminations among the above list, as the accusative and dative are identical with the simple nominative.

3.—ON ADJECTIVES.

The adjective differs with regard to form in no wise from the substantive, it being susceptible not only of a dual and plural number, but also of all the suffixes contained in the preceding paragraph.

Adjectives may be formed of substantives or indeed any other part of speech, except the verb, by affixing the termination *bidni* to them, or dropping the consonent *b,—idni.*

Kalkarridni from *kalkarra, wiltyarridni* from *wiltyarra, wiltyadllidni* from *wiltyadli.*

Often the vowel *i* coalesces with the terminating vowel of the word; as:

Yerkullüdni from *yerkullu, yauullüdni* from *yau-ullu.*

The particle *bidni* sometimes stands by itself as a distinct word, but even in this case it merely indicates some connexion or relation between the person or thing spoken of and the word preceding it; as:

Ngai warra bidni, I am far off, *i.e.* my place of residence or my country is at a distance.

Ngai yatta bidni, I just now of, *i.e.* I arrived only just now.

Ngai paru bidni, I game of, *i.e.* I have been hunting.

Another particle of less frequent use which seems to form adjectives is *ndo* or *nto*; as:

Mannando from *manna,* plenty; *paityando* from *paitya,* fight; *walbunto* from *walbu,* bone.

A sort of comparative is produced by attaching the syllable *lla, lli* or *llu* to an adjective; as:

Karralla, higher; *parrilli,* deeper.

It is not necessary that the substantive and its adjective should both take the suffixes forming numbers and cases; it is sufficient if one of the two (which however must always stand last) is thus distinguished; as:

Mangalla yurarri innamatta, friendly men (are) these; not.

Mangallarri yurarri inna matta.

But if the adjective stand by itself so as to be descriptive of the subject and the auxiliary "*is, was,*" etc. is to be understood, it then assumes the same termination as its substantive; as:

Nauurri irabukarri, kadla willururri, the Nauos (are) teeth rotten and long rumped.

4·—ON PRONOUNS.

The pronouns form an interesting and very important feature in this language, showing a degree of regularity and niceties of distinctions truly surprising in so rude a people. They are very numerous, and since without the correct use of them it is impossible for a native to understand what is said, it will be advisable to give them at full length. They are naturally divided into three classes viz :—

1.—Personal and possessive pronouns, the latter of these two being merely a modification or the genetive case of the former.

2.—Demonstrative pronouns.

3.—Interrogative pronouns.

Note.—Relative pronouns their are none in this language, their place being supplied partly by demonstrative pronouns, partly by repetitions and circumlocutions.

1.—PERSONAL PRONOUNS. First person singular:

Nom. (1)	Ngai, *I*		
Act. Nom.	Ngatto, *I*		
Possessive	Ngaitye, *my*		
	Ngaityidni, *of*, or *from me*		
	Ngaityidninge, *with me*		
	Ngaityidniru, *to* or *towards me*		

Second person singular:

Nom.	Ninna,	or	nuro, (2) *thou*
Act. Nom.	Nunno		nuro, *thou*
Possessive	Nunko		nurko, *thy*
	Nunkurni,		nurkurni, *of*, or *from thee*
	Nunkurninge,		nurkurninge, *with thee*
	Nunkurniru		nurkurniru, *towards thee*

Third person singular:

Nom.	Panna, *he she, it*
Act. Nom.	Padlo, *he*
Possessive	Parnüntyuru, *his*
	Parnüntyudni, *of, from him*
	Parnüntyudninge, *with him*
	Parnüntyudniru, *to him*

First person dual:

Nom. Ngadli, ngadlaga, (3) ngarrinye, (4) *we two*
Poss. Ngadluru, ngadlagguru, ngarrinyuru, *our*
Ngadlidni, ngadlagadni, ngarrinyidni, *of us*
Ngadlidninge, ngadlagadninge, ngarrinydninge, [*with us*
Ngadlidniru, ngadlagadniru, ngarrinyidniru, *to us*

Second person, dual.

Nom. Nuwalla, nuwadnaga, (3) nuwarinye, (4) *you two*
Poss. Nuwalluru, nuwadnagguru, nuwarinyuru, *your*
Nuwallidni, nuwadnagadni, nuwarinyidni, *of you*
Nuwallidninge, nuwadnagadninge, nuwarinyid-[ninge, *with you*
Nuwallidniru, nuwadnagadniru, nuwarinyidniru, [*to you.*

Third person dual :

Nom. Pudlanbi, (5) *they two*
Poss. Pudlanbiru, *their*
Pudlanbidni, *of them two*
Pudlanbidninge, *with them two*
Pudlanbidniru, *to them two*

First person plural

Nom. Ngarrinyelbo, *we*
Poss. Ngarrinyelburu, *our*
Ngarrinyelbudni, *of us*
Ngarrinyelbudninge, *with us*
Ngarrinyelbudniru, *to us*

Second person plural.

Nom. Nuralli, *you*
Poss. Nuralluru, *your*
Nurallidni, *of you*
Nurallidninge, *with you*
Nurallidniru. *to you*

Third person plural :

Nom. Yardna, *they*
Poss. Yardnakkuru, *their*
Yardnakudni, *of them*
Yardnakudninge, *with them*
Yardnakudniru, *to them*

NOTES.

1.—The nominative or first case of the above pronouns answers also for the dative and accusative cases.

2.—The pronoun *nuro, thou,* is only used by a father and his children addressing each other.

3.—The pronouns, *ngadlaga* and *nuwadnaga,* apply only to certain relatives, as a mother and her children, uncle and nephew; as: *pappidnuru ngukat' adlaga, ngammiá,* to father let us two go, mother.

4.—*Ngarrinye and nuwarinye,* apply to a father and one of his children only.

5.—*Pudlanbi, they two,* is more especially used for husband and wife, for instance, *pudlanbi padnamatta,* means they two are husband and wife.

2. DEMONSTRAVE PRONOUNS. Singular number.

Nom.	Inna, *this*	ngunna, *that*
Act. Nom.	Innanga, *this*	ngunnanga, *that*
Poss.	Innaru, *this one's*	ngunnaru, *that one's*
	Innardni, *of this*	ngunnardni, *of that*
	Innardninge *with this*	ngunnardninge, *with that*
	Innardniru, *to this*	ngunnardniru, *to that*

Dual number.

Nom.	Innalbelli, *these two*	ngunnalbelli, *those two*

Declined in the same manner as the singular

Plural number.

Instead of the plural *innarri, ngunnarri* it is more usual to say:

Inna matta, *this mob*	ngunna matta, *that mob*
Inna mattanga	ngunna mattanga
Inna mattaru, ect.	ngunna mattaru, ect.

3. INTERROGATIVE PRONOUNS.

Nom.	Nganna, *who, what*
Active. Nom.	Ngannunga, *who*
Poss.	Ngankuru, *whose*
	Ngankurni, *of whom*
	Ngankurninge, *with whom*
	Ngankurniru, *to whom*
	Ngannanga, *in what, wherein*

Ngannalbelli, *Dual.* Ngannatanna, *Plural.*

Wanna, *which,* Wananga, *wherein*

There are no other cases in use of this pronoun.

5.—ON THE VERBS.

The verb of the *Parnkalla* language consists of a simple root which is always a dissyllable, except those that are derived from nouns or other verbs. According to the general tendency of the Australian idiom, these roots are susceptible of a variety of terminations, some of which constitute *voces verbi* or conjugations, others moods and tenses.

This language seems to be destitute of Auxiliary verbs, such as: *to be, have, can, will,* ect, for the first of these, *to be,* the particle *ta* is often used in short sentences; as: *mantyarri ta'* it is good or well. When the sense admits it, the following words are frequently used, where we would employ the auxiliary to be viz. *yuwata,* to stand; *ikkata,* to sit; *padnata,* to go; *kariti, v.* to continue; *wanniti,* to lie down; as: *kutyo yurarri yarlanga padnatanna,* the other men are hunting; *pallarri kangaranga karitanna,* the women are among the *kangara* or grass tree roots. Another means for obviating the want of auxiliaries is found in the terminations *iti and nniti* by affixing which to adjectives they are rendered into verbs; as: *ngallanniti,* to be great, from *ngalla*; *paityanniti,* to be hostile, from *paitya*; *waieriti,* to be right or well, from *waieri*; *mantyarriti,* to be good, fine, from *mantyarri.*

But very often the auxiliary verb is omitted altogether; as: *paru buka,* the meat (is) rotten. The verb to have is expressed by the suffixes, *ilka,* having; *marraba and wakka,* not having; as: *ngai palta-marraba,* I have no cloak; *kaya-ilka padnatanna,* they have spears.

The auxiliaries *shall and will* are expressed by the future tense of the verb.

The proper verb may, both with reference to form and signification, be divided into the following classes or conjugations:

1.—The simple verb, which may be either active or neuter, as: *kundata,* to strike; *yuwata,* to stand.

2.—The continuative form of the verb, which is derived from the root by the addition of the termination, *ntutu,* and denotes the continuation or repetition of an action; as: *ikkantutu,* to continue sitting, remain; *ngammantutu,* to keep running.

3.—The medial and reciprocal conjugation, signifying, that the action, expressed by the verb, has no relation to any particular object or that it is preformed by two or more parties reciprocally. It is derived from the root by the termination, *rriti* or *ngarriti;* as: *yabmirriti,* to abuse each other, quarrel, from *yabmiti,* to scold; *wittirriti, v.* to spear each other, from *wittiti; millingarriti,* to work, from *milliti*; *nungkungarriti,* from *nungkutu.*

4.—The causative conjugation which is always an active or transitive verb. It may be derived from any of the preceding forms, except the continuative by dropping the last syllable and adding the termination, *ngutu;* as: *birkibirkiringutu,* from *birkibirkirriti; ngallanningutu,* from *ngallanniti*; *ngammangutu,* from *ngammata.*

Also adjectives may be thus made into verbs; as: *marnitingutu,* from *marniti,* good.

Observe that this termination is only applicable to neuter verbs, if therefore the simple verb have an active or transitive meaning, you cannot form this conjugation, there being no occasion for it. It changes the signification of the verb from which it is derived, so much as to require frequently an entirely different word in English to translate it, for instance: *yuwata,* to stand, *yuwangutu* to make stand *i.e.* to raise: *worniti,* to fall, *worningutu,* to make or let fall, to throw down, drop.

5.—To express the intensity of an action, the natives

double the root of the verb; as; *munnimunniti,* to breath quickly, pant. *Tuttututturriti,* to produce a creaking noise.

6.—An other congugation is formed by the termination—*nturrutu*; as: *mankunturrutu, nakkunturrutu, nungkunturrutu*

The subjoined paradigm will show the conjugation of the verb, which is applicable to all the six classes just mentioned. It should however be born in mind, that the language is as yet but imperfectly known, and that consequently many more modifications of the Verb may be used by the natives of which we have no knowledge

I have noticed only three tenses of the verb, namely the Present and the Future which do not differ in form, the Imperfect and Perfect. The latter of these is made use of when speaking of an action as completed, while the Imperfect relates to past events.

The moods of the Verb have always appeared to me as the most difficult subject, and I think that with regard to them a great deal of information is still wanted.

To show the application of the two nomitive cases of the Pronouns, I have selected one Neuter and one Active Verb.

NEURTER VERB.—Root *Nguka,* Go.

Present and Future. Characteristic termination, *ta, ti, tu,*

Indicative Mood.

Sing. 1. Ngai ngukata, *I go,* or *shall go*
2. Ninna ngukata, *thou goest*
3. Panna ngukatawo, *he goes.*

Dual 1. Ngadli ngukata, *we two go*
2. Nuwalla ngukamatta
3. Pudlanbi ngukamatta

Plur. 1. Ngarrinyelbo ngukata, *we go*
2. Nuralli ngukatanna, *you go*
3. Yardna ngukatanna, *they go*

Subjunctive Mood.

Sing. 1. Ngai ngukara, *I might go* or *would go*
2. Ninna ngukara, *thou mightst go*
3. Panna ngukarawo, *he might go*
Dual 1. Ngadli ngukara, *we two might go*
2, Nuwalla ngukamara, *you two might go*
3. Pudlanbi ngukamara, *they two might go*
Plur. 1. Ngarrinyelbo ngukara, *we might go*
2. Nuralli ngukaranna or ngukarna, *you might go*
3. Yardna ngukarna, *they might go*

Optative and Imperative Mood.

Sing. 1. (Ngai 2) ngukai, *let me go, I wish to go*
2. (Ninna) ngukakka, *do thou go*
ngukannaka } *thou shalt go*
ngukakkaitye }
3. (Panna) ngukawo, *let him go*
Dual 1. (Ngadli) ngukamadli, *let us two go*
2. (Nuwalla) ngukamakka, *do you two go*
3. (Pudlanbi) ngukamai, *let them go*
Plur. 1. (Ngarrinyelbo) ngukarrinyelbo, *let us go*
2. Nuralli) ngukakanna, *do you go*
3. Nguka anna *or* ngukarna, *let them go*

Imperfect or Preterite, Characteristic Termination.—na.

Sing. 1. Ngai ngukanna, *I went* or *did go*
2. Ninna ngukanna, *thou didst go*
3. Panna ngukannawo, *he went*
Dual 1. Ngadli ngukanna, *we two went*
2. Nuwalla ngukamanna, *you two went*
3. Pudlanbi ngukamanna, *they two went*
Plur. 1. Ngarrinyelbo ngukanna, *we went*
2. Nuralli ngukanna, *you went*
3. Yardna ngukananna, *they went*

The imperfect has only the Indicative mood.

Perfect, Characteristic termination intya.

Indicative Mood.

Sing. 1. Ngai ngukaintya, *I am gone*
2. Ninna ngukaintya, *thou art gone*
3. Panna ngukaintyawo, *he is gone*
Dual 1. Ngadli ngukaintya, *We two are gone*
2. Nuwalla ngukamantya, *you two are gone*
3. Pudlanbi ngukamantya, *they two are gone*
Plur. 1. Ngarrinyelbo ngukaintya, *we are gone*
2. Nuralli ngukaintyanna, *you are gone*
3. yardna ngukaintyanna, *they are gone*

Subjunctive Mood.

Sing. 1. Ngai ngukaintyara, *I should* or *would have gone*
2. Ninna ngukaintyara, *thou wouldst have gone*
3. Panna ngukaintyarawo, *he would have gone*
Dual 1. Ngadli ngukaintyara, *we two would have gone*
2. Nuwalla ngukamantyara, *you two would have gone*
3. Pudlanbi ngukamantyara, *they two would have* [*gone*
Plur. 1. Ngarrinyelbo ngukaintyara, *we would have gone*
2. Nuralli ngukaintyaranna or ngukaintyarna, [*you would have gone*
3. Yardna ngukaintyaranna or ngukaintyarna, [*they would have gone*

Intensive Future, (3) *Characterised by the letter* ng.

Sing. 1. Ngukangai, *I will go*
2. Ngukanginni, *thou wilt go*
3. Ngukanggawo, *he will go*
Dual 1. Ngukangadli, *we two will go*
2. Nuwalla ngukamangka, *you two will go*
3. Pudlanbi ngukamangka, *they two will go*
Plur. 1. Ngukangarinyelbo, *we will go*
2. Ngukangkanuralli, *you will ge*
3. Ngukangkardna, *they will go*

Infinitive Mood.

Ngukayu, *to go*
Ngukayuru, *for to go*

Gerunds

Ngukantanga, *in going*
Ngukanturlungu, *in* or *during going*
Ngukaintyaranga, *for going, on account of going*
Participle.—Ngukanyalla

NOTES.

1.—Although the present and future tenses do not differ in form, as far as I know, yet the natives make a distinction between the present and the future time, as appears by their adding an appropriate adverb, when the latter is to be understood: as: *ngai yata ngukata,* I shall soon go; *ngai kari ngukata,* I shall go by and bye; *pityarri ngukatia,* I shall go presently.

2.—It is not necessary to use always the pronouns in connexion with the imperative mood, but only in those cases when it is intended to lay a particular stress upon them; as: *ngannaru ngai kapmarra ngukayuru, ninna ngukakka,* why am I always to go, do thou go.

3.—I have called this tense the intensive future for want of a more suitable name. The meaning of it is that the person, speaking or spoken to in this tense, is willing or resolved to do something.

ACTIVE VERB.—Root *witti,* to spear.

Indicative Mood.

Sing. 1. Ngatto wittiti, *I spear*
2. Nunno wittiti, *thou spearest*
3. Padlo wittitarru, *he spears*
Dual. 1. Ngadli wittiti, *we two spear*
2. Nuwalla wittimatta, *you ditto*
3. Padlanbi wittimatta, *they ditto*

Plur. 1. Ngarrinyelbo wittiti, *we spear*
2. Nuralli wittitanna, *you ditto*
3. Yardna wittitanna, *they ditto*

Subjunctive Mood.

Sing. 1. Ngatto wittiri, *I might* or *would spear*
2. Nunno wittiri. *thou mightst ditto*
3. Padlo wittiru, *he might ditto*
Dual. 1. Ngadli wittiri, *we two might ditto*
2. Nuwalla wittimara, *you two ditto*
3. Pudlanbi wittimara, *they two ditto*
Plur. 1. Ngarrinyelbo wittiri, *we might spear*
2. Nuralli wittiranna or wittirna, *you ditto*
3. Yardna wittiranna, or wittirna, *they ditto*

Optative and Imperative Mood.

Sing. 1. (Ngatto) witti, *let me spear*
2. (Nunno) wittikki, *do thou spear*
3. (Padlo) wittiarru, *let him spear*
Dual. 1. (Ngadli) wittimadli, *let us two spear*
2. (Nuwalla) wittimakka, *do you two spear*
3. (Pudlanbi) wittimai, *let them two spear*
Plur. 1. (Ngarrinyelbo) wittirrinyelbo, *let us spear*
2. (Nuralli) wittikanna, *do ye spear*
3. Yardna wittiadna, *let them spear*

Imperfect.

Sing. 1. Ngatto wittinni, *I speared*
2. Nunno wittinni, *thou ditto*
3. Padlo wittinnarru, *he ditto*
Dual. 1. Ngadli wittinni, *we two speared*
2. Nuwalla wittimanna, *you two ditto*
3. Pudlanbi wittimanna, *they two ditto*
Plur. 1. Ngarrinyelbo wittinni, *we speared*
2. Nuralli wittinnanna, *you ditto*
3. Yardna wittinnanna, *they ditto*

PERFECT. *Indicative Mood.*

Sing. 1. Ngatto wittintya, *I have speared*
2. Nunno wittintya, *thou ditto*
3. Padlo wittintyarru, *he ditto*

Dual 1. Ngadli wittintya, *we two ditto*
2. Nuwalla wittimantya, *you two ditto*
3. Pudlanbi wittimantya, *they two ditto*

Plur. 1. Ngarrinyelbo wittintya, *we ditto*
2. Nuralli wittintyanna, *you ditto*
3. Yardna wittintyanna, *they ditto*

Subjunctive Mood.

Sing. 1. Ngatto wittintyara, *I should have speared*
2. Nunno wittintyara, *thou ditto*
3. Padlo wittintyararru, *he ditto*

Dual 1. Ngadli wittintyara, *we two would or should have [speared*
2. Nuwalla wittimantyara, *you two ditto*
3. Pudlanbi wittimantyara, *they two ditto*

Plur. 1. Ngarrinyelbo wittintyara, *we would have speared*
2. Nuralli wittintyaranna or wittintyarna, *you ditto*
3. Yardna wittintyaranna or wittintyarna, *they [ditto*

Intensive Future.

Sing. 1. Wittingatto, *I will spear*
2. Wittingunno, *thou wilt ditto*
3. Wittingarru, *he will ditto*

Dual 1. Wittingadli, *we two will spear*
2. Nuwalla wittimangka, *you two ditto*
3. Pudlanbi wittimangka, *they two ditto*

Plur. 1. Wittinggarrinyelbo, *we will spear*
2. Wittingka nuralli, *you ditto*
3. Wittingardna, *they ditto*

Infinitive Mood

Wittiyi, *to spear*
Wittiyuru, *for to spear*

Participle

Wittinyalla, *spearing*

Gerunds.

Wittilidni } *spearing*
Wittilambo }
Wittintingi, *in spearing*
Wittinturlungu, *during spearing*
Wittintyaranga, *for, on account of spearing*

In the above paradigms the pronouns have been placed before the verb to show the full form of both verbs and pronouns; but the natives very commonly pronouce the pronoun after the verb and more or less contract the two into one word, as will be seen from the following specimen :

		NEUTER VERB *Present.*		ACTIVE VERB.
Sing.	1.	Ngukatai or ngukatia, *I go or shall go*	1.	wittitatto, *I spear or shall spear*
	2.	Ngukatinni, *thou goest*	2.	wittitunno
	3.	Ngukatao, *he goes*	3.	wittitarru
Dual	1.	Ngukatadli	1.	wittitadli
	2.	Ngukatuwalla	2.	wittituwalla
	3.		3.	
Plur.	1.	Ngukatarrinyelbo, *we go*	1.	wittitarrinyelbo
	2.	Ngukaturalli, *you go*	2.	witturalli
	3.	Ngukatardna, *they go*	3.	wittitardna

The other tenses to be formed in a similar mannner.

The following terminations which can only be connected with the verb, seem to be here in their proper place, viz.

1.—*alka*, *ilki*, *ulku* } are often attached to the imperative mood with intensive meaning; as: *ngukaiilki,* let me go, or I will certainly go; *kambarrulku,* let him cook, *i.e.* he shall or must do it.

2.—*adla*, *idli*, *udlu* } may be affixed to any form of the verb, to signify the doubtfulness of what one says: as : *ngukaintyannadla,* perhaps they are gone *Innaityinge pony padnatawudlu,* it may be that the horse is here.

PART II.

VOCABULARY.

VOCABULARY

A

A, ò or Awo, *adv.* yes, just so

B

Ba-ata, *v.a.* to scrape; plain; as a spear or skin
babmata, *v.* to rise; come up
babmababmata, *v.* ditto *mudla babmababmata*, to sneeze
babmantiti, *v.* to come; return
bakka, as *kurdli bakka*, a stunted kind of she oak
bakkalla, *s.* hoar frost
bakkamba, *adj.* full, as *worna bakkamba* belly full, satisfied
bakkambiti, *v.* to be full
bakkanbata, *v.a.* to dig round, lay bare by digging as *yadlanna bakkanbata*, to bare the root of a tree
bakkanna-williti, to pierce; spear
bakkarra, *s.* lump; clod; as *yurra bakkarra* a clod of earth
bakkarta, *adj.* sore; festering; as *mena bakkarta*, having sore eyes
bakkartangata, *v.* to canter; gallop
bakhata, bakkata, *v.* ditto
bakkebakkiti, *s.* knife; chisel; consisting in a sharp edged piece of quartz joined to the end of a stick
bakkubakku, *s.* a species of bird; Bell bird
bakkullu, *adv.* onward; along; as *ngai bakkullu*, I along, i.e. I will go with you
bakkullu, *pastfix*, this side of; as *yakkalla bakkullu*, on this side of the island
bakkullumbo, ditto

baku, *s.* the point or catch of the *midla* or *wommara* that fits into a hole at the butt end of a spear
bàkukku, *interj.* behold; look there; as *bakukku kaya yapurubidni paru ngarrinyuru, kaitya!* behold child! the game is ours, being hit by the spear
bamba or bamballa, without
bamburriti, *v.* to stand still; be stationary; as *wariyoko bamburritawo murdliringi,* the ship is stationary in the calm
bammallammalliti, *v.* to break out; form eruptions on the skin
bathubathutu, *v.* to shake out; empty a bag
batta, *s.* a species of grub
battara, *s.* a species of gum tree, commonly called scrubby gum, being very crooked and unsightly
battara yurrarri, the appellation of a native tribe, so called from their country abounding with the scrubby gum
battata, *v. a.* to drive away; scare off
battabattarriti, *v.* to disperse
battarriti, *v.* as *metye yurringi kutta battarritao,* the name remains not in the ear; i.e. I have forgot it
battiti, *v.* to wake; rouse from sleep
bau-urru, *s.* pot; kettle; any large sized vessel
bebi, *s.* egg; any jelly like substance, as the brain, marrow, &c.
beku, *s.* eyebrow
beku walbara, pert; impudent
beku walbo, eyebrow strong; i.e. not sleepy
bidla, *adj.* & *s.* dry, hard, any dry substance, as rind, crust
bidlangarriti, *v.* to walk slowly; tarry
bidlata, *v.* to cut; scrape
bidlyo, *s.* the white female grub of a species of ants eaten by the natives
bidna, *adj.* permanent; as *bidna kano* permanent water
bidni, an *affix.* which when attached to nouns and other

parts of speech gives them the power of an adjective as karnkurtu bidni yura, a man of the boat or ship, a sailor, from *karnkurtu*, a boat

yerkullüdni yura, an ancient man; ancestor from *yerkullu*, before

wiltyaridni, of yesterday, from *wiltyara*, yesterday

kallkarridni, of old, from *kalkarra*, a long time ago

yatanyarüdni, of to day, from *yatanyaru*, to day

***Observe that in most instances the first consonant of the affix is dropped.

bila or gadla bila, *s.* charcoal

birka, *adj.* ripe

birka, *s.* stick; end, as *gadla birka,* fire stick

birki, *s.* light; as *pirra birkingi,* by moon light

birki birki, *adj.* piece meal, consisting of many small pieces

birkibirkiringutu, *v.* to break in pieces; spill

birkibirkirriti, *v.* to crumble to pieces

birri or marra birri, finger nail; claw

bithu, *s.* a species of redbill; said to accompany the souls of the departed on their flight to the islands

boka, *s.* steam; breath; as *ya boka,* breath of the mouth

bokalla, *s.* a species of ant, often called *bokalla wipa*

bokirri, *s.* anything to rest one's feet upon, hence it is applied to shoes and boots

budlu, *n. pr.* Lipson's Cove

budnata, *v.* to come; return

buka, *adj.* old; rotten; offensive

bukanniti, *v.* to decay; putrefy

bukalla, *s.* a fatherless orphan; a person bereft of his father

bukarra, *s.* fine weather; hot weather

bukkininye, *adj.* of old ancient

bulka, old; aged; an old man; an old kangaroo

bulta, *s.* flesh; meat; also, the pulse

bulta wappirritao, the pulse beating is

bumba, *adj.* thick; large; full; as *kanti bumba* having a stout leg

bumbabumbaningutu, *v.a.* to enlarge
bumbara, *adj.* plentiful; abundant
bumbarriti *v.* to be plentiful; abound
bunta, *s.* a species of mouse
buntunniti, *v.* to blow with the mouth
bunturarriti, *v.* ditto
burkalla, *v.* the stretching of one's limbs
burkata, *v.* to throw water; to sprinkle
burko, *s.* dew
burtu, *adj.* short: stunted
burtu, *adj.* done; sufficiently cooked. There is a scarcely perceptable difference of pronunciation between these two words.
butta, *s.* womb
butti, *s.* hair; fur; as *pilla butti*, oppossum hair

G

GADLA, *s.* fire; wood; fuel
gadla bila, *s.* charcoal
gadläira, *adj.* hot; heated by fire
gadla gudna, *s.* the clouds of smoke produced by a running fire
gadla marraba, without fire
gadla murru, *s.* embers; ashes
gadla puyu, *s.* fire smoke
gadla walba, *s.* small wood: branches
gadla yadlu, *s.* fire flame
gadla yaltata *s.* light; candle

I

Iä, iändi or ya, yandi, yes, so it is
iä ta, *s.* North East country or coast. The natives of Port Lincoln have four distinct words in their language descriptive of the bearings of their Peninsular country, and totally unconnected with the directions of the heavens. They are: —
Iäta, North East coast and country

worrtatti, South East country
wailbi, South West country
kayalla, North Western, and Northern country
They use entirely different words to express the directions of the winds.

ibirri, *s.* a small species of lizard, said to have separated the sexes. The women call it by the name of *waka;* whenever one of these little animals makes its appearance, it usually is the cause of merriment and jokes

ibma, *adj.* green ; raw

idla, *adj.* light colored

idla, *s.* or *idla wadlata,* branch ; twig ; bush

idli, part of the abdomen ; as *worna idli*

idlya, *s.* hamstring

idna *s.* foot

idnambata *v.* to approach softly ; walk on tiptoe

idni, round about ; out of the way

idnawardnu, *s.* heel

idnidlyi, *s.* a kind of fungus

idnya, *s.* a cat ; wild and European

idnyalla, *s.* flank ; groin

ika, obstructed, as *mudla ika,* having an obstruction in the nose ; speaking through the nose

ikara, *a negative affix,* not so ; not it ; as *nnina ngarra wanggata,* you tell a lie ; *ngarra-ikara,* it is no lie

ikarniti *v.* expresses the rapid motion of a spear ; to fly, as *mirra ikarnitao kaya,* swiftly flies the spear

ikkata, *v.* to sit ; dwell ; live

ikkantutu, *v. intens.* ditto ; to remain ; stay

ilari, *adj.* strange ; unknown

ilga, *s.* a prickly kind of shrub ; thorn

ilga ilga, *adj.* pretty ; fine with respect to personal appearance.

ilgaringutu, *v.* to track

ili, *s.* lap ; womb.

iliti, *postfix.* on account ; for the purpose of ; as *birkiti iliti wara karnkungu wannitanna*

ilka, *affix* having, possessing, as *kaya ilka*, provided with spears; armed, *kakka ilka*, having a head, i.e. obstinate
ilkanna, ditto
ilkari, sky or ether
ilkata, *v.* to look askance; scowl
ilkaringutu, *v.* to envy
ilki ilki, among; as *nauurri ilki-ilki* among the Nauos
ilkiri, as *kaya ilkiri*
illa, *adj.* ready; prepared, *illa mai*, food ready to be eaten
illa, not hitting or not killing the game aimed at, as *illa wittiti*, *v.* to throw a spear past the object; miss
illa nungkutu *v.* to shoot past; miss
ilpi, or oftener plur. ilpirri, drops; as *mena ilpirri* eye drops, i.e. tears; *kauo ilpirri*, rain drops
ilta, or iltalla } choked; full with; as *mudla kunimpi iltalla*, the nose is choked with mucus
iltalliti, *v.* to be choked; breath heavily
iltya, *s.* muscle; sinew; vein, *kauo iltya*, water vein, i.e. spring; streamlet
iltyarreri, *s.* crevice; crack
iltyi-iltyiti, *v.* to hiss like boiling water
illyirriltyirriti, *v.* ditto
ilya, *adj.* loose; open, as *ilya ngutaka*, cast loose
ilya, *s.* an opening; open place; passage
imbanna, *s.* ashes
imini, *adj.* sacred; forbidden; anything that must not be seen, said, or touched, is *imini*. The ceremonies of bleeding, circumcising, tattooing, &c. are *imini*; with regard to women and children, they being on no account allowed to see them.
inata, *v.* to sink in; bog; stick fast, as *warru inata madlyanga*, the kangaroo sticks fast in the mud
inba, straight; as *inbarri yuwalanna pitraarri*, the soldiers form a line
inbarriti, *v* to be in a line with another object, or to be close to it
inda, *adj. & s.* bloody; wounded; shattered; wound;

abscess, as *inda nallata, v.* to crush; kill, *inda kambata* to foment a wound

indirrindirriti, *v.* to creak; to produce a creaking noise

ındo, *affix.* likewise; also; as *ngai piri indo* I (am called) *piri* likewise

ini, *s.* a pointed bone used as a needle or awl

inki or inkirri, in a circle; in a row; as *inkirri yurarri ikkitanna,* the men are sitting in a circle

inna, *pron. dem.* this; that

innaitye, ditto

innaityinge, in this; here

innarra, there

innarambo, there along

innaru, *gen. case.* this person's, his

innelli, tired, as *innulli yura ngukatao wittintyaranya,* a man becomes tired by diggigg

inninye, *s.* rib

inyalla, *s.* a species of burrowing animal

ipi, *adj.* alive; living

ipinniti, *s.* to be alive; live

ipillippilli *s.* bell

ira, *s.* tooth

ira buka, decayed teeth, having a smelling breath; as *nauurri irabukarri kuyabidnarri,* i.e. the *Nauo* people have an offensive breath, being fish eaters.

iralbo, *adj.* sharp, having a sharp and hard point as the spear when hardened in hot ashes

irallu. *s.* black cockatoo

irapa, *adj.* sharp edged

irata, *v.* to keep off; defend; protect, as *kutyu yurarringe iratann " winni winni " wanggaintyaranga,* the other men keep us off by saying "winni winni."

ngarrinyelbo ninna iratanna, we will defend you

irangarriti, *v.* to disengage oneself

irangutu, *v.a.* to protect; defend; claim, as *ngaityc karnko kutta irangukka,* my house do not defend, i.e. do'nt keep other people away from it. *Mundulturringe*

irangutannn yerta. the Europeans protect or claim the country
iraworta, *s.* jaw, gum
irbi, *s.* information ; news ; message
irbi kattiti, *v.a.* to carry a message
irbi wanggatta, *v.a.* to deliver a message
irebilye, *s.* cockroach
irerinye, *.s* a species of sea bird
iridniti, *v.* to separate ;*bulloki iridnitana*
iridningutu, *v.a. as karpanga iridningutu adli*
iri, irinnirinni
iriti, *v.* to move ; be moving ; shift ; as *pallarri iringtutarru yuranga yadni : karra pudnuru irikanna.* A man bids the woman to move thus : remove up to the scrub
irirriti, *v.* to keep moving or shifting ; be restless
irkanda, *s.* scrub
irkarra, *s.* bush : layer of the wallaby
irkelli, *s.* salt
irpata, *v,a.* to rub ; file ; saw ; *wallaranga irpata,* to cut with a saw ; to say sharp or witty things ; to fop ; joke; tease ; as *pallarri irpatanna,* they fop with the women
irparriti. *v.* to fop each other ; joke
irri, *adj.* clean
irrinniti, *v.* to be clean
irrinnignutu, *v.a.* to make clean ; purefy
irta, *s.* bird generally
ita, s. shag
ita wadlata, *s.* a kind of shrub
italla, *s.* a burrowing animal ; rat
itha, *pron. dem.* that
ithara, there
itharu, thither
iti, s. the jugular vein
iti, as *pilla-iti, iti wortalbo, as ngai iti wortalbo mai murlu ngalgungutanna*
itinya, *s.* granite
itirriti, *s.* to be dejected, or in a pet ; as *karnbanga*

itirritao yura, a man is dejected when hungry.

K

Kabmi, *adj.* as *kabmi palkara,* a species of Eucalyptus
kabminye, *s.* morning star
kabmiti, *adj.* wise, aware, knowing, as *ngai kabmiti,* I (am) aware
kabmirriti, *v.* to get better, convalesce
kabmititi, *v.* to become wise, learn
kadalyili, *s.* a species of shark
kadla, *s.* tail
kadlarti, *s.* flesh fly, maggot
kadlayini *s.* a species of fish
kadlayini marra, *s.* a small kind of fish
kadli, behind
kadilli, father behind
kadliri, slipping, grasing, as *kadliri kaya wittinnarru padlo,* he speared the fish so as only to grase it
kadlirindi. *adv.* ditto
kadlirriti *v.* to slip, as *kadlirrinao winna,* the fishing spear slipped
kadliti, *v.* to peel, skin
kadlo *s.* the large black species of ant, lion ant
kadlo, or kadlo bebi, *s.* testicle
kadlukko, *s.* a grown up kangaroo
kadnanya kadnanya, very slowly
kadno, *s.* a yellow striped species of lizard
kailko, *s.* pus, matter
kaitya, *adv. & s.* small, little, infant, child
kaityaba, *n.pr.* Stamford Hill
kakka, head
kakka bebi, *s.* brain
kakkalle, *s.* a belt or girdle made of the hair of the head and consisting of many separate strings
kakkamita, *s.* name for a relative
kakka murtilli, thick head, stupid
kakkaninye, *s.* a species of fish

kakkannara, *adv.* from the surface, on the top, above
kakkanniti, *v.* to rise, come up, grow
kakkanningutu, *v.* to make grow, rear
kakkaputti, *s.* the hair of the head
kakkarra, *s.* pillow, anything to rest one's head upon
kakka tandutu } very common expression of reproach
kakka yailti, }
kakkelli, *s.* mangrove tree
kakkiti, *adv.* in two, as *kakkiti kundata,* to beat in two, break
kako, *s.* an edible root
kakkurriti, *v.* to wish, desire, like
kakkurrindi, *v.* wish, intent, as *kakkurindinge wappetanna* they do it intentionally
kakurru, on end, upright
kakurru wirri, *adj.* ditto
kakurru yuwata, *s.* to stand on end or upright
kakkurru yendata, *v.* to put on end, upright
kalalballa, *s.* sand fly
kalalta, *s.* torch, dry bark lighted and used in fishing at night
kalanbi, *s.* ashes, lime
kalawidna, *s.* a coarse, reedy sort of grass
kalba, *s.* cheek, side of the head
kalba, *s.* lap, as *kalbanga ngai mankukka*
kalba, as *kalba ngalla metye yendat unno,* you name it repeatedly
kalbanna, *s.* emu feathers, shavings
kalbanya, *s.* Australian pheasant
kalbelli, *num.* two, a pair; as an affix it forms the dual number of nouns dropping the first two letters, as *yuralbelli,* two men, *marralbelli* two hands
kalbi, *s.* leaf
kali, *s.* leaf of the cactus, commonly called the native fig
kalka, open, openly, public, as *yurarri kalka ikkatanna,* the men sit openly, i.e. you can see them
Tő wittirrimadli, pardni palkakka kalka ngai yuwata

come on, let us two fight, run hither, I stand openly i.e. unscreened
kàlkara, *adj.* narrow, close
kalkarra, *adj.* long time ago, of yòre
kalkaridni, *adj.* ancient
kalkarriti, *v.* to tremble, heave, feel great desire, as *kalkalkarrimatta ngaitye pinkalbelli warra ngukaintyaranga* my hips ache from travelling far. Or, *yura kalkaritao pallaradnuru*
kalkiti, *v.* to become loose, undone, slip
kalkulliti. *v.* to forget
kalkullalkulli, *adj.* forgetful
kalkutu, *v.* to be in pain
kalkurriti, *v.* to be sick, ill
kalla, *s.* voice, speech, dialect
kalla, *s.* sleeping lizard
kalla, *s.* pond, pool, as *kauo kalla,* water pool
kallanbi, i.e. *gadlabidni*
kallalla, *s.* a species of fish
kalla pùdni, *s.* a beautiful blue flowered creeper, native lilac
kallara, *s.* tea tree
kallanniti, *v.* to call
kallata, *v.* to call, hail
kallakallanniti *v.* to call repeatedly, neigh
kallangarriti, *v.* to call to each other, speak with a person at a distance
kallikalliti, *v.a.* to chip
kallilliti *v.* to cover with earth, bury
kallinyala, the site of Port Lincoln
kalliworra, *s.* sea gull
kalluru, *adj.* unripe, green
kaltanye, *adj.* asking, begging, stingy, as *maii kaltanyilbellinge ngai yeringumatta,* the two beggars ask me for food. Or *ninna piyi kaltanye,* you are (always) begging for clothing
kalti, *s.* husk, peel, bran

kalti, i.e. *mai kako mirrinye*
kalterinye, i.e. *yerdna walbo,* vertebrae, back-bone
kaltirriti, *v.* to be clamorous, beg, i.e. *kaltirrtao kaitya ngaminge mankoyuru,* the child cries for the mother to take it
kaltirringutu, *v.a.* to ask, desire, want
kaltya *s.* resin, gum
kaltya, *s.* great number, mob
kaltyini, *v.* level, *as kaltyininge kuri kuri ngkatao bebi,* the egg turns round on the level
kalunu, *s.* a species of fish; whiting
kaluru, *adj.* bold, fierce, as *kurdninni padnatao kaluru,* the wild dog walks boldly, *i.e.* does not run away
kalya, an interjection, *as kalya kutta kundakka,* don't strike, I say
kalyautu, *v.* to beckon away ; to make a motion with the hand to another person to keep at a distance
kalyirkiti, *v.* to slip, glide, stumble
kalyoru, *adj.* chill, bleak, whizzing *as warri-kalyoru* bleak wind; *kalyoru ngukatao warriyoko* the ship goes whizzing
kambata, *v.* to cook, bake, roast, foment
kanbangurru, *s.* whiskers
kammala, *s.* a species of fungus
kammalla, *adj.* as *kadla kammalla nau urri*
kammata, *v.* to tell, intercede for, ask
kammangutu *v.a.* to invite
kammirri, *adj.* hopping, *as kammirri kammirri ngammatao warraitye,* the Emu hops along
kammirriti, *v.n.* as *yurti kammirriti gadla kundaintya ranga,* the arm aches by beating the wood, this word expresses the painful sensation, that is produced by hitting a stick that another person is holding
kammullu, *adj.* dejected, pensive, *as kammullu ikkata*
kananna, *n. pr.* Emu bottom
kananna purre, Winter's Hill
kanbara, *adj.* fertile good soil

kanda, *adj.* choked, swollen, *as yurdne kanda* swollen throat

kandara, *adj.* as *yumballa kandara,* wallaby hunter, expert in spearing wallaby

kandarra, *s.* eructation, belching

kandi, *s.* hammer, tomahawk, axe

kandideri, as *waiiti kandideri,* to be sore afraid

kandulguru, *s.* a species of fish

kanganye, *s.* side of the human body, flank

kangara *s.* the root of the grass tree which at certain seasons of the year constitutes an excellent article of food for the natives

kangai, *s.* a sea bird, bozen bird

kanggata, *v.* to drive, lead

kangi, *adj.* self willed, impetuous, resolute

kanginniti, *v.* to act resolutely

kangi worta, *s.* a self-willed, impetuous person

kangiti, *s.* grass tree

kangkarru, *s.* whale!

kangu, *s.* an edible kind of root

kankarra, *adv.* together, in common, as *paru ngalgumarinyelbo kankarra,* let us eat the meat together

kannalla, *s.* current tree

kannata, *v.a.* to wait for, as *ngatto ninna kannata,* I shall wait for you

kannarriti, *v.* to awake, get up

kannelli, *adj.* old, abandoned, as *kairko kannelli,* an old hut; it also means an old complaint, especially of a rheumatic nature, to which the natives are frequently subject

kanti, *s.* thigh, shank

kantya, as *kaya kantya*

kantyiti, *v.a.* to lead, conduct, as *karteti kantyiti,* to take a wife, or to have a wife

kantyingarriti, *v.* to carry about with one, as food &c., to save

kanya, *s.* stone, rock

kanyalla, *s.* a pebble or round stone, carried about in the knapsack or net, used in breaking bones &c.
kanyamai *s.* a species of fungus, mushroom
kanyangkunu, *n.pr.* Point Bolingbroke
kanyanniti, *v.* to become stone, to harden, be obstinate, persist in
kanyanungkutu, *v.a.* to detain by force, prevent
kanyi, *s.* name for a relative
kapi=kauo, water
kapiti, *v.a.* to cut off, make a short cut, surround
kapmarra, *adv.* only, or always as *kapmarra innaityinge ikkat'ai,* I shall always live here
kappakkata, *v.a.* to love, court
kappalliti, *v.* to go back, return home
kappaltiti, *s.* to be tired
kapparna, *s.* gravy
kapparnka, as *kutta kapparnka ngukatao wilya, makkandara ngukatao*
kapparra, *adj. & s.* weak, tired, lazy, laziness
kapparra worta, *s.* a weak person, lazy fellow
kapparriti, *v.* to be weak, tired, lazy
kappattiti, *v.a. kappakkata,* to love or court a woman
kappikarnka, *n.pr.* an Island in Spencer's Gulf, on which *Midlalla* is said to reside
kappo=kulbarri, three, several
kappúrru, *s.* arm pit
kapurru, *a. & v.* down, out of sight, as *yurno kapurru ngnkanao,* the sun is gone down
kara, *s.* spider, tarantula
kara, *s.* grass
kardlaintye, *adj.* fledged, able to fly
kardnarriti, *v.n.* to bend, lean back, as *muyn kardnarritao,* the back is bent.
karai, *adj*=mau-urru, dark, black
kara yalga, *s.* cobweb
kara yurdla, *s.* a good sharp edged piece of quartz
karata, *v.a.* as *vaitya karata* to commence a quarrel

karangarriti, *v.* to quarrel
karakarata, *v.a.* to commend, praise
kardi, or karthi, *interj.* calling attention ; I say, listen
kardma, *n.pr.* Mount Gawler
kardni, *s.* girl
kardnirriti, *v.* to stretch one's limbs
karkuru, *s.* a whizzing or or rustling noise, as *karkuru ilkanna kauo wornitao,* the rain comes rushing down
karkurarkuru, whizzing, as *karnkurtu karkurarkura ngukatao kauungu,* the boat goes whizzing through the water, i.e. very swiftly
kari, gradually, by and bye, as *ngai kari ngukata,* I shall go by and bye
kari kari, softly, gently, take care
kari kurru, later, not yet, by and bye
kariti, *v.* to be or exist stlil, be behind, as *parungu karitanna yurarri,* the men are still at the game, are hunting still
karkalla, *s.* kind of cactus, commonly called the native fig
karkantya, *s.* a species of hawk
karnba, *adj.* empty, hungry
karnbanniti, *v.* to be empty, hungry
karnda kutyo, otherwise or again
karnmarri, *s.* lues venerea
karnmi, *adj.* encircled, enclosed
karnmi karnko, *s.* prison
karnmi karnmi, *adj.* amorous, fond
karnmiringutu, *v.a.* to encircle, enclose, defend, screen
karnkarra, above
karnkata, *v.* to raise, lift, take up
karnko, *s.* hut, house, place of encampment, watering place
karnkurtu, *s.* boat, small vessel
karpa, *s.* inside, room, European house, as *karpanga ngalbakka.* come into the house
karpalla / karpallanna } alongside of, along, as *yartu karpalla ngukakka,* go along there

karpalla, sewn, stiched, *karpalla palta,* a cloak consisting of many small skins sewn together
karpata, *v.* to join, sew, build
karpa karparriti. *v.* to be joined together, as *mena karpa karparriti,* to have one's eyes closed with opthalmia or swelling
karpatye,=murtunyu, *s.* a small blue colored kind of fish
karpili, *s.* one of the burrowing species of animals
karra, high, above
karra-arra, *s.* noon, afternoon
karraitye, *s.* manna tree
karraityukkutu, *v.a.* to hold up to the wind, to winnow
karralbunto, *adv.* upwards
karralla, *adj.* yellow
karrakarrirriti, *v.* to be high, as *yurno wibma karra karrirritao,* the sun is already high
karrambi, *s.* a kind of edible berry
karranna. *s.* frog
karrara, *adj.* down, prostrate, as *karrara wvorniti,* to fall down, to die
karrarra, *s.* hot season, summer
karraru, *adj.* uncommon; every native claims the title of being either *karraru* or *matteri,* both which words appear to refer to some superstitious idea
karrata, *v.* to be lame, to walk lame
karranungkutu *v.* ditto
karrenni, *s.* east, easterly wind
karrenyé *s.* a species of lizard, ratling lizard
karrenyerenye, *adj.* of blue or purple color.
karrenyerenye, *s.* blister
karrulyuru, *s.* a species of ant
karta, *s.* dirt, dung, resin, gum
kartalla, *s.* dirty
kartanye, *s.* name of the first child, if a female
karteti, *s.* wife
karteti nallata, to take a wife, marry
karti, *s.* stem of a tree, the thick branches of a tree

kartipalka, *s.* the fatal instrument with which evil disposed persons render the objects of their malice ill and eventually kill them
kartintye, *s.* blood, sap, juice
kartintyaltarta, *adj.* bloody, blood stained
kartu, *adj,* short and thick, depressed, as *kartu mudla,* a short thick nose
kartuworta, *s.* a short and stout person
kartungulli, *adj.* bent, curved like a hawk's beak
kartunnu, *s.* coitus
kathai, North side hill
kathukathurriti, *s.* to be sad or discontented, as *mai madlanga yura kathukathurritao,*for want of food a man is sad
kato, *s.* cloak, waistcoat
katta, *s.* club, grubbing stick ; gun, musket
kattanga nungkutu, *v.* to shoot
katta bidni, Mr Browns's sheep station
kattaintya, *s.* a species of bird called goatsucker
kattappi, *s.* porpoise
kattapulba, *s.* gun dust, gunpowder,
kattara, *adj.* apart, distant, little way off
kattari, rain, as *kattari kauo,* rain water, surface water
kattarna, *s.* scorpion
kattiti, *v.* to bring, fetch
kattirriti, *v.* to overtake, meet
katturu, *adj.* greedily, as *katturu ngalgutu,* to eat greedily *katturu kudnata*
katyeti, *s.* a species of lizard
kauallu, *adj.* steep, rocky
kauanna, *s.* an animal of the burrowing species, rat
kauara, effectual, as *kauara wittiti,* to spear effectually, i.e. to hit or kill the object
kauo, *s.* water
kauoiltya, *s.* water vein spring
kauokauurriti, *v,* to swing to and fro, being suspende
kauopulba, *s.* water dust, drizzling rain, heavy fog

kauurkauurku, *adj* pregnant
kauurkauurkiti, *v.* to be pregnant
kauwalka, *adj.* open, apart
kauwarriti *v.*
kauwirtananya, *adj.* long, swinging
kauwirtauwirti, *adj.* ditto
kauwirtauwirtiti, *v.* to be shaking, going to fall
kauwiti, *v.* to bring up, vomit
kauwultu, hanging, suspended
kauwultiti, *v.* to be hanging
kaya, *s* spear
kayailka, armed with spears
kayalla, *s.* the north and north western country
kayaworta, *s.* a fighter, pugnacious man
kayiti, *v.a.* to cover all over, to incubate, hatch
ketyelli, *s.* name of a place, Charlton
kiya=kaya, spear
ko, *s.* shelter, fence
kokalla, *s.* hip
kokara, *s.* staff, stick
kokarniti, *v.* to lean upon
koltye, *s.* green paroquet, grass parrot
kolutu, *v.* to cough, groan
konye, *s.* a species of shark
korti, *s.* swan
korti purre, Mount Hill
kuara, *s.* plug, stopper
kubmanna, *num.* one, alone, sole
kubmalberi, once, only once
kudla, *s.* well
kudlakauo, *s.* well water
kudliti, *v.* to rub, hurt ?
kudlirriti, *v.* to be silent, sullen ; *ngannaru ninna kudlirriti ngannaruyalla ?* why are you so silent
kudlirindi, *adj.* silent, as *kudlirindi ikkata, to be silent*
kudlirringutu, *v.a.* to make silent, quiet
kudlu, *s.* louse

kudmirra or kurdmirra, *s.* circle, ring, picture
kudna, *s.* bowels, excrements, coitus
kudna ngangkella, *s.* stomach
kudnanna, *s.* large weed, tobacco
kudnannaga, *s.* a species of redbill
kudnapabmi, *s.* opprobrious term
kudna parto, *adj.* costive
kudnata, *v.a.* to evacuate the bowels, let blood, comprimere
kudnarriti, *v.* coire
kudna yardniti, comprimere
kudna yardnirriti, *v.* coitum habere
kudnulko, loose in the bowels
kukata, national name of a north western tribe of natives, said to be very numerous and ferocious
kulalye, *adj.* wet
kudlalyiti, *v.* to be wet
kulata, *v.a.* to sever, cut, break, tear
kulanniti, *v.* to be rent
kulangarriti, *v.* this word expresses the peculiar sound produced by the *pullakalli*, (which see)
kularriti or kulakularriti } *v.* to crack, break
kularra, *s.* sweat, perspiration
kularabmata, *v.* to perspire, sweat
kulbarri, three, several
kulbi, i.e. *pinnarabidni mai*
kulburko, *s.* gravy, as *paru kulburko yarlirritao* the gravy is spilling
kulilyala, s. the seed vessel of the casuarina
kulindi, round, surrounding
kulka, *s.* kangaroo rat
kulkutu, *v.* to imprecate, curse, rebuke. When it rains or a kangaroo or other animal escapes, the natives employ a long string of imprecations which they pronounce with great vehemence and believe to be infallibly efficacious

kullari, *s.* *a* fabulous bird, said to peck people's heads
kullarnu, *adv.* still, yet
kullilli, *s.* the name of a variety of eatable grubs ; as :—
kullilli numma
kullilli patta
kullilli yako
kullilli yulko
kullindi, *s.*=kurdli bakka, stunted sheoak
kulli purru, *n.pr.*.the name of a hill called "Cobler's friend"
kullirri, *s.* the blossoms of the male she oaks
kullu, *s.* snoring, *kullu ngutata*,to snore
kulpa, *s.* young man, youth
kulta, *s.* germ, fresh shoot
kultai, *s.* a species of fungus
kultimpiti,=wanniti *v.* to lie down
kulya,=pulka, old
kulyanniti, *v.* to be old
kulyara, *v.* young male kangaroo
kulyeritye, *s.* a small speckled species of paraquet
kulyunnu, *s.* native lark
kuma,=kubmanna, one, alone
kumanni, alone, by one's self
kumbara,=yabmarra, a species of fish, groper
kumbu,*s.* urine
kumbukumbu, *s.* wave, billow
kumburunye, *s.* a species of ant
kumbutu, *v.* to make water
kumbutyukkutu, *v.a.* to wet with urine
kummarri, alone, as *kummarri mai ngalgutanna*, they eat the food alone, viz not giving me any
kunballa, *adj.* serious, modest
kunballiti, to be serious, to be in earnest
kundata, *v.a.* to strike, beat, kill
kundi=wirri, throwing stick
kundindi, *s.* belt, girdle, made of the hair of the head or of oppossum hair
kundo birra, *s.* a large shell, spoon

kundullu, *s.* heap, as *ngampa kundullu,* a heap of roots
kunga kunga, *s.* infantine voice, the cry of an infant
kunggullu, *s.* craw fish, sea crab
kungka, arm or fork of a tree
kunimpi, *s.* mucus; as *mudla kunimpi,* mucus of the nose
kunkurru, *s.* cluster, thicket ;as *kurdli kunkurru,* a cluster of sheoaks
kunmata, *v.* to kill
kunna, *s.* a species of kangaroo
kunnari, *s.* fat, suet
kunni, *s.* name of the third child of a mother if a male
kunnurru, of dark colour, brown
kunnulyu, *s.* a water bubble, a hollow sound
kunnurriti, *v.* to be wet
kunnütyullu, *s.* mosquito
kunta, *s.* name of the third child, if a female
kunta, *n.pr.* name of a river
kunti, *s.* horse fly
kunto, a *postfix.* as *Parnkalla kunto wanggakka,* speak in Parnkalla or the Parnkalla dialect
kunyalla, a friend or relation
kunyu, *adj.* dead
kupa, *adj.* ditto
kupi, as *kauo kupi*
kupilyipilyi, as *kupilyipilyi yurno,*—
kupiri, *s.* edge, margin, as *pinnara kupiringé,* on the margin of the lake
kupirri, *s.* a kind of kangaroo, white kangaroo
kuputu, *v.a.* to state, maintain, represent with vehement gesture; *Nantinge kurru midlantarri ngalla kuputarru,* Nanti represents the Adelaide natives as very numerous, *Yupinge irbi kupuntyarru* Yupi has confirmed the message
kura or kuranga, behind, after, as *kuranga ngukata,* to walk behind, follow, *Piriru kuranga Warri worninao,* Warri was born after or next to Piri

kura or **kuralye,** visible, in sight as *karnko kura palkatao*, the house may be seen, or is in sight
kurai, *s.* a species of fish
kurailtye, not far, or for a long time, as *kurailtye waiingukaintyao,* he has fled far away, or for a long time
kurakka, *adj.* young, green; as *kurakka kurdli* green sheoak
kuralbo, *s.* a small species of fish
kuralla, *s.* a well dug in sand or gravel
kuranna, *s.* thunder
kuranya, *s.* rainbow
kurata, *v.* to bore, dig a well in the sand, turn round; as *warri kurata,* the wind turns round
kurarriti, *v.* to hum, buzz; as *yurre kurarriti,* to feel a buzzing sensation in the ear
kurbo, *s.* smell
kurbu, *s.* side; as *kurbungu wanniti,* to lie on one side
kurdi, *s.* native peach tree
kurdi,mai, *s.* native peach
kurdla, *s.* strength, semen
kurdli, *s.* sheoak, casuarina
kurdli bakka, *s.* dwarf sheoak
kurdlu, *s.* an animal of the marsupian species
kurdninni, *s.* native dog
kurelli, *s.* rainy season, winter
kurrelli mudla, *s.* beginning of rainy season, autumn
kuri, *s.* ring, circle, song, dance
kuri kundata, *v.* to sing
kuri wawutu, *v.* to dance
kurilbi, *s.* grass seed, ear
kurilyelli, *n.pr.* Boston Island
kurinti, *s.* distance; as *kurintinge ikkata,* to be at a distance
kurinyarra, *s.* a pillar of dust produced by a whirlwind
kuriti or **kurikuriti,** } *v.* to turn round, wander about
kurkarra, *s.* native geranium
kurko, *s.* a species of owl

kurkullu, *s.* bandicoot
kurlo, *s.* side of the body, that part of the body between the shoulder and loin
kurni, *s.* hair, fur, *kakka kurni,* hair of the head
kurnunnu, *s.* elbow
kurpata, *v.a.* to sprinkle with water
kurra, *s.* magpie
kurrirrurriri, round about, uninteligible ; as *kurrirrurriri Nauurri wanggatanna,* the Nauos talk unintelligibly
kurroalla, *s.* crown of the head, vertex
kurroalla, *n.pr.* Mount Liverpool
kurru, *s.* stick, poker, tube, flute
kurrugadla, ditto
kurrungu kallata, to play upon the flute
kurrukkungutu, *v.a.* to make giddy, confound
kurrukkutu, *v.* to be giddy, stupid ; as *kakka kurrukkutu wanggaintyaranga,*my head becomes giddy by talking
kurrulkurulku gadla
kurrulkurrulkutu, *v.* to be giddy
kurrukurru, round
kurrumidlanta, national name for the Adelaide natives
kurrunnu, all ; as *mai kurrunnu nakkuntyarru,* he has seen all the food
kurruttiti, *v.* to become stiff
kurruwallu ; as *kutta kurruwallu yuralka yuwaintyarao*
kurrütyunnu, *adj.* all, whole
kurta, *s.* posterior
kurta milka, a reproachful term
kurtankiti, *v.* to lean upon one's elbow
kurti, *adj.* stiff
kurto, steep, steep place, precipice, hollow
kutta, not, no ; *kattadla,* perhaps not ; *kuttalka,*not at all
kuttara=kalbelli, two
kutyu, another, other, the rest ; as *kutyu yura purrakka,* call another man

kutyulkanna, the plural of kutyu, others
kutyubidni, other, some; *kutyubidni warraitye marniti kutyubidni milla*, some emus are good, some are bad
kutyupi
kuya, *s.* fish
kuyabidni, Sleaford Mere
kuyanna, *s.* the male grub of the mita ant which is not eatable and is separated from the female. *bidlyo*, by winnowing
kuyo, switch
kuyurkuru, *s* ditto
kuyurkuru, *s* Dragon fly, hornet
kuyuru, *adj.* slim, slender; as *battara kuyuru*, a tall slender gum tree; *kanti kuyuru*, a thin shank

M

Ma, mai, vegetable food
mabinye, *s.* cloud
madla paru, yailba mirrinye, a species of animal
madla, no, none
madlanniti, *v.* to be or become no more, to die
madla madla, ditto, as *mai madla madla*, having no food
madli, *s.* the place of infants on the backs of their mothers; as *madlinge ikkata* to sit on the back, i.e. to be of tender age
madlo, *s.* shade; *madlo yertata, v.* to throw shade, stand in the light; as *kalya madlo yertakka*
madlo kanti, *s.* ditto; as *madlo kantinge ikkata*
madlya, *s.* wet, soft, muddy,dirt mud
mai, *s.* vegetable food generally, such as roots &c.
maialla, *adv.* never mind, letting alone, notwithstanding
maí erri, *s.* a species of mouse
mai-ilkanna, having food, rich
mai-ilya, *adj.* liberal with food
mai-karnba, food empty; i.e. hungry
mai-marraba, having no food, destitute

mai-mintyuru, particular with food, stingy
mai-munta, liberal with food
mai-pinta, greedy, close
mai-pinta worta, a close or greedy fellow
maitya, *adv.* expressing assurance, indeed, then, now; as *maitya ngannaru*, why then (viz should it be) *maitya kulbarri ikkardna*, they are many indeed
maiworna, satisfied with food
mai yeri, tenacious of food, stingy, greedy
makka, a negation; not so, or it is not
makkarniti, *v.* to be no more, die
makkarndara ngukatao wilya
mako, *s.* a piece of quartz attached to the *wommara*, and used as a knife
malakunnu ninna ngukanna at the moment you went
malbara, *s.* haze, mist
malberinye, *s.* the coverlet of the male pubes, consisting in a bunch of feathers or a sort of tassels made of opossum hair
malbu, *s.* a murderer; any person that has killed another whether he be justified in doing so or not; author, owner
malka, *adj.* long
malkiti, *v.* to press, knead
malkingarriti, *v.* to wash one's self
malta, thicket; as *pundarri mallanga wanniti*, to lie in a thick scrub
malla palba, *s.* ditto
malko=mabinge, cloud
malleri, peaceable, friendly; as *worna malleri* ditto
mallaityamallaitya, showery; as *mallaityamallaitya kauo wornitao*
mallilparriti, *v.* to slip
mallirriti, *v.* to dissolve, become powerless
malliti, *v.* to become undone, slip, fall
mallimbiti, *v.* ditto
mallimbarriti, *v.* ditto

málo or malomálo, *adj*, not heeding, unconcerned ; as *ngia-malo ngukana*, I went unheeding by, i.e. I took no notice
maltarra, *s.* a bunch of emu feathers over the top
malti, *s.* darkness, night ; *parri malti*, deep darkness
malturlo, morning, morrow
maltyata, *v.*
maltyangarriti, *v.*
malyarra, *adv.* long, for a long time ; *diu*
mambarna, *s.* lad, boy.
mamba. knee ; as *mamba madla*
mambutu, *v.* to set on, as dogs, to instigate, encourage, persuade, seduce
mammata, *v.* to share, partake of anothers property, as food, meat &c.
manga, *s.* thread or yarn made of oppossum hair, and worn round the head
mangalla, *adj.* peaceable, friendly, friend, the reverse of hostile, *paitya*
mangalliti, to be peaceable, friendly
mangallingutu, *v.a.* to make peace, pacify
mangirri, *adj.* well, healthy
mangirriti, *v.* to become well, convalesce, heal ; as *mangirriti mingka*
mangu, *s.* face
mani, *s.* a relative, nephew ?
mangkunnu, *adj.* strong, stiff ; as *yurti mangkunnu*, a powerful arm
mangkunniti, *v.* to be strong
manka, *s.* dots, tattoo scars
mankailkanna, having dots, a grown up man
mankutu, *v.* to take, receive,
mankulbarriti, *v.* to take away, liberate
mankunturrutu, *s.* to take again ?
manna, *adj.* much, plentiful, large
manna, *s.* ground grub
mannallara, *s.* mutton bird
manna murri, very much

mannando, ditto
mannandutu, *v.* to become large, grow
mannanniti, *v.* to be or become plentiful ; as *ngai kudlu mannannintyara,* I might have become full of lice
mannara, slowness, laziness, slowly ; as *mannara kundangarri yata*
mannarriti, *v.* to be slow, lazy, behind
manngu, *s. semen*
mannu, together, near each other
manta, *adj.* moist, wet
mantalliti, *v.* to become weak, fail, as *pinka mantalliti,* to be lame
mantarriti, *v.* to be moist, wet
manti, *adv.* repeatedly, continuingly ; as *manti kundata,* to beat repeatedly
mantimantirriti, *v.* to be thin, lean ; *mantim pulta mallanga*
mantyarri, *adj.* fine, right, nice
manu, *s.* back
manutu, *v.* to carry on the back
manya, i.e. *mita pulyo,* ant grub
manyanna, i.e. *ngallira* ; as *nuwalla manyanna yurramata*
manyartini, rain ? as *kauo manyartini,* rain water ? *kartinty(eg) altrata wittinarru ai, manyartini ngarrin yelbo wittinarru*
manyutu, *v.* to lay hold, grasp
manyurriti, v, to break, an an egg
mappa, *s.* rubbish, dirt
mappara, full of rubbish, dirty
mapparniti, *v.* to be dirty
mapparningutu, *v.a.* to make dirty
mappiti, *v.* to rest
mara, *s.* arm of a tree : hair ; as *kakka mara*
mara, *s.* pond, pool ; as *kauo mara,* water pond
mari, willingly ; as *mari ngukatao' pallara yerdlinnuru*
marka, space of twenty four hours, day
markaru kunto, for one day

markalla, *s.* shell
markata, *v*, to be fast, jammed in, to stick, pull tight; as *markatarru poninga wandurru*
markutu, *v.* to bark
markunyu, *s.* quarrel about a woman, jealously
marni, *s.* fat, grease
marni tappa, very good
marniti, *adj.* good; *marniti mai*, good food
marniti, *v.* to smell; as *kurbo marniti*
marningarriti, *v.* ditto ditto
marnitingutu, *v.* to make good, ornament, improve
marnko, *s.* elbow
marnta, *s.* animal of the marsupial species
marnpi, *s.* pigeon
marpalya, brokenly, incorrectly; as *marp wanggata*, to speak brokenly
marpu, *s.* bush, branch
marra, *s.* the young offspring of animals, pup, pullet, &c.
marra, *s.* hand, finger, quantity; as *kutta pulyo marra*, not a small quantity
marra, *s.* point
marraba, *affix*; as *mai marraba, palta marraba*, without food, without clothing
marrabirri, finger nails
marrakatu
marràlye, *s.* boy
márralye, *s.* fiend, devil. The Marralye is described as a man belonging to the Kukata tribe, who assumes the shape and action of a bird, if he has a spite against an individual, he pounces upon him at night, while he is asleep, stabs him imperceptibly, and then leaves him to die in a short time after. Whenever the cause of death is not apparent to the natives comprehension, such as old age and wounds, they have no doubt that the dreaded Marralye is the author.
marramarrarkuru, *s.* intensitive form of, *marra*, a great quantity

marramunka
marrangalli, *v.* the palm or hollow of the hand
marrangangkalla, *s.* thumb
marrangukata, *v.* to show, point with the hand
marrangultu; as *marrangultu wiltinarru,* with a ruthless hand he speared him
marranya, slowly, leisurely
marrapalba, *adj.* even, smooth
marrapappa, *s.* little finger
marrara, *s.* wild duck
marrata, *v.* to crawl, walk on the hands
marra warra
marra willuru, forefinger
marrenye, *s.* snapper fish
marreri, *adv.* far away
marri, *s.* name of fifth child if a male
marritye, i.e. *idnya,* cat
marru or marruntu, different; as *marruntu wanggatanna iäta matta,* the north eastern people speak differently
marru, *s.* black paint, a mixture of the ashes of the grass tree and grease with which the natives ornament their faces
marrukko, *s.* name of the fifth child if a female
marrurko, *s.* a widow
marruyu=marri
marrutu, *v.* to creep
marta, *s.* place, former place, or the place before inhabited or spoken of; as *wana ngaitye nurti? martanga,* where is my bag? in the old place or where you left it
martanna, *s.* an acquaintance, friend; a person seen before
martanniti, *v.* to remain, survive; as *mart yerdli kartati kunyunga,* the man survives his wife
marti, *adj.* well, healed up; *s.* a scar, a sore healed up
martinniti, *v.* to heal
martiti, *v.* to embrace

martu, *s.* *mons veneris*
matta, *s.* tribe, nation; as *Parnkalla matta,* the *Parnkalla* nation
matanya, *s.* designation for one of the actors in the ceremony of tattooing
mattara, *adj.* ignorant, not used to, inexperienced
mattata, *v.* to pick up, gather
mattantutu, *s.* ditto
mattata, *v.* to stick fast
matterri, the reverse of *karrarru*
matu or martu, a tree bearing a yellow berry
mau-urru, *adj.* dark, black
mauurrurriti, *v.* to be black
mauurruringutu, *v.a.* to make dark, blacken
mau winya, a lightly clouded sky, favorable to oppossum hunting
meka, *adj.* bare, bald; as *kakka meka* bald head
mekkalla, bare, clean; as *karnko mekalla,* as *kutta mappa ilkannu*
méllakka, *s.* a name of the seventh child, if a female
mélalla, shining, glittering; *melalla kariti,* to shine, glitter
melara=meka, bare,
melata, *v.* to feed, eat; applied to animals only
melingutu, *v.* to clean,, smooth, plain
melokunyo, *s.* a species of mouse
melli, *s.* wattle tree
mena, *s.* eye
mena, theft, a word that expresses the idea of hiding in a variety of ways; as *mena karnko,* a strange house not seen before
mena galba, the depression below the eye
menakaka
menakanya, eye stone, of hard eyes, not easily weeping, unfeeling
mena kurto, having sore eyes
menalla, *adj.* invisible; as *menalla wilya padnatao,* the soul is invisible

mena mú, anything that one is not allowed to see, sacred
menamulka, *s.* tear
menanda. *adv.* unseen, clandestine
mena ngalla, thievish
mena nganta, visible, apparent, plain
mena ngurtiti, *v.* to accuse, make ashamed
mena palkata, *v.* to look, open one's eyes
menata, *v.* to take away unseen, to steal
menangutu, *v.* to hide, conceal
menaringutu, *v.* ditto *ngara menaringutu* to belie
menaringarriti, *v.* to deny
menawaiata, *v.* to prevaricate
menawaiangarriti, *v.* to deny, prevaricate
mena wakka, honest, not theivish
menawalbo, (eye-bone) of a strong eye, i.e. not sleepy, awake
mena walka,
mena wapo, eye-covered, i.e. blind
menayalga, *s.* eyelid, properly eye skin
mena yalga willara, having no eyelids
mena yernbi or } *s.* eyelid
mena yernbinye }
mena yulkata, *v.* to weep, shed tears
mende, *s.* net bag, basket
menka, *s.* a shrub growing on the sandy coast, and bearing a pod similar to French beans
métullu, *s.* a species of fish, shellfish
mettullu pira, *s.* a kind of shell
metye, *s.* name; as *nunko wantye metye?* what is your name?
meya, *s.* sleep
meya ngarrara, feigning sleep, pretending to be asleep
meya wanniti, *v.* to sleep
meya nniti, *v.* to be sleepy
mialla=mena, *s.* eye
midla, *s.* a wooden lever to throw spears with wommarra,

midlilbelli, double; as *midlilbelli yendata*, *v.* to double fold up
midliti, *v.* to pinch
milka, *adj.* thick; as *kurta milka*
milkarra=kallawidna
milkitye, *s.* poinard, dagger, also used for key
milla, *adj.* bad, wicked, evil
millaniti, *v.* to be or become bad
millari, *s.* a kind of rushes, of which the natives make their net bags
millari, yarnu, *s.* a net made of *millari* rushes
milli, *s.* name of the seventh child,if a male
milliti, *v.* to do, make, dig up
millingarriti, *v.* to busy oneself, to handle, work
milta, kanya, *s.* a kind of stone, slate
milti, *s.* a sort of red ochre used for ornament
miltyinye, *s.* bat
mindi mindi, gently, stealthily
minmirri, swift, quick; as *kaya ikarnitao mira* the spear flies swiftly
mingka, sore, sick, ill
mingkarriti, *v.* to become sore, ill
minna=pulyo
minna, *s.* navel
minna, *s.* a species of stingray
minnara, *s.* a kind of eatable berry
minnarka, far, at a distance; as *minnarka palkatao*
minnangutu, *v.* to watch a bird or animal, it jumps far
minnirriti, *v.* to produce a humming sort of noise like the *witarna*
mínngatta, *s.* a species of fish
minno, *s.* a shrub bearing an edible fruit, *menku mirrinye*
mintapa, witch craft, supernatural power; as *kukata mintapa ilkanna*, the *kukata* are possessed of witch craft
mintidli, as *yakkudla mintidli*, I don't know
mintyilli, as *nganna mintyili*, an approbrious expression
mintyuru *affix.* nice, particular; as *palta mintyuru* par-

ticular with one's cloths, stingy
minyara, *adj.* cool
minyarriti, *v.* to cool, be cold
minye=mirrarri, the Orion
mirkapa, *s.* a person bereft of a relative, mourner
mirkarriti, *v.* to startle, being taken by surprise
mirkarringutu, *v.* to surprise, frighten
mirko, as *mirkomirko pinnat ai,* I shake weakly
mirra, as *mirrangukata parchi nunkurnura,* quick, swift
mirrara, swamp, bog, mortar ; as *mirraranga karpa karpatanna,* they build houses with mortar
mirrarri, *s.* the Orion, a constellation
mirrarri, *s.* pimple
mirrata, *v.* to rub, scratch
mirraütu, *v.a.* to sprinkle oneself all over with sand to assuage one's thirst
mirreri, *adj.* itchy, prurient ; as *palba mirreri*
mirriki or *mirriki miririki*
mirrilti, *s.* a white delicate species of flower
mirrinye, an *affix* or *adj.* like, similar ; as *warru mirrinye pilla mirrinye,* similar to a kangaroo, to an oppossum
mirrinye yura, a native, the reverse of *mundultu yura,* a European
mirru, *s.* large, grown up.
mirrurriti, *v.* to grow
mita, *s.* a species of ant, or ant heap, the grubs of which the natives eat
miti, fast, firm ; as *miti pirrinyit'atto,* I hold it fast
miyerta, *s.* a man of mature age, *vir*
mokalla, as *mai makalla maiworna,* satiated with food
mokalla yulalyiti, *v.* to fret, sympathize
mokanya, as *mokayna kundata,* to beat so as to produce swelling
moko, *s.* knot, knob, button, any round and hard substance
moko irta, button bird, a small species of bird
mokuntu, *adj.* spotted

mona, *s.* the net with which boys of the age of about sixteen or eighteen (pardnapa's) secure their hair, hat, cap

mudla, *s.* nose, the extreme point of any thing, point of land

mudlababmata, *v.* to sneeze

mudlailta, insolent, impudent, *nasutus*

mudlannu, *s.* a large species of snake, carpet snake

mudla parkata, *v.* to blow the nose

mudlata, *v.* to make love, court

mudlayappa, *s.* nostril

mudlayurkuru, *s.* mucus of the nose

mudlirirri, *s.* calm, still weather

muinma, *adj.* fat, corpulent

mukurbo, *s.* envy, jealousy; as *paru murkubo,* envy about meat

mukurbo yabmiti, *v.* to scold, abuse, being envious or jealous

mulka, *s.* tear, cry, lamentation

mulka nungkutu, to hold a lementation

mulla, *adj.* dry, dry land, *terra firma*

mullai, as *mullai karkalla mirrinye,* the mullai is similar to the native fig

mullanniti, *s.* to be or become dry

mullaru, *s.* flood, tide

mulla-utu, *v.* to scratch like a dog, to burrow

mullu, *adj.* ripe; as *karkalla mullu,* ripe fig

mullullullu, panting, blowing; as *mullullullu ngukata,* to run one's self out of breath

mulpata, *v,* to save, reserve, to rub out, cut, reap?

multyuru, *s.* intestines, bowels

mulu, *s.* leech

mundalya, *adj.* sweet, nice; as *paru mundalya,* the meat (is) nice

mundalyabmiti, *v.* to be fond of; *ninna mundulyabmiti kuyurkururu*

mundultu, European; *mundultu yura,* a European dog,&c.

mundultiti or } to become a European or white man, to
mundulturriti } live in European manner

mundütya, at once, quick; *mundutya wittiti, mundütya ngukata,* to dig, go at once or directly

mungaltiti, *v.* to be satisfied; as *mungaltiti maiinga* to be satisfied with food

mungaltanna, *n.pr.* of an Island in Spencer's Gulf; as *wilyarri ikkatanna mungaltannanga,* the souls live or reside in Mungaltanna

mungarra, *adj.* still, silent

mungkullu, *s.* staff, mast

mungkulyu, *pinnare bairi mai*

muni, *s.* a small black snake

munkunko, *s.* shoulder

munka, or *munka karnko,* the layer or cover of an animal

munna, *s.* chest, breast

munna mantyarri, *adj.* brave, bold

munmalla, bruised all over, *munmalla walbo pittata,* to pound the bones in order to suck the marrow out

munna, *s.* jealously

munnanga paityanniti, *v.* to be enraged, jealousy

munnaka, *s.* name of the fourth child if a female

munni, *s.* name of the fourth child if a male

munniti or } *v.* as *worna munniti,* to have a disordered
munnimunniti } stomach, to heave, pant, have fever

munnikkiti, *v.* to hiccup

munno, *adj.* blunt, dogged; *idna munno,* having short toes, *kadla munno,* dogged tail

munnudnutu, *v.* to sink in, bog

munnu munnu, at once; as *munnu munnu wittikki, kutta nurreri,* did at once, not long, i.e. finish what you have to dig and be not long about it

munnumunnirriti } *v.* to be tired of; as *ngai tolai inga*
munnumunniti } *mannum,* I am tired of pinguins

munta, *adj.* all, the whole

muntyanta, *s.* brother in-law

muntyalla, *s.* manducating

muntyo=kunyo, dead
munu, *s.* stubble
munu, *s.* a venomous sea animal, often found dead on the sea beach
munyanna, *s.* mustache
munyarra, *s.* a small species of fish
murdla=mulla, *murdla yura ikkatao karngunga,* the man sits dry in the house
muriti, *v.* to wipe ?
muringutu, *v.* ditto
murringarriti, *v.* ditto
murka, *s.* yolk of an egg
murkilli, *adj.* as *worri murkill imurri*
murkurkurko, gradual, swelling
murkunkiti, *v.* to swell
murkiti, *v.* to assemble
murra, *affix ;* as *paru murra.* a good hunter
murreri, *adj.* in health, well, healthy
murreriti, *v.* to be healthy, well
murreringutu, *v.a.* to make well, mend, as *gadla murreringutu,* to mend the fire
murrerinye, *s.* a species of bird
murri, together ; as *murri ngalgumarrinyelbo,* let us eat together
murrippi, *s.* ebb tide, low water, shoal, sand bank
murru, *adj.* soft, yielding
murru, sand, soil, ashes
murrunyu, not strong, or lasting, breakable ; *murrungu palta*
murrullu kauo, water in the sand
murrumparriti, *v.* to live on the ground, creep like snakes, &c.
murti, *s.* salmon, a species of fish
murtilli, *adj.* stiff, hard ; as *kakka murtilli,* a hard head, i.e. blockhead
murtilliti, *v.* to be stiff ; as *kudna murtilliti,* to be costive

murtiti, *v.* to rejoice, exult, shout; as at sight of a shoal of fish, or of other game, when the natives will express their joy by saying: *ngaitye kuya, ngaitye kuya,* my fish, my fish; or *ngaitye paru, ngaitye paru,* my game, my game, &c., &c.
muwai, *s.* an edible kind of berry
muwarriti, *v.* to be employed in, to remain or stop; as *kuyanga yurarri muwarritanna,* the men are employed in catching fish
muwaringutu, *v.* to wait, await, to delay
murtu, different, separate; as *murtu ngai nungkakka mai,* give me (my) food separate
murtuitya, ditto
murtünyu, *s.* a species of fish
mutya, *adj.* ripe
muyu, *s.* back
muyunga ikkata, to sit on the back, i.e. to ride
muyunnarra, *adj.* safe, unharmed, preserved; as *muyunnara kauo marroba padnatao mirriye,* a native can travel safe without water
muyukartu, *adj.* very desirous, greedy; as *mai muyukartu*
muyukartukartu, out of breath, panting
muyukartukarturriti, to be out of breath, blowing
muyu wawutu, to breath heavily, to be out of breath

N

NAI, *adv.* first; as *kauo nai kattikka,* first fetch water
naieri, *s.* the sky, heaven
nakkulpiti, *v.* to look for, seek
nakkungarriti, *v.* to be of dim sight, to be on the point of dying
nakkuttu, *v.* to see, understand, know
nalbata, *v.* to bend
nalka, right, just; as *nuro nalka ngai pallanna,* you named me right; *nalka kundaintyanna ngarbi malbu mannu para* justly have they killed, *ngarbi,* a great murderer he
nallanta, *adv.* loud; as *nallanta wiliti, v.* to laugh loud

nalara, moving, restless ; as *nalara yuwatao, warri yoko* the vessel pitches
nallata, *v.* to break, sever ; *karteti nallata,* to marry
naltiti, *v.* to stir ; as *gadla naltiti,* to stir the fire
naltyata, *v.* to feel about, grope ; as in a hole for game
nalya, *s.* lock, ringlet ; as *kakka nalyaranna,* a curly head of hair
nalyarinye, as *kakka nalyarinya,* curled hair
nambarni, *adv.* a little while ago, this way, hither
nambarriti, *v.* to cover oneself
nambata, *v.* to cover
nambingarriti, *v.* to lick
nambiti, *v.* to lick
namminni, how many
nanganna=maialla, never mind, let be
nangka=ningka
nangka=milla, bad
nani, harmless, lightly ; as *nani paiatarru wabmanya,* the bite of the *wabna* snake is harmless
nankata, *v.* to taste, immitate
nanna, wrong, bad ; as *nanna nganninguntyaru nuralli Kungkanga,* badly has Kungkanga guided you
nanni=inna, this
nantiti, *v.* to whine, lament ; as *nantitao yura yadni ; ngaitye midla ngeirtye midla nallaintyar'atto,* a man laments thus : my midla, my midla, I could break it
nanya, *adj.* lean, ugly
nara, i.e. *wilya kunyo,* ghost or departed soul
naralya, *s.* ditto
narna, near, close to ; as *nurkurni narna,* close to thee
narranda, *adj.* fast tough
narranditi, *v.* to be fast, tough
narru narru, quick ; as *narru ngukakka,* go quick
natta, *s.* back, spine, ridge, *wortanna natta,* ridge of the sea, i.e. wave
nauwe=nganna, what, who
nauwindi=ngannaru, what for

nauo or, nawo, } the national name of the native tribe inhabiting the country about Coffin's Bay
nemi,=yalluyu, a species of fish
nemi, *s,* lip
nemi pendulliti, *v.* to let one's lip hang down, to look sour, sullen
nengki, *s.* seal
nidlata, *v.* to stop remain; as *ngai karnkunge nidlata,* I shall stop in the house, i.e. at hcme
nikarra, *adj.* ripe; as *nikarra ngallitao mai yurra yullurungu*
nilai, *s.* an edible species of root
nilkata, *v.* to squeeze
niltenni, *s.* a small species of snake
niltyarra,
ningka, *interj.* let see, give me
nimmata, *v.* to pinch, touch, feel, squeezc; as *pendunnu nimmata*
ninmilye, *s.* a water bird
ninna, *pron.* thou
ninga ningariti, *v.* to imitate
ninka palla, *s.* spouse, concubine
nunka palliti, ditto
ninnata, *v.* to accuse, suspect
nintyalla warnitao kauo,
nintyattalla, perhaps, quick; as *nintyatalla parreri ngukatao,* he goes perhaps down
nintye, so, thus, such; as *ninna kappara worta,* you are a lazy fellow, *nintye ninna kutyo,* such are you also
nintyernanna, enough, sufficient
nirrariti, *v.* to assemble
niri, *s.* a part of the abdomen
nirkiriti,
nita, *s.* spring, fountain
nita kayu, *s.* spring water
niyarra, *s.* glutinous kind of berries, eaten roasted

nondo, *s.* a shrub bearing an edible fruit, in the shape of beans, which the natives roast between heated stones
nondomai, *s.* the fruit of the nondo
nudla, *s.* the large bag carried by the woman
nudlutu, *v.* to put in, imprison, bury
nukunnu, *s.* national name of a native tribe inhabiting the country about the head of Spencer's Gulf
nulkünyu, *s.* the eggs of lice, nits
nundalla. *n.pr.* Thistle Island
nungkunturrutu, *v.* to give; *mai nungkunturrukka*
nungkutu, *v.* to give, impart, to shoot; as *kattanga puru kungkukku* shoot the animal
nungkurriti, *v.* ditto
nungkulputu, *v.* to infect
nungkung karriti. *v.* to confess lie on one side
nungurru, careful, not wasting; as *nungurru kundatanna mai mundulturringe kutta batta battarrini*, the Europeans beat out the food (wheat) carefully, not spilling any
nunkurni, of thee
nunko, thy, thine, of thee
nunkurninge, with thee
nunkurnuru, towards thee
nunata, *v.* to push
nunangarriti ngungkurninyinge, to lie sleeping
nunantata, *v.* to tie up
nunnata, *v.* to swallow, consume; as *kartetinge nunna tarru yerdli*
nunnarriti, *v.* to swallow
nunno, thou, the agent; as *ngannuru nunno ai kundata*, why dos't thou beat me?
nunyara, surviving, or restored to health; as *nunyara ikkata, kayabidni kutta padlutu*, he will survive, he wont die of the spear wound
nunyarriti, *v.* to recover, survive
nunyata, *v.* to make wet and cold; as *kauunga nunyatarru yura*, rain makes a man wet
nuralli, *pron.* second person, *plur.* ye, you

nurallidni, of, or from you
nurallidninge. with you
nurallidniru, toward you
nuralluru, of you, your
nurbata, *v.* to catch, lay hold
nurbarriti, *v.* as *kunyo nurbarriti*
nurko, of thee, thy
nurkurni, from thee
nurkurninge, with thee
nurkurniru, towards thee
nurnara, *s.* low gum scrub
nurni, *s.* neck, nape
nurnikkiti, *v.* to break the neck of an animal, extinguish it's life
nurni marti, *s.* neck scar, a fleshy knob in the necks of the male natives produced by tattooing
nurni moko, ditto
nurni malka, thick throat, opprobrious
nuro, thou, the form used by father and children
nurnpiti, *v.* to be with, remain
nurnpinyutu, *v.a.* to approach
nurreri, far away : for a long time, *nurreri ngukanaına*, they are gone far away
nurrerinye, *adj,* distant, remote
nurru, *s.* a species of snake, black snake
nurti, *s.* knapsack, net bag, carried by men
nurtutu, *v.* to fill, press in, *paipa nurtutu* to fill the pipe
nurtungarriti, *v.* to rub ; as *mena nurtungarriti,* to rub one's eyes
nutu, false, incorrect, joking
nutu, wanggata, to make an unfounded statement
nutu-ngalli, sad, sorry
nuwalla, you two
nuwallidni, of, from you two
nuwallidninge, with you two
nuwallidnuru, towards you two
nuwalluru, of you two, your

nuwadnaga, you two, viz. *ngammanna* and *wintya*, uncle and nephew, husband and wife
nuwadnagadni, of, from you two
nuwadnagadninge, with you two
nuwadnagadnuru, towards you two
nuwadnagguru, of you two, your
nuwarinye, you two, father and child
nuwarinyidni, of, from you two
nuwarinyidninge, with you two
nuwarinyidnuru, towards you two
nuwarinyuru, of you two, your
nuwirri=nurreri, far away
nuwutu, *v.* to stab
nga, *adv.* yes
ngabitye, not eatable, useless
ngadlaga, we two, (*ngammanna* and *wintya*)
ngadlagadni, of, from us two
ngadlagadninge, with us two
ngadlagadnuru, towards us two
ngadlagguru, of us two, our
ngadlamba, *s.* an actor in a native ceremony
ngadli, *pron.* dual, we two
ngadlidni, of, from us two
ngadlidninge, with us two
ngadlidnuru, towards us two
ngadluru, of us two, our
ngadlirriti, *v.* to be sad, sorry
ngadluru, the fleshy part of the abdomen
ngai. *pron.* first person, *sing.* I
ngaityaba, *s.* younger brother
ngaityara, *s* hunting party In summer when food is plentiful and the grass sufficiently dry to burn, the natives assemble in large numbers for the purpose of hunting on a large scale, by selecting whole districts of country and surrounding the game upon it
ngaityaranga ngukata, to go upon a hunting expedition
ngaitye, my, mine

ngaityurni, of or from me
ngaityurninge, with
ngaityurniru, towards me
ngakunya, acter
ngakunya parti, ditto
ngakunyu, *s.* rectum
ngala, the thick part of the thigh
ngalapa, *s.* lap
ngalballiti, *v.* as *marni ngurko ngalballitao*
ngalbata, *v.* to enter, go down
ngalbarriti, *v.* to stoop, creep through or under
ngalgutu, *v.* to eat
ngalgungutu, *v.a.* to make or let eat; as *ngai iti wortallo mai murtu ngalgungutanna.*
ngalku, i.e. *wadlata pinnaranga yuwatao,* a tree standing in a lake
ngalla, much, plenty, many
ngallai, *s.* name of the ninth child if a male
ngallka, *s.* name of the ninth child if a female
ngallanniti, to become large, grow
ngallanningutu, to make grow, increase
ngalli, *s.* liver. The natives consider the liver as the seat of the feelings, wherefore many compounds are formed with it.
ngalli-bakka
ngalli bakkamba, *adj.* sympathizing
ngallibakkambiti, *v.* to relent, sympathize
ngalli kuri kariti, *v.* to sympathize
ngalli ngutarriti, *v.* to grieve, fret
ngalli parnkato
ngalli wapperriti, *v.* to feel anxious
ngalli wawutu, *v.* to be sad dejected
ngalli yaltata, to rejoice, exult
ngallira, a friend, confident, *ngallira yura*
ngalliti, *v.* strong, able; to burn, take fire
ngalta worta, Tod River, so far as salt
ngaltya, sweet, eatable, drinkable

ngalu
ngalyakka, brackish
ngamma, *s.* female breast, milk
ngammaityu, mother
ngammama, *s.* uncle
ngammata, *v.* to go, run, come
ngammangutu, *v.* to make come, fetch
ngammantutu, *v.* to keep going, running
ngammi, *s.* mother
ngammiri, *s.* orphan, a person bereft of his parent
ngammirünye, *s.* two brothers, a pair of brothers
ngammiti, a female animal, having born young ones
ngampa, *s.* an edible species of root
ngampa wallara, *s.* a yellow flower
ngampurko, *s.* a root smaller than the *ngampa*
ngandalla, *s.* a species of kangaroo rat
nganderi, of different colors, spotted
ngandi, *s.* sunshine, light, the reverse of *madlo,* shade
ngando, *s.* upper arm
ngandowalbo, strong-armed, powerful
ngangkalla, *s.* stomach
ngangkalla, *s.* male bird, cock, of any species
ngangkurninye, side, sleeping posture
ngangunge, *s.* chin
nganiti, *v.* to return
nganingutu, *v.* to send, carry back
nganinganningutu, take back; as *yarru ikkai, mai maialla ngalgunnu wakko wittintyaranna, nganinganingutu,* let me sit down, take the food back and let it not be eaten, as they have not dug
nganka, interference in a quarrel, prevention of a fight protection from aggression
nganka worta, a person interfering, preventing a fight, protector
nganka yabmiti, to remonstrate, interfere
ngankuru, whose

ngankurni, of, from whom
ngankurninge, with whom
ngankurnuru, to whom
nganna, *pron.* interrog, who, what
nganna, *s.* forehead
ngannabunta, opprobricus expression
ngannalli, musk duck
ngannanda, *adj.* friendly, hospitable
ngannanna, *s.* palate, roof of the mouth
ngannara, *s.* north-east wind
ngannaru, to what purpose, why
ngannayalta, opprobrious term, knitted brows
ngannelli, *s.* a species of water bird
nganninni, who or what is it, was it, let me see, a soliloquising phrase
ngannumba, *s.* cave, hole in rocks
ngannunganuu, coming gradually back
ngannunge, *pron.* who, the agent; as *ngannunge ninna yernbaintyarru*, who has sent you?
ngantungantu, fast, secure; as *karnko ngantungantu*, prison
ngantya, dear, sweet, pretty
ngantyangantya, ditto, very dear
ngantyarniti, *v.* as *ngantyarniti pallara yerdlinnuru*, the woman is making up to the husband, endearing herself to him
ngantyangantyarringutu, *v.a.* to treat kindly
nganyara, sweet
nganyata, *v.* to praise, commend
ngappa, fat, corpulent
ngappalya, *s.* saliva
ngappalyarriti, *s.* to be salivated, foam
ngappata *s.* fat
ngappiriti, *s.* daughter
ngarka, incision, (see *worringarka*
ngarkabakko, *s.* wattle-bird
ngarkarko, *s.* species of wattle-bird

ngarkenni, beyond, on the opposite side
ngarkiri, *s.* head dress, the tying of the hair with an oppossum hair girdle
ngarkundinye, a species of bird; *yurdne pitara, mungkulyu ngalgotarru,* redbreast
ngarnka, *s.* beard
ngarnka paita, to bite the beard, an expression of great fury
ngarnkidi, *s.* a kind of shell, used for peeling roots
ngarra, error, deception, falsehood, lie, wrong, astray
ngarradda, *adj.* clear, transparent
ngarradditi, *v.* to be clear, transparent, settle
ngarrakungarriti, *v.* to be pretty
ngarralbata, *v.* to miss, not hit the mark
ngarra mankutu, *v.* to lead astray
ngarra nungkutu, *v.* to deceive, tantalize, viz. to promise and not give; as *mai ngarra ai nungkunnarru,* he did not give me food, gammoned me
ngarrara, *adj.* feigning, pretending
ngarrata, *v.* to conceive, hatch, bring forth
ngarrarriti, *v.* to increase, multiply
ngarrarrita, *s.* heap; *kutta kubmanna ngarrarta ngalla ngarrata*
ngarra wangatta, to tell a falsehood
ngarra yappa, liar
ngarra yarnata, to belie, deceive; as *nunno ngai ngarra yarnanna,* you did belie me
ngarri, *s.* sight, face
ngarrilli, *adj.* high, tall; as *kurdli ngarrilli,* tall sheoak
ngarrinye, *pron. dual,* we two father and son
ngarrinyidni, of, from us two
ngarrinyidninge, with us two
ngarrinyidnuru, towards us two
ngarrinyuru, of us two, our
ngarrinyelbo, *pron. plur.* we
ngarrinyelburni, of, from us
ngarrinyelburninye, with us

ngarrinyelburniru, towards us
ngarrinyelburu, of us, our
ngarrinyi, *s.* level; as *ngarrinyinyi kuri kuri ngakannao bebe,* the egg ran round on the level
ngarru, *s.* breaker, roller
ngarru, circle, enclosure; as *ngarrungu willitanna ngarrinyelbo,* they will surround and spear us
ngarruru, *s.* an edible kind of root
ngarta, *s.* region about the genitals
ngarta putti, hair about the genitals
ngartara, *s.* bank, precipice
ngatto, *pron.* I the agent
ngattutu, *v.* to weep, cry, howl
ngattungutu, *v.a.* to weep for, lament, bewail
ngauurru, shallow
ngauwalla, word language, dialect; as *Parnkalla ngauwalla,* the Parnkalla dialect
ngauwalla marru, a different dialect
ngauwalla wadli wadli, a person speaking incorrectly
ngauwirri, about, round; *ngauwirri ngukakka,* go round
ngauwirrauwirri, ditto
ngauwirriti, *s.* to go round, double
ngkalli, *an affix* indicating a question; as *wibma ngkalli* already?
ngudityc, yon, yonder
ngudityinge, in yon place, direction
ngudlalli, *s.* a mother, a woman having born children
ngudli, *s.* pouch of the kangaroo and other marsupial animals
ngukaulku, growing; as *ngarnka pullinye ngukaulku,* fat, or grease makes the beard grow
ngukata, *v.* to go, walk
ngukeli, s. a small kind of native figs
ngukurko, blister, pimple
ngulbu, *s.* a species of fungus
ngulko, *s.* cheek
ngulluko, *s.* the fat near the genitals of the kangaroo

ngulta, *s.* coverlet over the male pubes
ngultapa, s youth, young man
nguctu, importunate, bold, greedy ; *mai ngultu,* clamourous for food
ngultunniti, *v.* to be bold, reckless
ngultu wittiti, *v.* to spear ruthlessly
ngulu, *s.* knee joint, hough
ngumiti, *v.* to tie round, fasten
ngummunnummunnu, *s.* spring, fountain
ngunda, tight, whole ; as *kauo ngunda,* water tight or proof
ngundunyu, *adj.* broad, thick ; as *bullorki nganna ngundunyu*
ngunna, *pron.* demonstrative, that, you, *ngunna yura, inna yura,* that man, this man
ngunnara, yonder
ngunnaramba, ditto
ngunningutu, *v.a.* to show, offer, present
ngunningunningutu, *v.* to carry home
ngunniti, *v.* to motion with the hand, beckon to come
ngunnirriti, *v.* to show with hand, count
nguntinguntirriti, *v.* to whirl, twirl ; as *karra nguntinguntirritao pulba, yarru mirrinye,* high whirls the dust, like a whirlwind
ngunya, over ripe, decayed, *karkalla ngunya,* the figs (are) over ripe
ngunyalla, *adj.* as *yurre ngunyalla,* mindful
ngupi, *s.* darkness, pitch dark night
ngupinniti, to be dark
ngupinningutu, *v.a.* to make dark,
ngupurrupurriti, *v.* to be pitch dark ; *ngupurrupurrintyaranga gadla kattitarru,* he carries a firestick because it is pitch dark
ngurata, *v.* to turn round, throw the waddy, grind, draw water, &c.
ngurdli, crooked
ngurdlingurdli, round about, serpentine

ngurdlirriti, to bore turn round, squeeze
nguriti, *v. paityanna nguriti,* to quarrel, fall out
ngurko, sap
nurgok mai, the flower of a very small shrub, which tastes very sweet; by shaking the stem the flowers drop and the natives often collect a considerable quantity of them
ngurko, deep, abyss; *ngurko kauo,*an unfathomable water
ngurkunniti, *v.* to be happy, rejoice
ngurrinniti, *v.* to be sore, running; as *mena ngurrinniti yataranga,* the eye is running, being hurt by a blade of grass
ngurro, hair, *kakka ngurro*
ngurtiti, *v.* to accuse
ngurtu, *s.* cheek
ngutata,, *v.* to loosen, untie, break
ngutarriti, *v.* to break out; as *paitya ngutarrity,* to begin quarrelling
ngutha, yonder, *ngutha warradla* yonder, away
nguthatu, in yonder direction
nguwata, *v.* to ask, entreat, pray
nguwangutu, *v.a.* to implore, ask for
nguwangarriti, *v.* to entreat
nguyarriti, *v.* to shake one's leg, dance

P

Pá, pá, *interj.* hush, hst
pa, an *affix,* as *marnitapa,* very good, *mantyarrappa,* very fine
pabmi, *s.* a small bag, purse
pabmi, *s.* dirt; *kudna pabmi*
padityi } strange, unknown
padityidli }
padlata, *v.* to wash
padlarriti, *v.* to play
padla padlarindi, play, joke
padlo, *pron.* he, she, it; as *padlo ngai mai kutta nung*

kunnarru, he did not give me food
padlutu, *v.* to die, be extinguished; *gadla padluntyao,* the fire is gone out
padlunyunu, all, the whole
padnata, *v.* to go. This word is often used where the English language would require the auxiliary verb *to be*; as *ninna yurreyappu padnata?* you are aware? *ngai kubmunna padnata,* I am alone, i.e. have no relatives
padnantutu, *v.* to keep walking about
padnangkutu, *v.* to make go, send; as *padnangkutu kubmanna,* he sends me alone
pai alla, cold
pai alliti, *v.* to be cold
paiata, *v.* to bite
pai irkiti, *v.* to feel acute pain, suffer intensely
pailba, *s.* bush, shrub
paitya, angry, hostile, quarrel, fight
paitya ngalla, very angery, quarrelsome
paityando, fierce, strong, able; as *paityando kundakka,* strike fiercely, hit hard
paityanniti, *v* to be or become angry
paityanningutu, *v.* to attack, quarrel with
paityarta, noxious, dangerous, venomous
paityarta wadlata, thorn bush
paityartiti, *v.* to hurt, injure, endanger
paitya yalturu, warlike, brave
palba, *s.* ticklish, ticklishness
palba, *s.* dry grass, rubbish; as *gadla palba,* combustible matter
palballa, ditto, as *palballa piyirritao bukarranga,* the grass withers from the heat
palbanniti, *v.* to be ticklish, itchy
palkanyalla, whitish, grey; as *ngarnka palkanyalla.* white or grey beard
palkárra, white, *palkarra yura,* a white man
palkara, a species of eucalyptus, blue gum
palkata, to shine, extend, jump, run; *warra palkatao*

ngaitye mena, far extend my eye, was the remarks of a native when let out of prison

palkerrintye, *s.* a species of bird, shrike

palkiti, *v.* to crackle; as *gadla palkitao*, the fire crackles

palkirriti, *v.* to crack, break, become loose; as *kakkalle palkirritao mai madlanga*, the girdle becomes loose for want of food

palkirringutu, *v.a.* to crack, break, as an egg, &c.

palkurru, yellowish, cream colored

palko, *s.* knee pan

palla, level, or fertile; as *palla yerta*, fertile or level land

pallai, as *kayapallai*

pallakarriti, to rise, get up, hasten; as *pallakarritao yura padnayuru*, the man hastens to go

pallanna, *n.pr.* of a place, the fountain

pallanniti, *v.* to produce, pronounce, name

pallanningarriti, *v.* to be named, have the name

pallara, *s.* woman, dual; *pallalbelli, plur. pallarri*, women

pallarra, light, candle, seeing; as *ngai mena pallarra, kutta mena wapo ngai*, I can see, I am not blind

pallaru, thin; as *kadla murniti, kutta kurta pallaru*

pallarri, (woman) a constellation, the Pleiades

pallarriti, *s.* to shine, be lighted, enlightened; as *yullupunge yura pallarritao*, by truth a man becomes enlightened

pallarringutu, *v.a.* to enlighten, instruct, inform

pallata, *v.* to pull, draw, let loose, start

pallapallata, *v.* to jerk one's tongue, express surprise

palli, *s.* flank, groin

palpanda, plain, even, smooth

palparni, a kind of rush or tree

palparta, *s.* the fag ends of the *kangara* or grass tree roots; that part of the grass tree which grows above ground and cannot be eaten. When *kangara* is in season, the country is strewed with this *palparta* and the natives are easily tracked by it.

palpata, *v.* to move, shift; as ***madluru palpakka,*** move into the shade
pulta, cloak, clothing
paltalta purdnu, the flower of the native geranium
palta piyi, thin clothing, shirts
paltarra, *s.* gum scrub
paltata, to knock, thrust, beget
paltimbiti, *v.a.* to broil, roast; as ***kuya paltimbitanna,*** they are broiling fish
paltu, *s.* sound, noise
paltu babmantiti, *v.* to sound, make a noise
paltu paltu, decayed, rotten
palturriti, *v.* to diminish, decrease
paltyarra, *s.* a species of rat
paluworra, *s.* light clouds in a hot day, haze
palya or palyapalya, cool breeze, evening breeze
palyamba, feeble, weak; as *marra palyamba*
palyo, slowly, gently
pana, crack, crevice, gap, wrinkle
pana kulakularriti, *v.* to crack burst
pana gudna, a person bleeding, letting blood
pandanya, striped, rifled, florted
pandarri, *s.* sky, heaven
pangarriti, *v.* to be ripe, ripen
pangkurru, weak, sick
pangkurriti, *v.* to be sunburnt, brown
paniti, *v.* to dig, burrow, bury
panna, he, she, it
pannai, *s.* a species of fungus
pannara, *s.* knee cap, patella
pannara, *s.* a stone with a rough surface used as a rasp in sharpening the grubbing sticks
pannitye, he, she, it, that there
pannityinge, in that, there
pannityuru, that way, thither
pannu, even,flat, level
pannüntyaru, of him, his

panta, brackish, salt, bitter
panta kauo, fermented liquor, wine, spirits
pantapantarriti, *v*, to be thirsty
panyaltiti, *v.* to be thirsty
pappa, *v.a.* young one, pup, whelp ; *worru pappa,* joey
pappalya, ditto
papparniti, to become a young one, i.e. be born
papparnko, *s.* old acquaintance, friend
papparta, opposite or near ; *karnko papparta* opposite the house
pappi, *s.* father
pappiranye, father and son
pappullu, *s.* reins, kidneys
pará, he, she, it, this word occurs only at the end of a sentence ; as *kundakka pará,* strike him
pardla, *s.* ancle
pardna, *s.* a species of lizard
pardnapa, *s.* a circumcised youth, distiguished by having his long hair secured in a netting
pardnapparu, *s.* a young forward fellow
pardni, hither, this way
pardnitye, this here
pardnityinge, here
parkata, *v.* to shake, dust, as clothes, &c.
parnata, *v.* to push, drive, scare away
parnbaparnbarriti, *v.* to reel, stumble
parnbilli, as *mena parnbilli,* squinting
parndabirru, *s.* bozenbird
parndalla, *s.* lime
parndalla kadnya, limestone
parndanna, *s.* a kind of gum scrub
parnda worra
parndeti, *v.* scar, lump
parnipinye, *s.* wart
parnkalla, *s.* national name of the native tribes, inhabiting the western coast of Spencer's Gulf and the adjacent country

parnkalla ngaurralla, *s* the *Parnkalla* dialect
parnkalliti, *v.* to be Parnkalla, to speak the Parnkalla language ; as *ngarrinyelbudninge ninna Parnkalliti,* through us or with us you are *Parnkalla,* i.e. you have learned the language from us
parnkata, *v.* as *ngalli parnkata*
parnkumbu, *s. crepitus ventri*
parnma, *s.* chip ; as *kurdli parnma,* chip of sheoak
parnma, *adv.* ere before
parnmanna, ditto before hand ; as *parnmanna mai nungkukka,* give the food befere hand
parpa, *s.* South
parra, *s.* thing, something ; as *parra kutyo ninna wangganna,* you said something else
parra, *s.* fork of a tree
parradla, *adj.* still, unmoved ; as *parradla yuwattao warrinyoka murdlirinyi*
parrakutyu, *adj.* until ; as *ninna Adelaidiru parrakutyungu ngukaintyaranga yalgaltanga kanaru* ; *yalgalta* may wait till you go to Adelaide
parri, deep, below, river
pàrriri, very ; as *mantyárri parriri,* very fine
parriti, *v.* to disappear be silent
partalye, *s.* scar
partaparta, *s.* brothers in law brothers having one wife
parti, *s.* grub, catipillar, egg
partu, stiff or bent *muyu partu,* stiff backed stooping
partütyuru, as, *madla partütyunu,* long rumped, *kantipartütyuru*
paru, animal, game, meat, as *warruparu* kangaroo meat, *paru ikara manna wondakka,* no game plenty let alone i.e. to be sure
paruntu, deceased dead
parupà, *adv.* very well, do, so ; as *pallarri nudluo' atto parupá,* I shall imprison the women, very well
paruparu, gray
paruparurriti, *s.* to be gray

patha, there
pathar, there
patharu, thither
pathitye, that
patta, as *patta kauo; kauanno wornitao patta kauunga*
pattarnda, open glade, an open plain surrounded by scrub, oasis
pattata, *v.* to scold, abuse, accuse; as *badlo ngai ngan naru pattainyarru,* why did he abuse me?
pattiti, *v.* to be silent wait, consider
paú, a call, halló, cooeè
payipayirriti, *v.* to be exhausted, tired
mingkanga payipayirriti, exhausted by pain
karnbanga payipayirriti, exhausted by hunger
peki, *s.* small dots on shoulder or arm produced by tattooing
peli, as *mita peli* the hardned paste found on the ant heaps, and serving as partitions of the cells
peli, *s.* the white of an egg
pelintya, a yellow flower, retaining its color in its dried state
pelukko, *s.* pit of the stomach
pelupelu, as *yurre pelupelu* not mindful, forgetful
peluru, a hard root growing in the scrub, the thick skin of which is eaten when roasted
penduliti, *v.* as *nemi pendulliti,* to look sour, make mouths
pendunnu, as *pendunnu wittiti pendunnu nimmata*
pengi, *affix.* for, in exchange for, for the value of; *gadla pengi mai nung kutanna,* they give food for firewood
pentye, shoulder blade
penu penu, crooked, clumsy; *kurdli penu penu,* a crooked unsightly sheoak
penyi *s.* smart, pain
penyiti, *v.* to be painful, smart
perru, *adj.* small; as *perru ka'tya,* a small child
peru or perdu, strong, firm fast, immoveable; as *wandurru perru,* a strong tough rope

perudu, *s.* a species of hawk
perutu, *adj.* startled; as *perutu waü ngukutao warru*
perutala, *v.* to be startled, start off
pidlara, *affix.* skilled in, used to, expert; as *yerla pidlara*, skilled in swimming, swimmer
pila, *s.* charcoal
pilalye, fine, pretty?
pilba, little bit, piece; as *mai pilba nungkukk ai* give me a bit of food, in two, to pieces
pildari kintye, a species of bird, plover
pilderilderi, *s.* plover
pilgata, *v.* to open find
pilgalpiti, *v.a.* to open
pillalla, *s.* plate
pilla, *s.* oppossum
pilla putti, oppossum hair
pillara, thin, scarce, scattered; as *kardli pillara*, the she-oaks are scarce
pillarriti, *v.* to be scarce scattered
pillarringutu, *v.a.* to make scarce, diminish, consume: as *mai kuita pillaringutanna*
pilla worta, Mr. Driver's station
piltilye, *s.* spark
piltiti, *v.* to sparkle, crackle; as *gadla piltitao*, the fire throws out sparks
pilturpilturpu, the flashing of a fire stick carried about at night
pirturlpiti, *v.* to light, to carry a light to see by
pilyilye, *s.* butterfly
pilyuru, extensive, wide spread; *gadla pilyuru*, an extensive fire
pimba, coal black, shining black
pinba, pine tree
pinba moko, pine apple
pinda, slow, gentle; as *pinda padnato*
pinba, *s.* cherry tree
pindamai, *s.* cherry fruit

pinda pinda, *s.* large species of fly, horse fly
pinderi, *s.* shears, scissors
pinka, *s.* a small bone near the hip, used for peeling roots knife
pinkinya
pinkyata, to call, name adopt
pinkyangurriti, to be named
pinmanta, not doing the thing promised or desired; as *pinmanta ngukannawo,* he is gone without doing it
pinmanta worta, *s.* a person flinching from his duty, lazy fellow
pinmata, *v.* to refuse, shirk out of it; as *pinmatanna kutyo matt-anga wittiuru,* the others refuse to dig
pinna marra, *s.* a name for a relative
pinnata, *v.* to tremble, quiver, shiver
pinta, *affix.* stingy, tenacious of; as *mai pinta*
pinta, *adv.* through; as *pinta kulata,* to cut through, *pinta ngukata,* to go through, i.e. away
pintata, to poke, pick, prick
pinyapinyata, *v.* to call, hail.
pintya=pentye
pintya kakka, shoulder bone
pípara, *s.* ring tail oppossum
piralla, *s.* black magpye
pirata, *v.* to spread extend; as *gadla pirata,* the fire spreads
piri, *s.* name of the first child, if a boy
piri, enough; as *ngai, piri wangganna,* I have said it often enough
piri or pirthi, as *pirthi malo,* not heading, or noticing; *pirthi malo ngukata,* to forget
piri piri, or pirthi pirthi, ditto
piri manka, *s.* dog fish
piri mepunnu bidni,
piriti, *v.* to be ripe, ripen
pirra, *s.* moon
pirra, *s.* shell, nautilus shell

pirrata, *v.* to pluck
pirri, *s.* forked stick, fork of a tree
pirrinyiti, *v.* to touch, lay hold, detain
pirriti, *v.* to carry in the hand, draw, pull
pirthi pirthi, see piri piri ; as *pirthi pirthi ngattutao ngammi kaityaru,* i.e. it is nothing but the mother crying for the child
pita, *s.* needle case, hollow bone in which is placed the pointed bone used in sewing
pita, *s.* *libido,* lust
pita=ilka, pita manna, pita ngalla — *libidinous*
pitara, *s.* red, *pitara yura,* soldier
pi ta, *v.* to knock, pelt, stamp, kick, *kauunga pitatarru* the n is pelting
p tata, *v.* to knock
piter teri, afraid, cowardly
pitha, *s.* lungs
pitha pitha, ditto
pithara, winded, blown
pithara pithara, ditto
pithara kattu kattu, ditto
pithara kattukatturriti, *v.* to be winded, out of breath
pittiti, *v.* to pick up
pityarri, by and bye ; presently
pityerki, timber, board, door, any smooth piece of wood
pityindi, smooth, soft
pityurnu, scale of fish
piya, as *kurdli piya,* sheoak leaves
piyakularriti, *v.* to be angery, enraged
piyi, *s.* the skin of the human body, any thin skin like matter, as paper, linen, &c.
piyirriti, *v.* to dry up, whither,
piyipiyirriti, to whither, blush, be shy, ashamed
piyipiyirringutu, *v.* to make ashamed, say things to blush at

pudla, *s.* a species of fungus
pudlalye, *s.* a species of parrot, black head
pudlanbi, *pron.* they two, husband and wife ; as *pudlanbi padnamatta,* they two are married, husband and wife
pudli, *s. anus,* the butt end of anything
pudli-irra, afraid, a coward
pudli katteri
pudli narra, bold, brave
pudli punata, *v.* to turn over, roll
pudliti, *v.* to turn upside down. invert, pervert ; as *nunno ngauwalla pudliti,* you pervert the language
pudlirriti, *v.* to turn one's self, change
pudlipudlirriti, *v.* to be giddy ; as *pudlipudlirrini wornin ai* I fell being giddy.
pudli walga, pregnant
pudli yalta, *s.* an opprobrious expression
pudli yappa, an opprobrious expression
pudni, *s.* nest ; *pudni pilgata,* to find a nest
pudnu, *s.* scrub generally
pudnu malla, low scrub, heath
pulba, *s.* dust ; *katta pulba,* gunpowder
pulballa, *s.* sponge
pulbanniti, *v.* to be dusty, mourn, bewail, to shed, drop as seeds
pulbullu, *s.* a kind of berry, native gooseberry
pulburu, dusty
pulka=bulka, old, old man kangaroo
pulkanto, ditto
pulkarra, a species of tree producing a black sort of raisin, manna tree
pulkarra, the raisin of the *pulkarra*
pulki wituru, survivor ; as *ninni pulki wituru padnata,* you will survive
pulku, *s.* mouse
pulku ulku, i.e. *yernbayanbanyalla,* commanding, domineering
pulla, pond ; *kauo pulla*

pulla } warm
pullaitye }

pullakalli=witarna

pullapulla, as *mai yakkatanna yurra pullapullanga*, they seek food in different places

pullamba, *s.* porcupine grass; a crustacious species of fish

pulli, *s.* fat, grease; as *warru pulli*, kangaroo fat

pullimai, a species of fungus

pullipullilbi, *s.* a species of beetle

pulli yukirriti, *v.* to be painted with black paint

pullu, light; *yuranga pullu wayandatarra, paityanga*

pullulyita, sugar

pullulyu, *s.* as *burkalla pallata pullulyu*

pullutu, *v.* to wipe, brush, sweep

pullungarriti, *v.* to wipe one's self, wash

pullunniti, *v.* to be light

pullunnungutu,

pulta, again, oft; as *pulta wanggakka*, say it again

pultinultini, *s.* mustache

pulyo, small, little, young

pulyurkuru, dwarf, pygmy

punailgurriti, *v.* to become loose, undone

punalkiti, *v.* to break, give way

puna punarriti, *v.* to crumble to pieces

punata, *v.* to pull up or down, break; as *karnko punnata* to tear the hut or the house down; to put out; as *worri punnata*

pundarri, *s.* tall scrub generally

punda, *s.* ball, cake, dumpling

pundarningutu, *v.* to make into a ball

punga, inflammable, combustible; as *punga piya*, dry leaves

pungkutu, *v.* to stab, bite, wound, kill

pungkurriti, *v.* to fight, quarrel

pungurru, *s.* dagger, a pointed bone

punnu, lagoon; as *kauo punnu*; rushes, reedy grass

punnu mudla, Kirton Point
punta, *s. paru marnta mirrinye,* i.e. an animal similar to the *marnta*
puntyullu, pin, needle
pura, low scrub, heath
purarra, weak, feeble, tired
purarriti, *v.* to be weak, tired ; *ngai kakka purarriti,* I have head ache
purdli or purli, star
purdnu, *s.* flower, blossom
purdnu, pin, peg, nail, key
purkabidni, an imaginary being ; invisible companion
purlu, porous, light of weight
purlupu, *s.* the string of hair dividing the abdomen into two halfs
purnda, round stone, pebble
purperinye, *s.* a species of bird
purra, *s.* knee
purrai, *s.* a large species of kangaroo rat
purralla, *s.* a species of fungus
purrata, *v.* to call, hail
purri, *s.* hill, mountain
purrelli, *s.* hedge hog fish, any crustacious species of fish
purrenye, *s.* a shrub producing an edible kind of raisin
purri, *adj.* blunt, docked ; as *idna purri,* having short mulitated toes
purro, *adj.* yet, still, applied to anything that remains in its original state ; alive
purrulye, ditto ; *ngai purrulye mai madla,* I am still without food
purrudu, crumb, bit ; *mai purrudu,* crumbs of bread
purrudu purruditi, *v.* to crumble to pieces
purrullu, *s.* quail
purrununnutu, *v.* to cram, eat greedily
putta, *s.* heap
putti *s.* hair

puttinggarri, the hairside of a skin
puttiperinye, *s.* a species of bird
puttutu, *v.* to ache, tear ; *kakka puttutu,* to have head ache
puttungkutu, *v.* to make ache ; as *nunno yura kakka puttungkutu,* you make people head ache
puttütya, in two, to pieces
puttutyaputtutya, ditto
puttutyáttata, *v.* to break to pieces
putye, *s.* mist, fog
puyu, smoke
puyullu, *s.* name for a relative, adoptive son
puyuru, smoky ; as *puyuru kauo,* smoky drizzling rain
puyunniti, *v.* to smoke

T

TA, it, or it is ; as *innaratà* there it is
tadli, *s.* spittle, foam
tadlimbarriti, *v.* to be salivated, to water ; as *tadlimbarrit'ai paru makkanga,* my mouth waters for want of meat
tadlitye, foaming, boiling ; as *kavo tadlitye ngadlitao,* the water boils
taitya, jerk, far ; as *taitya palkatao idnya,* the cat jumps far
tallalla, *n.pr.* White's Station
talli, *s.* the young of a bird, pullet
tallillillilli, full to the brim, running over
taltatalta, *s.* noise, rumbling
taltye, the gums
tanya, *s.* raisin, gum
tannanna, Sleaford Bay
tardnintyiti, *v.* to be tired
tarkalla, hard, swollen, inflamed ; as *ngai worna tarkulla,* my stomach is hard
tarkalliti, *v.* to be hard and swollen
tarndatarndata, *v.* to smack one's lips

tarna, fast, strong
tarralla, as *tarralla yawatao warriyoko*
tarrala, seed, grain
tarri, *postfix*, over, by way of, in the direction of; as *mungkullutarri*, in the direction of the flag staff
tartatarta, *s.* a species of bird
tàúalla, *n.pr.* the swamp
tólai, *s.* pinguin
tolilye, Biddle's Station
tsú, an expression of anger; *tsù milla yura*, out! you wicked fellow
tuin-nga, *s. yarnerinye mirrinye*
tulatularingutu, *v.* to forgive, conciliate
tultumai, a species of fungus
tumba, as *worri tumba*
tumburru, high, steep; as *karnko tumburru*
tunda, i.e. *kutta kurru kurru*, straight
turkalta, wet, moist
turlko, inside; *karnko turlkunga*, inside of the house
turnba, *s.* death struggle
turnba milliti, *v.* to be struggling with death, on the point of dying
turnnguwarri, *s.* south easterly wind
turru, thin; as *kanti turru*, thin shank
tuttu. *s.* song; *tuttu kallata*, to sing
tuttu worniti, to cry
tutturru. *s.* a species of sea bird
tuttututturriti, *v.* to creak
tyedityenkata, *v.a.* to tickle
tyeduwalla or tyiru walla, knowing; as *ninna kubmanna Parnkalla tyeduwalla* or *tyiru walla*, you alone understand *Parnkalla*
tyeka, *s.* hole in the rocks, *pillu tyeka*, an oppossum hole, layer for oppossums
tyelai or *tyelai battara*, a species of gum tree
tyepa, as *yo gadla tyepa*
tyidaru, *adv.* suddenly, rapidly; as *tyidaru pudlirritanna*

pitararri, the soldiers turn suddenly round
tyilla or tyillamarra } skilled, experienced in; *kuya tyillamarra* skilled in fishing an expert fisherman
tyimba or tyimballa } ashes; *gadla tyimba*
tyindara, *s.* light, candle
tyingkalla, sprig, dry branch
tyingkalliti, *v.* to dry, wither
tyipalla, *v.* the blossom of the nilai root
tyirkullu, *adj.* stiff, hard
tyirkulliti, as *kudna tyirkulliti*, to be costive
tyirrera, *s.* a species of parrot, blue mountain parrot
tyitarta, close, fast, shut
tyitarta yertata, *s.* to close, shut, lock
tyityapi, *s.* a species of bird, honey sucker

W

wabma, *s.* a species of snake, diamond snake
waburtu, *interj.* hallo
waburtukkutu, *v.* to hail, accost
wadla, tree, fallen timber, block
wadlata, *s.* tree, bush
wadlata, *v.* to tell, say, communicate
wadlangutu, *v.* to call, invite, persuade
wadli, wrong, incorrect, *wadli wangata*, to talk incorrectly
wadlimi=marru, black paint
wadlu, behind, *wadlu ngukata*, to walk behind
wadna, *s.* a species of bird, crane
wadna, *s.* boomarang used in Port Lincoln only for killing fish; horn, sword
wadnara, as *wadnara kauo*
waduirri, *s.* a kind of red berries growing on the beach and of a sweet saltish taste
wai, probably, contracted form of *wa ngai*; as *wai paityalli*, I am not hostile or *wai malbullu*, i.e. *kutta malbu*

wai-eri, right, correct
waieridna, *s.* a species of bird
waieriti, *v.* to be right, in good health
waii, afraid, fear
waiilkinyi, afraid, a coward
wai-imanna, much afraid, coward
waiikukarnka, *adv.* get up, get out of my way
waiikummata, to fear
waiingukata, to run from fear, flee
waiinniti, *v.* to be afraid
waiiningarriti, *v.* ditto
waiingutu } to make afraid, frighten
waiinungkutu }
wailbata, *v.* to swing round; as *witarna wailbakka*, swing the *witarna*
wailbawailbata, *v.* to shake; as *kakka wailbawailbata*, to shake the head, nod
wailbi, *s.* south west country
wailkanniti, *v.* to be careless, indifferent
wailkanningutu, *v.* to neglect, slight
wainballa, as *wainballa wanggata*
wainbata, *v.* to leave, forsake
wainbarriti, *v.* to feel forsaken, lovely, to long for
wainbarringutu, *v.a.* to forsake, abandon
wainmata, *s.* to stir round
waityúru, *s.* sore, boil
waiwaieringutu, *v.* to put one in the way, instruct
waka, *s.* a small species of lizard, (see *ibirri*)
wakaityakaitya, *adj.* spotted, striped
wakalta, *adj.* shining, glittering
wakarra, *s.* neck
wakka, *a privative affix,* answering to the English ending less; as *kakka wakka,* headless, stupid, *kuya wakka,* having no fish, or being no fisherman
wakkarrata, *v.* to make fall, fell
wakkarri, *s.* female kangaroo, doe

wakkarri, asunder, to pieces, broken
wakkarriti, to go assunder, break, fall
wakkarringutu, *v.* to tear, break
wakko, *a negation;* as *wakko millako,* not bad indeed. i.e. very good, *wakko, wantyako,* no? what then
wakkunyu, *s.* an actor in some native ceremony; a person administering a sacred rite
wakkurninye, wakurninyewakurninye } alternately, in turns
wakkumanna, *s.* a person bereft of relative
wakkumballa, *s.* ditto
wakutu, *v.a.* to throw up or out; as *wortannga ngarrinyelbo wakuntyarru karralbuntu,* the sea has thrown us up
wala, *s.* male? as *wala ngukatao yura ibirringe,* a man is a *wala* by the *ibirri*
wala, *s.* an administerer of a sacred rite; as *walanga manka warnitarru,* i.e. the *wala* cuts the incision
wala, *s.* a heap, multitude; as *wala ikkatanna pitarrarri*
walba, *s.* sand
walbadli, *v.* strong powerful
walba moko, sand hill
walbara, bottom of the sea
walbara, *s.* rake, fork
walbo, *s.* bone, strong, hard
walbullu, bony, strong; as *walbullu katta,* a hardened grubbing stick
walbung garri, the flesh side of a skin
walbunniti, *v.* to be strong
walbuntu, hard
walbu peli, rotten, decayed
walbúrru, *s.* a species of eagle
walburru, *adj.* strong, headstrong
walburriti, *v.* to be strong, persist in; as *nuralli walburritanna paityanga,* you persevere in hostility
walga, *s.* bag, protuberance, the protruding part of anything

walgalgiti, *v.* to be full, crammed
walgalgingutu, *v.a.* to fill cram
walganniti, *v.* to protrude, rise, swell. be pregnant
walga purre, Green Hill
walkiti, *v.* to roll, swing; as *pityerki walkinni,* the door is swung to, is fast
walkingutu, *v.a.* to roll, swing
walko, *s.* hail stone ; *kuranna walko,* hail storm
walkutu, *v.* to praise, commend
walla, *s.* wild turkey
walla, *s.* fun, joke, *nintyananna walla,* enough fun ; i.e. cease joking
wallara, joious, funny, droll, witty, intelligent
wallara, *s.* saw
wallaranga yuturriti, *v.* to saw
wallarangarinye
wallilli, *s.* a species of fish, cod fish
wallira, *s.* day, daylight, the reverse of *malti*
wallu, *s.* space between two objects, gap, interval, opening, in two, to pieces ; as *wallu puttukka,* cut in two
wallumba, *s.* common rat
walta, *adv.* I say pray; as *ngaitye walta*; or : *kauo nungkúkka, walta,* pray give me water
waltirriti, *v.* to examine, look into
waltullu, as *palta waltullu,* clothed
walyari, *s.* a species of mouse or rat
wamba, *s.* side ; as *wamba kutyo,* the other side
wamba kutyo yendata, to put the other side down, to turn
wambara, *s.* ambush, treachery
wambaranga ngukata, to be in search of an enemy
wambaranga wittiti, *v.* to spear unawares, treacherously
wambarutyo, otherwise, again
wambiri, *s.* seacoast
wambiri bidni yurarri ; or wambiri, yurarri, coast people coast tribe
wammurru=wornalyaranna, corpulency, big belly
wana, which, what, where

wananga, in which, wherein ?
wananda, where ; as *mai wananda*, where is food
wanambo, where along, in which direction ; as *wanambo ngai ugukata*
wanburru, *adj.* fast closed
wandara wandara, thin, scattered, here and there
wandurru, *s.* string, rope
wandurru, *s.* a shrub with fine yellow blossoms
wangara, as *wangara warri wirritao*, the bleak west wind is blowing
wanggata, to say, speak, talk
wangangutu, *v.* to tell, inform
wanggangurriti, *v.* to converse, talk together
wanggalbarriti, *v.* to speak to, tell
wanggurtu, *s.* name of the eight child, if a female
wangguyu, *s.* name of ditto if a male
wangi wangi
wangini wangini, one over the other, double ; as *nunno wanginia-palta yarriti*, you put one coat over the other
wangirinye, striped
wanniti, *v.* to lie ; as : *meya wanniti* to lie sleeping
wanningutu, *v.a.* to give ; as : *mai wanningukka*, give me food
wannintutu, *v.* to remain in a lying posture
wannata, *v.* to trace ; as : *idna wannata*, to track, *kurbo wannata* to scent
wannawannangutu, *v.a.* to deprive, or abdicate ; as : *nauuringe kungka wannawannanguntyanna*
wantirriti, *v.* to stop, remain
wantye, how ; as : *nunko wantye metye*, how is your name?
wantyiti, *v.* to pour, bale water
wantyukko, s. young kangarroo
wapparra, *s.* speech, address
wappara manna, *s.* spokesman, speaker
wappilye, better, restored to health
wappirtiwappirtiti, *v.* to swing from one side to the other, slouch

wappiti, *v.* to do, make
wapu, covered, hidden, cover ; as : *kauo wapu,* the water is covered, *mena wapu,* covered, blind
wapunniti, *v.* to be full, *worna wapunniti,* to be satiated
wapuwapu, unintelligible, nonsense
wara, Happy Valley
wardlubu, hidden, underneath
wardnu, *s.* heel
wardnu, *s.* the shell of an egg
wari, or warri, name of the second child, if a male
warkutu, *v.* to put in the bag, pocket
warnbata, *v.* to bale draw water
warndi warnditi, to heave ; as : *worna warndi warnditi paityanga,* the belly heaves in rage
warndu, *s.* tree, billet of wood, dead root
warniti, *v.* to cut off or through
warnirriti, *s.* to be hanging, suspended
warnko, *s.* i.e. *wabma pulyo,* small snake
warnpi=multa, *s.* one bereft of a near relative
warnpurtu, *s.* a woman bereft of her elder brother
warnpuyu, *s.* a person bereft of his elder brother
warpara, *postfix.* at the time of, when ; as : *kauo warpara,* at the time of rain
warpata, *v.* to jump, dance about, frisk ; as : *paitya warpata,* to make hostile gestures
warpuru, all, the whole
warpuru kutta, not at all, by no means
warra, out, far away, absent
warraitya, *s.* emu
warrakka, *s.* swallow
warramurru, farther, beyond
warrara, *s.* a boy gone through the first sacred rite ; *warrara mankutu,* to make a boy a *warrara,* which is done about the age of twelve, when the boy is enjoined to speak in an undertone of voice for a month or two
warrautu, to lighten, *warrautao,* it is lightening

warri or warréri } about, hither and thither, *warri ngu-*
warri warri } *kata*, to wander about
warri, *s.* wind; *warri wirritao*, the wind blows
warrirriti, *v.* to be about, to live, exist
warrirringutu, *v.a.* to keep about, frequent
warriyi, *s.* a father bereft of his child
warriyoko, *s.* ship
warru, true; *warru wanggata*, to speak true
warru, *s.* kangaroo
warrukatta, kangaroo hunt, consisting in surrounding and closing in upon the game till the men are near enough to spear them
warrulputu, *v.* to go far, make a long journey
warrunnu, i.e. *wadlata*
warrumulyu, *s.* dwarf native fig
warrutu, *v.a.* to throw about; as *gadla warrutu*
warrunturrutu, *v.a.* ditto
warrutu, *v.* to bake in hot ashes, roast
warrurriti, *v.* to be roasting, shrivel up; *ngai iltya warrurrini bulkanga*, my sinews are shriveled up by age
warto, *s.* wombat
wartuwarturriti, *v.* to stretch one's limbs
wata, *s.* whale
watha, where
watharu, whither
watiku, desert, inhospitable, waterless, *watiku, yerta*, a country destitute of water
wattaka, *s.* side of the abdomen, flank
watti, middle, *wattinga*, in the middle, between
wattiri, *adj.* middle
wattitirdi=warra
wato, *s.* shelter, wheather shore
watyewatye, *adv.* as *watyewatye wittitarru*
wawirriti, *v.* to ask, seek, look for
wauwultiti, *v.* wag; as *wauwultitao wilga kadla bilia*, the dog is wagging its tail
wawanta, right away, for a long period; as *wawanta*

ngai waiingukaintya, for a long time I fled
wawartawarta, *s.* eddy of wind
wawartawartiti, *v.* to eddy, turn about
wawutu, *v.* to waver, move from one side to the other
kuri wawutu, to dance; *kakka wawutu,* to nod
wawurtuwawurtu, head over heels, tumbling over; as
ninna ngatto wawurtuwawurtu pittata, yata para, I shall
directly knock you head over heels
wayandata, *v.* to throw, pour, fill
wayi. where; as *wayi maitye nunko yurdniru palta?*
wayiwayirriti, *v.* to ooze out, fester
wayuru, *s.* name of the second child if a female
wedli, *s.* corner
welintye, *s.* scoop, spade
welku, narrow, tight, straight, narrow strip
welli, *s.* want, hunger; *wellinge padnata,* to be in want
wellinge ngalgutu, to eat less than will satisfy one's
appetite
wellu, *s.* hearth, fire place
welu, *s.* punk
welu, *s.* curlew
welunnu, *s.* a species of fish
welutu, *v.* to sweep, harrow
weluwelutu, *v.* to handle, press; *mingka weluwelutu,* to
press a sore with a view to cure it
welu-welu or willu willu, not heeding, noticing past
wendu or winda / wendu wendu } long, always, constantly
werbi, *s.* the place before a running fire, where the natives take their station to knock down the game disturbed by the flames
wi, directly, this moment; perhaps, may be
wibma, already
widla, path, road
widlara, slow, slowly
widli, *s.* pelican
widlukko, *s.* spring: as *widlukkunga mai kulta kak-*

kannitao, in the spring the herbage grows up
widluyu, *s.* one whose elder brother is dead
widna, thin, emaciated
widna widna, *s.* an evil person said to be *milla pulka yura,* a wicked old man
widnanniti, *v.* to become thin, poor, fall off
widni, thin, small
wiiti, *v.* to laugh, rejoice
wikarra, as *wikarra ngammata*
wikullu, narrow
wilballa, *s.* small gum scrub
wilbullu, remote, distant
wilbullunniti, *v.* to be far distant
wilga, *s.* a domesticated wild dog; any domesticated animal, as: a cat, &c.
wilgarra, *s.* mane
wilkintya, *s.* grave
wilkintyappa, *s.* grave
wilkiti, to toss, jerk, shy
willagillaga, *s.* a yellow fine scented flower
willara, bare, uncovered, naked
willata, *v.* to name, call
willu, a species of eagle
wallullu, a species of eagle
willupappa, *s.* a term of reproach
willuru, long, tall
willurriti, *v.* to be long, tall
willurungutu, *v.* to make long, lengthen
wilpata, to set fire to, burn
wilturru, fast, tied; *wandurru wilturru,* tied with a rope
wiltyadli, in future, by and bye
wiltyallidni, *adj.* relative to the future, future
wiltyaparrari, to morrow *wiltyaparrari malturlo,* to morrow morning
wiltyarra, yesterday, some days ago
wiltyarridni, of yesterday, yesterdays
wilya, soul, spirit. The human soul is believed by the

Port Lincoln natives to be removed to some Island, there to be changed into a white man

wilyalkinye, *s.* a youth of about eighteen years, who has gone through the ceremonies of circumcision and tattooing; when they must for some months keep out of sight of women and children, and speak in a low tone of voice, till the old men release them from this obligation

wilyamarraba, insensible, unconscious

wimanna, an interjection, expressing doubt or ignorance; as: *nunko pappi watha, wimanna,* where is your father? I don't know

windelli, as *kunyo windelli, windelli ngutata*

windi or winni, angle, fishing hook

windutu, *v.* to dripple, trickle down

wingunne, from now, from this moment

winkurru, *s.* barb of a spear

winma, *adj.* thin, lean, poor

winmanniti, *v.* to become thin, lean

winmirriti *v.* to whistle

winna, *s.* large spear, fishing spear

winna, *s.* chalk

winnalla, *adj.* long, lengthy; as *yardla winnalla,* with legs stretched

winna. or *plur. winnarri,* seaweed, any tough rushy plant fit for basket work

winnata, to plait, make basket work

winni, *s.* fishing hook, see *windi*

winni, *adv.* indeed, certainly

winninya, dry grass, any other soft matter to lie upon, bed

winninyiti, *v.* to put something underneath to lie upon

winnu, *s.* a red species of root

winta, *s.* a species of owl

winturru, bubbling up; *winturru babmata,* to bubble up

wintya, *s.* name for a relative

wipa, *s.* a species of ant

wipanda, satiated with food

wira wadlata, *s.* a kind of shrub
wira, *s.* bachelor, spinster, unmarried
wirata, *v.* to make the fire up, trim it
wiriti, *v.* to be averted; as *mangu wirritao, bukaranga ngadlintyara,* his face is averted lest it become sun burnt
wirringutu, *v.a.* to avert
wirirriti, *v.a.* as: *iberringe worri wirrirritarru*
wirkata, *v.* to dry by the fire, handle
wirko, heart?
wirpa, *s.* a fence across a creek, to keep the fish in that have gone up with the tide
wirra, *s.* scrub, bush, *wirranga padnatanna,* they are gone in the bush
wirra, *s.* the air, ether, rain
wirra kauo, rain water
wirrakalla, as: *palta wirrakalla*
wirrapa, as: *yata wirrapa, yata wirrapa ngunatanna*
wirri, *s.* shoulder, *gadlanga wirri penyiti,* the shoulder aches from the wood, from carrying wood
wirrilbi, *s.* a person bereft of a relative
wirri karkurru, the whizzing of a waddy
wirrinni, *s.* a species of fish
wirrintya, forest? as: *kurdli wirrintya*
wirriti, to blow, *warri wirritao,* the wind blows
wirrirriti, to storm, rage; *wirrirritanna yurarri paityanga,* men are raging in fight
wirru=ibma, raw
wirrukku, *s.* species of bird, cuckoo
wirrukkutu, *v.* to flow
wirruppu, *s.* row, line
wirrupparriti, to be in a line, form a line or row
wirruru, tall slender; as: *kurdli wirruru,* a tall sheoak
wirrurarriti, *s.* to be tall, slender
wirrutu, *v.* to scrape, chip
wirruwirru, in a heap, close together; as: *wirruwirru yurarri padnatanna*

wirti, *s.* the lower part of the spine
wirtu, bundle, tied in a bundle
wita, *s.* leg, shin
witarnda, *s.* an edible kind of root
witarna, *s.* an oval piece of wood, about two feet long and four inches broad, which is fastened to a string and swung rapidly round when it produces a deep humming sort of sound It is used principally at the performance of natives' ceremonies
witti, as : *nganna witti,* a term of reproach
wittiti, *v.* to spear, pierce
witu, *s.* reed
witullu, away ; as : *wittullu waiyukkuku,* run away
witullunu, as : *nurti witullunu*
witurko, *adv.* stand to one side, get out of the way
wityalliti, *v.* to become brown ; *bukarranga wityalliti* to be sun burnt
wityiwityirriti, *v.* to flow, roar
wityurru, flowing, liquid, violent ; as : *kartintye wityurru,* flow of blood ; *yalla wityurru,* violent gale
wiyerni, *s.* west
wiyerni wallu, north-west
wiyidni, (from *wi* and *bidni*) direct, instant
wolgarra, *s.* a species of shark
womballa, *s.* female oppossum
wondata, *v.* to let be, alone
woppa, *s.* a bunch of emu feathers, stuck as an ornament in the hair on the forehead
Worna, *s.* abdomen, belly
worna bakkambiti, *v.* to fret, grieve
worna kartintya, glad
worna kuriti, to be in great rage ; as : *worna kuriti paityanga*
worna malleri, content, peaceable
worna mundalye, glad, merry
worna mundalyiti, *v.* to feel glad, merry
wornandata, *v.* to hang

wornarriti, *v.* to abound, crowd, be confused
wornata, *v.* to abound, be plentiful
worna wadla, big belly, gormandizer
worna waieri, glad, pleased
worna waieriti, *v.* to be pleased
wornawarkuyu, dead
worṇa yulalyiti, to feel sad, grieve
worna yuwata, to be satisfied, satiated
wornikkiti, *v.* to fall, climb
worniti, *v.* to fall
worningutu, *v.* to let fall, drop
wornka, *s.* a species of fish
wornkạrra, *s.* crow
worrarriti, *v.* to have the menses
worri, *s.* penis
worribidla } sensualist
worribuka }
worri kartintye, catamenia
worri katti
worri kudla manna, strumpet
worringarka, the extraordinary incison in the male pubes of the Port Lincoln natives
worri palba, *s.* lust
worta, stump, stem
worta kutyo, again
worta pala, a small obnoxious insect
worṭanda, *s.* continent, terra firma
wortanda yappa, orcus
wortanna, *s.* sea
wortatti, *s.* south east coast and country

Y

Yᴀ, yes, *yandi,* ditto
ya, *s.* mouth
yabirri, full
yabma, *s.* back of a man
yabmauna, i.e. *wadlata* or *willanna*

yabmata, to carry on the back
yabmarra, *s.* a large species of fish, groper
yabmiti, *v.* to scold, abuse, rebuke
yabmirriti, *v.* to quarrel
yadlanna, *s.* root
yadnanni, like that
yadni, thus, so, such
yadnintye or yadintye, so, such, thus
yadnyiti, *v.* to claim; as: *yadnyitao yerdli nintye, ngaitye karteti. ngaitye karteti*
yailba, *s.* an animal of the burrowing kind
yailbo, *s.* far away; *ngai yailbo ngukata,* I shall go away
yailbudni, off from, far
yailgu, together, in company
yailgutu, *s.* to put together, mix
yailgurriti, *v.* to assemble
yaitya=yalla, as: *yattarurlo wondatanna yaitya,* they will leave off for the present
yakka, *s.* sister
yakkalla, *s.* island
yakkanya, *s.* the fat or thick part of the abdomen under the navel
yakkarra, *s.* level country, plain
yakkarrarriti, *v.* to blow, sweep along; as: *warri yak karrarriti,* the wind blows fresh
yakkata, *v.* to seek, look for
yakkangutu. *v.a.* ditto
yakkantutu, ditto
yakkarta, *adj.* hard, firm
yakkartautu, *v.* to be hard, heavy
yakkilli, dry, dried up; as: *yakkilli kauo,* the water is dried up
yakkudla, I don't know, cannot tell
yakkunya, deep; *yakkunya yappa,* deep hole
yakkutto, *s.* bag, pocket
yakulata, *v.* to tear the mouth, yawn
yalanya, fresh; *yalanya kauo,* fresh water

yalbata, *v.a.* to roll
yalbata or yelbata, *v.* to hate, destine to death ; as *: ngai yalbaintyanna Battara yurarringe mundulturri yauurru kattintyanna,* i.e. the *Battara* tribe have declared to kill me, having fetched the Europeans straight (because I have been guide to them)
yalbarriti, *v.* to hate each other, to hide one's self, shift, change place
yalbarringutu, to look out, choose
yaldu, *s.* black, shag
yalkalla, *s.* a message of somebody's death
yalkambi, *s.* a kind of berries
yalkanya, *adj.* new
yalkata, *v.* to warm, stand near the fire
yalkalparriti, *v.* to make oneself warm
yalkirriti, *v.* to yawn
yalla, indeed ; *yalla paialla,* indeed it is cold
yalla, *s.* gale, storm ; as : *yalla wityuru wirritao,* it blows a violent gale
yallanyi, *s.* sea beach
yallara, *s.* grave
yallarta, *s.* oyster
yalleki, *s.* a species of fish
yalliyaltata, *v.* to shine, be visible
yalliri, *s.* deaf adder
yallu, flame
yallu, *adv.* quick, hasty, violent ; as : *yallu kallata,* to neigh ; *yallu yuwatialla,* instead *yuwata yalla*
yallülpata, *v.* to light
yallurko, reddish, brown
yalluru, light, not heavy
yallutu, to rebound ; *kurdlinga kaya yallunna,* the spear rebounded from the sheoak
yallu wanggata, *v.* to neigh
yalluyallu, red hot
yalluyu, *s.* a species of fish
yalta, crack, fissure, fold, wrinkle

yaltalta, as: *yaltalta pinnata,* to shake one's legs, dance
yaltami, joke, false promise, lie, gammon
yaltami wangata, to lie, not keep one's promise
yaltara, *adj.* fierce; as: *yaltara wilga,* a fierce dog
yaltarpi, fresh, sweet; *yaltarpi, kauo,* fresh water
yaltarta, as: *kartintye yaltarta,* blood shot
yaltata, as: *ngalli yaltata paru madlanga,* to feel dull or sad for want of meat
yalta yalta, as: *yaltayalta ngukata*
yalturru, bold, fearless, brave
yamba, strange; *yamba yura,* a stranger
yambarra, away, out of sight; *yambara ngukata,* to go away, disappear
yambinna, *s.* widower
yammara, *v.* embrace
yammara mankutu, to embrace,
yanata, *v.a.* to use, employ; as *palta piyi yanatanna mundulturringe*
yanata, *v.* as *yarli yanata,* to put the tongue out
yanayanata, *v.a.* to abuse, insult
yandarri, *s.* comet?
yandütyuru, *s.* a species of sea bird
yangara, broad, wide
yangarriti, *v.* to extend, spread; as: *paitya yangarriti*
yangkalla, rendered fat, grease
yangkayangkarri, wide, all about; as: *yangkayangkarri, ngalgutanna,* they feed all about
yangku, *s.* left hand
yangkunnu, *s.* white cockatoo with a red crest
yanmurru, *s.* name for an actor in a ceremony
yanta, there, *yanta, ikkakka,* sit there
yanturrutu, *v.* to catch
yanyánya, whisper, speaking in a low voice
yao=kalliworra, sea gull
yapi, *s.* a parasitical plant on the sheoak
yappa, *s.* hole
yappaityappaitya, perforated, spotted; as: *idnya yap-*

paityappaitya, a spotted cat
yappallappalla, full of holes, perforated
yapparnda, as : *worna yapparnda*, hungry
yàpparndàpparndà, as : *tsu yàpparndàpparndà, tsu yàp-parndàpparndà*, a form of imprecation
yapparriti, *v.* to walk softly, steal on
yapparta, *adv.* through
yappata, *v.* to suck, kiss, drink
yappirti, close, near
yapurru, in, into ; as : *yapurru wittiti*, to spear into, to wound, or drive the spear into the object. *Yap-urrunganga*, among ; as : *Nauurri yapurru*, among the Nauos
yaralta, *s.* black cockatoo
yararta, *v.* bank, coast
yardla, *s.* the hide of the hind legs
yardna, they, others
yardnakurru, of them, their
yardniti, *v.* comprimere
yardnirriti, *v.* coïre
yariti, *v.* to be poisonous, or to spread ; as : *wabmanga yaritao yura*
yarka, *s.* reef, bank
yarkarriti, *v.* to long for ; as : *nurkurniru yarkarrit ai*
yarkata, *v.* to spread out, unfold, unfurl
yarlanni. blabbing, talkative ; as : *yarlanni wanggata*, to blab, give the alarm
yarli, *s.* tongue
yarli ngalla, talkative, garrulous
yarlipappa, pointed, sharp
yarli yanata, *v.* to put the tongue out, which is a common habit with the natives when something un-expected is said
yarliyarlirriti, *v.* to hiss, like boiling water
yarliyarlirringutu, *v.a.* to address, call, order
yarnata, *s.* as : *ngarra yarnata*, to belie
yarnballa, *adv.* together, in company ; as : *yarnballa*

ikkamatta
yarndi, as: *yarndi kurbo,* denotes the peculiar smell of opposums
yarndi kurbunniti, as: *pilla marninge yarndi kurbunniti*
yarneri, *s.* youth, youngster
yarni. ticklish?
yarnkarra, *s.* a species of edible root
yarnkutu, *v.* to be sleepy
yarnta=yanta
yarnu, *s.* eagle hawk
yarnu, *s.* net
yarnutu, *v.* to construct, build; *karnko yarnutu,* to build a hut or house
yarpara, as: *yarpara murtütye wanggatao,* or *ngadli yarpara pardni ngukanna*
yarpungutu, *v.* to hunt, pursue, run down
yarra, *s.* mill
yarra, *s.* search; as: *mai yarranga padnata,* to look for food
yarrabidni, *adj.* anything found
yarra, as; *kutta yarra yabmit'atto,* or *milla yarra*
yarraityalla, quick
yarrakkata, *v.* to seek, search
yarranda, quick; as: *yarranda ngukata*
yarranta, *s.* name of the sixth child if a female
yarrapalla, *s.* a small species of lizard
yarrarriti, *v.* to speed, spread; as; *gadla yo yarrarriti,* the fire is spreading
yarrayarrarriti, ditto
yarrata, *v.* to fly
yarrautu, *v.a.* to spill, throw about
yarredi, *s.* goose
yarrera, bold, brave; as: *ngai yarrera ; yarrera pungkutu*
yarri, *s.* name of the sixth child if a male
yarri, *s.* wing, feather, quill
yarrindakarriti, *v.* to be or become feathered, winged; as: *yura mirrinye maitye yarrindakarritao marralye*

yarriti, *v.* to put on, cover one's self

yarrirriti, *v.* to be covered; as: *penyinge yarrirriti*, to be covered with pain, feel pain all over the body

yarru, only, merely, for nothing, or no reason. The natives always employ this word when they cannot or will not make a direct answer; *ngannuru wittinnunno pallara? yarru.* Why did you spear the woman? for nothing, or I won't tell.

yarrupullu, light, not heavy; as: *yarrupullu yuranga wayandatarru karteti bidni*

yarruru, *s.* sponge

yarrutu, *v.* to be hot, oppressed with heat

yarruyalga, empty skin, hungry

yartarriti, *v.* to stretch one's limbs

yarti, *adj.* smooth, without stones; as: *yarti yakkara, kutta kanya*

yartini, *s. paltyarra mirrinya,* a species of rat; spotted bandicoot

yartu, there, that one, *yartu yura,* that man there

ya ta or ya-ata, *v.* to hunt, pursue, persecute

ya arriti, *v.* to fight

yateri, *wadlata,* a kind of tree

yateri, as: *nuralli yateringe,* with you

yati, *adv.* a long time ago, or thus, there

yatta, now, soon, directly

yattallungu } speedily, hastily
yattallatallungu }

yattanda, just now

yattanya, a little while; as: *yattanya ngai meya wanniti,* I shall sleep a little while

yattanyarru, to day

yattanyarudni, of to day

yattanyingutu, *v.a.* as: *irbi yattanyingutu, v.* to bring news

yattarru, directly, by and bye

yattarrurlo, untill, by and bye, or for the present

yathutu, *v.a.* to grow, produce

yatturriti, or yathurriti, *v.* to grow, become stout; as *widna widna maiinga yathurriti*
yaturru, *s.* right hand
yaúara, *s.* spine
yau ullu, behind, later, backwards
yauullüdni, of late, later; *yauullüdni yurarri,* the later people, progeny, present generation
yau-urru, straight
ya-wapo, mouth shut, silent
yawata, *v.* to be gathering; as: *kauo yawata* the rain is gathering, to put up, plant; as *pirri yawata*
yayardlu, *s.* cuttle fish
yelbi, *s.* flea. The natives declare that the fleas are an importation by the whites
yelbityelbitye, irritated, excited
yeli=ili, womb, lap
yelta, *adj.* stiff
yendata, *v.* to put down, give
yeni moko, *s.* glass
yerdla, *s.* a species of tree
yerdli, *s.* husband
yerdli-wirri, *s.* sticks over a grave. After the body is put in the grave and a little earth thrown on it, the natives place a number of sticks across its mouth, over which they spread grass or bushes to prevent the remaining earth from falling down, so that an empty space of about three feet in depth is left between the body and the top earth.
yerdlutu, *v.* to meet or pass on the road
yerdna, *s.* spine
yerdna widla, the hollow of the back
yeri, *affix.* tenacious of, stingy, greedy; as: *mai yeri* tenacious of food
yerilyeli, *s.* a species of fish
yériti, *v.* to be stingy, greedy, desire
yeringutu, *v.* to crave, ask, beg
yerkullu, before, in front

yerkullamba, *adv.* before, sooner, earlier ; *yerkullamba pardnapa yuwaaityao*
yerkulludni, former,preceeding ; as : *yerkulludni yurarri,* former men, ancestors
yerkullulpata, *v.* to precede, lead the way
yerla, *s.* hunt, chase ; *paru yerlanga padnata,* to go hunting
yerla, swimming
yerla kabmitl, skilled in swimming
yerlamattara, unskilled in swimming
yerlanga ngammata, *v,* to swim
yerlata, *v.* to cut through, circumcise
yerlarriti, *v.* to be spilling, leak out
yerlarringutu, *v.* to spill
yerlakkata, *v.* to pour
yerliti, *v.* to lay hold, detain
yerlingarriti, *v.* to hide one's self
yernata, *v.* to charm, bewitch
yernbata, *v.a.* to send, dismiss, order
yernbarringutu, *v.a.* to mention, speak of ; as : *nunno yernbarringuntyaranga kauo wornitao,*
yerndabirra, cart, waggon, wheelbarrow
yernka, *s.* sea beach
yernpinye, *s.* eyelashes
yernpiti, *v.* to be thirsty
yerra, different, otherwise ; as : *yerra wanggatanna* they speak differently
yerra murru, quite different ; as : *yerra murru kalla,* quite a different language
yerranneranna, *s.* a great noise
yerru or yarru, whirl
yerru warri, whirlwind
yerta, *s.* land, country
yertata, *v.* to cover, shut
yertayangarriti, *v.* to be choked, shut up ; as : *mudla yertayangarriti bukanga*
yaata, *v.* to gaze, stare

yilkarringutu, *v.* to look steadily at one
yinkinye, the stripes on the breasts of the natives produced by tattooing
yo, *s.* flame; *gadla yo,* fire flame
yoka, *s.* mud
yorunu, Louth Island
yubmarra, stopping, remaining; as: *ngai yubmarra,* I shall stop at home
yubmulliti, *v.* to be plentiful, abound
yubmullu warkata, *v.* ditto
yudlinni, as: *palkarra yudlinni,* a species of gum
yudni ngalliti, *v.* to be hot
yudniti, *v.* to wipe, clean
yudnu, *s.* a small hole in the butt end of the spear for the hook of the *midla*
yuka, dark, black
yukanniti, *v.* to become black, blacken
yukarta, heavy
yukirriti, *v.* to shine black, to be painted with black paint
yukirringutu, *v.* to paint, blacken
yukupata, *v.* to gather, collect
yulalyiti, *v.* to sigh, long for
yulgo, *s.* the heart
yulgo kulata, the heart breaks, to be very sad; as: *yulgo kulatao yura mai madlanga,* a man's heart breaks when he has no food
yulgo moko, heart, pulse; *yulgo moko wappirritao,* the heart or pulse beats
yulkara, *adv.* for a while; as: *ngatto nunko palta yarru yulkara yarriti*
yulkarra, *s.* fright, fear
yulkata, *v.* to flow over, weep
yulkumbo, sore, wounded, festering
yulkurru, as: *yulkurru ngalgutu,* to swallow loudly, eat greedily
yullu, *s.* milt, spleen

yullupu, true, indeed, certain
yullupullu, ditto
yullupunnu, ditto
yullupunye, *adj*. accurate, correct; as: *yullupunye yurre*
yulluru, *postfix*. with; as: *irkelliyulluru ngalguyurungkalli?* is it to be eaten with salt?
yullutu, *v*. to knock on the head, kill; as: *pallaranga karpili yullutarru*, a woman knocks the *karpili* rat down
yulpararrata. *v*. to swell
yulpuru, as: *kauo yulpuru*, or *yulpuru yappatarru*
yulputu, *v*. to quench, put out; as: *yulputarru gadla kauunga*, the water quenches the fire
yulta, time; as: *yulta kubmanna*, one time, once
yulta kalbelli, twice
yulta kutyo, once more, again
yultata, *v*. to tread upon, press down
yultarringutu, *v*. to squeeze through or out
yulti, *s*. dry bark
yultu, spreading, wide; as: *yultu ngukata*, to spread out
yultungalla, spreading far
yultunnu, *s*. shell
yulturu, *adj*. as *kudna yulturu*
yulyurriti, *v*. to assemble
yultyutu, *v.a*. to obtain, get; as: *karteti yultyutu*
yumballa, *s*. wallaby
yumbarra, *s*. common fly
yumbu, as *gadla yumbu wirakka padlareyuru*
yumbuntu, as *yumbuntu kauo*
yummarri, name for a relative, mother-in-law, wife's mother
yunga, *s*. elder brother
yungara, *s*. wife
yungarungara, *s*. a species of fungus
yunkutu, *v*. to recollect, know; as: *karnko kutta yunkutatto*, I don't recollect or know the place
yunneri, piecemeal, cut up; as: *warru yunneri warkutu*,

to carry the kangaroo piecemeal, cut np
yunnu, *s.* an edible species of root
yunnuyu, *s.* a species of fish
yuntata, *v.* to drive, speed; as: *warringa yuntata warri-yoko pardni,* the wind drives the ship hither
yüntyata, *v.* to incite, impel, encourage: as: *ngarradla yuntyatanna ngai wayawayarurlo*
yüntyarringutu, *v.a.* to prevail upon, persuade
yünyalla, *s* a species of bird
yupa mai, *s.* bread
yupara, *s.* pig
yupiri, fertile, loamy
yupunnu, *s.* kangaroo bird
yura, *s*· a man, male
yurbalye, *adj.* fertile, good soil; as: *yurbalye yerta*
yurdla, *s.* quartz, flint
yurdlakka, a star or constellation
yurdlu, fertile; as: *yurdlu karnko,* fertile place
yurdlu munta, liberal, bountiful
yurdlu yeri, stingy
yurdnu, *s.* flour
yuridni, *s.* a species of wallaby
yuriti, *v.* to vent one's rage upon, or to desire; as: *kar-teti yuriti*
yurka, sandy sea bottom
yurkunye, *s.* kind of eatable berries
yurkuru, *s.* the mucus of the nose, cold
yurkunye kadnya, iron stone
yurla, home, at home, *yurla karnko,* resting place, camp
yurlanta, *s.* a species of yellow flower of a globular shape
yurlu, *s.* throat
yurlu, farther, beyond
yurndulyu, *s.* steam
yurne, *s.* thirst
yurne itarta, thirsty
yurne itartiti, *v.* to be thirsty
yurna yappa, having one's thirst quenched, not thirsty

yurne yappattiti, *v.* to be not thirsty, moist
yurno, *s.* sun, day
yurno ngarri day light
yurno worta, sunset, evening ; morning
yurpullu, before hand ; as : *yurpullu ngukata*
yurra, *s.* earth, soil
yurranniti, *v.* to hear, attend
yurrayurrata, *v.a.* to tell, persuade
yurre, *s.* ear
yurre kurrara, *s.* a humming sound in the ear
yurre kurraranniti, *v.* to hum, buzz
yurre mantyarri, in good humour, glad, merry
yurre marniti, *adj.* ditto
yurre mantyarriti, *v.* to be pleased, in good humour
yurre mantyarringarriti, ditto
yurre milla, disliking, loathing, disgusted
yurre millanniti, *v.* to be disgusted, dislike
yurre ngunda, deaf, disobedient, obstinate
yurre ngundanniti, *v.* to be deaf, not listen to
yurre ngundarkuru, very obstinate, stubborn
yurre walbo, of good hearing, willing, docile
yurre wayata, *v.a.* to slight, disregard
yurreyappa, attentive, tractable
yurre yertarriti, *v.* to hear with difficulty, forget
yurrimbarriti, not to think of
yurrimbiti / yurrimbirriti } to forget
yurrinniti, *v.* to have a mind to do something, wish, like
yurriti, *v.* to hear
ynrringutu, *v.* to understand
yurru, *s.* chain of mountains
yurrukkutu, *v.* to hear
yurrullu or / yurruyurrullu } later, by and bye, afterwards ; *pony-nge yerkuyerkullu ngukakkanna, ngarrinyelbo yurru-yurrullu ngukata,* i.e. go ahead on the horse, we shall follow afterwards

yurrullüdni, later, younger
yurrulputu, *v.* to accompany, bring, follow
yurrulpungarriti, *v.* to follow, accompany
yurrulyurrulyu, *s.* a species of bird
yurrundo, *adj.* very large
yurta, *s.* rear ; *yurtanga,* in the rear, behind
yurti, *s.* lower arm
yurti, *adj.* withered, faded
yurtinniti, *v.* to fade, wither
yurtu, looking down, stooping
yuta, *s.* the bark of a pine tree made into a sort of a fan from four to six feet long by one foot wide, and presenting the form of an open water spout. The natives very dexterously clean the eggs of ants with this simple apparatus
yuta padlo, *s.* punk
yutara, *s.* grass
yutirri, *s.* a species of bird, *gannyte*
yutiti, *v.* to bury
yutirriti, *v.* to be burried, under water
yutu, *s.* waist, loin
yutu, *adj.* troubled, muddy; as: *yutu kauo,* muddy water
yuwa, good, very well
yuwari, *adv.* indeed very well
yuwannuwanniti, *v.* to fly, run away
yuwata, *v.* to stand upright
yuwangutu, *v.* to make stand, i.e. raise
yuwindi, friendless, without relatives
yuwiti, *v.* to ward off?
yuwirriti, *v.* to sink, soak in ?
yuwityallata, *v.* to skewer an animal
yuwunnu, i.e. *mai minno mirrinye*
yuwunyu, *s.* musquito